Blood Stained Feathers

My Life Story
By Mordechai Lustig
from Nowy Sącz

Translated and Edited by William Leibner
Additional Editing by Toby Bird

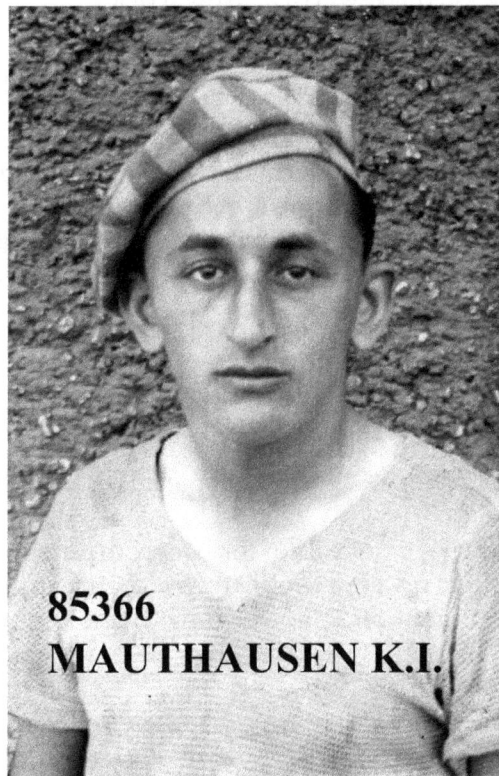

85366
MAUTHAUSEN K.I.

Mordechai Lustig aka Markus Kannengisser with his concentration camp hat and concentration camp number at Mauthausen Concentration Camp

Published by JewishGen

An Affiliate of the Museum of Jewish Heritage - A Living Memorial to the Holocaust
New York

Blood Stained Feathers
Translation of *Nutzot Adumot*

Translator and Editor: William Leibner, Jerusalem, Israel
Assistant Editor: Toby Bird, New York, New York
Layout: Joel Alpert, Woburn Massachusetts
Cover Design: Nina Schwartz, Alexandria, Virginia
Indexing: Adar Belinkoff

Published by JewishGen, Inc.
An Affiliate of the Museum of Jewish Heritage
A Living Memorial to the Holocaust
36 Battery Place, New York, NY 10280

Printed in the United States of America by Lightning Source, Inc.

Library of Congress Control Number (LCCN): 2017934030
ISBN: 978-1-939561-50-3 (422 pages, alk. paper)

Front Cover photograph: by Sally Hinchcliffe, https://SallyHinchcliffe.net
Back Cover: Photo Courtesy of Mordechai Lustig

JewishGen and the Yizkor-Books-in-Print Project

This book has been published by the **Yizkor-Books-in-Print Project,** as part of the **Yizkor Book Project** of **JewishGen, Inc**.

JewishGen, Inc. is a non-profit organization founded in 1987 as a resource for Jewish genealogy. Its website [www.jewishgen.org] serves as an international clearinghouse and resource center to assist individuals who are researching the history of their Jewish families and the places where they lived. JewishGen provides databases, facilitates discussion groups, and coordinates projects relating to Jewish genealogy and the history of the Jewish people. In 2003, JewishGen became an affiliate of the **Museum of Jewish Heritage - A Living Memorial to the Holocaust** in New York.

The **JewishGen Yizkor Book Project** was organized to make more widely known the existence of Yizkor (Memorial) Books written by survivors and former residents of various Jewish communities throughout the world. Later, volunteers connected to the different destroyed communities began cooperating to have these books translated from the original language—usually Hebrew or Yiddish—into English, thus enabling a wider audience to have access to the valuable information contained within them. As each chapter of these books was translated, it was posted on the JewishGen website and made available to the general public.

The **Yizkor-Books-in-Print Project** began in 2011 as an initiative to print and publish Yizkor Books that had been fully translated, so that hard copies would be available for purchase by the descendants of these communities and also by scholars, universities, synagogues, libraries, and museums.

These Yizkor books have been produced almost entirely through the volunteer effort of researchers from around the world, assisted by donations from private individuals. The books are printed and sold at near cost, so as to make them as affordable as possible. Our goal is to make this important genre of Jewish literature and history available in English in book form, so that people can have the personal histories of their ancestral towns on their bookshelves for themselves and for their children and grandchildren.

A list of all published translated Yizkor Books in the project with prices and ordering information can be found at:

> http://www.jewishgen.org/Yizkor/ybip.html

Lance Ackerfeld, Yizkor Book Project Manager

Joel Alpert, Yizkor-Book-in-Print Project Coordinator

JewishGen
Yizkor Book Project

This book is presented by the
Yizkor Books in Print Project
Project Coordinator: Joel Alpert

Part of the
Yizkor Books Project of JewishGen, Inc.
Project Manager: Lance Ackerfeld

These books have been produced solely through volunteer effort
of individuals from around the world. The books are printed and
sold at near cost, so as to make them as affordable as possible.

Our goal is to make this history and important genre of Jewish
literature available in English in book form so that people can have
the near-personal histories of their ancestral towns on their bookshelves for themselves and for their children and grandchildren.

Any donations to the Yizkor Books Project are appreciated.

Please send donations to:
Yizkor Book Project
JewishGen
36 Battery Place
New York, NY 10280

JewishGen, Inc. is an affiliate of the
Museum of Jewish Heritage
A Living Memorial to the Holocaust

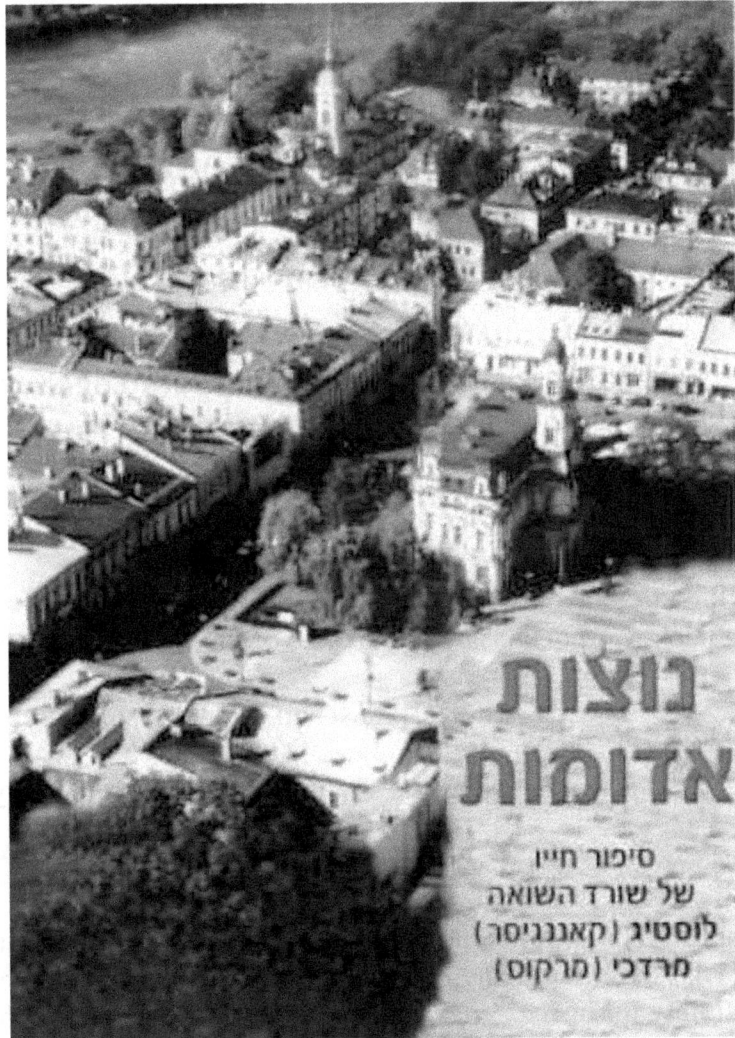

Cover of the original Hebrew book *Nutzot Adumot*

Translation:

Red
Feathers
The Life Story of a Shoah Survivor
Lustig (Kannengisser)
Mordechai (Marcus)

Translation of the Original Hebrew Title Page of the Book

'Blood Stained Feathers'
On The Background Of the City Of Sandz

The Life Story of a Shoah Survivor
Mordechai Lustig/Markus Kannengisser
Docostory Inc.

Hebrew editor; Rachel Manor
Managing editor; Docostory Inc.
Graphic artist; Niva Itzuvim
The book was published with the help of the following organizations:

Yad Vashem Holocaust and Memory Authority
The Azrieli Group
The Conference on Jewish Claims Against Germany

The authenticity of story and facts are the sole responsibility of the author.
The Docostory Company, the shareholders, managers, workers take no
responsibility for the contents and facts reported in the book. They are solely
the responsibility of Mr. Mordechai Lustig. Any lawsuit resulting from the
publication of the book has to be directed at him. The company merely
printed the material as submitted by the author. The company has in no way
shaped or influenced the story.

The Publishing Company Docostory Inc
Post Office Box 926, Ra'anana
www.docostory.com
Published 2012 in Israel

IN MEMORIAM

The book is dedicated to the memory of my dear parents; my father Yaacov Lustig the son of Esther and Levy Kannengisser. My dear mother, Ita, daughter of Miriam and Shalom Lustig. My dear sister Rachel, daughter Ita and Yaacov Kannengisser, my dear brother Moshe Yossef, son of Ita and Yaacov Kannengisser.

To my paternal and maternal relatives who underwent terrible sufferings before they were killed by the Germans and their helpers during the war and whose places of burial are unknown.

Mordechai Lustig

MAY THEY REST IN ETERNAL PEACE

The City of Sandz

The city of Nowy Sacz (Nowy Sonch in Polish and called Sandz in Yiddish) was established by royal decree about 1258 on the site of a village named Kamienica. Sandz was a royal city located between Krakow and Lemberg, Galicia, Poland. The hamlet developed rapidly since it became a commercial center and handled most of the Polish-Hungarian trade. Sandz received many royal privileges, notably tax reductions and the right to hold annual trade fairs. The city had a royal residence where the king stood when he visited the city. Throughout the ages, the city was plagued by fires, wars, invasions epidemics and floods. Following a series of disasters, the city faced total economic disaster and decided to call on the Jews to help. Jews were allowed to move to the city and open businesses so as to give the city an economic boost. The easements were promulgated in 1765 and had the desired economic effects. Jews began to move to Sandz in larger numbers. Of course there were some Jews in Sandz before this date but little is known about them. The stagnated economy of the city started to thrive with the arrival of the Jews. The Jews concentrated in lending money, textiles, wines, honey and tobacco.

In 1763 there were already 23 Jewish homes located near the royal residence of Sandz. The Jewish community or "Kahal" was established in 1765 when the Jewish population reached 509 souls. The Jewish population steadily grew and built a synagogue and a school for Jewish children. In 1710, Jews started to move to the center of the city or more precise to the market square and vicinity. As the Jewish population increased in Sandz, Jews also started to settle in the vicinity of the city, namely in the hamlet of Grybow where 200 Jews lived already in the year 1800.

The Jews of Sandz operated the flour windmills and provided a variety of services to the local population. Jews also run the inns and pubs in the city and periphery. In 1770 Sandz was occupied by the Austro-Hungarian Empire with the collapse of the Polish Kingdom. The Austrians incorporated the city into their empire. Many of the Polish feudal restrictions against the Jews were eased or removed. Jews could now leave their places of residence and move to the city of Sandz. The Austrians liberalized trade regulations but almost doubled the taxes of the citizens and they enforced the tax collections to the penny. Tax arrears were collected without mercy. There were still commercial laws aimed at the Jew like the trade in wheat was forbidden to them. Jews could not hire Christian workers or buy Christian homes. The Jews appealed to various authorities to reduce the tax burden but the Austrians refuse to budge. The situation improved slightly following the 1848 revolution when most of the restrictions were slowly reduced or eliminated . Most of the merchants in Sandz were Jewish. In 1880, the Jewish population reached 5,163 while the total population of the city was about 11,158. About 1830 Rabbi Chaim Halberstam also known as Divrei Chaim (name of his book) was appointed rabbi of Sandz. He converted the city to a Hasidic bastion. Sandz became the most influential Hasidic center in Europe under the rabbi's guidance. The rabbi greatly influenced Jewish life in the city of Sandz.

The fires of 1890 and 1894 almost wiped out the Jewish quarters of the city and impoverished the Jewish population. These disasters were followed by a wave of anti-Semitic pogroms that the army had to put down. Still, the Jewish population kept moving to the city where it hoped to improve its lot. By 1910, the Jewish population reached 7,900 while the total city population reached 25,004. The non-Jewish population grew much faster in the city than the Jewish population. The Russians invaded Sandz during World War One and caused havoc amongst the Jewish population. The Russian army was known for its brutality to Jews. The Cossacks went on a rampage and broke into Jewish stores and homes, robbed and stole what was at hand. Many Jews had fled Sandz prior to their arrival to the interior of the empire. Many of them decided to stay and not return to Sandz. Others returned and found their homes vandalized and their business structures in shambles. The Jewish economic recovery in the city was slow. The American Joint Committee stepped in to help the poor Jews as did the American Association of Sandzer Jews. Jewish welfare agencies also actively helped the poor people. The Polish government enacted laws that were directed against Jewish businessman and weakened the recovery programs of the Jewish help organizations. In 1921, the Jewish population reached 9,000 people; the Jewish population still grew but very slowly. Most of the commercial activities in the city were in the hands of Jewish merchants, namely the food and textile sectors.

Religious orthodoxy dominated the Jewish community of Sandz. Rabbi Halberstam's descendants continued to rule Jewish life in the city. This domination was being challenged by the Zionists especially the Zionist youth. The struggle stopped during World War I but resumed following the end of hostilities. Zionist organizations opened branches in Sandz, notably the " Mizrahi" or moderate religious Zionist party. The members of the party were harassed by the more orthodox elements in the city and even chased out of the synagogues when they came to pray. The General Zionist or middle of the road Zionist party was well represented in the city as was the Zionist labor group, notably the "Poalei Tzion group that soon split into a right faction and a left faction. The latter attracted the Ringelblum brothers namely Emanuel Ringelblum who would later become the historian of the Jewish ghetto of Warsaw. Another personality that joined this group was Raphael Mahler who would become a famous Jewish Polish historian. The Revisionists and Wizo also had branches in Sandz. All of these Zionist groups made serious inroads into Sandz and challenged the orthodox leadership of the community.

The Jewish youth movements ranging from the Aguda or anti-Zionist orthodox party to Betar or militant revisionist party were very active and highly competitive. They provided an outlet to the Jewish youth that was slowly being excluded from the Polish youth clubs. Sandz even had a strong " Bund" or Jewish workers party branch and even a communist group that had to operate underground since the party was outlawed in Poland. The Jewish community supported a variety of cultural and social activities in the city. Jewish schools were opened where Hebrew or Yiddish were used as the medium of instruction. Anti-Jewish incidents continued to take place in the city. Boycotts of Jewish stores or acts of vandalism occurred quite often. Despite everything, the Jews volunteered en masse to join the Polish civil defense organization in the city. The young Jews were of course drafted to the army where they fought against the German army. But nothing could stop the German war machine and they entered the city of Sandz on September 6, 1939. The city had a total population of about 34,500 inhabitants that included about 13,000 Jews. The fate of the Jews under the German occupation would be described in the following pages by the shoah surviving native son of Sandz:

Mordechai Lustig

BALTIC SEA

LITHUANIA

RUSSIA

Vilnius ●

POLAND

BELARUS

GERMANY

● Poznan   Warsaw ●

● Lodz

● Prague

CZECH REPUBLIC

● Krakow

● Nowy Sacz

UKRAINE

SLOVAKIA

250 miles

0

0   250 Km   500 Km

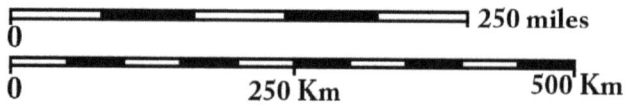

POLAND - Current Borders

Map of Poland showing Nowy Sacz

Geopolitical Information:

Nowy Sącz, Poland
49°38' North Latitude 20°43' East Longitude
181 miles South of Warsaw

Alternate names: Nowy Sącz [Pol], Nay Sants [Yid], Neu-Sandez [Ger], Nový Sadec [Cz], Nový Sacz [Slov], Újszandec [Hun], Neisantz, Novi Sach, Novi Sansh, Nowy Soncz, Naya Sandets, Sandets, Sandec, Sandz, Sants, Sanz, Tsants, Tzanz

Region: Krakow

	Town	District	Province	Country
Before WWI (c. 1900):	Nowy Sącz	Nowy Sącz	Galicia	Austrian Empire
Between the wars (c. 1930):	Nowy Sącz	Nowy Sącz	Kraków	Poland
After WWII (c. 1950):	Nowy Sącz			
Today (c. 2000):	Nowy Sącz			

Jewish Population in 1900: 5,163 (in 1880), 7,990 (in 1910)

Notes: Yiddish: סאַנץ (Santz) or סאַנץ-ניי (Nay-Santz).

Located 47 miles SE of Kraków, 29 miles SSW of Tarnów.

Nearby Jewish Communities:

Stary Sącz 5 miles SSW
Maciejowa 10 miles SE
Grybów 10 miles E
Rytro 10 miles S
Bobowa 11 miles ENE
Limanowa 13 miles WNW
Czchów 14 miles N
Ciężkowice 15 miles NE
Zakliczyn 17 miles NNE
Szczawnica 17 miles SW
Krynica-Zdrój 18 miles SE
Gromnik 19 miles NE
Rzepiennik Strzyżewski 19 miles NE
Krościenko 19 miles SW
Gorlice 20 miles E
Dobra 21 miles WNW
Muszyna 22 miles SSE

Nowy Wiśnicz 23 miles NNW
Stará Ľubovňa, Slovakia 23 miles S
Hniezdne, Slovakia 23 miles S
Spišská Stará Ves, Slovakia 23 miles SW
Brzesko 23 miles N
Wojnicz 24 miles NNE
Tuchów 24 miles NE
Biecz 25 miles ENE
Ryglice 25 miles NE
Čirč, Slovakia 26 miles SSE
Bochnia 26 miles NNW
Łapsze Niżne 26 miles SW
Podolínec, Slovakia 27 miles SSW
Malcov, Slovakia 28 miles SE
Lukov, Slovakia 28 miles SE
Mszana Dolna 29 miles W
Tarnów 29 miles NNE

William Leibner also wrote the following books:
     The <u>Nowy Zmigrod Yizkor Book</u>
     <u>Krosno by the Wislok River,</u> a Yizkor Book
     The <u>Zabrze-Hindenburg Yizkor Book</u>
     <u>Brichah</u>
     <u>The Unlikely Hero of Sobrance, Slovakia</u> with Larry Price

William Leibner also translated the following books:
     <u>The Korczyna Yizkor Book</u> from Yiddish to English
     <u>The Yizkor Book of Jaslo</u> from Hebrew to English
     <u>Blood Stained Feathers</u> from Hebrew to English

Notes to the Reader:

In order to obtain a list of all Shoah victims from Nowy Sącz, Poland, the reader should access the Yad Vashem web site listed below; one can also search for specific family names using family name option. These lists are continually updated by Yad Vashem, so it is worthwhile to periodically search these lists.

There is much valuable information available on this web site, including the Pages of Testimony, etc.

http://yvng.yadvashem.org

A list of this book and all books available in the Yizkor-Book-In-Print Project along with prices is available at:
http://www.jewishgen.org/Yizkor/ybip.html

Translator's Note: The author of the original Hebrew book used many expressions and terms that needed explanations and some research. We tried to explain and clarify the terms and ideas that were used. We also felt that the author frequently moved from item to item abruptly. We abridged certain passages to clarify and render the text more comprehensible.

Table of Contents

Notes

Chapter I
Blood Soaked Feathers
"...וָאִמָּלְטָה רַק-אֲנִי לְבַדִּי, לְהַגִּיד לָךְ..." (איוב א' 16)
...And I am one of the few escapees to tell you...
Joab, section A, line 16

Family Background

Names
Nowy Sacz
The Kannengisser Family
The Lustig Family
My Father
My Mother
Village Vacation
Life at Home
Our basement

Evening in the ghetto of Sandz

The noises from the streets carried bad omens. Heart breaking screams, shootings, killings, supplications followed by deadly silence. Jews were being killed left and right and Jewish blood was flowing in the homes and in the streets. No pity was shown to the Jew. Everybody was killed: children, women and old people. The bloodthirsty Germans stopped at nothing but continued their methodical and systematic killing. I, Mordechai, laid in my warm bed wrapped up from toe to head in the blanket. I could not fall asleep as I heard the noises from the streets. My brother Moshe Yossef slept well, knees bent. We slept in the same head but our heads were at different ends of the bed. He was in a deep slumber as a twelve year old can be after a busy day. His head pointed to the door; he was always curious to know what was going on in the hallway.

I heard my parents whisper in the next room. My mother and my sister, Rachel, were sleeping in the bed. Rachel was fast asleep, exhausted from the fears of the day. I heard my father's footsteps. Perhaps he went to the window to see what was going outside or perhaps he was moving items from place to place or perhaps he was still praying. I listened to the breathing of my brother and tried to relax. Loud and heavy boots seemed to approach our apartment. I prayed that they skip our place. But not this time. Our luck had run out.

Impossible to relax. I suddenly heard doors opening and closing doors downstairs. German curses directed apparently at the inhabitants of the apartment. Then a burst of gunfire, followed by another round. Heavy furniture was being moved and I heard the sound of broken glass. I began to tremble and could not control my hands and feet.

Silence ensued. Perhaps they forgot about us and went to another place. No, I heard heavy steps ascending the stairs to our apartment. I slid under the blanket and covered myself completely. I thought that perhaps they will skip our floor and head upstairs to the apartment under the roof. I was shaking beyond control. I was afraid. They probably killed the Hertzberg family that lived under us. There is no sound in that apartment. Now it is our turn to die. I heard them enter the apartment of our next door neighbors, the Sheinfelds. I knew the sound that their entrance door made. They left the apartment intact. They entered the next apartment and a burst of fire rang out. I slid further under the blanket. My brother continued to sleep; perhaps he would manage to survive. The shootings moved closer and closer, furniture pieces hit the floor and the sound of broken glass was heard everywhere. German orders. I also heard voices crying.

The main door to our apartment burst open. They entered our room where my brother and I slept. They quickly headed to my parents' room. I was wondering what would happen there. Meanwhile I stopped breathing and intently listened to what was taking place in the next room. What would they do to my father or mother? What fears I had. I heard one of the German murderers ask my father what he did for a living. He answered very softly, "I am a bookbinder." These were probably his last words. The German ordered my father to turn around, I heard a shot and my father fell to the ground. I shriveled in fear. I whispered, Dad. My mother broke out in hysterical screams and she too was killed. Silence ensued. My mother, I said to myself under the blanket. I heard my sister crying and shouting mother, mother. A shot was fired. Quiet. I closed my eyes tightly under the blanket. I broke out in a cold sweat. I could not control my fears. The Germans were now leaving my parents room and heading back to our room. I heard them approaching. And hoped that they would leave already. They looked at the bed, and one German said, look what we have here. Another one said, it is merely a child. The former pulled out his pistol and fired directly into the head of the sleeping Moshe Yossef. I held my breath and did not move. I felt my brother's blood dripping on my legs. At last, they left the room. One of the murderers said in Polish, good night. I remained in bed not knowing whether they would return. I was frozen with fear. I did not cry, I did not scream. My tongue seemed to be glued to the inner palate. I remained in bed until the shooting stopped. An eerie silence followed. I saw feathers soaked in blood cover the floor.

I must get up from the bed, I said to myself. But I remained sitting. My feet were shaking on the floor and my body seemed to sway. My eyes saw the horror and death everywhere. I saw my brother still laying with his head on the pillow as though he was still sleeping. His head was shattered. I closed my eyes. I looked at the room of my parents and saw my father on the floor amidst a pool of blood. He was shot in the head. I said to myself, Father, what have they done to you? My mother and sister were sprawled on the bed profusely bleeding while feathers from the quilts soaked in blood covered them. The walls and the floors looked like a slaughterhouse. Mother, Rachela, I whispered, but no response. I now realized that I was an orphan without father, mother, sister or brother. Was this my destiny, my luck? I would never know. The picture of my dead family would remain with me as long as I live. It would inspire me to continue to live and forge ahead. The determination would drive me to survive and establish a nice family that would be my living proof that I survived Hitler's plan to eradicate the Jews from the globe.

Copy of Markus Lustig's birth certificate

My family

Below are listed the members of my dear family from the city of Nowy Sacz or Sandz in Yiddish. The city is located south east of Krakow, in southern Poland near the Slovakian border.

My father was Yaakov Kannengisser and my mother was Ita Lustig. My parents married at a religious ceremony that was not recognized by the Polish state. So all the children were listed under my mother's maiden name Lustig. Notice my birth record listed me as Markus Lustig. I was born on May 28, 1925. My parents gave birth to a previous child who died in infancy. My sister was born in 1926 and my brother was born in 1930. We lived on Piarska Street, number 34 that met Zelazna Street, the Jewish section of Sandz.

Nowy Sacz

Nowy Sacz was established in 1292. Jews lived in the city for centuries. Already in the 14th century, a Jewish community existed in Sandz. The Swedes conquered the city in the 16th century. The city experienced fires that caused large destruction including the synagogues that were later rebuilt. At the beginning of the 19th century, the Polish government forced the Jews of Sandz to live in the Jewish quarter. "Sandz Hasidut" was created and established by Rabbi Chaim Halbershtam, author of the famous Hasidic book "Divrei Chaim" or The Words of Chaim. He was frequently referred to as the Divrei Chaim. He was born in 1793 in Tarnograd, in the Lublin region in Poland, and was invited to Sandz in 1828 to be the spiritual leader of the community since there was an officiating rabbi in town. He refused the post and accepted the postion when the officiating rabbi passed away in 1830. The event occurred three days after the Passover holiday. This day was celebrated in Sandz by assembling all the children who studied in the yeshivas. They marched to the cemetery where the rabbi was buried. The children carried charity boxes to collect donations. Thousands of Hasidim used to come to Sandz from all over Poland, mostly Galicia and Slovakia. The Polish railways placed special trains at the disposal of the Hasidim who came to visit and pray at the tomb of the rabbi. The latter's grave was enclosed by a dome where the entire family was buried. Near the dome, stands were erected that sold religious articles and food. This tradition continued year in, year out until the Germans conquered Poland. The rabbi had seven sons who established their own courtyards in various Jewish communities in Galicia, Poland. The family extended its influence throughout the area. The various Hasidic courts frequently scrimmaged with each other. The Germans practically wiped out the Halberstam dynasty. Between the wars, the Jewish community had already established many Jewish institutions to study torah. The city had many yeshivas where religious study was exclusively taught. There were also many study halls where young men continued to study religious texts.

The Jewish community

Lewi Kannengisser

The Jewish community was very conservative and tried to maintain a strict religious life in the city. The Jewish community in Sandz was predominantly orthodox and had large Hasidic followings.

My father's family - The Kannengissers

My paternal grandfather, Lewi Kannengisser, and his wife, Esther, had six children. My father Yaakov Kannengisser was the oldest. He was followed by Awraham, Zwi, Bluma, Frida and Moshe. Lewi Kannengisser grew up in the village of Mszana Dolna or in Yiddish "Amsane" on the outskirts of the city of Sandz. From 1909 he lived in a big house in the village of Slomka. The house had many rooms as was the custom in those days. The outhouse was in the yard next to the small warehouse and the water well nearby provided water to the house. My grandfather was involved in many business ventures, namely: he cultivated a piece of land, raised turkeys, ran a small saloon where the farmers could relax and drink sharp spirits. He also dealt with wood. He would go to the forest and select trees that would be cut down. He or his brothers would estimate the number of cubic meters of wood that the tree would give. They would then hire haulers who would transport the logs to the saw mill, The haulers would receive a portion of the wood for their labor as did the saw mill for cutting the logs. He also bought raw skins from animals that t hat were not cured and sold them. He was a very busy person and made a nice living. In 1937 my grandfather and his wife left the village and moved to Sandz. They moved to the house where my maternal grandmother lived on Romanowskiego Street that led directly from the main market to the river. Three rivers crossed the city: the Dunajec, the Kamienica and the Lubianka. We lived near the Dunajec River.

My uncle Moshe Kannengisser, also lived in the same old building under the roof. He was drafted in 1937 and took part in the dismemberment of Czechoslovakia in 1938 when Poland demanded and received pieces of territory in Czechoslovakia, He continued to serve in the Polish army until the war. My aunt Frimed Kannengisser was single until 1937 when she married Yidel Mastboim. They gave birth to a daughter in 1938. They moved to Neimark. My aunt Bluma Kannengisser married Moshe Odzer. They lived in the village of Grybow, She often went to Krynica to sell merchandise. Uncle Zwi Kannengisser married and lived in the village of Mszane Dolna. Uncle Awraham Kannengisser married and lived in Sandz.

Frimed Kannengisser

**Sara Jakubowitz,
a sister of Esther Kannengisser**

The Lustig family

My great grandfather Moshe Yossef owned a big building in Sandz with many apartments to rent. Precisely opposite this building lived my maternal grandfather Shulem Lustig who was a fur merchant. My mother's uncle Mechel Lustig was a known alcoholic; he could not budge without a small flask in his possession. His wife divorced him. He took me on many excursions that I enjoyed. He had two children, a daughter and a son Nathan. Nathan lived in Krakow and managed to flee to the Soviet occupied zone in Poland. Later, I will describe what happened to him.

The bride is on the right, Mania, a niece of Yaakov Kannengisser

Zwi Kannengisser with his wife

Mother's aunt, Itta Lustig- Raich, was married to Dawid Raich. They had two sons: Aaron Reich who left for Kashou, Slovakia, where he was the cantor at the synagogue, and Eliasz Lustig who dealt with animal skins, mainly rabbit skins. When Moshe Yossef Lustig died in 1938, the children decided to sell the house and divide the money between the three children: Shulem Lustig, Mechel Lustig and Ita Lustig. They sold the house for 6,000 zlotys. Each was supposed to get 2,000 zlotys. Ita and her mother refused to give the money to Mechel, fearing that he would spend it on spirits. Instead, an arrangement was made whereby he ate permanently at our house. Sleeping accommodations were also made for him with the shoemaker family, Mendel Miller, nicknamed Mendel Top. They treated him very nicely. He died of liver cirrhosis caused by excessive drinking.

Grandfather Shulem Lustig and his wife, Miriam nee Brandshteter, born in the hamlet of Stryi-Doniec, had eight children: Abish, Ita, Yehoshua, Nathan, Yecheskel, Chaim, Rivka, and Aaron. Shulem Lustig dealt with fine leather.

Shulem Lustig in this house lived in 1937.
A year later he moved into the house of Lewi Kannengisser

Abish Lustig married in 1912 in Poland. They had a daughter named Riwka. He served in the Austrian Imperial Army during World War One. Following the end of the war, the family moved to Berlin, Germany. He lived on Muller Street 8. He was forced to leave Germany by the Nzis and settled in Palestine in 1933. Yehoshua Lustig married and moved to Krakow.

Nathan Lustiger married and lived in Sandz. Yecheskel Lustig married and moved to the city of Chrzanow near Auschwitz. Chaim Lustig visited his brother Abish Lustig in Berlin. After a few days of staying with his brother, Chaim overheard the wife of Abish complaining about her brother-in-law's extensive vacation in their house. Chaim Lustig felt hurt and next morning left the brother's house without saying a word. He went to work in the coal mines. For years the brothers did not keep in touch until they met in Palestine. Chaim Lustig worked very hard and managed to save some money that enabled him to sail to Brazil. In 1931, he returned to Poland to take his sweetheart, Rodala Prokesh, to Brazil where he intended to marry her. Meanwhile he ordered a cottage for a month in a lovely place called Glemboka, situated on top of a mountain not far from Sandz. To get to the place you had to take a riverboat. He invited the whole family to spend time with him at the place. The place had a variety of springs that emitted different kinds of mineral water. We drank the mineral water all the time. We even bathed in tubs full of mineral water. The place also filled large barrels of mineral water for distribution. I managed to open one of the barrels and the content poured onto the floor. The attendants chased after me but I managed to escape. Next to the cottage was a big sewing where we took pictures with Chaim's camera. When the latter visited Sandz, I walked with him and he gave me 20 groshen or cents, which was a lot of money, to buy chocolate or sweets. None of the aunts or uncles ever gave me such a big gift. Sometimes on a good day, I would get 5 cents from them. Following his stay in Sandz, he left for Brazil where he married his sweetheart and opened a shop, a hat factory. They gave birth to two children: a daughter Laura and a son Luiz.

Seated are Shulem Lustig and his wife Miriam.
Standing from right is Riwka Lustig, Yehchezkel Lustig, Ita Lustig, Nathan Lustig and Aaron Lustig

Rivka Lustig married Boguchwall in 1938 in Sandz. They opened a store selling writing materials on Kazimierz Street. Aaron married in 1940 during the war. He married the baker's daughter who lived on Walowa Street. They gave birth to a baby. They always had bread. Shulem Lustig died in 1936 of hernia rupture.

Abish Lustig

Chaim Lustig and his sweetheart

Father, Yaakov Kannengisser

Yaakov Kannengiser, my father

In 1920, Yaakov Kannengisser was a cavalry soldier in the Polish army stationed in Bielec Bialy. His anti-Semitic master sergeant drove him crazy. Whenever he wanted to pray, the sergeant would give him orders to carry out. Finally, Yaakov could no longer tolerate the situation and deserted the army. The Polish military police chased him but he managed to escape and jumped over an obstacle. He managed to elude the military police but injured himself in the jump, and he developed a hernia. He managed to reach Sandz where he was in hiding and studying at the study hall for some time. Eventually, the Polish government proclaimed an amnesty for all deserters from the Polish army. My father was at last free to appear in the street. He was then introduced to my mother Ita who was ten years older than him. He was born in 1900 and she was born in 1890. They married in 1924 and received a nice dowry. But there was serious inflation in Poland at the time and the money soon shrank. They opened a store where they sold supplies to the tailors. The business was a failure and my father went into bankruptcy.

Meanwhile I was born in 1925. My parents again opened a similar store and again failed to make a go of it. They could never get another permit to operate a store. So they converted a corner of their apartment into a store. They assembled a few boards, sheets and shelves. They brought their merchandise home and started to sell from their house. They sold a bit cheaper than the regular stores. They had a variety of buttons, bands, beads threads and tissues that tailors needed. Competition was stiff but the home business was successful. Many tailors came to buy their supplies from the Kannengissers' store. The Zeifert family was one of our best customers. That family had several sons who survived the war and reached Palestine where they have since passed away. One of the brothers named Naphtali sewed clothes for the famous Israeli actress Hannah Robino. He married and adopted a daughter. I maintained contact with him until he passed away. In 1930, my brother Moshe Yossef was born at home. There was a great commotion and many doctors were there. I was sent away to grandfather Shulem Lustig where I remained until things settled down and mother resumed her duties.

Mother- Ita nee Lustig-Kannengisser

Ita nee Lustg Kannengisser, my mother

During World War One, the Jewish community in Sandz opened a kitchen that was called "People's Kitchen," which distributed free meals to the poor people and orphans. My mother was the cook and volunteered her services. She was an educated woman. She worked and studied Polish, German and Yiddish. Although she was a housewife, she helped my father in many ways.

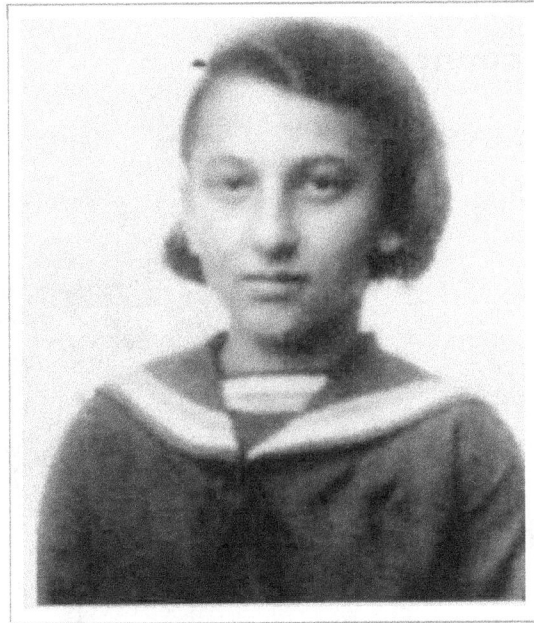

My sister, Rachel Lustig

**Standing is Mrs. Lustig-Kannengisser and her children:
Mordechai, Moshe Yossef and Rachel**

Vacations in the countryside

**Mordechai Lustig-Kannengisser visited the farm in the Slonka village
where he spent many summer vacations with his family**

I started spending my vacations in the country at the home of grandfather and grandmother from the age of five years. I loved the trips by train. On arrival, I immediately went for hikes with my uncles and picked berries and blueberries in the nearby forest but first we had to cross underneath the rail lines. The forest was about three hundred meters from the house. We ate the berries and admired the trees. I could spend hours watching the trees and the railways that were passing in front. At grandfather's home, I became acquainted with the beauty of nature that existed in the world. I became familiar with the domestic animals and the ones that roamed the area. I familiarized myself with the different kinds of trees. As I walked in the forest I saw the beauty of the valleys, mountains and small lakes. I met the neighbors' children who were non-Jewish. On occasion grandfather took me with him on his various errands to the farmers in the area to buy untreated skins and other items.

Grandmother Esther had two sisters, Libe and Sarah, who lived in Germany. Grandmother was an excellent housekeeper. She baked and cooked for the entire family and we appreciated the homemade food. All items were fresh from the country that the farmers brought to the house: butter, cheese, eggs, chickens, fruits in season like apples, plums, peaches. On occasion I was sent to the nearby grocery called "Maletz" to buy bread, candy or fly traps. The countryside was full of flies in the summer. Next to the grocery lived another Jewish family named Schechter. Close to the hamlet lived Baruch Mastboim who owned a minimarket. The local Jews prayed at the place. On holidays, the Jews went to the nearby hamlet to pray at the study hall.

Life at home

Uncle Moshe was discharged from the Polish army early in 1939 and he was never recalled. We lived in an apartment where the rooms were big. In one big room lived the five of us: three children and our parents. We paid rent to the owner, Itzik Sheinfeld, as did the other tenants. Everything was in the room. The building was hooked up to the electrical system in 1937 and also to the water line. Our place had a water faucet but no sewage pipes. We could only use the faucet for water. The faucet was located in a corner of the room where there was also a chair with a hole in the seat. At the bottom of the chair was a basin to collect the water when we washed ourselves. Under the basin was a pail where the dirty water from the basin was emptied. We considered ourselves lucky since we did not have to bring pails of water from the well. The building was big and toilet facilities were downstairs in the yard. Usually, at night, we used a night pot if we had to go and then emptied it in the morning. This saved us from running in the middle of the night to the outhouse in the yard, especially in the winter. The laundry was hung to dry in the attic in the winter.

Itzik's wife gave birth to four children: Gusta, Zwi, Ella, and Baruch. Itzik's father, Yossef Pivnik, sold leeches and I followed him for hours watching him sell his merchandise to the farmers and smoking a long pipe. Yossef died at a ripe old age during the war. All the tenants in the building dealt in commerce. Two tenants dealt in illegal merchandise. They traded in flintstones and saccharine. They stored the merchandise outside their apartments, in the cellar or in caves. Two other tenants were religious teachers: Shmuel Braber and Hershel the tall one who taught Talmud and Eliasz Lustig who taught Yiddish and other languages (he was not related to our family) lived in an apartment in the building. In the yard lived and worked Zonderling who built tombstones. I loved to stand and watch him draw and chisel the letters that he later colored in a gold color. A woman lived in the building who sold pieces of bread and also entire breads. There was also a hauler of goods who lived in the building. He transported goods from place to place or village to village.

Our basement

All the tenants had access to the cellar where coal and wood was kept to heat the building in the winter. Well-to-do tenants had small shafts on the ground floor through which coal was dumped and reached their private small cellar. Most people had access to the cellar where they had small areas to store food, potatoes, apples, cabbage, marinated cabbage and meats. The cellar kept

everything fresh and cool.

Father worked in a butcher shop where he removed the veins from the meat before it was koshered. He was paid five pennies for each cleaned kilo of meat. We had no lack of money or meat and food. We always had enough to meet our needs. Sometimes, the butcher gave my father extra parts of the cow, like liver, brain or lungs. He also received a kilo of meat a day. Sometimes he sold the extra meat. We had plenty of meat and fish and had Friday night dinners where we sang songs. My father drank a bit of vodka and enlived the evening. My mother even had a maid, a somewhat retarded girl, who washed the floor and removed the garbage. She slept in the attic at the house of my maternal grandfather and grandmother.

Chapter II
The Sandz that I Knew

The Cheder
Children games
The Shoemakers
The evangelist church
The Turkish bathhouse
Part of the castle
Work
The River
The Great Floods
Veterans Day
Nicknames
Prostitutes
Crazy people
Thieves in Sands
Sabbath
Rosh Hashanah, Kippur and Sukkoth
Chanukah
Purim
Passover
Lag B'Omer
Shavuot
Tisha B'Av
My Bar Mitzvah
Pretty Girl
Special Events

The famous "Great Synagogue" in Sandz
(Picture donated by Jean Krieser of Paris, France)

The Synagogue was the nicest synagogue located at 12 Berka Joselowica Street in Sandz. It was called the" Great Synagogue" and referred to as the "Magistrate Synagogue" or "Gorotzka Synagogue." It was built in 1746 and survived to the present. The synagogue received the official Polish political leaders who came on May 3 (Polish independence day) and November 11(when Poland received its Independence following World War One. On these days, Jewish soldiers who served in the first mountain regiment known as the "Podhalanski unit" were brought to the synagogue. They would present arms to the official Polish dignitaries that arrived to participate in the festivities. The synagogue survived the war as a German warehouse. The building was returned to the municipality of Sandz in 1974. It underwent extensive restoration and was opened as "Galeria Dawna Synagogue," a museum dedicated to Judaica.

The Great Synagogue has become an art gallery
dedicated to Jewish motifs and is open to the public
(Picture courtesy of Jean Krieser of Paris, France)

When I was young, Sandz was known as a bustling city. The Jewish community was headed by Shulem Yonah Tentzer. One of the most important Jewish institutions was the religious Jewish court that ruled the community with a firm hand. There were also mutual financial support groups, health support groups, various welfare groups to help the needy. Many of these groups belonged to the various Hasidic courts that existed in the city; Grybow, Bobow, Siniowa, Gur, and Sandz proper. Each group had its own synagogues, study halls and cheders. There were of course groups that included Hassidim and non–Hassidim like the "Tehilim group" or psalm reciters. When I reached the age of nine I joined the choir at the synagogue and the cantor taught me the musical scale notes. There were also various political groups in the city: the Aguda or orthodox religious party, Mizrahi or moderate Zionist religious party, Poalei Tzion – left or Socialist Zionist party, Hanoar Hatzioni or Zionist youth movement. There was even a cell of Communist party members. At the Hebrew school, Hebrew was studied. Even prior to my Bar Mitzvah, my friends and I helped the cantor Shaul Bronfeld to prepare the prayers for the various Jewish holidays. At the synagogue called "Hevrat Shomrim" or association of guardians that was located on our street, preparations for the cantorial parts of the services started two months before the high holidays. There were constant rehearsals so that we reached perfection on the holiday in question. When I went to morning services during the week days, the dairy man gave me three liters of milk to give to the wife of the rabbi, Nechema and to the caretaker. I was paid 5 pennies for the work.

Sandz always had some "Halutzim" or pioneers that walked about the city. Most of them were not locals. They were members of the training farm to prepare themselves for agricultural work in Palestine. They took on very difficult jobs like cutting down trees. Volunteering and giving charity were particular Jewish traits and Sandz was no exception. Every Thursday, poor Jews went from house to house and begged. They usually received a penny. If they visited 100 homes they managed to accumulate 100 pennies or one zloty. A zloty bought a kilo of sugar or a kilo of meat. The houses were open for beggars only on Thursday. On Friday, my mother would give me a kilo of meat and a "challah" or braided Jewish bread to give to a poor Jewish family with many children. Ceirale was a warm-hearted woman who helped poor people and concerned herself with kosher food for the Jews. Some of the Jewish soldiers observed Jewish dietary laws and existed on bread alone. The Polish army did not provide kosher food for the Jewish soldiers. She organized and collected food from the rich families and put it in containers that her grandchildren and I took to the military base where we gave it to the soldiers. There were there even two Jewish officers; lieutenant Moniak Shteinberg and captain Templer, son–in–law of Gelb who also partook in the kosher meals.

We prayed at the Hassidic synagogue of Sandz–Grybow; this particular Hassidic court continues to exist to the present. Amongst the worshippers at our services was the late rabbi of Sandz, Rabbi Arieh Leib Halberstam who fled Sandz and reached the city of Tarnow. He was forced to move to the ghetto of Tarnow where he disappeared with many other Jews. There were also other rabbis affiliated with other Hassidic groups like Rabbi Bnei Tzion, a Satmar rabbi and a Sinawer rabbi. The studies at the study hall lasted all day except for interruptions during the morning and afternoon services. The study hall was open daily to the students except for Shabbat or holidays. During the winter the study hall was heated day and night. The oven was big and emitted enough heat to heat the place. There was also a small kiosk where one could buy tea, cakes and fruits.

Children's Games

Our games went from generation to generation. Older brothers and sisters would teach their brothers and sisters all the games. There were no toy stores where you went and purchased toys. We created games with everything we found and made do. Some of the games were familiar like hop scotch on the side walk or placing five items on the ground and throwing something in the air while picking up the items and catching the falling item. Another game was pitching pennies against the wall, or spinning a bicycle wheel with a rod, or drawing a circle on the ground and throwing knives into the circle from a distance. Girls jumped rope and the boys played mainly hide and seek or pitched wall nuts or marbles. We all loved to play store where we measured and weighed imaginary products. We all paid attention to the rickety scale that very professionally almost like the adult merchants. We also used pieces of glass against the rays of the sun that created a flame where we burned some items. We also played cards whenever we had them. There was a kiosk in the market that sold packages of candy with animal pictures. We collected these pictures and traded them amongst ourselves.

Shoemakers

There was a small house next to ours where a Christian shoemaker lived named Pietrek. He fixed shoes and also sewed new shoes. He also raised goats and sold their milk. In the summer we went to him in the evening to buy goat milk. We paid 5 pennies and received milk that was very tasty although slightly sour. We of course liked to pet the goats and to watch the girl that was selling the milk. Her nose did not protrude from her face. We could not accept this genetic deficiency and kept looking at the nose and did not understand what had happened to her nose. There were other shoemakers in town like Mendel Top Miller, Henrik Mahler and others.

Beginning Cheder

I remember at age three I started the cheder. My parents invited the entire family to celebrate the event. I was dressed with all kinds of jewels. The religious teacher Fishel placed raisins and candies on the little board that contained the Hebrew alphabet. The sweets were supposed to motivate the study of the alphabet. Our cheder was part of the bakery owned by Dawid Leib the baker nicknamed

"Dupa Lala." At the age of five, I left this cheder and went to a higher learning cheder where I would study the bible and commentaries. The family gathered to celebrate the event and I was decorated with jewels belonging to my grandmothers. The new cheder was part of a "Talmud Torah" that was located in a building. The teacher was not from the area and was nicknamed

"Phonie," a designation attached to all Russian Jews by Galician Jews.

As a yeshiva student I never attended elementary school. During the summers I received private lessons namely in the Polish language by Berish North's wife. In 1936 I was joined at the lessons by two friends; Moshe Dawid Laor and Zwi Friedman. I took all the examinations following the summer and passed the tests. I received a report card that allowed me to go to the next grade. Of course, I did not attend the next grade but took lessons and passed all the tests at the "Kochanowka" school and was again granted a report card that would enable me to go to the higher grade in 1937. Above is the report card that indicates that I was an externist student namely I did not attend regular school hours since I was studying at the "heder" but showed up for the final end of the year examinations that I passed with the help of a tutor and was granted the elementary school certificate.

A copy of the examination sheet that enabled Mordechai to pass to the next grade

The Evangelist Church

Sandz had many churches, amongst them an evangelist church that served Poles of German descend. They were called in Poland "Volksdeutche". The religious services were conducted in German in the Protestant manner while most of the churches conducted their services in Latin and belonged to the Catholic religion. The evangelist church stood on Piarski Street next to our house. The church had a large school that had a nice auditorium where theater performances were held. Whenever the opportunity presented itself, I would sneak into the theater to watch Jewish theater groups perform various Yiddish plays like " Tuvia the Dairy Man," "Cyrus" and "The Purim Shpiel." We had many actors who played at the theater: Moshe Shlanger, Awraham Lustbader, Moshe Dawid Shapiro, Benyamin Rey, Shlomo Teitelbaum, Ratzel Golberg, Mala Weissbard, Mela Geller, and Eidel Buchner. Sandz also had a few Yiddish publications that enriched the cultural life of the city.

The Turkish Bath House

Sandz had a few "mikvot" or ritual bath houses and a few Turkish type bath houses. Two ritual bathhouses belonged to Jews and one bath house was owned by a non–Jew. One of the ritual bath houses belonged to the Hassidic group and was located at the exit of the city near the Helena Bridge. Next to it was the Christian bathhouse. There was also a Jewish mikvah along the road to Przetakowka.

Each year the Polish army drafted Poles to the armed forces. Jewish youth were also drafted to the first unit of the "Podhalanski Regiment". Their day of induction was a memorable day to see young Jewish civilians enter the mikvah dressed in civies and emerge as soldiers dressed in their Polish military uniforms.

A Section of the Castle

Next to the synagogue stood the remains of the castle that once housed the Polish kings. The place was referred as the "Schloss" in Yiddish. The place bordered the residence of the rabbi of Sandz, Rabbi Halberstam. The place was used extensively during the days when the Polish army inducted the new recruits into military service. The army presented lively shows to entertain the audience that assembled to witness the induction. From the rabbi's house and garden one could see the entire proceedings that included folk dances and military bands. The rabbi house was different from the houses of other rabbis. The rabbi's house had a large garden and in the center stood a permanent "Sukkah." The wonderful item was the roof of the rabbi's roof that could be closed and opened. The path from the rabbi's house led to the road that led to the Dunajec river and along the slope to the Kazimierz Street named after the Polish king by the same name. The path also led to the mikvah not far away from the slaughterhouse. In the winter the slope was covered with snow and we brought sleds that slid down the slope. Some children did not have sleds, so they improvised all kinds of gadgets and used to slide down. Prior to the war, the city built steps that changed the whole area. Presently, the steps are gone and there is a road there. Next to the mikvah lived Markus Friedenbach with his two beautiful daughters. Marisha was an exceptional beautiful girl. I frequently came with friends just to catch a peek of her. Nearby lived some of my friends like the Timbergs, and Hannah Greenberg of the tailor family, Zabla and Yossef Schochet. Not far from there, just before the Przetakowka bridge leading to the cemetery or to Tarnow, stood the candy factory owned by Poles. We always received 5 pennies to get sweets on Friday for the Sabbath.

The market

The city hall of Sandz. The market took place around this building
(Picture courtesy of Jean Krieser of Paris, France)

Like every city, Sandz also had a big market place located in the center of the city around city hall. The market was bustling with activities from early morning. Tuesday and Friday were market days in Sandz. Some farmers brought their produce on carts while others carried it on their backs. Some farmers walked barefoot until they reached the city and then put on the shoes.

Sometimes they sold their merchandise to a Jewish middleman in the market place or they would stand behind the stand and sell their produce. The market prices were the cheapest in town. The market spread and occupied every parcel of land around city hall. Sandz also had many other specialty markets that were located in different parts of the city; the turkey square, the place of pots, the 3rd of May lot, the wood lot, and the egg and dairy lot where milk was sold by the liter. Rows of women were sitting on the floor selling their products in front of them. Others stood behind stands loaded with all kinds of goods. Chickens were carefully examined if they were kosher and fat enough to put into the pot to make chicken soup. Fruits, vegetables, eggs, turkeys, ducks, pigeons and even chicks, ready to wear clothing, everything was on sale. The market even had a section where used items were sold and bought. The market also attracted the usual cheaters who would sell a box of sugar. The box would have a slim coat of sugar and the rest caustic powder. There were also the card sharks with their tricks of placing three cards on the table. The simple peasants lost most of their bets in these tricky games. At the sight of a policeman, the tricksters disappeared.

One day I noticed a sizable neck cut on one of the grandchildren of Tzirel. I asked him where he got the cut. He answered that they played the game of Itzhak being sacrificed. Obviously, he did not want to admit that he was involved in one of these trickster's set-ups that resulted in a knife fight.

Besides the market, Sands had a large selection of stores that sold many goods like the store of Menashe Yeheskel Baugrund that sold metals and construction items, or the Lustig store not related to our family that sold building materials mainly to a Franco–British company that was building a dam across the Dunajec river with the Poles in 1935. Most of the builders were related to the Kinderman family. The city commercial life set a good tempo of activities and provided a livelihood to many people in the city.

Many people were of course employed in the various workshops that provided many jobs in the city. Small tailor shops provided many jobs to the ready to wear clothing stores like Lew, Braun, Kolber, Shimel, Neishtat, Bitersfeld and Berliner. One of the Berliner's worked at Jagielonska Street while another one worked next to the "Talmud Tora Yessod Hatorah." Some like Zwi Teller received finished merchandise while others finished the materials themselves. About 90% of the commercial activities of the city were in Jewish hands. The rest were in the hands of the Poles. I remember especially the well-known pastry chef Szeracki or some of the broom and brush makers.

The days that Sandz did not have a market, the stores were busy and some streets concentrated on particular products like Franciskanska Street devoted itself to fish stores and fish stands; even in the winter they sold fish there. It was freezing but the vendors were there, selling all kinds of fish. To keep warm, they would place a smoldering log of wood in a pail and keep their feet next to it. On Thursdays, the sale of kosher fish would start and last until

Friday afternoon. The main suppliers of kosher fish were the family Bauman and the family Miller in the fish street. The slaughterhouse was an important institution that provided kosher meat to the Jewish population. There was the slaughterhouse where cows and sheep were slaughtered and there was also the smaller slaughterhouse where turkeys and ducks were slaughtered. Every Friday and the eve of holidays, I was sent to the slaughterhouse with a rooster, or chickens. The sight was unbelievable as many chickens and roosters were brought to be slaughtered. These were some of the religious slaughterers; Gribel, Zimel, Lustbader, Samuel Dorenter, and others. In the corner of the market stood the pharmacy called "Drogueria" owned by the Klausner family. Whenever someone was ill, they immediately sent someone to buy aspirin. In Polish they called it "Kogut" and a rooster picture was attached to the pill box. If the pain persisted, you would usually see a doctor. There were several doctors: Stater, Amazein, Syrop, and Ringelbaum who later left for Warsaw. There were also dentists: Shapiro, Schimel and others. The patients that the doctors could not save, usually reached the hands of the gravediggers, namely Arieh Bielas who lived near the cemetery.

In the center of the market near the city hall stood Schwimmer's kiosk. He lost an arm and two fingers in the other arm during the war. He sold cigarettes, sweets and other goodies. In the winter he heated his place and people came to warm themselves from the bitter cold outside. In the summer months, people used to hang about the kiosk and discuss politics and sell American dollars on the black market.

At the shoe store " Sport" worked my neighbor Gusta Sheinfeld whose parents owned our apartment. Her co-workers were Sima Kolber and Eva Rabi. Sima had a sister named Janka and two brothers, one of whom was a close friend of mine. They lived in the "Kaduk" neighborhood along Jagielonska that lead to old Stary Sandz. There were other Kolbers that lived there but they were not related. The Stein family and Awraham Mastboim sold gas and grease to the carriages at their store. The two Sapir brothers had a big warehouse where they kept wood and wood products. During the war they helped us by providing us with wood to heat our place. The Birenboim family had a big locksmith shop and the Bluzenstein family owned a large carpentry shop. Flour wholesalers in Sandz were the Laors and Moishe Mendel Rheinholt. The Topper bookbinders controlled the book market.

The wine cellars that provided Jews with their vines were the rich families; Kalman Lustbader, Shmayahu Halbershtam, Abramowicz, and Knabel. The family also owned the hotel

"Imperial" in the city. The restaurant "Biageloinska" on the Jagielonska belonged to the Folkman family. There were several steady waiters that worked at Jewish weddings: Peretz, Nissim, and Chaim Yossef Kishenboim. There were of course Jewish kleizmers but unfortunately I do not remember their names. There were several very rich Jews in Sandz namely Shulem Tenczer who headed the Jewish community. There was also Reicher, Wolf, the family

Rhainhold, Schlissel, Menashe Chaskel Blaugrund, Nayel, Lustig not related, and others. The rich banking family Mashler dominated the financial life of the city.

Many factories were owned by Jews that provided employment to the Jewish workers. There were two large soda factories "Burgenicht" and "Orenstein." I worked in one of the factories during the war. There was also a shoe polish factory, a candle factory, an oven factory, and a candy factory owned by the Englender family.

Sandz had a large vacant lot called the " Duck Lot" where an occasional circus parked its tents and amusements stands. A big tent was erected. Loud music was blared through loudspeakers; parades of elephants, zebras and circus hands dressed in their colorful uniforms marched through the streets advertising the show. As a child I was very impressed by the show and occasionally I managed to sneak my way to the performance by joining the animals or clowns as they entered the performance hall. To me the performance was breathtaking.

Along our street, in the Jewish center, there was also an inn called "Ici–Bober" where Hassidim sat on Friday afternoon and drank a glass of beer and ate chickpeas. And further away there was another inn called "Eber Anderland–Eber Shenker" where they served fine meals. At the end of the street was the jail house. The city of Sandz had two railways stations. One was close to us and the other one was a distance away. The first station also had a factory where locomotives were repaired. We as children loved to play along the rail lines in spite of the dangers. Children of course are fearless. We used to place nails on the rails and the train would flatten the nails into flat items similar to knives that we used in our childish games.

The River

The beautiful Dunajec river flowed at the entrance of the city from the railway bridge to the Helena bridge, this section of the river was used by the hassidic Jews to bathe. From the bridge in the direction of Venice was used by all inhabitants beside the Hassidim. I once went to swim at the river when they removed a 15 year-old girl from the river who had drowned. There was a great commotion and people tried to resuscitate the naked girl but she was already dead. Along the river edge stood a two story house that the brave youngsters used as a diving board, amongst them Tzina. There were also bowling alleys where the players played the game and we watched. Every Sunday, the Polish army organized concerts with a minimal entrance fee. The military band played various tunes. There were also stands that sold various knick-knacks, toys and foods. Occasionally dance music was played and youngsters took to the dance floor. At the sport center we used to ride bicycles and jump in the sand pits. During the summer we went fishing and tried to catch fish with our fishing rods at the end of which we attached worms. Sometimes we were lucky and caught a fish or two.

The Flood

In 1934, there was a great deal of rain and the rivers kept rising; the waters soon reached the height of the bridges of Piekale, Pshetkawowkaa, and Helena. The waters continued to rise and went across the riverbeds. Parts of the city were flooded. The roads and railways were disrupted. When the waters receded, the extensive damage could be seen; many buildings were covered with mud. It took months for the city to restore the roads and railways. Slowly the city returned to normalcy. The same year, a convention of Zionist youth took place at Mozer's home; I still remember vaguely some of the events around the meeting.

Veteran's Day in Sandz

Veteran's Day

Jewish and non–Jewish veterans of the First World War who served with the Austrian or Polish army units paraded as a unit. They were followed by the mailmen with their rifles and cartridge belts. Also the railway men in their special uniforms paraded. Each group was preceded by a musical band. Youth movements also participate in the parade. I played hooky from the yeshiva to attend the parade.

Nicknames in Sandz

In Sandz it was customary to refer to people by their nicknames and almost everybody had one. Some made sense others were totally unrelated to the party but still the party was stuck with the nickname. Some nicknames; Golda Ratzti, Chaya Dicki, Grabski Shtinker, Dupa Lala, Leizer Kori, Eilish

Fresser, Moshe Bonk, Mechale Piok, Yidel Bentcher, Tchaski Traski, Jumin Shabis, Chaim Lewi, Kiggel Fresser, Moske Mahrl, Yossele Sherrer, Zelikl Shames, Zelig Frachter, Motci Jopa, Motci Maciornik, Moshe Socki, Tovia Meshugener, Fonie Ganev, Di Yuklech, Yehoshua Yapciosh , Chaim Yossel Sarver, Peretz Katchke, Yechezkel Shmoder, Shlom Jasler, Shimon Kakao, Chaiml Chazan, Duvid Mach Dir, Alipo Mendel Blachaz, Shabse Melamed, Yona Karabin, Zlata the Bakerin, Eber Shenker, Itche Bober, Trany, Di Shene Olga, Tchutchu Babki, Trana Nacht Top, and other nicknames.

Prostitutes in Sandz

Prostitutes also made their rounds in Sandz along the Pioterskargi Street near the Shtengel store. There was an inn in the same house, the cantor Dov Moishe Awraham Gottlieb lived above and there was another apartment where the prostitutes provided services. The woman started as a milk saleswoman from a distant village named Wistaweica. She had a son and a daughter. During the war her daughter provided services while the son became a mean "kapo" according to rumors.

Mentally ill people

In Sandz, like in many other towns, there were some people with mental problems. One such person in Sands was Yumin Shabos and another was Chaim Levi nicknamed Chaim Levi Kugelfresser.

The latter would go from home to home on Shabbat and collect the leftover kugel from each family. He lived on this food the entire week. He had three daughters and a son. One of the daughters was intelligent and joined the Communist party; perhaps the son also joined the party. When the war started, they left for Russia and survived the war. Chaim Levi died, and his wife and two daughters died of starvation during the Shoah. I would add later some more information on the family.

Thieves in Sandz.

There was no shortage of Jewish thieves in Sandz. Mendale Miller headed the list. When the Polish farmers used to drive to the city market in Sandz, they usually brought a calf or a sheep or a goat attached to the rear of the cart. They left a child to guard the possession and they went to purchase items that they needed. Mendale used this time to trick the child and removed the calf or sheep from the cart and stashed it away until the farmers left for home. He would then slaughter the animal and distribute the meat to the poor Jews in town. In 1929 there was a cold winter. Mendale went to the head of the Jewish community, Shulem Yona Tenczer, and asked him to give some coals for the poor Jews that were sitting and freezing in their apartments. Shulem gave Mendale two sacks and led him to the basement where he had the sacks filled with coal powder and dust. Mendale took the sacs and went upstairs to the apartment of Shulem and spilled the coal powder on the floor and the carpets. Shulem was furious but decided to give Mendale sacks of coal for the poor Jews in town.

Shabbat

The Jews of Sandz observed strictly the religious laws pertaining to Jewish life especially the rules pertaining to the holy day of Shabbat. The religious Jews devoted the entire week to the preparation for the Shabbat. Every Jewish matron prepared and baked challot and cookies for the Shabbat. Some even rolled out the dough and cut fine noodles that would go into the soup. Already on Thursday I started on errands to the stores. Bring two decagrams of raisins, or 3 decagrams of cinnamon, cacao, or yeast. The next day I was sent to the market to buy a few decagrams of jam, butter and other things. Cheeses and milk were bought fresh daily. Pickled herring was bought in slices. Go the store and buy two center-pieces of herring my mother ordered. I was going and coming. Purchases were made the entire week for the Shabbat. Slowly everything was prepared for the Shabbat. The challot were baked in the oven where the food was also cooked.

In anticipation of the Sabbath, Shabbat songs started to be sung at our synagogue. My father did not attend morning services every day in the synagogue for he prayed at home. But on Friday he attended services to prepare himself for the Shabbat. My father and I went to the mikvah on Friday that also had a sauna with steps and each step was steamier than the step below. We paid an entrance fee of a few zlotys and received a bunch of whip branches that we would use on ourselves in the sauna. The sauna attendant was a Christian and he poured cold water on the heated stones to increase the amount of steam. Of course we sweated profusely and inhaled the hot and moist air in the coldest days of the winter. Cleaned and purified we returned home very hungry. Awaiting us at the table were plates with buckwheat mixed with fried onions that my mother prepared and to this day I still have their taste in my mouth. We then dressed in our Shabbat clothes and headed to the synagogue. Meanwhile my mother was setting the table. When we returned from the services, my mother received us warmly. The table was set, the candles were lit, the wine was on the table as were the challot. We sat down at the table and started to sing the traditional song of "Shalom Aleichem" or peace unto you. Then my father blessed the wine followed by the blessing of the challot. Fish was the first item of the family menu. Then we started to sing the special chants that religious Jews sing at the Shabbat meals. Chicken soup with noodles or beans followed; then came the cooked chicken with potatoes. More chants at the table. The dessert consisted of compote or fruit cocktail. The meal ended, the final prayers were recited thanking the almighty for having granted the people at the table with food. Tea was then served.

Saturday morning we awakened early and went to the baker to pick our thermos of hot coffee that remained in the baker's oven all night. We brought the coffee home. Shabbat was devoted to prayers that were long and went on for hours. With the end of the services, we had to run to the baker and take our "cholent" or stew that stewed all night in the baker's hot oven. Sometimes, we also had a noodle kugel. Since religious Jews did not heat the kitchen stoves. There was no way in which one could have some warm food except through the use of the baker's ovens that were extremely hot and kept closed to prevent the heat from escaping. This food was especially precious in the cold winters. While eating the Shabbat meal, we of course sang Shabbat songs at the table. My father made Kiddush late in the afternoon on Shabbat. We then went to the synagogue where the rabbi was conducting the third meal ceremony. The ceremony was rather simple; the rabbi tasted the foods and spread the rest among his followers. It was a great honor to receive a piece of chala from the rabbi's table. The rabbi gave religious sermons followed by Shabbat songs that continued until the evening services. The sexton of the synagogue then conducted the service called "Hamavdil" that announced the end of the holy Shabbat and the beginning of the regular week.

When we came home, father blessed the wine and lit a candle. He receipted the prayers terminating the Shabbat. The entire family was home in comfort. I still remember these precious moments of family warmth and unity. In the summer months, some storeowners opened the stores Shabbat evening: the Kleintzeler, the Brovar, and the Kirshenboim, families. Chaim Yossel Kirchenbaum and other vegetable merchants took carts and horses and went to the hamlet of Krenica to pick up fruits and vegetables for their stores.

Summer passed very fast. We approached the season of our holidays that I liked very much. Each holiday had a special significance, special foods, and special tunes. Our hearts looked forward for these festivities.

The High Holidays

A month prior to the High Holidays, we started to attend regularly services where special penance prayers were recited for the entire month to prepare the congregants spiritually and mentally towards the holidays. We felt the approaching air in the holidays. Services were much longer and started early. Frequently, I had to be awakened from my deep sleep and warm bed to get dressed and proceed to the synagogue. I went readily to the services since we received prior to the services a warm glass of tea with milk and a lump of sugar. Following a month of penance we were ready to receive the high holidays. Mother prepared special dishes for Rosh Hashana or the New Year. She cooked carrots as a good omen for plenty of coins meaning that we should have a prosperous year. She then prepared grapes mixed with sweet apples and dipped in honey as an omen for a sweet and happy New Year. The synagogue was packed since many guests arrived and took their seats. The attendance for the Yom Kippur services was expected to be even larger since most Jews attended these services. Father purchased several roosters so that we can ask forgiveness by offering the rooster as a sacrificial lamb and hope for forgiveness for the sins we committed. The rooster was twirled above the head of the party and prayers were recited for forgiveness. Mother was busy cooking the dinner that would be served prior to the commencement of the fast. We were dressed in white and headed to the synagogue. As we entered the synagogue, we lowered our head and received four imaginary hits on the backside as a token of punishment for the sins that we committed throughout the year. We then headed to our seats. Father was dressed in a white "kittel" or white robe and wore sneakers since religious Jews do not wear leather shoes for the Yom Kippur services. He wrapped himself in a big talit or prayer shawl and prayed throughout the day until the blowing of the shofar announced the end of fast. We came home and broke the fast with a slice of cake and then began to eat the festive meal.

With the end of the fast, some neighbors met and planned to build a big "sukkah" or booth in the empty lot opposite our house. The men assembled planks and beams and began to hammer and build the sukkah. We children handled the decorations. We bought colored paper and made paper chains and cut out various paper wings that were attached to the hollow shell of eggs creating the impression of birds that were hung in the sukkah. We tried to make it as attractive as possible. At a special section in the market we bought the lulav or palm branch, the etrog or related fruit to the lemon, the willow branches and the myrtle branches. Together the combination was carried to the synagogue where a special blessing was recited. Then the prayers began at the synagogue. Following the services, the men went to the sukkah where the wives had set the tables and brought the food that they prepared at home. The menus were similar with some minor exceptions. Roasted turkeys with various additions were the most popular items. The women of course tried to embellish their meals with a variety of color and extras that were eaten on the Sukkot holiday. With the end of Sukkot, we reached the "Simchat Torah Holiday" or rejoicing with the torah. This was a very festive holiday, all the children had various small flags and they were called up to the torah. Following the services, people were invited to the homes of some congregants to make Kiddush and taste holiday specialties. This was indeed a very festive holiday.

Chanukah

On this holiday, the yeshiva was closed and we played " dreidel," damke, dominoes, chess, and even took the sleds to ride them on the snow.

Tu– Bishvat

The holidays of the trees that falls on the fifteenth day of the Hebrew month of Shevat is dedicated to the tree and plants. On this day we received fruits from Palestine; figs, dates and boxers.

Purim

Every child prepared in advance a mask, an outfit and a noisemaker. We all went to the synagogue where the "Megillah" or story of Purim was read. Every time the name of Haman was mentioned, all the noisemakers went into action. My mother papered the special cakes. She also prepared baskets loaded with all kinds of candies and goodies that were sent to relatives and friends. Children went from house to house and sang Purim songs for which they received candies. It was a joyful holiday especially for children.

Passover

Spring was in the air and pushed the people to greater activity. The lethargy of the cold and harsh winter was making room for warmer days. Commercial activities increased, stands appeared everywhere selling cookies, coconut pastries, sweets wooden spoons, and pots and pans for the approaching holidays. The atmosphere was jovial and invigorating. Following Purim, we started to clean the apartment, room-by-room, and bed-by-bed. Father started to prepare wine for the holidays during the Purim holiday. He took grapes and sugar and mixed the ingredient in bags that were then hung above a container. The drips that dropped into the container were the wine for Passover. The wine was strong and tasty and served during the holiday. When I was permitted to drink wine at the table, I got drunk. This repeated itself several years in a row. The bakeries started to bake matzot for the holiday. Some Jews bought machine made matzot but the Hasidim refused to use machine made matzot.

They used "Shmira matzot" that were baked on the eve of the holiday under the rabbi's supervision. Following my bar mitzvah, I worked by Palishniok to prepare shmira matzot. Generally the bakeries were located in the basements. One of the better-known bakers in town was Zlate the baker. There were also Goldfinger and Dawid Leib. My job consisted of pouring water into the dough so that it would not harden and started to ferment. I made some money and enjoyed the work. I was also attracted to the sister of Palishniok. She was fifteen years old and very attractive. She came to the bakery quite often. Mother bought lots of shmira matzot and stuffed them into clean pillow cases that were then placed on top of the Passover closet. We received new clothing, from hats to shoes for the holiday. Everything was clean and polished for the holiday.

We went to services and when we came home, father put on his white kittel and sat down on a chair propped up by cushions. We started to recite the "Hagadah" or story of the exit of the Jews from Egypt. Father then blessed the wine and the matza. We then proceeded to eat. Mother had prepared an abundance of food that was served on special holiday dishes. After the holiday, the dishes were packed away for next year. We started with fish, chicken soup with kneidelach, potatoes, pancakes from eggs, matza flour and potato flour, we ended with dessert. We resumed reading the story of the exit of Egypt. The Seder or Passover dinner was celebrated outside of Palestine two succeeding nights. During the following days mother took matzot and broke them into small pieces, added eggs and butter. This mixture called "a matzah brei" was then fried for some time and very edible. Juice from red beets we also consumed. We ate various delicacies prepared from potatoes and matzo flour during the holiday. With Passover gone we returned to normalcy.

33 Days in the counting of the Omer

The Jews count the days between Passover and Shavuot. This count is called the Omer. The period is somewhat a sad period, religious people do not shave, do not swim and avoid scheduling parties namely weddings. The thirty-third day of the Omer is an official break to the sadness. The yeshivas are closed and we celebrated by walking through the countryside and inhaling the fresh air. When I was a bit older, my friends and I hired a horse and a cart and we traveled out of the city. We crossed the various bridges, the Dunajec alone had two major bridges one for the railway and the one for pedestrians and carts. We traveled passed the Helena bridge, near the cemetery in the direction of the village Zbiszits until we reached the farm of Reibsheid. There we built a huge camp fire and opened our supplies of food that we brought from home. In my case I had a hard boiled egg, buttered slices of bread, some vegetables, and water diluted with lemon juice. We enjoyed the freedom and party and then returned to the city.

Shavuot

The holiday of booths. We did not eat meat dishes on this holiday. Our apartment was decorated with green branches.

Ninth day in the month of Av

The day supposedly when both temples of Jerusalem were destroyed. We were very sad on this day, we fasted, and went to the synagogue where they read the "Megillah Eicha" written by the prophet Jeremiah.

Bar Mitzvah

In 1938 I celebrated my bar mitzvah. One week before Passover I started to put on tefilin. There was a big celebration where they distributed cigarettes and raised glasses of vodka to wish me a happy bar mitzvah. My parents saved every penny prior to my bar mitzvah, especially regarding clothing. They took my well-worn "bekeshe" or black silk coat worn by Hasidim and gave it to a tailor who restored it and made it presentable. My mother mended the torn socks for nothing was discarded in Sandz. Shoes and clothing were constantly patched. Almost every family had a sewing machine that was operated by a foot pedal. Most of the fixing and sewing of clothing was done by the women. The tailors in town had a serious complaints that the women were taking away their jobs.

The pretty girl

In Sandz there were two important institutions; the hospital and the orphanage established by the banker Mashler who also supervised the institution. The orphanage celebrated Passover and invited each year the soldiers to attend the party. The orphanage was surrounded by a large garden with many slides, swings and playgrounds for children. We played there a great deal. Some of my friends were also there. Then I saw this pretty girl with her braids. I could not resist myself and said to her, my name is Mordechai Lustig. She replied I am Chaike Wasner. We became friends and continued our relationship until the beginning of the war. During the Hol Moed days of Sukkot in 1934–35, it became known to my parents that I was riding a bicycle, something that was not acceptable for yeshiva student. I was sent packing to Mszana Dolna and from there to my grandfather in the village of Slomka. My parents also arranged that I would have a hot meal once a day at different homes. Friday afternoon I would reach my grandfather's home by walking or hitchhiking. I spent there the Sabbath. I lived like this for one year. I was terribly home sick but also gained independence. From the window I saw the rail lines leading to Sandz but I remained at grandfather's place. My mother sent packages with goodies via the train. The conductor would drop the packages at a specific place where I would pick it up. The packages contained sweet cookies and chocolates and reminded me of home. I also slept by Urish who played his fiddle in the summer and grated potatoes in the winter. This family had a small inn where the small buyers would sleep to make it in the morning to reach the market and sell their products. The house was big but not terribly clean. Towels were changed every two weeks Even here I also started with girls. Then the year was up and I returned home.

In 1938, I met again Chaike Wasner. She was standing on the balcony and asked me whether she can borrow my big boots for her Purim party. We exchanged a few more words and I left. I of course did not know that some of the yeshiva boys followed me and picked up the conversation. They immediately reported the event to my father. He nixed the whole idea. I was helpless and could do nothing, but it hurt. She disappeared during the war but I never forgot her. Following the war, I met Wolf Kempner in Israel. He had a large collection of pictures from the Sandzer ghetto. Amongst the pictures, I saw the picture of Chaika Wosner.

She was born in 1925, her father Mendel Wasner was one of three hundred Jews that were executed at the Jewish cemetery on April 29, 1942 at about 6.30 in the evening according to reliable witnesses.

Chaike Wozner

Wolf Kemfner was the hero of the Jewish population in the city. He was the son of Awraham Sheiss and dealt with milk. Each year in April, young and health men had to present themselves to the draft board to be inducted. Wolf helped many Jewish boys to avoid the draft by long marches, abstention from food intake and other devices whereby the medical officer rejected them for service. Some were underweight others were exhausted mentally and physically. Wolf worked with these Jewish boys until they dropped from their feet and of course were rejected from service for a variety of reasons.

Mszana Dolna where Mordechai spent his year of banishment

Special events

In May 12,1935, Josef Klemens Pilsudski, leader of Poland died. He kept the country together in spite of the many large minorities in the country. He broke the various peasant strikes. Suddenly he died. The country went into shock.

In 1936, Sandz buried minister Pieracki, an important member of the government. He was a native of Sandz.

In 1937, the ND Polish Nationalist and anti–Semitic party began to launch boycott campaigns aimed at Jewish stores. Members of the party would stand in front to Jewish stores and urge the Poles not to buy from Jews. The same tactics were also used in the market place to oust Jewish stands. The campaign was vicious and continued until the war started.

Chapter III

The Winds of War

1938–1939, Feeling of war
End of the Family Business
Outbreak of War
Under German Occupation
Chanukah Pogrom
The Death of Grandmother Esther Kannengisser in 1941
Ghetto Wall Constructions
Life or Death in the Ghetto in 1942
More Death than Life
The Bestial Killings Continue

Sandzer Jews returned home

The Jews of Sandz as well as those of Poland were accustomed to seeing Jews leave Poland. Mainly they headed to Germany, Austria and the United States. This trend continued for many years until the United States established a quota system following World War I that, in effect, barred Polish Jews from entering the United States. This act was soon followed by other nations that faced massive unemployment caused by the severe financial world depression. Each country tried to stop the flow of immigrants. Hitler assumed power in Germany and not only stopped Jewish from entering Germany but proceeded to expel them by any and all means, especially non-German citizens. Jews who lived in Germany for many years suddenly faced expulsion. Most of them were deprived or stripped of everything and sent to Poland. The expulsions were rigidly enforced and sometimes split families that consisted of German and foreign citizenships. The Jewish expulsions were vividly described in the German press, which launched vitriolic attacks against Jews. Of course, the Germans saw to it that the anti-Jewish campaign also appeared in the neighboring countries under various disguises. The Polish press, or rather a good part of it, fell prey to this anti-Jewish campaign and further incited the Polish public against the Jewish population.

The Polish government was not crazy about accepting the German Jewish residents of Polish descent but it had no choice. The refugees returned usually to their native places. Sandz received a number of them. These Jews had left Sandz in the hope of finding a better life in Germany, which they did. But with Hitler's rise to power, they were persecuted and finally chased out of Germany under one or another pretext. The community launched an appeal to help these refugees. The refugees described in great detail the situation in Germany, particularly the Jewish situation. Many Jews found it hard to believe that the Germans who behaved decently to the Polish Jews during

World War I had sunk to such bestial behavior. Slowly the facts were digested but the Jews could do very little about the situation. The world was closed to the Jews and they had no place to go. Even Palestine slowly closed the doors to Jewish immigrants. The Sandzer Jew like all Jews in Poland and Eastern Europe became trapped with no exit.

The Polish government encouraged Jews to leave the country for it wanted to reduce the Jewish population in Poland. Following the official census of 1921, the Polish governments never published precise demographic information regarding the number of Jews in Poland. The estimates were that the Jewish population reached about 10% of the population of the country or about 3.5 million people. Various Polish governments tried to reduce this number by various manipulations of the actual figures. The fact remained that the Jewish community and the non–Jewish Polish community believed in the 10% figure. Yet, the Polish government had accurate statistics regarding the Polish population since people did not move from place to place without notifying the local authorities. The minister of interior had the exact figures but they were never published.

As the world depression spread and the entrance gates to most countries closed, the Zionist movement in Poland began to illegally ship young Jews to Palestine. The demand for passage steadily increased. A number of Sandzer Jews left Poland for Palestine.

We already mentioned that Marshal Pilsudski died in 1935. General Edward Smigly–Rydz took over the reins of Poland. A wave of anti–Semitic propaganda descended on Poland. Anti–Semitic Polish parties and groups began openly to agitate against Jews, notably the National Democratic Party known by the letters ND. The members were familiarly called the "Endekes." They refused to recognize the Polish Jews as Polish citizens. They staged violent campaigns against the Jewish manner of slaughtering animals, claiming that it was cruel to animals. Apparently hunting animals was humanitarian. The "anti–Schitah" or anti–ritual slaughter laws were passed in a modified manner that immediately increased the price of "kosher meat." Illegal slaughtering appeared on the Polish scene. The entire meat business industry received a serious shock and affected the Jewish butchers and customers. Other laws aimed at Jewish economic and financial interests were passed. The Polish street was incited against Jews. Polish students returning from schools for their summer holidays organized boycotts of Jewish stores and prevented buyers from entering the stores. Part of the Polish press encouraged these activities and created the illusion that the Polish Jew was the enemy of Poland, while the real enemy of Poland, Germany, incited the Polish masses against the Jews. Of course, the German press and radio did their best to incite the Poles against the Jews. Hitler wanted to detract attention from his military activities in Germany. Planes, tanks, cannons rolled speedily off the production lines and were given to the army. Germany had the best army in the world but was telling the Poles that the Jews were the cause of all Polish economic ills. Hitler smiled at Poland and the Poles ate it up.

Germany was very pleased with this anti–Jewish campaign in Poland. It also supported and encouraged Poland to insist on territorial changes along the Polish–Czechoslovak border in favor of Poland. The Czechs refused to negotiate. The Poles were furious and waged an aggressive publicity campaign against Czechoslovakia in the Polish press. Germany was of course interested in keeping these two Slavic nations apart, for Czechoslovakia was an industrialized country with a large military industry at its disposal that could provide military hardware to its allies in time of need. And the Polish army needed modern weapons. The Germans were determined to keep the feud going between the two Slavic countries to prevent any logical Polish–Czech alliance. Hitler succeeded beyond his wildest dream. Poland joined Germany militarily in dismembering Czechoslovakia. My uncle took part in the Polish military attack on Czechoslovakia. Czech prisoners of war soon appeared in Poland. Now Poland faced Germany alone in the east. Exactly what Hitler planned.

The Polish press soon began to discern minor German animosities toward Poland. The mood of the country began to change. Hitler, now in possession of Austria, Sudetenland and Czechoslovakia, began to change his demands. We also heard the events of the "Broken Glass" in Germany on our neighbor's radio. We heard the frightening speeches of Hitler. Then we read in the Polish press that France and England would protect the Polish borders. The street mood changed radically. The Polish authorities began to make preparations for war. There was fear of gas attacks so the Polish administration began to organize civil defense units. Courses were offered to train first aid workers. Some civil defense exercises were held to instill morale in the population. Nurses were instructed how to act in war and lessons were given in the use of gas masks. The fire department was instructed to act in case of war. But life in Sandz continued to flow.

The end of our business adventure

Our illegal store at our apartment continued to work until the end of 1938 or the beginning 1939. A Jewish merchant informed the authorities that we operated a store without a license. The authorities came and saw the merchandise. They took everything and placed it in a big closet that was sealed with the official seal of the tax department. Now we had no business and began to live from hand to mouth. My father was very optimistic and always used to say that even from a bad situation something good could be derived The locked merchandise would come in very handy during the German occupation of Sandz. It would enable us to sell pieces of goods and to maintain ourselves. My father now began to work at removing the hair from rabbit skins. He made a nice living at it.

The outbreak of the war

Germany was lately demanding territorial land from Poland in the Danzig area. Poland refused to discuss the matter. Other incidents began to be mentioned in the German press regarding the Polish mistreatment of German citizens in Poland. Suddenly, Germany and the Soviet Union signed a secret agreement called the Molotov–Ribbentrop agreement. One week later, on Friday, September 1, 1939, Germany attacked Poland from Silesia in the west, from Prussia in the north, and from Czechoslovakia in the south. The country that Poland helped to dismantle was now being used as a springboard for the attack on Poland. The German forces in the south soon pierced the Polish defense lines along the Carpathian Mountains and advanced at a furious pace in the direction of Sandz. Meanwhile, people in Sandz began to worry what to do. The same day, the city sirens screeched while I was outside, strolling along Jagielonska Street. I rushed into a building with other people. We all waited for the clear sign. Needless to say, I was terrified. On Saturday, September 2nd, I walked to the center of the city to see what was taking place. I saw a battalion of Polish soldiers heading west. I suddenly remembered that some time ago I saw carts and horses that were drafted from civilians to provide transportation for army supplies also headed west. On Sunday, I strolled again in the city and saw people with big bags and some carts heading along Jagielonska to the tobacco and cigarette warehouses where they loaded up.

On Monday September 4th, I went to the Dunajec river and saw Polish officers preparing a defensive line for the city and some privates carrying postal pigeon cages. I also saw many people heading from west to east across the bridge, some on foot and others in carts. On Tuesday, September 5th, many Jews began to leave the city. They headed to the railway station that was packed. Some left the city on foot and others hired carts. They were all heading in an easterly direction. Among the Jews who left the city were some of my uncles. It seemed that the city's population shrank. At the corner of Lewowska Street, I saw a policeman distributing tobacco and cigarettes to the people leaving the city. Explosions could be heard in the distance. We were ordered to leave our house since it was located near the city defense line.

We hurriedly ate breakfast and headed to the Zupnik family in the center of the city. They welcomed us. German artillery was bombing Sandz. We all had to go to the cellar. The shelling continued through the night. At 5 o'clock in the morning there was silence. Of course, we did not sleep a wink. We heard through the cracks the sound of engines moving along the streets.

On September 6, 1939, the Germans occupied the city. The streets were full of tanks, artillery pieces, various armed vehicles, infantry units, mountain troops with their special boots. All of these units were heading east. Some units were resting in the small parks, washing themselves and eating. When I left the Zupnik house, I saw Polish prisoners of war without their weapons sitting on the floor waiting to be shipped to prison camps or city prisons. Huge stocks of Polish weapons were assembled in a neat pile on the floor. We soon reached our house that was damaged as were many other houses on our street. Our building took a direct hit and the roof apartment had a huge hole. In the street we suddenly saw people with white armbands with swastikas in the center. These were Poles of German descent who had lived in Poland for centuries and suddenly felt part of the German nation. These so-called "volksdeutsche" immediately began to harass the Jews they encountered in the streets. The German army began to grab Jews for work details. Some Jews who had left the city prior to the German arrival began to return to the city, including some of my uncles. Later, some of the Jews would try to smuggle their way to the Russian side while others would try to return home to Sandz. These smuggling activities would last until June 1941 when Germany attacked the Soviet Union.

Prior to the outbreak of the war in 1939, two large kiosks that sold ice cream opened in Sandz. One was called the "Penguin" and another was opened near the main railway station. The Polish military intelligence became suspicious of both places and surveyed the places. The places were raided and in one place they discovered a radio transmitter linked to Germany. Three "volksdeutsche" people were arrested, among them Jekner, whose father had a flour mill and was friendly to Jews. Prior to the German entrance to Sandz, the Polish authorities released all prisoners from the city prisons except for the three spies. The Polish army took them to the city of Mielec where they were tried, found guilty and shot. The Germans retrieved their bodies and brought them back to Sandz where an honorary burial procession was held for the three German spies. The S.S. tried to accuse the Jews of having taken part in the discovery of the plot but Jekner's father said bluntly that the Jews had no part in the story and the S.S. dropped the issue. In a way, Jekner's father saved the Jews of Sandz from a possible planned pogrom by the S.S.

During the next two months, September and October, the situation remained fluid, no major upheavals or changes; life continued at a somewhat limited pace. The Germans even ordered all stores and stands to open their businesses. My father had the keys of the Teller family warehouse and store on Jagielonska Street. The store sold jackets. My father and the servant of the Teller family who remained in the store began to sell merchandise. The queue to buy jackets soon extended for a distance. The Germans soon aryanised the store or appointed a German supervisor. Still, the store sold merchandise. A few days later, Yeshayahu Bergman, brother-in-law of Teller, moved into the store with his family. My father handed him the keys and Bergman gave him a few jackets for his work. Bergman had good connections with the German authorities.

As the days passed, there developed a shortage of bread or specifically a shortage of flour. The bakeries tried to stretch their flour, and the bread became saggy and heavy. A curfew was imposed on the city. No one was permitted in the street before daybreak. I had to get up very early in the morning to go to the bakery where there was a huge line for bread. I stood a long time until I finally managed to get a loaf of bread. It was very difficult to get used to the situation that went from bad to worse. Our neighbor, the hauler Hertzberg, managed on several occasions to bring breads to the tenants of the building. The Germans eventually caught him and put him to work for the German army. Luck had it that while working for the German army he met an old Viennese acquaintance from prewar days who was now a master sergeant. The latter paid him in bread for his work. He brought the bread to the building and shared it with the neighbors.

Since the occupation of Sandz, the Hasidim stopped praying in their synagogue for fear of being seized for work details. Random check posts were everywhere and the Germans sought Jews for work details. At the end of October the office of the "Judenrat" or Jewish committee was established, headed by Yankel Marin. A Jewish police force was also established that wore blue hats along with a sanitary police that wore white hats. The Polish police, armed with pistols, controlled the city and the black market. Some of the policemen like Swoika from the Rozilla area had a particular fine nose for spotting food contraband, namely eggs. Polish farmers continued to bring food to the city despite the risks of being caught dealing in the black market.

The Judenrat surveyed the entire Jewish population from age 16 to 60 that would enable them to provide labor to the Germans. Each person who appeared on the list had to give a few days of work to the Judenrat per month or pay three or four zlotys for the exemption. The Germans, for their part, imposed all kinds of regulations aimed at the Jews. Every Jew had to wear a white armband with the Star of David on it. Jews could not travel on the railway. Jews could not leave town without permission. S.S. bullies grabbed Jews and demanded money or gold as ransom. These blackmail operations took on widespread form and proved very costly. Economic conditions became harder with each day. People with food supplies or clothing stashed away managed to sell items and survive. Those who had jewelry, cash or gold also managed to stay alive. We were selling the merchandise that was locked by the Polish tax department and managed to buy food. In November the Germans deported all the Jews from Sieiac near Lodz to Sandz. The Judenrat assigned them to live in the empty study halls that used to be full of yeshiva students. Some of the refugees had small children. These refugees were installed in the Jewish flats that the owners had left.

The Chanukah Pogrom

During Chanukah the Germans decided to search all Jewish houses for weapons. The Gestapo, the S.S., the German military police and the territorial police were called into the city to participate in the search. The Germans stole everything of value: money, jewelry and antiques. The homes were turned inside out in order to find things that soon disappeared into pockets. Our apartment was thoroughly searched, beds were turned over, mattresses removed from beds, and closets were emptied. The action started early in the morning and stopped at about 11 A.M. During the entire action, the men had to stand outside while the search took place. Of course, no weapons were found, but many homes were vandalized. My father was upstairs under the roof and the Germans did not go up there. As the Germans were leaving their searches, they came across a large group of Hasidim with beards and earlocks who were finishing their morning services still dressed with their prayer shawls. They ordered them to march to the center of the city. Here the show began. The Germans began to rip wrist watches and clothing from the Hasidim and threw the items to the Poles who were standing and watching the show. The Germans began to burn the beards and clipped the earlocks. Then the Jews were told to dance and sing while the Germans were beating them with their rifle butts or clubs. Many Jewish participants including some Lelower, Gorlitzer and Satmar rabbis wound up in the hospital with serious wounds.

There were new ordinances. Jews were not permitted to have radios, foreign currency, copper items, gold and valuables. We read the new orders. In the evening, we met with friends at someone's house and played cards, dominoes or chess and talked. Once we were so involved that we forgot to look at the clock and the curfew was already in force. We had to spend the night and only in the morning did I get home. My parents let me have it and rightfully so since they were worried the whole night about what had happened to me.

The Gestapo not only persecuted rabbis. They had a list of all Polish intellectuals including priests. Many were arrested and murdered. Once German soldiers caught me and forced me to work at the Polish military barracks. I had to clean the lavatories and to move some furniture from one place to another. On another occasion, I was forced to remove the bottles of wine from Abramowitz's liquor store. When we finished working, we received some bottles of wine. We drank the wine and I managed to reach home totally drunk

Jews living in the vicinity of Sandz were ordered to move to the city. The Judenrat helped them settle. Our apartment was in a large complex and there was always the availability of a quorum for services. The son of Rabbi Shmuel Praver was in charge of the services. In December 1939, my aunt Primet, my father's sister, arrived in Sandz. She came with her husband Yehuda Mastbom and their small infant. They had lived in Neu–Mark since they were married. They did not intend to stay in Sandz. They came to prepare the necessary arrangements to smuggle their way into Slovakia. On December 24th, they indeed succeeded and reached Slovakia. Life there was no picnic but they survived the Shoah.

My parents decided to send me to learn a trade. They chose the shoe making trade. I started to learn how to cut leather and prepare the various shoe parts. The peasants brought heavy, worn boots to the shoemaker and he stripped them and converted them into new shoes. They paid with flour, wheat or other food products. I worked there until May 1940. I left the place since I was not paid and started working for a soda factory where I was paid. I no longer remember how much I received. I received a bicycle and horse and cart and began to make the rounds of the city selling soda bottles, soda balloons and orange drinks. One day, I received two orders: one was from a Polish restaurant along Jagielonska Street where members of the Polish underground met and the other place was a restaurant at the main railway station where there were always many German soldiers.

One morning I was riding the bicycle with two baskets of bottles and soft drinks on each handle bar. I was pedaling fairly fast when suddenly a child burst from the sidewalk onto the road and headed straight into my path. I stopped the bike and hit the ground. The child was slightly injured with a nosebleed. The parents of the child who let him run onto the road started to scream that I wanted to kill the child. Luck had it that a Polish police officer rode by in a coach and saw the scene. He picked me up and took me to the police station. There a Jewish secretary shifted my papers to the Polish desk rather than to the one of the Gestapo.

I was pushed into the basement of the city hall that also served as a jail. It was freezing. There was another person there. I lay down on the ground but could not sleep since it was so cold. The police wrote a protocol and my boss was notified of my arrest. After a day, I was freed and resumed working for the soda place until the beginning of the winter 1940/1941. In order to make a few extra zlotys, I also started to deal in cigarettes, tobacco, flint stones, saccharine and yeast. The farmers continued to visit the city and many of them did not have money but they exchanged their products for the items that they needed. I would exchange my merchandise for bread and potatoes. We have to remember that the Jew received 100 grams of bread a day with his food coupons. So in order to live, we had to buy food on the black market. I conducted my business from the May 3 Square near our house. I also made the rounds among the carts that were parked in the area. I had two partners, Bulo Sheinfeld and another one. I became the sole supporter of the family. Not far from our house, there were storage places that kept eggs in special vats where they were preserved for the summer. Then they were packed in cases and shipped to the markets. Some of the crates were not tightly closed and this enabled my small hands to get to the eggs and remove some of them without being spotted.

With the beginning of 1941, Sandz saw an influx of German troops in the city. The soldiers bought and sold items. They would buy eggs in exchange for military bread or other such deals. These transactions stopped with the beginning of the German–Soviet war in June 1941. On Purim 1941, my grandmother Esther Kannengisser passed away and she was buried at the Jewish cemetery in Sandz. Grandfather remained alone in the apartment. My uncle Moshe lived in the same complex at 4 Romanowskiego Street. He visited grandfather and slowly took over a small room under the roof where the Zionist youth movement used to meet. The organization disbanded and Moshe took over the place. He began to sleep in grandfather's place. This uncle was a real handy man, especially in plumbing. He gave me the first lessons in this trade. He was very busy with frozen pipes that did not permit the water to circulate. He heated the pipes in the basement until the ice melted and the circulation of water resumed. I frequently joined my uncle in his plumbing errands. His talents were soon discovered by the Jewish employment office and Moniek Grin used him for all kinds of work. Even the German Svoboda used him. The office could not open a safe, so they called Moshe and he managed to crack the safe open. He became a permanent worker for the office that soon moved to the Lwowska Street after the bridge above the River Kamienica on the left side.

The Judenrat of Sandz appealed to the Slovakian Jewish community to send them matzot for Passover. The appeal was successful and in March 1941, 2,500 kilos of matzot arrived in Sandz. The next month a further shipment of matzot arrived in Sandz. The matzot were distributed to the Jewish population. Aunt Primet also sent us a package of matzot from Slovakia. Once again the Polish police arrested me for selling cigarettes and took me to the city prison located in the municipal building. I was again showed into the detention room in the freezing basement. I lay down on the cold floor alone since I was the only detainee. Apparently the police called my parents who showed up. I was released following 24 hours jail time. I returned to selling cigarettes but became more careful. I had a fresh encounter with a Polish policeman who wanted to arrest me but I managed to escape to one of the houses and disappeared. The policeman gave up. I continued with the cigarette business until the month of March 1942, when the Gestapo decided to stop all tobacco trade. They arrested all tobacco dealers, led them to the cemetery and shot them. I stopped with the cigarettes for it became too dangerous.

The employment office was first located in the house of Abramowitz on Swedska Street and then it moved to the building next to the Judenrat building on Wosowicziow Street. In the winter, coal was distributed to the poor people in the building. Bauman, who was supposed to keep order, behaved badly toward all the people. He was the distributor and the supervisor. We received wood dust from the Sapir family to heat our place. They had a huge warehouse of wood planks and trees.

In April 1940, I took my father's place and joined a gang of workers who took the train to a place called Marczonkowicz. There a Polish supervisor joined us and we continued our train journey to the Dunajec River where there was a work camp. We started to work when a heavy downpour drenched us and we had no place to seek cover. We were all soaked and wet to the bone. They took us back to the city of Sandz. On occasion, I worked at other places for three or four zlotys. Sometimes I worked in the military barracks and sometimes at the military kitchen where I received food. My parents decided to take advantage of the free time that the curfew provided. They took advantage of the German teacher Eliasz Lustig who lived in the complex. He started to give me German lessons for a small fee. With me were two other male students and two female students.. In one of the rooms we frequently met to pray or discuss or converse. That room had a table consisting of wood without nails. Some Hasidic students were familiar with spiritualism and we had a few seaance sessions but nothing came of it.

Our neighbor, Mrs. Sheinfeld who lived the third door from us, lived with her daughter Ella and her son Bulo Itci. Her husband Itzi, her daughter Gusta and her son Tzvi had escaped to Russia where they remained during the war. Some evenings, we used to enter their apartment and sit next to the ceramic stove that provided heat and coziness. Sometimes kissing or petting ensued. During the day, other friends joined and we played cards. Until 1940-1941 we lived in the apartment and next door lived an elderly woman who snored something terrible. One day she passed away and we received the room. We opened a door and joined the room to our existing room and now we had a two–room apartment.

In 1941 I was sent instead of my father to a German farm outside the city to pick potatoes. At the farm, we received breakfast and lunch and also 15 kilos of potatoes for our work. In March/April 1941, the father–in–law of our neighbor, Rhingold, asked me to join him on his tours to collect old debts from the farmers near the city. He had a horse and a cart as well as a proper license. On Sunday we started to travel to the villages of Czeczowina, Wisoka and others. The farmers were cooperative and settled their old debts. Many of them had no money but they paid in flour, wheat, potatoes, vegetables and other foods. We slept in the villages and continued our collection the next day. So it went until Thursday when we returned home. We came back to the city with the food and I received a nice food commission for my part of the work.

The Ghetto Wall Construction
Nowy Sacz Ghetto Maps
Drawn by Markus (Mordechai) Lustig (Kannengisser) / Translated by Bill Leibner (February 2006)

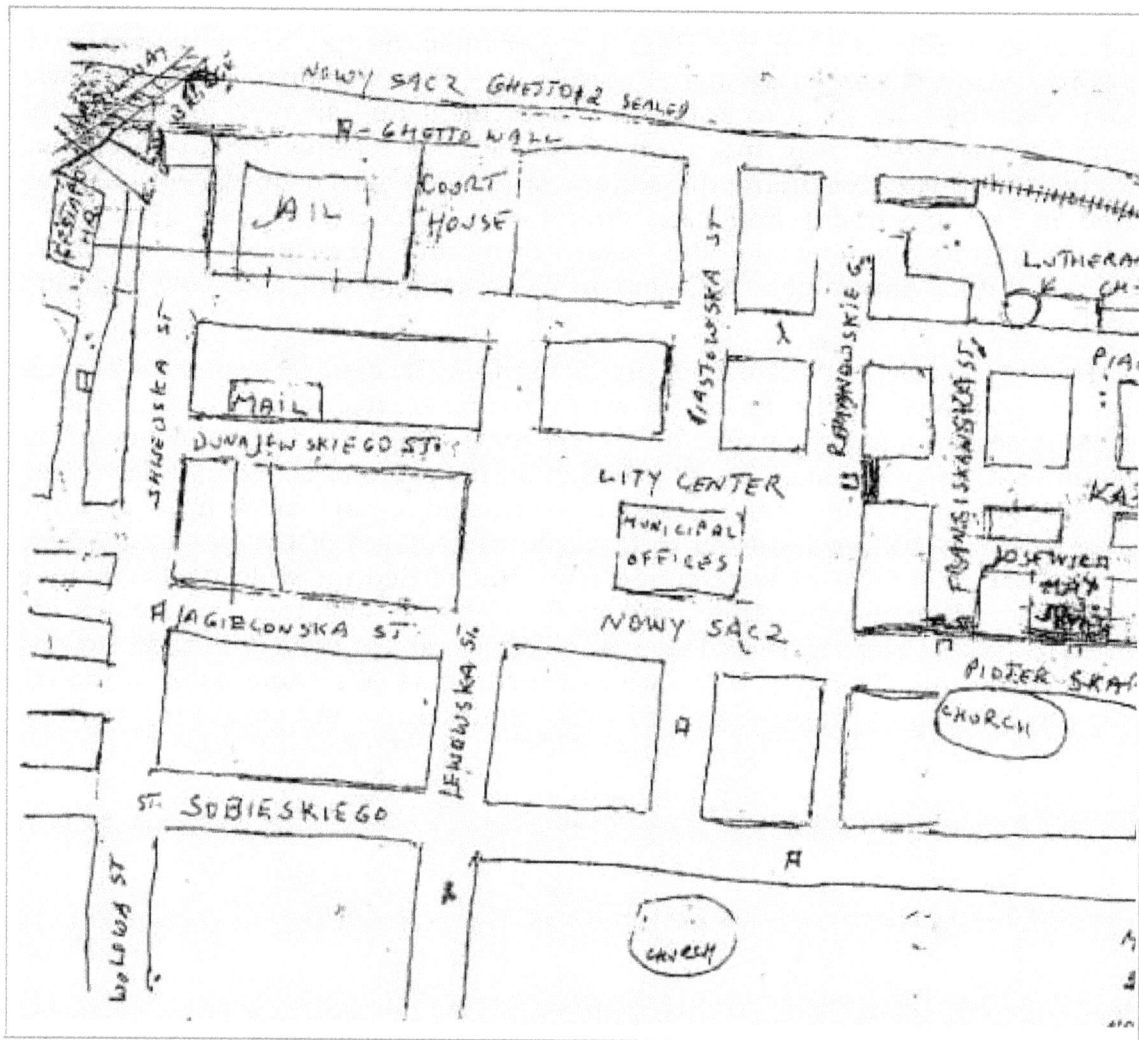

Nowy Sacz or Sandz ghetto. This ghetto was sealed. The entrance was on the right next to the letter A

Toward the end of the summer of 1941, the Germans started to build ghetto walls. The first wall extended from the entrance to the market to the intersection between Romanowska and Kazimierz Streets, known as the Yiddishe Gasse or Jewish Street. The second wall was built along Franciskanska Street, known as the Fish Street. The third was built around the 3 May Square. The fourth was built near the synagogue, at the corner of Pioter and Skargi Streets. The fifth wall was built along Kazimierz Street toward the Helena Bridge.

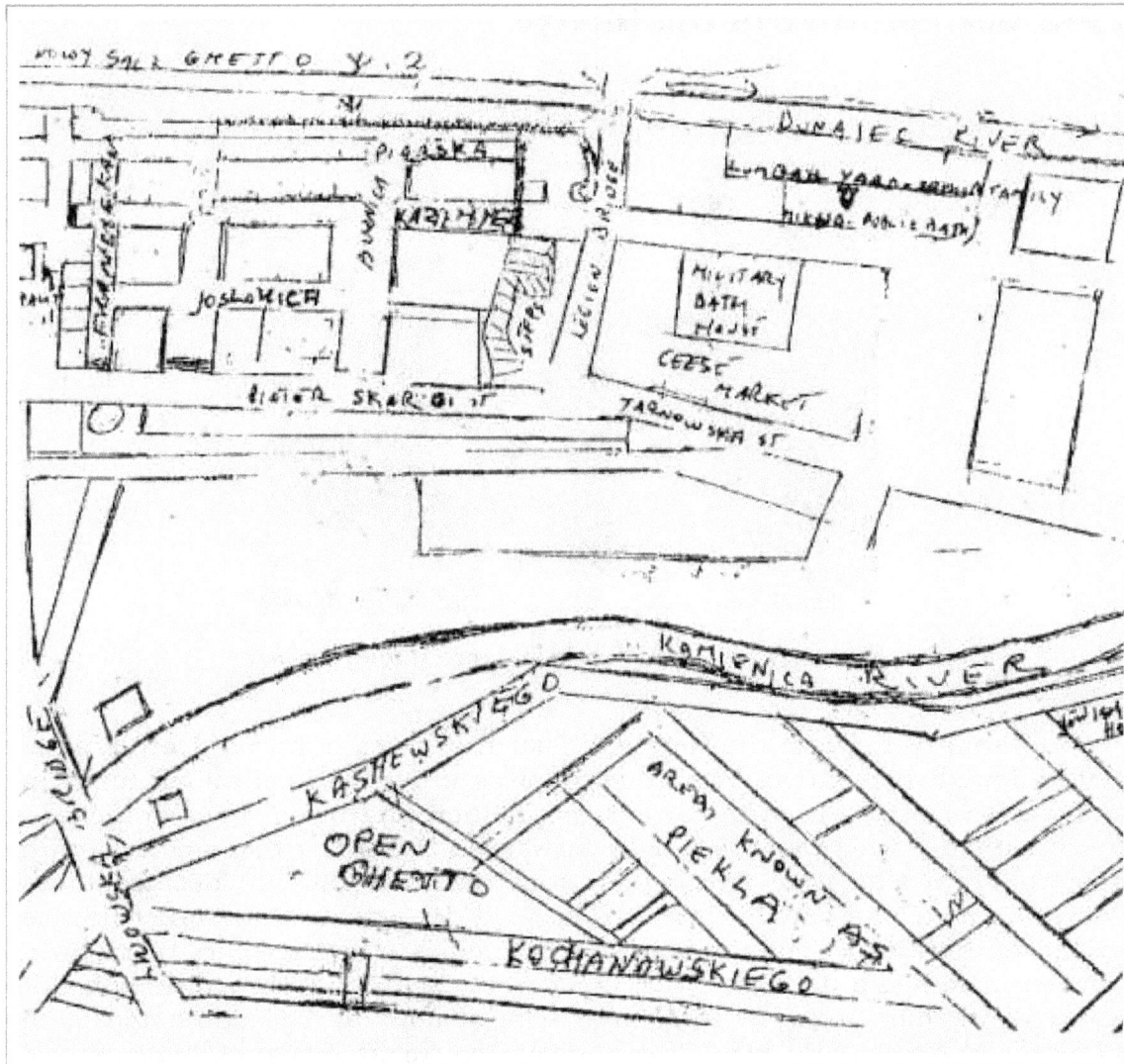

The Open Ghetto of Sandz that basically enclosed the area known as the Piekale

The second ghetto was concentrated in the so–called Piekle area and had no walls. You could enter it without difficulty by walking along Piarski Street to Swedska Street and then crossing Jagielonska and Lwowska Streets until the bridge over the Piekle above the Dominica River.

The number of friends in the ghetto kept shrinking. Still, we had a close circle of friends that consisted of Yossel Henig who lived in our building, Moshe Wint and Peretz Petrezeil who was called Peretz Katchka; there were also several girls, namely Ella Sheinfeld and others. We played dominoes and cards in our free time. At the end of 1941, a typhus epidemic started in our complex in the ghetto. The Judenrat quarantined the building but provided some food that consisted of soup and bread. The epidemic stopped at the end of December and the quarantine was lifted.

1942 Dead or Alive in the Ghetto

Jews with white arm bands in Sandz during the war

On January 1, 1942, the Germans issued a series of harsh decrees aimed at the Jewish population. The Judenrat was ordered to collect all fur items and woolen clothing from the Jewish population and bring them to the main collection place where they would be forwarded to the German soldiers on the Eastern Front who were freezing. At that time, my parents decided to sell flour. The flour was bought from Berish Nord. He was an undertaker licensed by the authorities to remove dead Jewish bodies and transport them to the cemetery. He had a deep cart with two horses. My friend Shragai Kleintzahler worked with him. Berish would buy sacks of flour and place on top of the sacks dead bodies. He would unload the sacks at designated places and continue his trip to the cemetery. On his way back from the cemetery he would collect the money. My parents knew Berish and made a deal with him whereby they would take took a sack of 100 kilos of flour and pay him when they sold the flour. The merchandise was sold kilo by kilo. My parents earned one kilo of flour when the entire operation was finished. The sale went very fast since our building complex had about 250 people. The entire operation was dangerous but hunger was the driving force of survival.

In March 1942, the Jewish police started an action aimed at the Jewish black market cigarettes dealers. They arrested all known dealers. The Gestapo insisted that all of them be delivered to their office. The Germans took possession of these Jews and after three days in jail, murdered them all. Luck was with me since I was a small dealer or I was not listed.

In 1942, the People's Kitchen opened at the Hertzberg study above us. For one zloty, I received a plate of soup from the distributor, Hertzberg himself. Poles could still enter the ghetto area but in limited areas. From the market along the Romanowskiego Street, Jews were permitted to walk on the right side of the street and non–Jews on the left side. On the left side of the street was my friend, the shoemaker, Pietrek, who sold me yeast until the Gestapo killed all Jewish cigarette dealers. We stopped trading.

On April 27, 1942, the Polish police submitted to the Gestapo the complete list of Jewish activists in the Poelei Tzion left movement. The files pertained to the period before the war. The Gestapo ordered the Judenrat head, Folkman (the previous Judenrat head, Marin, had been sent by Harman to Auschwitz) to arrest all the people on the list and to bring them to the Gestapo. On April 28th, the entire ghetto was surrounded by the Gestapo and the German police. The Gestapo chief Heinrich Harmann (the name is similar to the name in the Purim story) wanted to make sure that the Jewish police executed the order. There was one problem: the so–called list was an old prewar list that included many Jews who had left or moved from Sandz. To fill the quota, the police grabbed members of the family or people who looked like the ones on the list. The Judenrat was also ordered to take six members of the Judenrat and send them to the Gestapo as hostages to insure that the order was carried out. The hostages were; Koiftche Aftergut, Leon Goldman, Chaim Holtzer, Mendyl Wasner, Israel Wentzelberg, Wolf Langsam our next–door neighbor.

The search for the people on the list was brutal. The screams and tears could be heard all over. The police kept asking where is this person? Of course, people had died or moved away. But some family members were still in Sandz so the police grabbed members of the family; even women were arrested if the party was not found.

Finally, the Jewish police brought 300 Jews to the Gestapo. The Gestapo received them brutally and distributed beatings right and left. Their dogs were constantly barking and some of the dogs actually attacked the hapless Jews. Then the Jews were pushed into the city jail. Later on, the younger Jews were forced to dance before a select audience of the SS and their wives in the gallery. Harmann shouted, This is your death dance."

My friend Awraham Segulim was hiding. At first they arrested his wife. He then went to the Jewish police and presented himself. They released her and took him into custody. The Gestapo received him and beat him mercilessly. He was thrown into jail with the other Jews. Then on Wednesday, they were all lined up by the Gestapo chief Heinrich Harmann. He pulled six people from the crowd and gave them jobs. Awraham Segulim was among them. The assembled Jews were beaten and kicked. Then three were taken and shot. The rest were marched back to the prison. Harmann addressed the six Jews whom he had given jobs and held a sermon for them. At the end of the service he let them go home. They, of course, brought greetings from the rest of the Jews who were locked up. Little did they know that the remainder of the Jews would be murdered. The entire story was told to me by Abraham Segulim when we were sent to the work farm of Ritro after the ghetto was liquidated.

More Sad News

Silence enshrined the ghetto. There were no people in the street after 5.30 in the evening. People were afraid and hid where they could. I went up under the roof and watched along Piarski Street at the end of which was the jail house. I managed to see three groups of prisoners surrounded by armed S.S. men and Gestapo men headed by Harmann. They were led away to Zelazno Street. I went over to the opening and faced the Zelazno Street and saw them heading along the street. To get a better view, I went down the stairs to our apartment and saw the Jews being led in the direction of the cemetery. I was certain that they were condemned to death.

Some people who were there witnessed the scene. The large mass grave was prepared in advance. The Jews were ordered to undress and neatly fold their clothes. They were then told to lie face down on the ground. Everybody expected to be killed instantly when suddenly a voice was heard loud and clear. It was the Jewish religious judge Yossef Moshe Zehman of Sandz who stood up erect and shouted: "Jews, you are being punished for the sins that we Jews committed against G-d's laws but our deliverance will soon arrive!" He turned to the German killers and said: "May the Jewish children who survive take revenge on you for what you are doing!" Ratzke stood up and began to curse the Germans and predicted their demise. A bullet cut her short and she fell to the ground. Shouting started all over. The Jewish police, the sanitation police and the cemetery assistants were dumbfounded by the butchery of innocent people. They could do little but watch. When the shouting stopped, the Gestapo ordered them to place the bodies in the grave in neat order. The policemen trampled on those bodies that were already in the pit in order to neatly place the fallen bodies. Some of the bodies were still alive. The action finished, the grave was covered with earth. The blood kept oozing above the ground and could be seen as black liquid spots for several days. The bloodthirsty killers then held a party and got drunk.

The German Horror Show Continues

The mass killings at the cemetery were not enough for the bloodthirsty Germans. When they sobered up a bit, they decided to continue their carnage. They entered the ghetto at about 9:30 in the evening and began to break into buildings and shoot Jews. They entered our building on the ground floor and opened the door to the Hertzberg family. They shot Moshe Hertzberg, his wife, his son Zalke who had returned from Russia in 1941 and their two daughters. The entire family was wiped out in an instant. The shooting stopped and the Germans headed up the stairs to the first floor where we lived. They entered our neighbor's apartment where the Sheinfeld family lived. She was blond and they left the apartment intact. Then they entered our apartment. What ensued in our rooms I have already described in great detail at the beginning of the book.

When the shooting stopped and silence descended on the ghetto I took another look at the horror show in our apartment and decided to go up to the attic under the roof. There I met some of the neighbors who had escaped the slaughter such as Itzi Dorenter and his wife Gusta Beck, with their baby. They were a young couple who had married during the war. Most of the people who survived that night in the attic would not survive the Shoah. They would be sent to the death camp of Belzec with the liquidation of the ghetto of Sandz.

The mass killings that evening resulted in the death of about 100 people including women and children. The murders with the Gestapo chief Harmann at their head then headed to the apartment of Aaron Neishtadt, where they encountered the Gestapo man Kestner. Harmann pulled his pistol and aimed at Aaron, intending to kill him and his family. Kestner interfered by saying that there was enough killing tonight. Without hesitation, Harmann turned his pistol to Kestner and fired. Kestner fell to the ground, seriously injured. He was rushed to the hospital where they managed to save him and extracted from him a statement of the events that occurred in the Neishstadt apartment. The Gestapo was already busy spreading rumors that the Jews killed a Gestapo officer. Kestner's statement demolished the rumors and quieted the situation in Sandz.

The next day, April 30, 1942, the Jewish sanitation police received the order to remove all dead people from their apartments. The caretaker Berish Nord and his assistant began to transport the bodies of the dead Jews to the cemetery where they were buried together with the Jews shot the previous day at the cemetery.

My uncle Moshe came and helped me clean the apartment. I then began to sit "shivah" for my family. My uncle joined me. Nobody came to pay their respects. Everybody was busy sitting in their own corner for their dear departed ones. Shabbat I went to my grandfather and prayed at the Berger house. After the mourning period I began to assume full responsibility for my life. I could not indulge in a long period of introspection as to the causes and actions of what had happened. Life continued and I had to swim with the stream. No time left for self-pity. I began to sell items from the house to the Poles in order to survive. There was a black market in the May 3 Square where they sold tablecloths, bed sheets and other household items. I was selling our belongings to buy bread and salami.

The Germans did not reach the house of grandfather Lewi Kannengisser where my uncle Moshe also lived. They were saved that day. As was my grandmother Miriam Lustig and her daughter Riwka, with her husband Shlomo Boguchwal and the Aaron Berger family and other families. But the Jewish youth who survived in Sandz turned to despair, seeing no hope or future. Those who had money started to spend it like water. The Wint family opened the Hollander Hall as a ballroom for dancing and drinking. Our apartment did not remain empty for long. A family was soon ushered in. They were from the village of Lelow. The family consisted of a father, a mother and a daughter. They had no money. They used to live downstairs. I helped them out occasionally with food. Their daughter invited me to spend the nights with her while her parents were sleeping in the same room.

Rumors started to spread that the Germans intended to liquidate the ghetto. German and SS officials came to inspect and make decisions regarding the situation of the ghetto of Sandz. My uncle Moshe told me that I must get a diploma or the Germans would deport me to one of their death camps. I consented and he managed to get me an official certificate attesting that I was a locksmith. Moshe had excellent contacts with the employment office. There is no doubt that this certificate helped me survive the war.

The certificate was written in German so that any patrol of the army or SS could read my trade with ease. The certificate in my pocket also gave me some self-assurance and enabled me to make decisions. The search for men was constant. The Germans needed constantly replacements for they mistreated the Jewish workers who died in large numbers due to the long work hours and very little food, especially in wintertime. To replenish the shortages roundups were carried out at a moment's notice. Sometimes the Judenrat was ordered to draft people for the German needs. The average Jew never knew when an action was about to commence actions and. Once it started, the Germans arrested everybody they could until they had their demanded quota of people.

The Jewish ghetto in Sandz. Notice the white armbands
(Courtesy of the Yad Vashem Archives)

[Page 106]

Chapter IV
The Liquidation
of the Sandz Ghettos

**Mordechai Lustig in the
ghetto of Sandz in 1942.
Notice the white armband**

We already mentioned that Sandz had two ghettos. The Jewish population was steadily pauperized in both ghettos to the extent of starvation. Jews died of hunger, disease, and hopelessness. Only those who could sell goods, jewelry or other valuables could survive since they depended on the black market for food. The Germans did everything in their power to reduce the Jewish population. All sorts of actions, arrests and terror methods were used to decimate the Jewish population of Sandz. Action followed action. The "Kapota Action" or "Kaftan Action" took place at the end of the summer when 10 rabbis and Hasidic–looking Jews were arrested and supposedly held as hostages for the explosion that took place at the Sandz railway station where tanks aboard a train were damaged. Among the rabbis were two sons of the Sandz rabbi Leibish Halberstam: Ephraim and Hersh Halberstam. Also arrested was Moshe Eichenstein. All of these people were sent to Auschwitz where they perished. This action was followed by the operation of rounding up all Jews who had left Sandz for Eastern Poland and returned later to Sandz; they were rounded up and murdered by the Gestapo. Indeed, the number of Jews from Sandz proper steadily declined. However, the Germans brought Jews from Krakow and Lodz to Sandz. They also forced some Jews in the area of Sandz to leave their homes and move to Sandz. These Jews were driven out of their homes practically naked. They arrived in Sandz and needed everything. The Judenrat helped but their resources were limited and steadily shrinking.

Ghetto wall in Sandz cuts street into two sections

There were two ghettos in Sandz. The so–called open ghetto was located in the Piekla area and relatively unguarded. The second one was generally closed and became sealed with the building of the walls around it in December and January 1942. There were also days when the Jewish police were looking for workers and seized Jews who were sent to places like Rabka. Rabka was a camp where the Germans had a school in which they trained the Gestapo and SS men to become professional sadistic killers. The course lasted six months and used live Jews as specimens for their sadistic kills. The school was located in the "Tereska" villa. No one survived the Rabka camp. Jews in the transports that arrived in Rabka were immediately shot or hanged. Two transports of elderly and sick Jews were sent from Sandz in May–June 1942 to Rabka. Most of the people were killed on arrival. The young and strong were used as guinea pigs for sadistic killings. All of the Jews perished, except for two people: Monek Lustig and Naftali Dershewitz. Both were natives of Stary Sacz. Naftali Dershewitz survived the war and went to Israel where he joined the police force. He was attached to a special unit that investigated Nazi war criminals. They prepared files and researched witnesses to testify against the war criminals. Some Jews were also sent to the labor camp Pustkow. We will describe this camp later.

At the end of May or beginning June 1942, I was ordered by the Jewish labor office to pack a small suitcase with clothing and to present myself to the office. There I met about 30 other Jews who had received similar orders. We boarded a truck and headed to a labor camp called Roznow. There were other Jews at the camp. The supervisor was a Jew named Liber Berliner. The camp consisted of barracks that had bunk beds with planks and straw. The place was located near the dam on the Dunajec River. On occasion the river flooded the nearby fields and the Polish government would pay the farmers damages. We did a variety of work details; mostly our work consisted of digging pits for construction. I also worked at unloading bags of cement that trucks brought to the site. The camp was a mess but we received enough food. Each month I received an envelope with money. I was paid three zlotys per day for heavy physical work.

I was then removed from the camp and sent to the hamlet of Czchow where I unloaded bags of cement and carried them to the warehouse. The hamlet was a typical religious hamlet and Jews lived here the way we used to live before the Germans arrived. The hamlet seemed to exist on a different planet. Jewish life flowed as though nothing happened. There was no Gestapo, no German army. I was invited to a Sabbath meal at the home of a local Jewish family and felt immediately at home. The dishes, the atmosphere, the singing, everything reminded me of my home that was no longer. The Jewish community of the hamlet was destroyed with the destruction of all the ghettos in the area.

Every two weeks I received a liberty pass and went home to Sandz to change clothes. The pass started Saturday noon and was valid until Monday morning. At home I washed my clothes and repaired some items. My grandfather and my uncle Moshe now lived in my apartment. During one of the visits at home, I noticed that my grandfather's face was bruised and black and blue. My uncle told me that the Gestapo had again raided Jewish homes and mercilessly beat people.

The conditions in the ghettos went from bad to worse. The closed ghetto was practically sealed. All Jews who arrived from nearby small hamlets and were penniless were sent to the closed ghetto. All elderly and sick Jews were also sent to the closed ghetto. Conditions there were beyond description. The mortality rate was very high in the closed ghetto. Most people who had money tried to buy their way into the open ghetto where there were factories and workshops – like the broom factory or fur or carpentry workshops – and worked for the Germans. Jews paid a great deal of money to get a work permit from the employment office that enabled them to work in an official place that was relatively protected from arrests and round–ups. Things were so bad that I was not permitted to enter the closed ghetto where I lived when I returned to Sandz during a weekend. The Judenrat assigned me another place in the open ghetto. I never saw my grandfather again.

Steps preceding the liquidation of the Sandz ghettos

In August 1942, the Gestapo in Sandz received orders to prepare for the liquidation of the ghettos of Sandz. The actual liquidation began in the district of Sandz. In the middle of August 1942 the Gestapo announced that the Jews of the four hamlets – Stary Sacz, Limanowa, Mszana-Dolna and Grybow – would have to move to the ghetto of Sandz. They even posted the exact dates: Stary Sacz would be liquidated on August 17, 1942, Limanowa on August 18,

1942, Mszana Dolna on August 19, 1942 and Grybow on August 20, 1942. All four communities also had to collect money to pay a German demand for blackmail. This contribution was also imposed on the city of Sandz. The Jews were forced to part with their last pennies. The liquidation program went into full swing. In Stary Sacz, the elderly and sick Jews, about 100–150, were told to assemble at a place where trucks would transport them to Sandz.

In reality the trucks took them to the nearby Poprad River and they were shot. They were buried in a prepared mass grave. The rest of the Jewish population was driven in the hot summer day to Sandz. Many collapsed along the road, others fainted from exhaustion; the stragglers were shot. Finally the survivors reached the closed ghetto of Sandz. The shrunken ghetto was already heavily overcrowded. The next day, the scene repeated itself in Limanowa. The Gestapo arrived with the trucks, they took about 160 elderly, sick and weak–looking people and assigned them seats aboard the trucks. The trucks rolled a distance whereupon they were forced to descend and were shot. They were buried in a mass prepared grave. The rest of the Jewish population was driven on foot to Sandz, a distance of about 26 kilometers. Next in order was the hamlet of Mszana Dolna. The Gestapo asked the Jews to provide a large sum of money as a contribution to the German authorities. The Jewish collection was a bit short. The Gestapo chief Heinrich Harmman took the contribution but was very angry. He ordered the entire Jewish population to assemble. All the Jews were ordered to mount trucks. They were taken to a prepared mass grave where 790 Jews were shot. One hundred twenty strong Jews were forced to march to Sandz. No Jews were left in the hamlet except for a group of Jewish workers who were supposed to collect and record the contents of the Jewish homes. The largest Jewish community of Grybow was next in order. The same procedure was used in the destruction of Grybow. The old people were taken and shot in several places. Then about 1,500 Jews were driven to Sandz. The ghetto was bursting at the seams. The Judenrat tried to help but was helpless. The Jewish population had reached 14,000 souls. The ghetto could not cope with such a large number of poor and desperate Jews.

On Friday, August 21, 1942, at 9 A.M., the Gestapo chief of Sandz Harmmann ordered the Jewish sanitary police, the block leaders and sanitary assistants to appear before his office. He told them that on Sunday, August 23, 1942 at 5 A.M. the resettlement of Jews would begin. All Jews would have to assemble between the Helena and the railway bridges along the Dunajec River. The Jews would have to be dressed in their Sunday best. They would be permitted to take with them 10 kilos of food and 15 kilos of goods and clothing. Everybody should lock their place and bring with them the key and a card with their name on it. The news set in motion a great panic and confusion. People had to decide what to take and what to leave. Some Jews did not trust the Germans and decided to leave for the forest areas. Others tried to use their connections with Poles and sought refuge with them. The great majority accepted the decision and hoped for the best. Many Jews tried to sell items for cash. The buyers had the upper hand since they knew that the Jews must sell the items. To keep the tension in motion, 200 Jews were arrested on Saturday and taken to the cemetery where they were forced to knock down the memorial tombstones.

With the end of the Sabbath, Jews already began to proceed to the designated place along the river. The furriers from the Piekale area were ordered to carry their work permits. Jewish forced laborers from Sandz were ordered to report to Sandz from their camps or workshops outside Sandz, among them Mordechai Lustig. I was awakened at 5:30 in the morning at the Rozinow camp and was told to get dressed and proceed outside where trucks were waiting. We were not permitted to take our belongings and had to leave everything behind. Outside, we mounted trucks that immediately started rolling to Sandz. They dumped us next to the Dunajec where the Jews were assembling for the so-called resettlement. Other Jewish workers began to arrive from the labor camps in Lipie and the barracks of the road construction gangs in Nowoyowek. The place was packed with Jews and I even saw two of my uncles, Awraham and Moshe Kannengisser, with their rucksacks on their backs. This mass of Jewish humanity was squeezed into a small area and waited. Meanwhile, more Jews kept arriving at the assembly area, street by street, each street headed by the block leader with a list of the Jews in his section. The streets of Sandz were being cleared of Jews. Finally, Harmmann and his assistants showed up and things began to move. He walked over to our Roznow group and selected several dozen workers including myself and told us to join the crowd of awaiting Jews.

At 6 A.M. Harmann and Swoboda, head of the security police and head of the employment office, the entire Gestapo contingent of Sandz, and some Polish policemen arrived at the scene. The place was surrounded by German soldiers in full battle gear. Dogs were barking. Harmann insisted that he must have another 250,000 zlotys to cover the expense of the resettlements. He claimed that the previous contributions were not enough to cover all the expenses. Money and jewelry were collected and Harmann took everything. Now the selection began. Swoboda announced that all professional workers including carpenters, locksmiths, plumbers and builders must move over to one little hill. One hundred one workers including myself stepped to the indicated place where trucks awaited and took us to the municipal slaughterhouse. We were told and warned to surrender all valuables to the guards. Anybody caught with money or jewelry would be hanged. Some gave, some threw their possessions into the sewers and some kept the valuables. We were then told to mount trucks and were sent to the Ritro labor camp. The camp consisted of two barracks and was next to the river Poprad. One hundred Jewish workers were sent to the Roznow labor camp, to Mszana Dolna were sent 50 workers, to Sandzaw 50 workers, to the sawmill in Nawoyowe 120 workers,

50 workers were sent to the fur workshop to repair furs for the Germans and 50 workers were sent to clean the Jewish apartments of Sandz. After the clean-up operation, most of them would be sent to the Tarnow ghetto and

then to other concentration camps. In effect, about 900 Jews were permitted to live. The rest of the 13,000 Jews were condemned to death.

The Jews condemned to death were driven back to the closed ghetto where there was hardly room to stand. Thirsty, hungry, fearful, the Jews were desperate and resigned. The Jews were sent to the Belzec death camp in three transports. The first transport left Tuesday, August 25, 1942. Most of the Jews were gassed on arrival. The second transport left for Belzec between Wednesday and Thursday and the third transport left for Belzec on Friday, August 28, 1942. All Jews were gassed on their arrival. Their bodies were buried in huge mass graves. Only one Jew survived Belzec. His name was Rudolf Leder, a native of Debice. He was in Belzec from August 17, 1942 to the end of November 27, 1942 and managed to escape and survive the war. He was the only survivor of the estimated 600,000 Jews that perished in the death camp of Belzec.

Bertha Korman

We already mentioned that some Jews tried to find hiding places among Polish friends in Sandz. Bertha Korman knew Stefan Mazor who worked for Mr. Barto. The latter was responsible for the maintenance of the municipal clocks that were set into the magnificent tower of the municipal building in Sandz. There were four clocks, one on each side of the tower. Mr. Barto had an assistant named Stefan Mazor who actually handled the cleaning and greasing of the big chains that kept the mechanisms in regardless of the weather conditions. Stefan managed to lead Bertha to the clock tower without being observed by anybody. There she remained in hiding until a safer place could be found. There was a serious noise problem in the clock room when the bells rang motion and with the steady grinding of the mechanisms. The noise was unbearable. Furthermore, there was always a Polish policeman on guard duty below the clock level where one can see a fenced balcony.

Notice the clock at the top of the tower of the municipal building.
There was a small room there where Bertha Korman was hiding
(Picture courtesy of Jean Krieser of Paris, France)

Bertha Korman

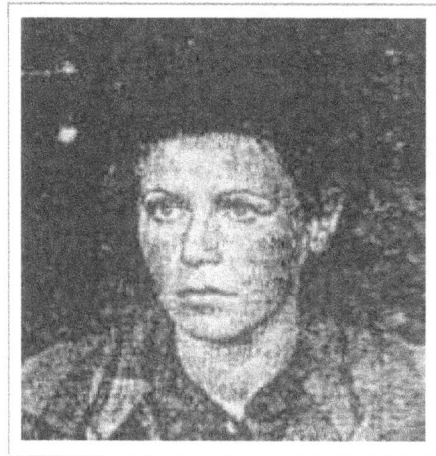

Stefan Mazor

Stefan made all kinds of plans to get Bertha out of the hiding place. He managed to get her "Aryan" or non-Jewish papers and they both left Sandz for another city, Przemysl. Both were arrested in Przemysl by the Gestapo and sent as Polish workers to Germany.

From left: **Riwka Lustig, Stefan Mazor and Mordechai Lustig in Lublin, Poland in 2001**

Following the war, the couple returned to Lublin, Poland, where they married and had two children, a son and a daughter. Their history became known when a Polish newspaper wrote an article about the family that had no clocks in their house. The story was picked by an Israeli film producer but the children objected to the publicity and the film production was cancelled. Mordechai and his wife met Mazor in Lublin, Poland in 2001.

Many Jews had built bunkers and hiding places prior to the liquidation of the ghetto of Sandz, including the Sapir family. They remained in hiding an entire month until one day someone reported their hiding place to the Gestapo. The Gestapo surrounded the place and took all the Jews to the cemetery where they were shot. In another instance, Yudel Weinberger hid in a bunker. He had made arrangements with a Pole to come and take him away to safety. The Gestapo followed the Pole and discovered the hiding place. Yudel Weinberg begged the Gestapo to kill him on the spot; they granted him his favor and shot him along the road. The Germans continued to search the ghetto areas for hiding places and bunkers.

The Jewish "cleaning commando" continued to clean the Jewish homes and institutions under the watchful eyes of the Gestapo. The smallest infraction could result in death. Jewish goods were sorted and assembled. Another group gathered furniture. All items were then sold in the open to the local population for peanuts. The Germans even assigned Shmuel Gutwein to sort books. Valuable treasures were assembled and sent to Germany. When his job was finished, Gutwein was sent to the Szebnie labor camp in Poland where he was murdered.

Toward the Jewish holidays in 1942, 50 cleaning workers from Sandz were sent to the labor camp in Mielec, Poland. Another large group was sent in October to the Tarnow ghetto. In the spring of 1943, there were still 100 Jewish workers in Sandz. In June 1943, 70 Jewish workers were sent to the

Szebnie labor camp. The last 37 Jews of Sandz were sent to Szebnie in July 1943. The city became officially "Judenrein." An entire old Jewish community was deracinated, never to regain life.

The Sandzer landsmanshaft in Israel collected money and sent representatives to Sandz where they placed a memorial plaque on behalf of the Jews who had lived and worked in the city and surrounding areas. The memorial is written in Polish, Hebrew and Yiddish.

May all the Jewish victims rest in eternal peace!

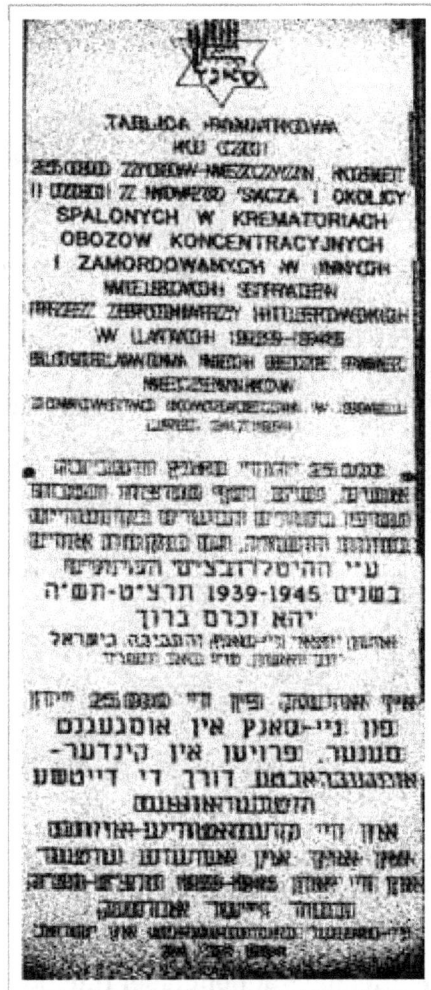

Monument to the Jews of Sandz and vicinity erected by the Sandz Landesmanzchaft association of Sandz in Israel following the war.
The inscription reads:
In Memory of the 25,000 Jews of Sandz and vicinity; Men, Women and Children who were murdered by German Hitlerites in the gas chambers and other killing sites during the war years 1939–1945 or Hebrew date Tarchat–Tasha.
HONOR THEIR MEMORY!
The Association of Jews of Sandz in Israel erected this monument July 24, 1994

Mordechai Lustig also erected a tombstone for his family at the cemetery in Sandz following the war

The memorial reads in Hebrew:
'Here rest, my dear relatives, who were shot on April 29, 1942.
My father Yaacov Kannengisser, my mother Ita, my sister
Rachel, and my brother Moshe.
May their memory be blessed.'
Mordechai Kannengisser (Lustig)

[Page 126]

Chapter V
The Hasidic City
of Sandz is No Longer

My synagogue of Sandz–Grybow was gone, my rabbi was gone and my family was gone. The Jews, the rabbis, the synagogues, the shtibelech and the study halls were destroyed. A deadly silence descended on the city that became "Judenrein" or free of Jews in July 1943. The bastion of the Halberstam rabbinical family was decimated and scattered throughout the world. Sandz was orphaned spiritually and physically.

Sandz was a small city where the Jewish population was predominantly orthodox. The city was basically devoid of industry and was a relatively small, dormant city where life flowed like the three rivers in the city. Then appeared on the horizon a Jewish scholarly star named Rabbi Chaim Halberstam, originally Halberstadt.[1]

Rabbi Halberstam then remained for the rest of his life in Sandz from 1830 to 1876 and became known affectionately throughout the world as Rabbi

"Chaimel the Sandzer." Sandz became a center of Hasidism[2] with the residence of Rabbi Halberstam. Not only Hasidim of Galicia came to the court but also Hasidim from all over Eastern Europe. Thousands of Hasidim came to the rabbi on Saturday and holidays from Galicia, Slovakia, Carpathian Russia, Hungary and the other parts of Poland. Together with the Hasidim also came famous rabbis and pious Jews, especially from the center of Galicia.

The economic factor cannot be minimized. The thousands of Hasidim that visited the rabbi had to eat, sleep and buy some souvenirs to bring home. The city's business community dominated by the Jewish merchants benefited tremendously from the large inflow of visitors to the city. The city of Sandz became a familiar place on the Jewish map. Even the Polish railway placed special trains at the disposal of the Sandzer Hasidim when there was a special occasion.[3]

All of his daughters married Hasidic rabbis in Galicia. The family became a very influential force in Jewish life in Galicia. The influence of the family was extremely powerful among the Jewish masses in Galicia. The rabbi himself assumed the leadership of Hasidism in Galicia and shaped it into a powerful instrument of conservatism. In many respects he accepted pragmatism but when it came to religion or religious tradition he would not budge an iota from the past.[4]

Rabbi Chaim Halberstam passed away in Sandz on April 19, 1876, three days after Passover. His son, Rabbi Aharon Halberstam, was appointed Rabbi of Sandz. The funeral was a massive event in Sandz. Many stores closed, most yeshivas and study halls stopped studying that day. A special memorial building was designated and built at the cemetery of Sandz for the rabbi. The rabbi was buried in the center of the hall. Later, his son Rabbi Aharon Halberstam would be buried on the Rabbi's right side and Rabbi Myer Nosom Halberstam on the Rabbi's left side. Added were the Rabbi of Siniawa, Rabbi Moshe and his son Rabbi Rabbi Leibush Mordechai. These five graves were fenced in.

**The memorial building where
Rabbi Chaim Halberstam was buried in Sandz**
(Courtesy of Yad Vashem archives)

**The memorial gravestone of Rabbi Chaim
Halberstam**
(Courtesy of Jean Krieser of Paris, France)

The Halberstam cemetery plot was extended several times to enable the burials of the son–in–laws Rabbi Tzwi Naftali and Rabbi Leibele the Glikser. His son, Rabbi Aaron Halberstam, was immediately assigned the post of Rabbi of Sandz. His father's death date became an annual pilgrimage site for the thousands of Sandzer Hasidim to visit the city and the grave of Rabbi Chaim. The Jewish community built a memorial building at the cemetery in the shape of bell in which the rabbi was buried. Buried there were also all the rabbi's sons and daughters. The entire family was eventually buried at the site.

The gravestone of Rabbi Arieh Leibush Halberstam
(Courtesy of Jean Krieser of Paris, France)

The gravestone of Rabbi Shulem Halberstam
(Courtesy of Jean Krieser of Paris, France)

לשרט נפלה עטרת ראשינו: כתר תורה

פ'נ

כ'ק אדמו'ר נזר ישראל גאון עוזנו
צדי'ק נשגב עובד ד' בקדושה וטהרה
בוק חום מאור הגולה רבים הלכו לאורו
מרן משה וצוק'ל בחנה'ק רשכבה'ז
מרן יחזקאל שרגא וצוקלהו'ה בהגאון הק'
רשכבה'ז בעל ר'ח וצוקלהו'ה: לפנים הי'
אבד'ק סטראפקוב וקק שינאווא ולבסוף
ימיד תקע אהלו בפהה'ק, דירכו בקודש
נפלא מאוד עבודתו ותפלתו במס'
כלהבת הקודש צדקת פזורונו לעני' ארצנו
ולעני' ארחק רבו מאוד וענייו ולבו
שם לפקח לטובת אחינו בא'הק, יען תול
דמע אל הלקח ארון הקודש ומשה עלה אל ד'
יום ועשוק י'ב מרחשון שנת נפלה עטרת ישראל
ת נ צ ב ה

Tombstone of Rabbi Yechezkel Shrahgai Halberstam
(Courtesy of Jean Krieser of Paris, France)

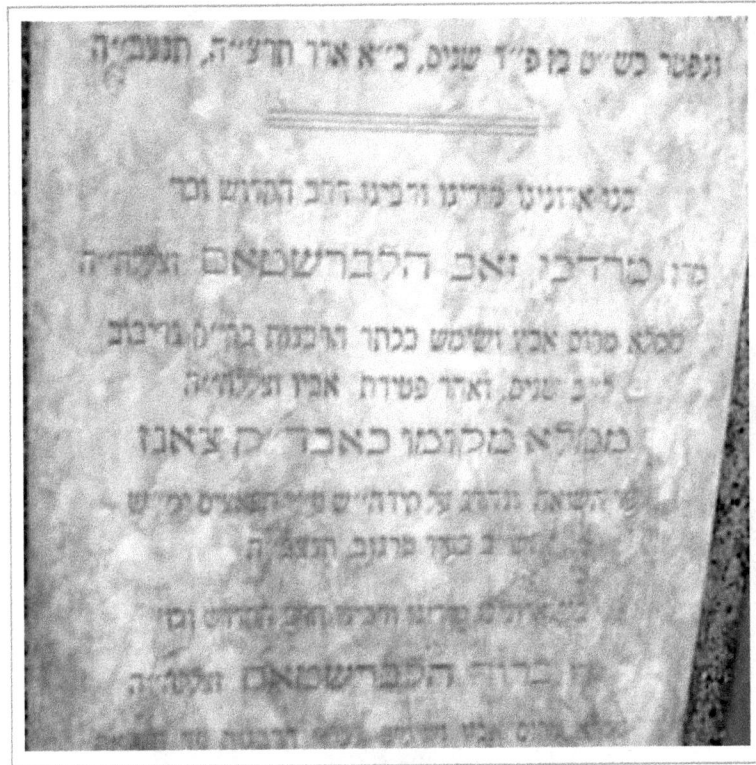

**The tombstone of Rabbi Mordechai Ze'ev
Halberstam and Rabbi Baruch Halberstam**
(Courtesy of Jean Krieser of Paris, France)

More tombstones were added until the Halberstam family decided to limit the total number of graves to 10. The place was kept in order but underwent serious damages during World War II.

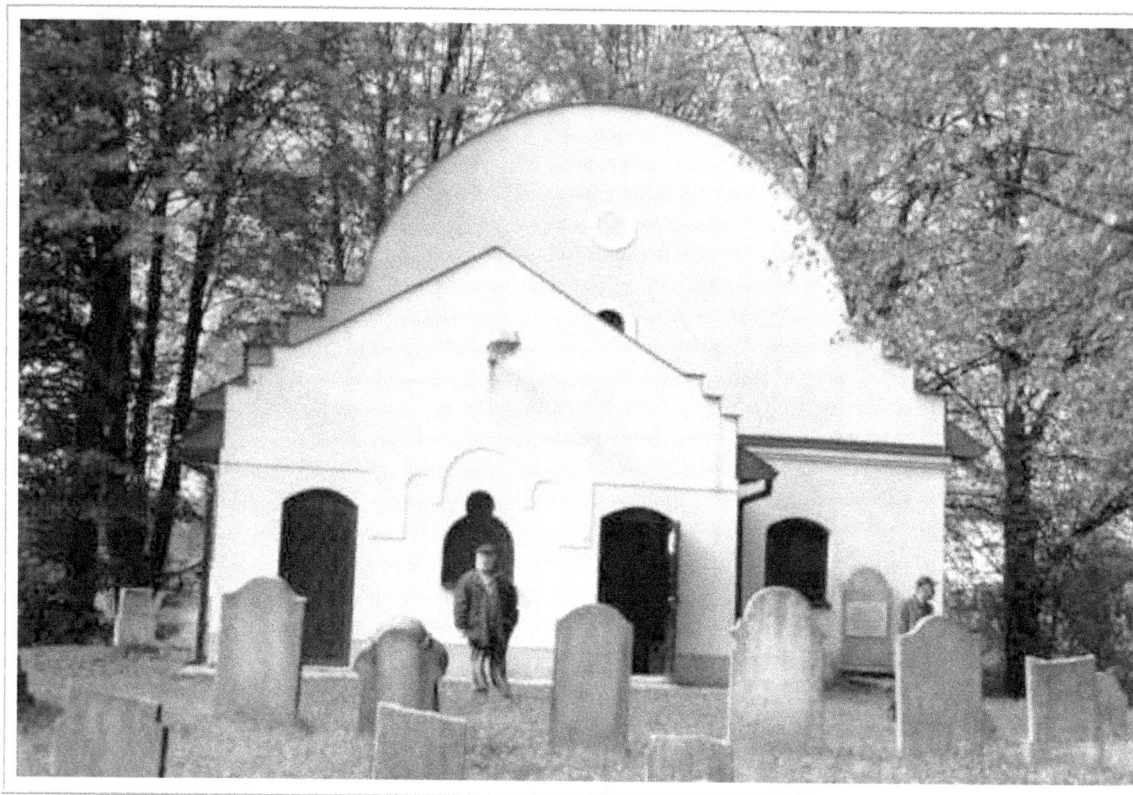

The renovated memorial building of the Halberstam family in Sandz
(Courtesy of Jean Krieser of Paris, France)

Following the war, the Sandzer memorial was in a poor state of affairs. Jacob Miller took it upon himself to restore the place. He lived in Sweden and spent many months in Sandz to supervise the restoration of the memorial tombstone to its previous splendor. After the war there were no Jews in Sandz so Miller lived a lonely life but was dedicated to the restoration of the Halberstam memorial building. Of course, many Sandzer Hasidim kept visiting Sandz and partook in services at the gravestones of the Halberstam family. Yaacov Miller died recently and the plaque below was erected in his honor.

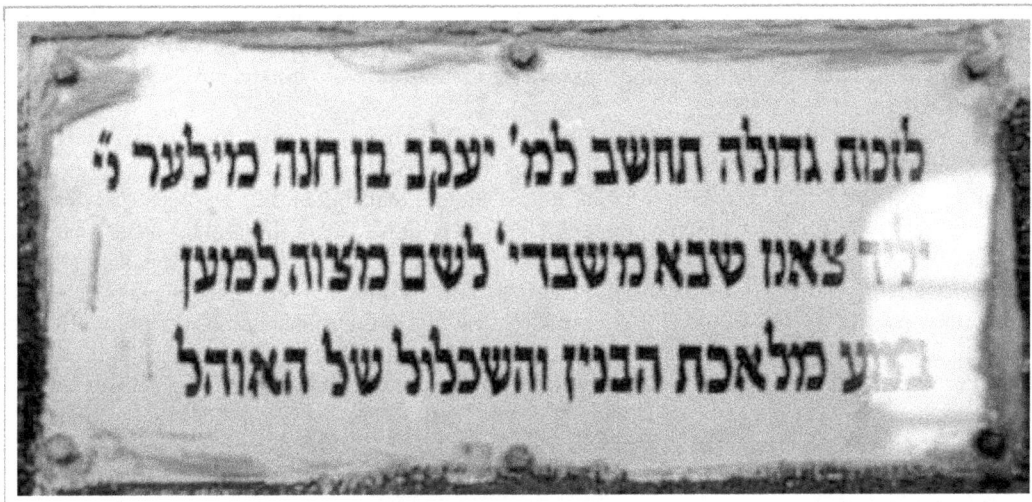

Memorial plaque in honor of Yaacov Miller, a native of Sandz who came from Sweden to supervise the remodeling and reconstruction of the Halberstam memorial building in Sandz
(Courtesy of Jean Krieser of Paris, France)

The rabbinical sons and grandsons created sub–branches of the Sandzer Hasidut in the years to come, namely: Bobower–Hasidut, Sandz–Grybow, Sandz–Gorlice, Sandz–Klausenburg and Sandz–Zmigrod. The Germans decimated the Sandzer Hasidut. Following the Shoah, some of the surviving descendants of the Sandzer Rabbi Chaim Halberstam re–established their Hasidic courts and continue to exist in many parts of the world.

Notes:

1. Rabbi Chaim Halberstam was born in the city of Tarnogrod in the Lublin region in 1793, the year of the second partition of Poland. His father, Arieh Leibush, was a great scholar and later assumed the post of "moyre–hoyroe" or spiritual supervisor of Przemysl. His mother, Miriam, was the daughter of Rabbi David in Brod. On his father's side, he was a descendant of Rabbi Tzvi Hirsh. According to tradition, the rabbi altered his name to Halberstam in order not to grant recognition to a non–Jewish place (Halberstadt is the name of a German town). Rabbi Chaim traced his paternal lineage to the "Maharashal" or Solomon Luria (1510–1574), one of the great Ashkenazi teachers of his time] and on his mother's side to the learned Rabbi, the Chacham Tzvi Ashkenazi of the 17th century.

    Rabbi Chaim was lame as a child and, it seems, he was lame his entire life. However in the Hasidic tradition of Sandz, the story is told that the "belfer" or assistant teacher hit him on his leg, causing a permanent injury. Tradition also has it that he cursed the assistant teacher all his life. Even as a young student he displayed great intellect and erudition and was famous as a great ilui or Talmudic genius. At the same time, he was fascinated and drawn to Hasidism. His first Hasidic rabbi was Yosele Halewi, a brother of the "Hozeh" or "Seer" of Lublin who lived in Tarnogrod.

Rabbi Chaim was so impressed by him that he continued to visit him until the "Hozeh" passed away in 1814. Even after his death, Rabbi Chaim always honored the memory of the Rabbi of Lublin and frequently quoted him or his writings and referred to him as our great saintly Rabbi of Lublin.

His great Torah idol was the rabbi and head of the Yeshiva of Leipnik in Moravia, present day Czechoslovakia: Rabbi Baruch Teumim Frenkel, who later became world famous as the author of the "Baruch Teum" book. Rabbi Chaim Halberstam married, at the age of seventeen, the daughter of the Rabbi of Leipnik, Rachel. He lived with his father–in–law for a full year and studied at his yeshiva. At the home of the Leipniker Rabbi, Halberstam developed a great interest in the book "More Nevuchim" – Guide for the Perplexed – by the Jewish religious philosopher Rabbi Maimonides. He continued to study Maimonides and became very familiar with his rational philosophy.

At the age of 18, Rabbi Chaim Halberstam was appointed Rabbi of Rudnik in central Galicia. The place was near the shtetl of Ropczyce where the famous Rabbi Naphtali "Ropshitzer" lived. The relationship between the two rabbis was very smooth despite the great age difference. The older rabbi treated the young rabbi as an equal. Rabbi Halberstam fell under the spell of the Ropshitzer Rabbi, adopting many of his views, notably with regard to charity, and the combination of Hasidism with scholarship. All three elements were basic forms of the Sandzer rabbinical dynasty. Rabbi Chaim always considered himself a student of the Ropshitzer Rabbi and always referred to him as "my saintly teacher and rabbi." He was imbued with the intelligence of the Ropshitzer court and borrowed from it many tunes that he brought to Sandz. Following the death of the Ropshitzer Rabbi in 1827, Rabbi Halberstam became restless and decided to leave the small hamlet of Rudnik. In 1828 he was invited to become "moyre tzedek" or righteous teacher of Sandz. The offer of rabbi could not be made since there was a rabbi functioning, in the person of Baruch ben Moshe Dawid Landau. Rabbi Halberstam did not accept the invitation. He left Rudnik for the small shtetl of Zolin in the same area. He remained for a short period of time in Zolin and moved to the city of Kalow in Hungary where he remained rabbi for two years. He finally accepted, in 1830, the position of Rabbi of Sandz when the officiating rabbi passed away.

2.   The city of Sandz became a Torah center. Rabbi Halberstam alone headed a yeshiva until age 70 and only then hired a supervisor to continue with the job. The first head of the yeshiva was Moshe Shmuel and when he died, the post was assumed by Fishel Gorlitzer (the father of one of the rabbi's biographers, Raphael Raker). Besides the yeshiva, the rabbi wrote and published a great many publications that spread the Hasidic word throughout the Jewish world with his questions and answers letters. He received many questions pertaining to Jewish law and answered them. He became renowned as an authority on "Halacha" or Jewish religious law. A great, steady stream of questions reached the rabbi's court from practically every Jewish community in Galicia. His answers were published and became familiar to the Jewish world. Sandz became a Hasidic and Torah center that inspired Jewish communities throughout Eastern Europe and even beyond.

3.   To Rabbi Halberstam the concept of charity was one of highest pillars in his kind of Hasidism. He not only espoused the concept but practiced it daily himself and saw to it that his Hasidim also adhered to it. He had a list of poor people and each morning distributed charity. He also used to distribute money to poor people who surrounded him. On his return from morning prayers he would usually distribute money to poor students who waited for him so that they could save and buy themselves shoes or clothing. Following evening prayers he distributed charity to the poor visitors (those invited to partake of the supper meal) with him. Saturday evening the rabbi would distribute money to the poor Jews so that they could have the traditional final meal of the day. The rabbi himself ate the meal on Sunday morning. On the fast of Esther

and on the eve of the Sukkoth holiday, the rabbi would distribute large amounts of money. He would say that God loved the poor people and so did he.

The rabbi never liked money hanging about the house and always distributed it among the needy. This beautiful concept of charity was deeply ingrained in his personality. The concept was not only derived from the Hasidic predecessors like the Baal Shem Tov but there is also a direct reference to it in the Talmud where there is an inference to the fact that rich people merely hold the money to be distributed to the needy. Many Hasidic courts indeed became vast charitable institutions that received vast sums of money and distributed them to the needy in the form of money or food, such as the large meal gatherings at the homes of the rabbis.

Rabbi Halberstam not only distributed charity but was also a very capable organizer of various schemes to raise money for charity. Chanukah or Purim would be excellent occasions to organize special affairs to raise money for charity. The Sandzer court was a very effective money raiser for the poor. The rabbi also took great interest in the weddings of the poor. He encouraged his followers to help entertain the bride and groom. When he was invited to the meals that followed the wedding of an orphan, he would always make sure that there was wine on the table (the wine was usually provided by the burial society where his grandson Shloymele was an active member, musician and a jester).

Rabbi Chaim Halberstam married three wives in succession. The first two were daughters of the Leipniker Rabbi mentioned above. He had a large family as one can see by looking at the genealogical chart. The rabbi had seven sons and seven daughters. The sons were:

Rabbi Yechezkel Shragai Halberstam (1814–1898), Rabbi of Siniawa

Rabbi Duvid Halbershtam (1821–1894), Rabbi of Chrzanow

Rabbi Myer Noson Halberstam (1827–1855), father of Rabbi Shlomo Halberstam , the first Bobover Rebbe

Rabbi Aharon Halberstam (1828–1903), succeeded his father in Sandz

Rabbi Borouch Halberstam (1829–1906), Rabbi of Gorlice

Rabbi Shulem Lazer Halberstam (1862–1944), Rabbi of Ratzfert, who was murdered by the Germans in the Shoah

Rabbi Yeshaye Halberstam of Czchow (1864–1944), who was also murdered by the Nazis.

Aryeh Leibish Halberstam, died at age of 7

4. He opposed education, even Jewish education. He vehemently supported the traditional "cheder" system and the yeshiva. Although himself an erudite scholar, he did not support such ideas for the majority. He insisted on absolute faith and devotion to it without hesitation. He wrote extensively and interpreted religious law. He answered and solved many theological questions that were written to him from many places. He has volumes of questions and answers that reveal a great deal of the period in question. He was accepted as a religious authority and as leader of the Jewish community of Galicia, especially the smaller townships. He was basically opposed to industrialization and sought the delay of implementing modern means of communication like the train.

[Page 143]

Chapter VI
From the Ritro Labor Camp to the Ghetto of Rzeszow

Ritro Labor Camp

I arrived at the Ritro labor camp dressed in summer clothes the way I left the Roznow labor camp in the morning for the selection at the ghetto of Sandz. All my belongings including money and papers and papers were left at the Roznow camp. The announcement about the departure for Sandz came after we had left the barrack and were on the way to work. The Germans did not permit us to go back to the barrack and get our belongings. Of course, there were some Jewish workers who arrived with back packs that contained all their belongings. I had nothing and could not complain. The Germans appointed Kuba Fuhrer to be in charge of the Jewish forced laborers. He selected as his assistant, his friend Awraham Segulim.

The wooden barrack contained two–tier bunk beds that had mattresses of hay or sawdust. Most of us received two blankets. Food was a serious problem at the camp. I worked with a Polish youngster at cutting leftover pieces of wood. The cutting was done near the living quarters; there were no guards there. There were German armed guards who belonged to the company. The supervisors of the sawmill were Germans and the place belonged to the German company known as "Hobag." All section chiefs were former soldiers who were disabled during the war. We worked 12 hours a day and received two meals per day. In the morning we received a cup of coffee and a slice of bread. At noon, we received a bowl of soup and whatever floated in it. At the morning break, we sat with the Polish workers who brought food from home that consisted of cooked potatoes, country bread, milk or sour milk. Since our breakfast was practically non–existent, we started to trade with the Poles, clothing for food. Shirts, pants socks were bartered for cooked potatoes, bread and milk. A black market of sorts developed in the camp between the Jewish forced laborers and the Polish workers.

We ate lunch in the big mess hall. I was lucky since one of the kitchen workers, Moshe Kriser, was from Sandz and knew me. The latter used to slip a cooked potato into my bowl of soup. The managers and supervisors also ate in the same mess hall but their section was closed off. Still, I waited whenever possible to sneak into that section to finish the food that was left on the plates by the Germans. With time, the food situation improved. We received three meals per day. On Sunday, the sawmill was closed but the Jewish forced laborers were forced to load sections of finished wood barracks aboard the train that headed to the front for the German army in the east. The railway station was opposite the sawmill. Attempts were made to establish contact with the few remaining Jews in Sandz. Some attempts succeeded. Contact was established with Yehoshua who was a fruit dealer who had survived the liquidation of the ghetto of Sandz. He employed a Polish maid who traveled between Sandz and Piwniczena. She lived in Piwniczena and worked in Sandz. Yehoshua began to send letters, money and even some packages to the Jews in the Ritro labor camp. Of course, she also provided the latest news regarding Sandz and the few remaining Jews there. Some of the money that was sent from Sandz disappeared along the road. At the time, one of my surviving uncles sent me some money but I never received it. To this day, I do not know what happened to it.

Toward the winter of 1942, the Jewish labor leader Fuhrer gave me some winter clothes since I had left everything in the Rozinow camp. Fuhrer wanted his Jewish workers to be content and not to create problems for him. The Ritro camp was not far from the hamlet of Ritro where there were no German soldiers or Gestapo men. It was easy to escape from the Ritro labor camp but the Jewish supervisor watched us like a hawk. He was afraid that someone might disappear and we would all be shot, including him. So he watched us very closely and tried to make life bearable.

One evening I worked the night shift with the Polish youngster. I was very tired and wanted to close my eyes for a few moments. I asked my Polish partner to keep his eyes open and if he saw a guard to wake me. He also fell asleep and the German guard making the rounds saw that I was missing. He started to look for me and found me asleep. He took me straight to the German commandant of the camp who ordered that I be given 25 lashes on my backside. The lashes were extremely painful but I survived. I could not sit for days on end since everything was raw. My big tragedy was the fact that I lost my position as a woodcutter inside the building. I was now assigned to work outside in the cold winter with no real warm clothes. My new job consisted of collecting used wooden planks and boards. I had to clean them and dunk them in large bathtubs containing chemical solutions that coated them against pests. The water solution was usually red.

I still remember some of the Jewish workers who worked with me at the Ritro labor camp.

Nechemia Sheingut	Romek Gut Hollander
Moshe Dawid Laor	Asher Brandstatter
Yeshayahu Bergman	Motci Blauzenstein
Zalman Fefer	Berek Hershtel
Iziv Kaempner	Awraham Segulim
Wolf Shimel	Kuba Fuhrer
Moshe Krizer	Mordechai Lustig
Menashe Wolf	

There were of course many more Jewish workers but I do not remember their names.

Flugmotorwerke in Lisia Gora, near Rzeszow

Suddenly, on February 23, 1943, we were told that we would be leaving the camp. Officers of the German air force came and took us to the railway station where we boarded a freight train and headed to an unknown destination. We traveled for hours and finally reached our destination. It was a former Polish air force installation. The letters PZL were still visible and stood for Polskie Zaklady Lotnicze or Polish Air Force Warehouses. The place now belonged to the German air force where there was a "Flugmotorwerke" or engine plane factory. It was located in Lisia Gora, near the city of Rzeszow. The aeronautical plant was operated by the German company Daimler–Benz. The place produced engines for the "Junker" planes.

We reached the camp at an early hour in the morning. We were received by two Jewish supervisors. One was named Bener and he was from the city of Przemysl in Poland. The name of the second one escapes me. We immediately received bowls of hot soup and bread. We were also accommodated in the barracks where there already were about 200 Jewish workers. The workplace had many metal machines. The living places were long halls with bunk beds that contained mattresses with hay. Our group was assigned to study theory and work on the metal machines.

The food situation was good. We started the day with an inspection of cleanliness, then a head count and finally we left for our workplace where we would spend the next 12 hours. There were two shifts. We also had to tend to the gardens around our workplace.

I was lucky that I found a big coat that would come in handy later. The work at the place was very hard and intensive. We worked and studied long hours. The place also had a policy of writing down the names of workers who broke or damaged instruments. The list was called the blacklist and was kept with precision. The first shift would wake up, wash and receive breakfast that consisted of coffee and bread. Then the head count and we headed to work at about 10 o'clock. We remained at the workshop until 10 o'clock at night. The night shift had difficulty sleeping in the day for there was always noise or other disturbances that prevented the workers from sleeping. During the month of March, I worked the night shift. I suffered from boils that prevented me from sleeping. I worked then with Wolf Schimel who was originally a dental technician. We operated this big metal machine that made specific metal plates that were fitted with big screws. I barely managed to stand on my feet. I told Wolf that I must get a couple of winks since I did not sleep in the day and I had the boils on my back. Wolf said: "Go ahead and rest I will watch and would wake you if the Ukrainian guard reaches the area." I sat down on the lowest step of the metal machine and fell asleep. Of course, Wolf fell asleep and the guard caught me sleeping. The Ukrainian guard caught me sleeping and started to shout and beat me mercilessly. He then dragged me to a water faucet and let the ice cold water run over my head. He held my head under the running water and I felt that my head would explode from the cold. Finally, he let go but he placed my name on the blacklist. I continued to work at the same machine. Ten hours of work and two hours of theoretical study and mathematics.

One day in April 1943, while working in the garden surrounding the barrack, I heard the announcement that all people on the blacklist are hereby ordered to leave everything and report. I left my work and joined a large group of Jewish forced laborers who were already assembled outside the workshop. I also saw the fully armed SS men who waited in the area. I thought to myself, where could they take us, what would be our future? Would they finish us somewhere over here? We marched out of the camp and began to march We marched and marched and finally entered the ghetto of Rzeszow.

Rzeszow or Reishe in Yiddish is located in southern Poland about 150 kilometers east of Krakow. Jews lived in the city since the 15th century. The city's Jewish population reached about 15,000 people in 1939 or one–third of the total population of the city. The Germans immediately started to harass the Jewish population. The crescendo of persecution of the Jews reached the peak in June 1942 when the Jewish population reached 23,000 souls. The ghetto was packed and poverty was rampant.

The process of concentrating the Jewish population of the region started as early as March 1941. All the Jews from small villages were ordered to move to ghettos in the nearest towns. They had to leave behind almost all their property. Jews moving to the Tyczyn ghetto were brutally beaten; all were robbed, a number killed. On 25–26 June, all Tyczyn ghetto Jews were resettled in the Rzeszow ghetto. Again, the march was accompanied by brutality and murders. A number of Tyczyn Jews were executed at the local Jewish cemetery. Jews living near Kolbuszowa were forced into the ghetto there in autumn 1941.

This ghetto was closed in February 1942. In Sokolow Malopolski the ghetto was formed in April 1942. At the time of the ghetto's liquidation in June 1942, 3,000 Jews lived there. During the resettlement to Rzeszow, 28 persons were killed. Most of the Jews from the ghetto in Glokow Malopolski were moved to Rzeszow in early July 1942. Jews concentrated in the ghetto of Strzyzow were resettled to Rzeszow on April 26 and June 9,1942 and those Jews of Blszowa on June 26,1942.

By the end of June 1942 all Jews from the smaller towns of Majdan, Kolbuszowa, Czudec, Niebylec and Staniszewska, together with some from Lancut, Sedzszow Malopolski and from small villages near Rzeszow were forced into the ghetto of Rzeszow. As a result, the population of the ghetto rose to almost 23,000 people.

Jews of Rzeszow being driven to the train station
(Yad Vashem Archives)

In June 1942, the responsibility for the entire Jewish population was transferred from the administrative authorities to the police and SD (security police). At the beginning of July, the Germans imposed a penalty on the Rzeszow ghetto of 1,000,000 zlotys, to be paid by its Jewish inhabitants. Between July 7–19, 1942, it is estimated that 20,000 were deported to the death camp of Belzec where they all perished. Yet there were still about 4,000 Jews in the ghetto of Rzeszow, for the Germans kept moving Jews from all the ghettos in the area to Rzeszow. We assume that most of the original Jewish inhabitants of Rzeszow were no longer alive when Mordechai Lustig arrived in April 1943 in Rzeszow from Gora, near Rzeszow.

Rzeszow had two ghettos: ghetto east and ghetto west. The ghettos were separated by a road that led to the eastern ghetto where there was no work. Both ghettos were surrounded with barbed wire and under the administration of the Judenrat and the Jewish ghetto police. The eastern ghetto had workshops that provided employment to workers. Many of the Jewish workers worked outside the ghetto and came in contact with the Polish population that sold them food that they brought home. The western ghetto was sealed and there were very few employment opportunities. If you did not have money, you could starve. Our group was taken to the western ghetto. The Judenrat officials assigned us – Shia Nagel, the two Kahana brothers, myself and a few other people whose names I no longer remember – to various buildings and apartments. I was assigned to an empty apartment where a Jewish woman and her two children had just arrived from the liquidated Krosno Jewish community. I went to sleep on the floor and covered myself with the big coat.

**Jews of Rzeszow being forced into deportation
train at the Staroniva station**
(Yad Vashem Archives)

The Judenrat assigned me to work on collecting and restoring bricks and maintaining sewer holes. I was given food that consisted of a bowl of soup that looked like carrots and a piece of bread. This was the food for the day. I realized that this was a starvation diet and many Jews in the ghetto died of starvation. On the other hand, if you had money you could eat at the restaurant like the Jewish policemen who ordered rolls with soup and eggs or potato puree with onion sauce. One day, I received a postal card from my two uncles, Moshe and Awraham. They informed me that they were alive and were in the ghetto of Tarnow. I was very pleased with the news. Following the end of the war, I looked for my uncles but did not find them. A childhood friend named Zvi who was in the ghetto of Tarnow told me what happened. My uncles decided to escape from the ghetto of Tarnow. They were spotted and shooting ensued. Both uncles perished.

Occasionally the Jewish police would seize Jews and send them to terrible places like Huta Komorowska or Bieszadka where the survival rate was very small. Whenever there was an action I hid very well in the septic sewer system where there were large manholes along the road. Yossef Niemiec and myself were busy unclogging the sewers so that the standing waters would disappear. We planned so that we advanced slowly toward the fence of the western ghetto. There we received food that consisted of soup and bread. People were standing at the entrance gate of the western ghetto but the Jewish police would not let them enter. Of course, black market operations took place along the fence. On occasion I managed to get some food and give it to the hungry people at the entrance gate. But this solution could not last.

I knew that the Judenrat had posted ads on the local bulletin board in the western ghetto that asked people with skills like carpenters, plumbers, to sign up for jobs. The jobs were located at the Skarzysko concentration labor camp at Juleg. People who signed up were permitted to enter the western ghetto and received food for about 10 days. This treatment improved tremendously the appearance of the workers. I asked someone to do me a favor and place my name on the board. I was soon called to report to the western ghetto. I barely spent one day in the camp when I came down with typhus. The epidemic raged in the camp. I had fever and was unable to move. My case was soon reported to the Jewish police and I was soon shipped back to the eastern ghetto to the hospital. I remained at the hospital for one month and thanks to the good care of a nurse who provided me with a constant flow of tea, I managed to return to myself. About 800 people of a population of 2,000 died of typhus at the ghetto. Following my discharge from the hospital, I was very weak. I approached a restaurant owner and told him that I would bring water to the restaurant and peel his potatoes for food. The water pipes to the restaurant did not function. The owner agreed and I worked for a short time as a water hauler until my strength came back to me.

You are probably wondering how a restaurant could function in the ghetto where there were few food supplies and the guards were instructed to prevent food from entering the place. The answer was very simple. The ghetto was surrounded by fences and Polish policemen patrolled the outside fences. But Polish youngsters managed to find loopholes and with the help of strings managed to deliver to the ghetto an ample supply of food that enabled the restaurant to provide rolls, eggs, potatoes, flour, sugar and onions.

My situation was getting hopeless. Then I met Yossef Niemiec who was with me in the engine plant. We discussed our situation and concluded that we must get to the western ghetto in order to survive. We decided to approach Lazarowicz. He arrived in Rzeszow with a transport of Jews from the area of Lodz in November or December 1939. He worked with the Jewish police. He was the official undertaker of the ghetto. He had a license, a horse and a cart. He was also permitted to travel outside the ghetto. We approached him and begged him to smuggle us to the western ghetto so that we could register for jobs. This was a very complex situation but we managed to get to the western ghetto. Lazarowicz even gave each of us 500 zlotys so that we could have a good meal and appear decent in the western ghetto. We entered the ghetto and signed up for work. Meanwhile we received food and rested for 10 days. Then the S.S. men came and took 50 of us. We climbed aboard trucks and proceeded to the labor camp of Pustkow near Debice.

[Page 158]

Chapter VII
From Pustków Concentration Camp

Due to its favorable location near a rail line from the city of Debice to the city of Tarnobrzeg, and away from large cities, the first trees were cut some three kilometers south of Pustków. Pustków is located in the district of Debice and in the region of Tarnow. As part of a massive Polish industrialization program, apartments for workers and blocks of flats and villas for managers and engineers were built in Pustków in 1937. A factory built manufactured ammunition as well as plastic materials for the Polish military establishment. Production started in April 1939, and on September 8, 1939, the first units of the German army entered the settlement. Germans completed the construction of blocks of flats, which they used as military barracks. All machines and plastics were transported to Germany.

In 1940, the Germans decided to expand the camp and to convert the entire area into a training area for German military units. The plan envisioned that the camp would be able to train up to 60,000 soldiers. Priority would be given to S.S. Waffen military units, especially foreign units like Frenchmen, Dutchmen, Ukrainians. Here were built large firing ranges, obstacle courses and various installations to train raw recruits. Of course, the base also had large warehouses where ammunition of all sorts was stockpiled. Additional buildings contained the signal communication unit and various facilities needed to maintain large military units. The area was covered with a dense forest. Clearing the forest was an immense job and required a large labor force. There was a small French prisoner of war camp in Pustków but the camp was moved. The Jews were chosen for the task. At first, the Judenrat of Debica sent daily Jewish workers to Pustków. Then some barracks were built and the workers remained for several weeks at the camp before they received passes to visit home. Some workers tried to avoid returning to Pustków but they were registered for the place and had to return or find someone to take their place. People with money or connections managed to get off the list but most of the people had to return to Pustków where the working conditions were pretty bad. The workers practically had to work with their bare hands to uproot the tall forest trees. They barely received food or clothing. Still, most workers continued to return to Pustków. This policy continued until June 1941. Then the camp was sealed. No more liberty passes and no more food from home. Starvation became rampant and the work load increased. The harsh labor conditions and the primitive or non–existent facilities caused many of the workers to die. The rate of attrition of Jewish workers merely increased with time since their energies were exhausted. Yet the building program continued at a rapid tempo and more Jews were brought to Pustków from all over Western Galicia, especially from Rzeszow, Tarnow and Krakow. The name of Pustków became a dreaded name and Jews were terrified of the name. But the place devoured workers and the Judenrats were forced to send more and more people to Pustków. Sometimes to fill the quota, Jewish children were grabbed and sent to Pustków and sometimes, old people. When a quota was not met, the Gestapo would seize Jews and fill the quota. The rate of decimation continued at a fantastic rate. Vast areas were cleared of trees, roads were laid, barracks were built, target ranges were constructed, and concrete bunkers were built. The work was progressing rapidly and so was the decimation of the Jewish workers. The Gestapo and the S.S. did not care about the Jews; to them, the Jews were a source of cheap labor supply. They forced the Judenrats of the various cities to provide Jewish laborers for Pustków that was killing them as fast as they arrived – starvation diets and the bestiality of the guards, namely Schmidt, Miller, Kleindienst, Hamann and Charke who took delight in firing at Jewish inmates heading to work. Jewish workers were being hung almost daily for no reason, according to Moshe Oster, a survivor of Pustków. Jewish forced workers continued to arrive to Pustków until the ghettos were liquidated and its inhabitants murdered. Almost no Jewish worker survived the first Jewish labor camp at Pustków according to Ben Soifer. author of the book "Between Life and Death," dedicated to Pustków. Between 1940–1942 there were about 14,000 Jews at Pustków concentration camp except for a few escapees and 216 skilled Jewish workers who had their own camp. According to Ben Soifer, half of the Jews died of starvation or were murdered. The murdered were burned at the crematory located on the hillside near the Jewish labor camp. Eventually most of the Jewish inmates of the Pustków Jewish labor camp perished. During the summer of 1942, 2,000 Jews were sent from Pustków to another camp. The rest of the Jews were sent to the Belzec death camp. The Jewish labor camp was closed. Only the needed 216 Jewish skilled Jewish workers remained at Pustków.

Pustków indoor firing range for the German army

Following the German attack on the Soviet Union, thousands of Russian prisoners of war arrived at Pustków. Some of them arrived by train while others walked from the Russian battlefields to Pustków. The Russian Jewish prisoners of war were immediately selected and shot. The others slept on the ground. No facilities were built for them. They were not fed and died of hunger, malnutrition and mass killings. Most of them died, especially during the harsh winter of 1942. There are no precise records; it is assumed that the number of Soviet deaths reached about 5,000 soldiers. The Soviet assembly ground camp was next to the Jewish labor camp. A few skilled Russian technicians survived.

Most of the Soviet soldiers died in Pustków. The rate of dying was soextensive that the Germans had to build a small crematorium to handle the dead bodies that accumulated in the camp. Dead bodies were kept in special bunkers until a sizable number accumulated and then the bodies were burned. Many executions took place in Pustków at the top of the hill that was later named "Krulowa Gora" or royal mount. The hill was next to the Jewish labor camp.

Bunker specially built in Pustków to hold dead bodies until they were disposed

Labor was decimated so fast that it had to be constantly replenished but the sources of cheap labor began to dry up. The Jewish ghettos were liquidated and Soviet prisoners had died by the thousands in German hands. In 1942, the Germans began to hire Poles to provide the labor but this proved a bit expensive and required extensive administration. It was simpler and cheaper to get slaves. So the Germans began to send Polish prisoners to a special camp in Pustków. There was no shortage of candidates since the Polish jails were full of Polish patriots and resistance fighters. These people began to arrive at Pustków. The Polish labor camp expanded with time. It was fenced and the rules were similar to all the German labor camps. There was no contact between the Jewish camp and the Polish camp. The Polish camp was well organized internally by the inmates. There was some contact between the camp and the Polish resistance movement in the area. The Poles worked extensively in the rocket launch programs of the V–1 and V–2 that were being developed by Germany. The work conditions at Pustków did not improve and thousands of Poles died at the camp despite the fact that they received food packages from home that slightly alleviated their food situation.

In the summer of 1943, The Germans decided to expand the small Jewish labor camp at Pustków. Calls were sent to the various places that still had Jewish skilled workers to send them to Pustków. The call was answered and transports of skilled Jewish workers began to arrive. The first large transport consisting of 130 Jewish workers arrived from the labor camp of Huta Komarowska in June 1943. Then a transport of 120 Jewish artisans arrived from the Szebnie concentration camp, followed by a group of Jewish skilled workers from the Rzeszow ghetto that included Mordechai Lustig. The Jewish camp now had about 416 skilled workers.

According to Mordechai Lustig, in the summer of 1943: "I arrived with some Jewish workers from the ghetto of Rzeszow or Reishe, Galicia. We were received by a German officer, Jewish workers who were specialists in their fields that consisted of tailors, shoemakers, plumbers, cooks, etc... and the supervisor of the Jewish workers, Leopold Waldhorn, who was a German Jew. Most Jewish inmates worked for the high ranking officers of the S.S. in the camp, including the S.S. commandant of the camp, Obersharfuhrer Ernest Kops'.

On reaching Pustków, we were given clean beds and two new blankets. We received clean mattresses. Our clothes were removed and burned since they contained too many lice. We received new clothing. We received shoes that belonged to the Soviet prisoners of war who had been killed in Pustków. We even received towels. Each morning we received coffee and we received for breakfast 250 grams of military bread, 10 grams of butter or honey or jam. After breakfast and the head count, we were divided into groups of four and began to drag parts of the barracks to their intended place that would be our camp and our workshops where we would create toys for the German soldiers so they could send these toys home to their families.

The new workshop was approximately three kilometers from the base camp where we slept. We received lunch at the place of work where there was a field kitchen. We were always led to the place of work by armed S.S. men and Ukrainians. Among the notorious Germans were Tchapeczka, Hamann and Charke. Once, prior to returning to our base camp at the end of the workday, we noticed that a Jewish worker was missing. Sharke went to look for him and reported that the Jewish worker had committed suicide in a barrack. We all knew immediately that Sharke hung him and told a lie. Sharke hung the fellow named Berger from the city of Krosno. We buried him and continued back to the old base. We continued to build barracks and by November 1943 two barracks were completed. We were now about 430 skilled Jewish workers. The camp had a service block as well as a kitchen, a sick room with a doctor named Shimon Sheingot. Our camp was surrounded by barbed wire that separated us from the Polish camp that was also surrounded by barbed wire.

One day following the head count, I was not assigned to a job. This was not a good omen. Three other inmates were also jobless. The kapo responsible for us started marching us back and forth as though we were preparing for a military parade. The kapo also tried to kill time. Then we were marched to our barrack where they brought wheat sacks that had to be fixed. We were soon assigned to regular jobs.

Every morning the beds were inspected and had to be perfectly arranged and symmetrical. In the winter we were also forced to run to the washroom half naked. Strange, none of us came down with a cold. Every evening the doors of the barracks were closed from the outside and reopened in the morning. Provisions were made for the workers who had to use the toilet facilities at night. Watchtowers were placed around our camp and the guards were S.S. men or Ukrainians. The entire area was lit by searchlights. Once a week, an S.S. man would bring a bag of parcels to our camp. The parcels belonged to Polish inmates who received them from home. Whenever the Poles committed infractions of the camp rules, the Germans used to confiscate their parcels and some of them were given to the Jewish workers. The Jews, of course, did not have parcels since their families had disappeared a long time ago. Each barrack received a bag that contained food parcels. The food was distributed evenly between the barrack inmates. We also had our own large field kitchen where we cooked food for our camp.

The daily schedule at the Jewish labor camp was as follows:

5:30 Reveille
6:00 Washing the upper part of the body at the wash basin
6:30 Morning roll call at the appeal place by the commander
7:00 March to work
7.00 P.M. End of work. March back to camp.

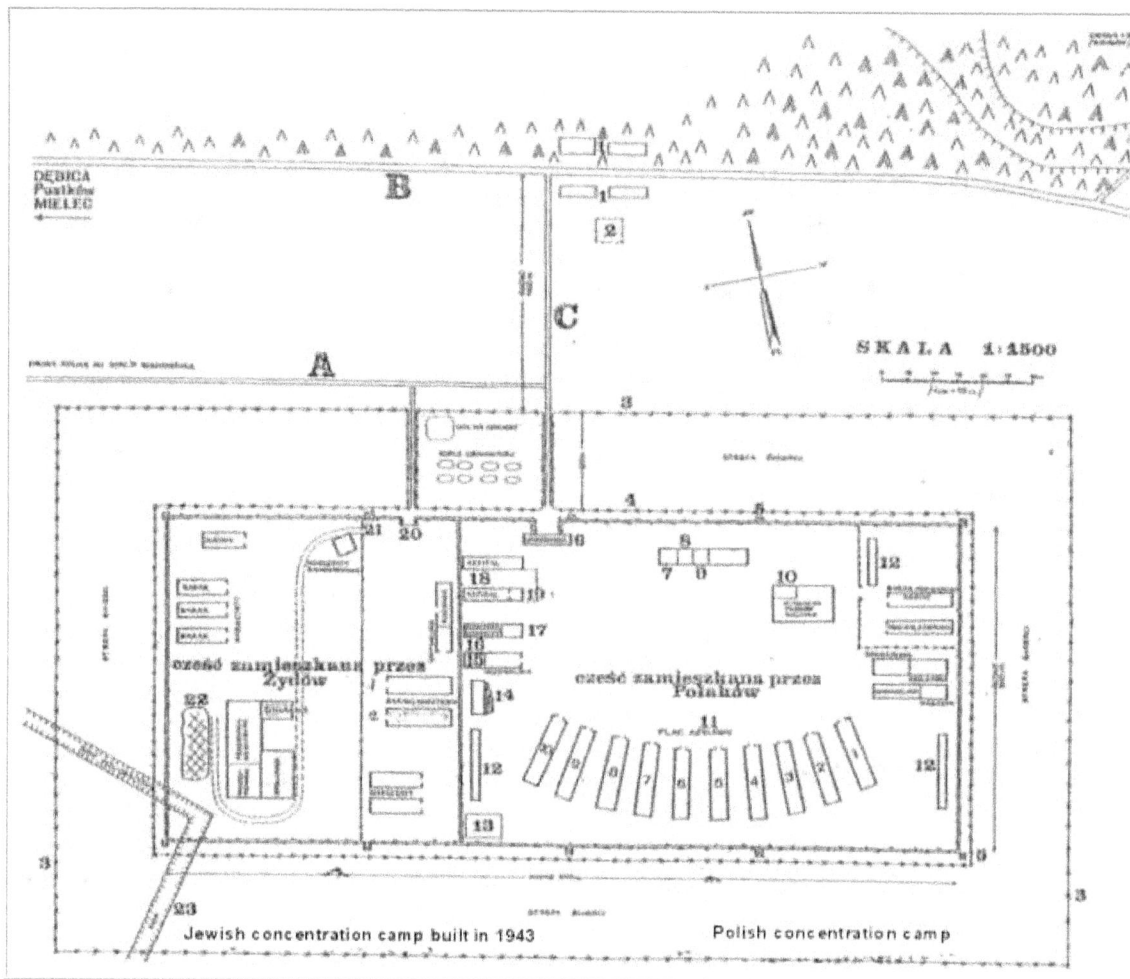

Pustków labor camps; on the left is the Jewish labor camp and on the right is the big Polish labor camp with many barracks

Every morning, The German commander of the Jewish concentration camp, Obersharfuhrer Ruf, was present at the head count formation. I can safely say that his conduct to us Jewish workers was exemplary in comparison to other German camp commanders of the period whose bestiality knew no limits. His tone of behavior set the mood for the rest of the German officials at the Jewish labor camp in Pustków. The commandant office on occasion left German newspapers that the Jewish inmates stole and became aware of the general situation in Europe. Occasionally, there were shows organized within the barrack by Jewish theater artists from Warsaw who were inmates of the barrack. Of course, there was a steady lack of food that caused many of us to think of food. Not far from our camp was the hill that was called "Chujowa Gurka" or the cursed hill. The Germans placed many cut trees on top of the hill and then brought the stored dead bodies and placed them on top of the trees. Torches lit the trees and the bodies were burned. Many Poles were thus burned. The Germans even sent a group of 50 Jewish workers in February 1944 to the hill and nobody returned.

Germany was crumbling. Soviet armies were already in Poland as of January 1944. These armies advanced rapidly toward Pustków and the German armies were steadily withdrawing The S.S. high command had to make urgent decisions. The Pustków labor camp had to move. Already in March 1944, I was sent to the Plaszow concentration camp near Krakow with a group of Jewish skilled workers.

Moshe Bart, a native of Rymanow, Galicia, and an inmate of Pustków, told me that the remaining Jewish inmates of the Pustków concentration camp including himself were sent in June 1944 to Auschwitz or, more precisely, to Birkenau. Prior to the departure, the inmates were told that the camp was being relocated for greater security. The S.S. commander of the Jewish camp, Obersharfuhrer Ruf, was aboard the transport and on arrival in Auschwitz he told the notorious Mengele that his transport consisted of skilled technicians that could still serve Germany. The oral intervention worked and the transport was given a reprieve; it was sent to the Mauthausen concentration camp in Austria. Most of the Jewish inmates of Pustków just walked away from the gas chambers. Their sufferings did not end but they were still alive and relatively much better off than most of the other concentration camp inmates as a result of their stay in Pustków. As the German armies retreated, camps were constantly evacuated and relocated and eventually most of the camps were liberated with the end of the war. The number of survivors from the Pustków Jewish camp was very impressive.

According to Moshe Oster, most of the Polish camp inmates at the Pustków labor camp were sent in July to Auschwitz, shortly before the liberation of the camp by the Russians in August 1944. The Germans put up a stiff resistance to the Soviets who lost about 1,000 soldiers but took Pustków. The camp was officially liberated in August 1944.

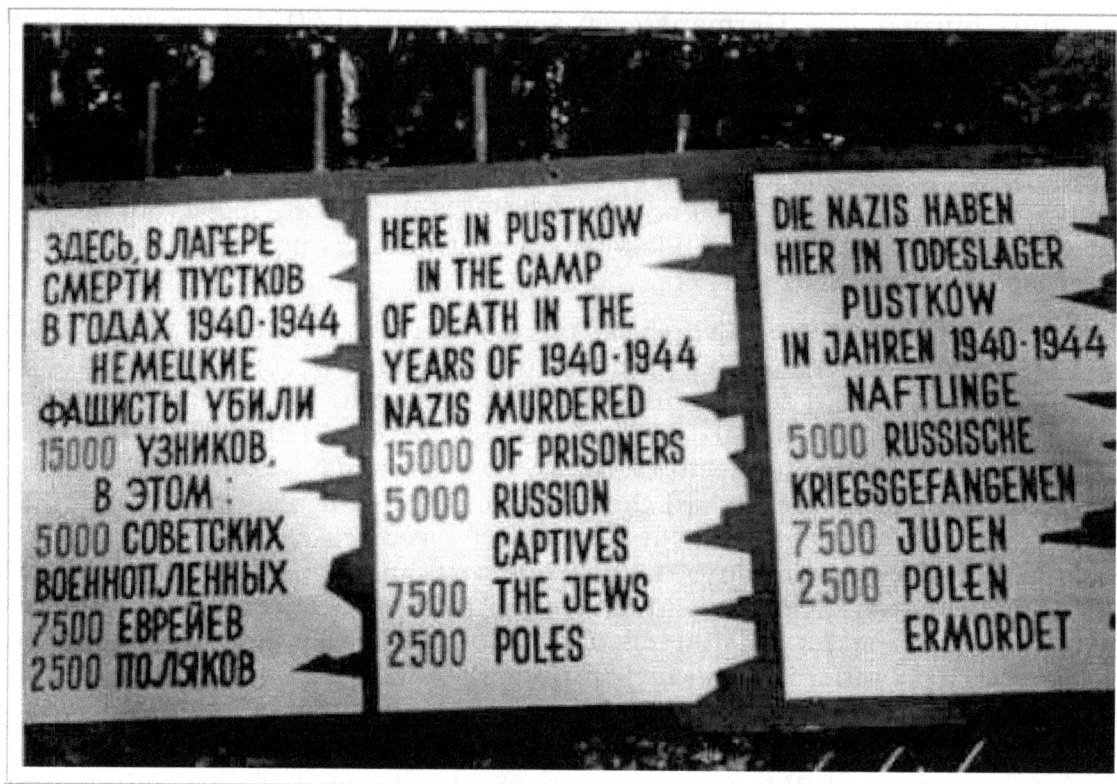

Memorial erected at the entrance to Pustków concentration camp.
No Yiddish or Hebrew or Polish inscription
(Courtesy of Yad Vashem)

Thanks to some former Jewish residents of Rzeszow, such as Moshe Oster and Leon Laor (Lambsdorf), Nathan Zebkowicz, Haim Grinszpan, Mordechai Lustig and other interested people, the idea of a Jewish monument to the Jewish victims of Pustków took shape. Jewish groups and survivors of Pustków started to push for a memorial dedicated to the Jewish victims of Pustków. They were assisted by several Polish professors, namely Mirek Kenzior, Tadeusz Pieta, Waclaw Wiezrbeniec, and Janusz Korbiecki. Finally, in 2007, a memorial was unveiled to the Jewish victims at Pustków. The event was widely publicized and many Polish officials, mayors, school principals and other important people attended the ceremony that was staged under government auspices.

I survived the war and reached Palestine as did most of the Pustkower camp survivors. I became very active in the association of former Pustkower inmates. The association was active during the 1960s and 1970s. The association was located at 35 Ezriel Street, Ramat Gan, Israel. We formed a secretariat that began to collect names and established contacts with Pustkower survivors throughout the world and especially in Israel. The secretariat consisted of:

Salo Sebel, chairman
Chaim Grinszpan, assistant chairman
Moshe Blassberg, treasurer
Yehuda Fuerst, secretary
Yossef Dreillinger, audit committee
Mordechai Lustig, audit committee
Dawid Eigler (Berglass), board member
Chaim Pfefer, board member
Yaacov Leizork, board member
Dawid Pearlberger, board member

We not only held annual membership meetings but also arranged social gatherings and tried to help the Pustkower members with their problems.

The Polish government erected a monument to those murdered at Pustków

A monument was placed at the top of the hill that was renamed "Krolowa Gora" or "Royal Hill." The memorial (in Polish) reads: "To those killed at the Pustków labor camps between 1940–1944 by the Germans." This monument was erected by the Polish government.

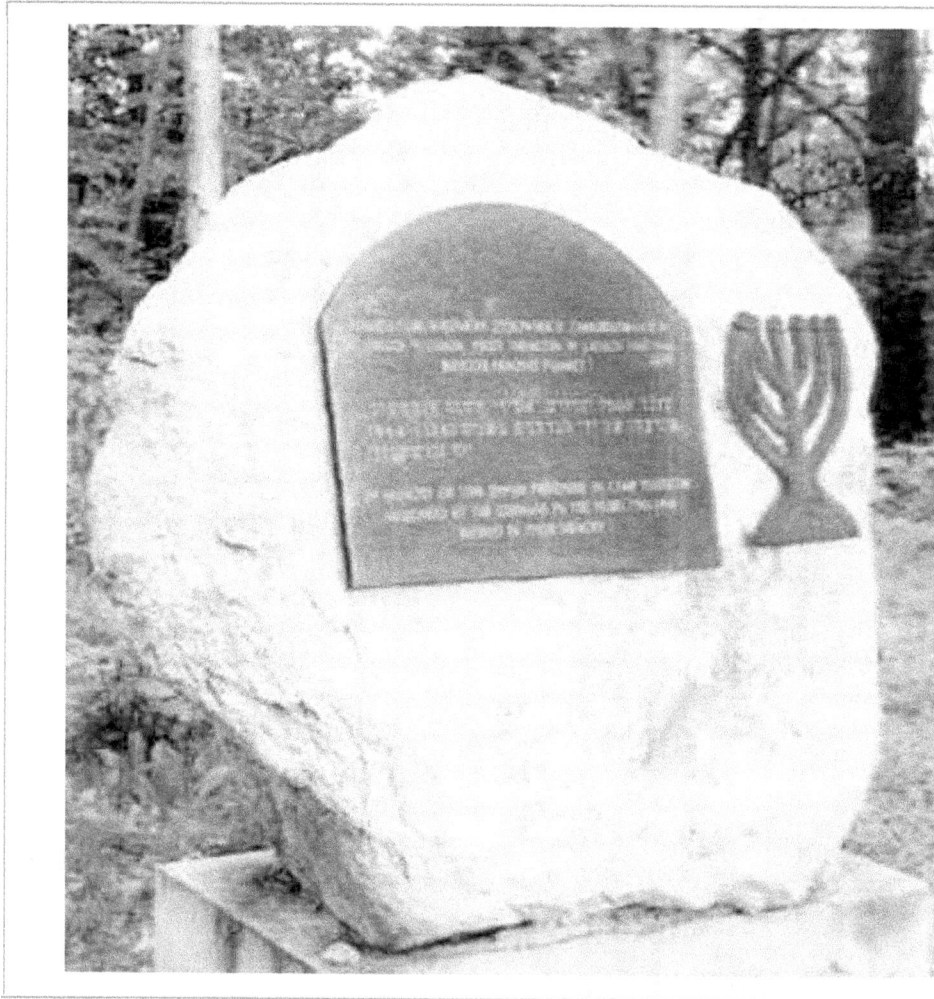

Memorial in Yiddish reads: "To the 7,500 Jews who were killed by the Germans at Pustków between 1940–1944.May their memory be blessed."

The monument was erected following the war in Pustków.

Members of the Pustkower Association in Israel

ALLWEISS	Moshe	FLIGELMAN	Naftali
ARONOWICZ	Abraham	FRANKEL (FRENKEL)	Marek
ATLAS	Yossef	FREILICH	Charles
BART	Moshe	FUERST	Yehuda
BEIL	Abraham	FUHRER	Yaakow
BERGMAN	Tzwi	FURST	Eliezer
BITTNER	Egon	GELDTZAHLER	Lezer Schlomo
BLASCHKOWSKI	Moshe	GOLDBERG	Zeew
BLASSBERG	Moshe	GOLDSTOFF	Baruch
BLEIWEIS (SUESMAN)	Salek	GOLDWENDER	Jechiel
BLUTTNER		GOLDWENDER	Zwi
BRZEZINSKI	Joseph	GOTTLIEB	Eliezer Dr
BUCHOLTZ	Dow	GRABER	Joel
DEGEN	Moshe	GRINSZPAN	Chaim
DEUTSCH	Moshe	GRUBER	Itzhak
DICHTENBERG	Moshe	GRUNN	Maximillian
DREILINGER	Yossef	HABER	Oskar
DRILLING	Benzion	HALICKI	Awraham
DRUCKER	Mendel	HAUSMAN	Herman
EIGLER (BERGLASS)	Dawid	HELLER (TENC)	Jeheskel Mo
EINHORN	Dawid	HERZBERG	Ignatz
EISEN	Yaakow	HIRSCHBERG	Dawid
EKSTERMAN	H	HOIDA	Dawid
ENTEN	Zeev	HORSKI (HOROWICZ)	Leo
EHRENFELD	Benyamin	JAKUBOWICZ	Henoch
EPSTEIN	Asher	JEKIEL	Dawid
FELSEN	Henryk	JERUCHEMSON	
FERTIG	Willy	KAPISZOW	Aaron
FIGOWI	Bernard	KATZ	Yehuda
FINK	Arie	KAUFER	Eliezer
FISCHLER	Zeew	KIRSCH	Naftali

KOHN	Markus	ROTH	Alter
KRISPOW (KRZYPOW)	Adam	RZEPKOWICZ	Nathan
KRONISH	Shlomo	SALZ	David
KUCZINSKI	Mordechai	SCHARF	David
KURTZ	Itzhak	SCHECHTER	Yaakow
LANDSMAN	Naphtali	SCHILDKRAUT	Naphtali
LANG	Israel	SCHNEIDER	Julius
LAOR	Asher	SCHOFET	Eliyahu
LEINKRAM	Yaakow	SCHONGUT	Shimon
LEISER	Nathan	SPIEGEL	Ziegfried
LENGEL		SEBEL	Salo
LIBAN	Chaim	SPIER (SCHMIER)	Leo
LIBERMAN	Dow	STANG	Zeew
LIEBOLD	Janek	STERN	Leo
LOW	Naftali	STERN	Leon
LUSTIG	Mordechai	SZAMIR	Dow
MAHLER	Henryk	SZAMIR	Yaakow
MARK (MARCHEWKA)	Sam	SZIFRIN	Benzion
MENDLINGER	Itzhak	SZPILMAN	Shlomo
MEYER	Fred	TAUB	Salomon
MULLER	Mordechai	TEIBLUM	Yaakow
NOWAK	Abraham	TEITELBAUM	Tzwi Zeew
OSTER	Moshe	TELLER	Moshe
PEARLBERGER	Dawid	TENCER	Itzhak
PFEFER	Chaim	TUCHMAN	Yaakow
PFLANZER	Benjamin	WAGNER	Szimon
PIASECKI	Henryk	WEINSTOCK	Yossef
PUTTER	Henryk	WIESENFELD	Kalman
REINER	Israel	WIMMER	Eliyahu
ROSSDEUTCHER	Samuel	WOHLFILER	Asher
		ZAPANOWICZ	Nathan

[Page 180]

Chapter VIII
Płaszów Concentration Camp

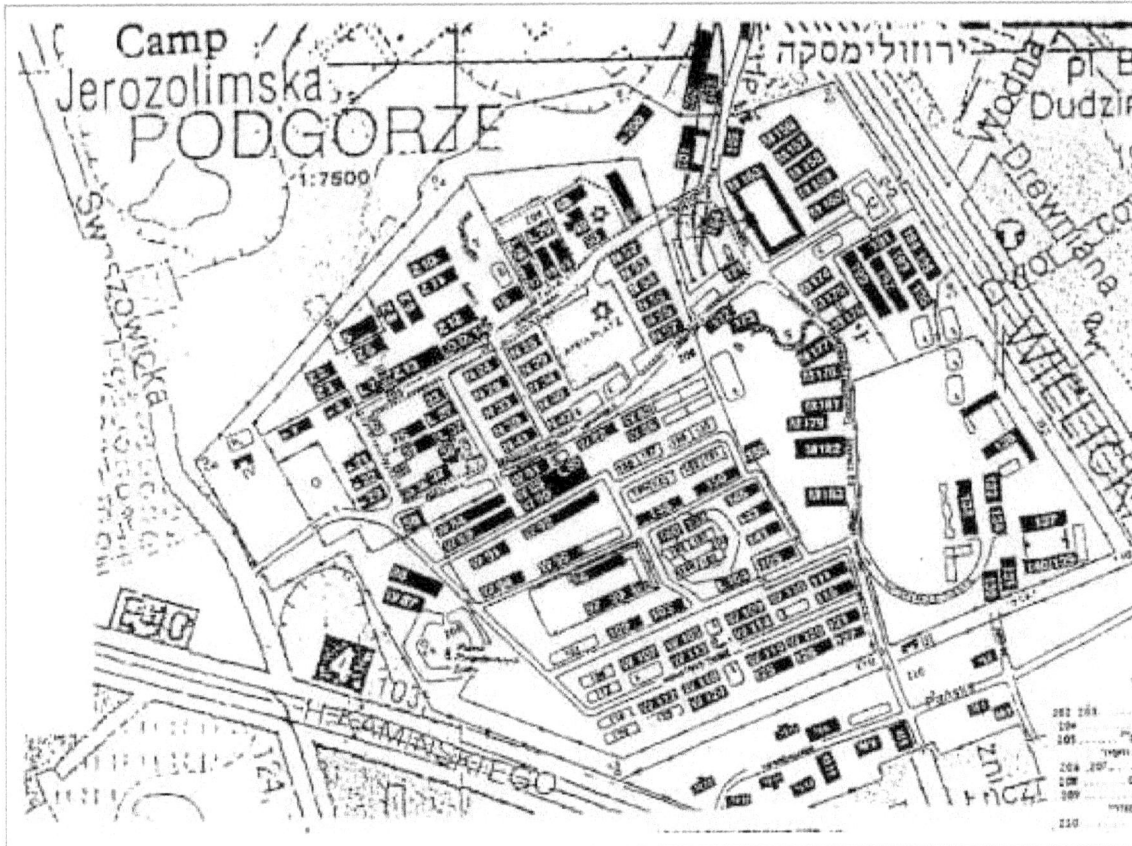

The Płaszów labor and later concentration camp were located in the Podgorze district near the city of Krakow

Plaszów was in the Podgorze district of Krakow, Poland, 10 kilometers from the center of the city. The place was made famous by Steven Spielberg in the movie "Schindler's List". The Plaszów camp started in the summer of 1940 when the German occupation authorities set up in the area a forced–labor camp for the Polish prisoners of war. In March 1941, the Jews in the Krakow area were put into a walled ghetto in Podgorze. It is estimated that between 60,000 and 80,000 people were squeezed into the small area. Krakow had an old and influential Jewish community that was well established in the historical Polish city. Jews were constantly sent from Krakow or Podgorze to the Plaszów camp where the attrition rate was extremely high.

The Płaszów labor camp where Jewish workers were forced to work in the quarry
(Courtesy of Yad Vashem)

In February 1943, Amon Goeth was appointed commandant of the Plaszów concentration camp. Shortly thereafter, on March 13–14, 1943, he supervised the bestial liquidation of the ghetto of Podgorze. All the Jews of the ghetto of Podgorze were selected. Those fit to work were sent to Płaszów Płaszów and the rest were sent to the death camp of Auschwitz or were shot on the spot. Prior to the arrival of the mass of Jews of Podgorze, Plaszów had about 2,000 inmates, all Jews. The population rose to 8,000 inmates with the destruction of the ghetto of Podgorze. In July 1943, a separate section was fenced off for Polish prisoners who were sent to the camp for breaking the laws of the German occupation government. Polish prisoners served their sentences and were then released from the prison. The Jews remained in the camp indefinitely. Many Jews were sent on to the Auschwitz concentration camp, only 60 kilometers southwest of Krakow.

Płaszów could easily compare with Auschwitz and Majdanek in their deadly beatings, punishments and killings. At its peak capacity the Płaszów camp contained 25,000 inmates at one time: men, women, and children. About 150,000 people were imprisoned in Płaszów, among them Jews, Hungarians,

Poles and Gypsies, Czechs, Frenchmen and Belgians. They were subjected to inhumane treatment, hellish living conditions, diseases, starvation, grueling slave labor, frequent beatings, and torture, and many fell victim to brutal killings. More than 80,000 of the Płaszów inmates died before the end of World War II, most in the gas chambers of Auschwitz–Birkenau. With the approach of the Soviet armies, the inmates were transported to other camps. The concentration camp itself was being dismantled brick by brick. Even the mass graves were exhumed and burnt to ashes. The last transport left Płaszów on January 14, 1945. Several days later, the Soviet Army entered to an empty place called the Concentration Camp of Płaszów.

In March of 1944 I was taken from Pustków with a few other Jewish skilled workers and sent to the Płaszów concentration camp near Krakow. We were not permitted to take anything with us except for a towel. We arrived at Płaszów and were directed to the bathhouse by the Jewish police in the camp. We emerged from the shower and were told to wait at a nearby grass mall. Meanwhile a transport of Jews arrived from the Bochnia labor camp that was being liquidated. The group in effect closed the camp. They all had backpacks and suitcases stuffed with a variety of foods. They too had to go to the bathhouse and, of course, had to leave their luggage outside. While they were bathing, the Jewish police ordered us to take all the belongings and move them to a small side hut that served the Jewish police as a warehouse and a detention hall until the arrivals were assigned to their barracks. The Jewish police ordered us to clear the area and place everything in the warehouse and ordered us to enter the isolation area and to stay put. While lugging the luggage we soon smelled the odors of foods like salami emerging from the luggage. We soon located the foods and removed them from the luggage. We ate the food like salamis, breads and other goods that were removed. The Jewish police spotted our feast. The police ordered us out of the isolation room and made us run several times around the area. Several days later, we were assigned to barracks. The barrack consisted of three–tier bunk beds. The food was skimpy and I was hungry. Of course, there were roll calls and formations. Then I was ordered to report to the tool shed. I was given a wheelbarrow and my job consisted of transporting sand. I dug the sand in the area of the Jewish cemetery. Frequently, I found bones or skeletons while digging for sand that was then transported to the villa of Amon Goeth, camp commandant of Płaszów. The sand was spread all around his place. Luck had it that he was still asleep when we spread the sand. I then walked to the kitchen where I met a Nowy Sacz acquaintance named Lew who was a tailor that used to live next to our family in Sandz. He worked at the Madritsch factory that produced uniforms for the German army and the workers there received plenty of food. He gave me a loaf of bread, a heavenly gift in Płaszów at the time.

At the end of 1940, Julius Madritsch, a native of Austria, was able to open a sewing factory in Kraków that employed about 800 Jews and Poles with 300 sewing machines that made clothing for the German army. Madritsch gained a reputation as a good man who treated his Jewish workers well; he was "wonderful" to his Jews. Madritsch saved the lives of thousands of Jews and also sought to make their lives more bearable. He employed many workers with no professional experience or training. Together with his factory manager, Raimund Titsch, he provided humane and comfortable working conditions. Every worker was well fed and received at the end of the day a loaf of bread. Jews were allowed to make contact with Poles outside the factory. The factory kitchens fed more than a thousand Jewish workers with food. A good part of the food was bought on the black market since the food rations for forced workers were abysmally low. Of course, the workers did not get paid since the S.S. received all salaries. So there was an extensive machinery whereby Madritsch managed to deflect large sums of money and buy food and bread for his workers. Thus Lew was able to give Lustig bread.

**Julius Madritsch, owner of
the Madritsch factories**

I ate the bread slowly and when it was finished, I was hungry again. I even raided the dump where the meat bones from the kitchen were tossed and grabbed a bone to suck on it. One day while collecting paper and loading it on a truck, I met an old friend named Samek Teitelbaum from Sandz who later became Samuel Bar Ilan in Israel. One morning, he awakened me and told me to follow him. I joined a small group of workers who boarded a German military truck that headed within the camp to a warehouse that contained all the goods that were left by the Jews when the ghetto of Płaszów was liquidated. Mostly women sorted the goods at the warehouse. We were told to take a few sacks of clothing for the Schindler camp.

Oskar Schindler

I had no bag so I took a backpack and filled it with undergarments, shirts, pants and whatever I could lay my hands on. I took as much as I could and we headed to the truck that took us to the Schindler camp.

Entrance to the Schindler factory in Krakow

The Schindler Jews at first lived in the Plaszów camp and walked 2.5 kilometers to and from Schindler's enamelware factory each day. The factory was in an ordinary–looking, modern, but dreary building in Krakow. Then Schindler bribed Plaszów Commandant Amon Goeth to let his workers move into barracks that he built in the courtyard of the factory. Schindler himself lived in a nondescript gray apartment building close to his factory. There were many small sub–camps, such as the Schindler factory, in the Nazi labor camp system, but none where the prisoners were so well treated. The Nazis provided food for the Schindler Jews, but Schindler supplemented the food rations through black market purchases of food.

Schindler was a Czech of the Sudetenland. He worked for the German secret service and was a member of the Nazi Party in Germany. He was a good man and helped save Jews like myself by providing us with jobs. The job gave me food and a certain amount of security. When I arrived at the Schindler camp I was assigned to a barrack. In the morning at the roll call I was assigned a job. The barracks consisted of long rows of double tiers where we slept. The food was good. Around the camp there were guard towers where the Ukrainian S.S. men observed the camp. The camp looked like any German concentration camp. The camp was actually called the Zablocie Camp in Krakow. In the camp there were Jewish policemen and policewomen, several group leaders and several kapos. Every day there were two roll calls: morning and evening. Schindler or rather his right hand man Itzhak Stern operated two factories in the camp; one produced all sorts of enamel pots and pans and the other plant produced all kinds of metal products, including hand grenades for the German army. The latter section had huge metal machines. German engineers worked together with Polish and Jewish workers. The Polish workers were regular salaried workers while the Jewish workers were forced workers. I was assigned to the metal factory but my real job was to transport the various finished ammunition parts from place to place in a wheelbarrow. When the press stamped the hollow hand grenade, it was filled with explosive material. I wheeled the filled hand grenades to a special furnace that sealed the grenades. When the grenades cooled down, I wheeled them to the enamel section where several female workers dunked the grenades into special tubs filled with chemicals. The girls sang Polish songs and the atmosphere was very pleasant. Among the girls was Lola Oppenheimer from Wieliczka near Sandz. The section chief was Lazar and the section was called Bounder. One day I was called to the office and tattooed with the letters KZ or concentration camp in German.

Next to the factory was the Zarna house that contained the bakery that provided the Schindler camp with bread. I had plenty of bread and also received very good soups that sometimes contained pieces of salami. I ate well at the Schindler camp. On occasion, I traded with Poles some of the clothing items that I took at the sorting place. The Poles brought chocolate, bacon, salami and other good foods for my clothing. Thus, I was able to enrich my food intake and accumulate more strength for the days to come. We also received money, medicines and food packages from an organization called J.S.S. that was financed by Swiss and American Jews.

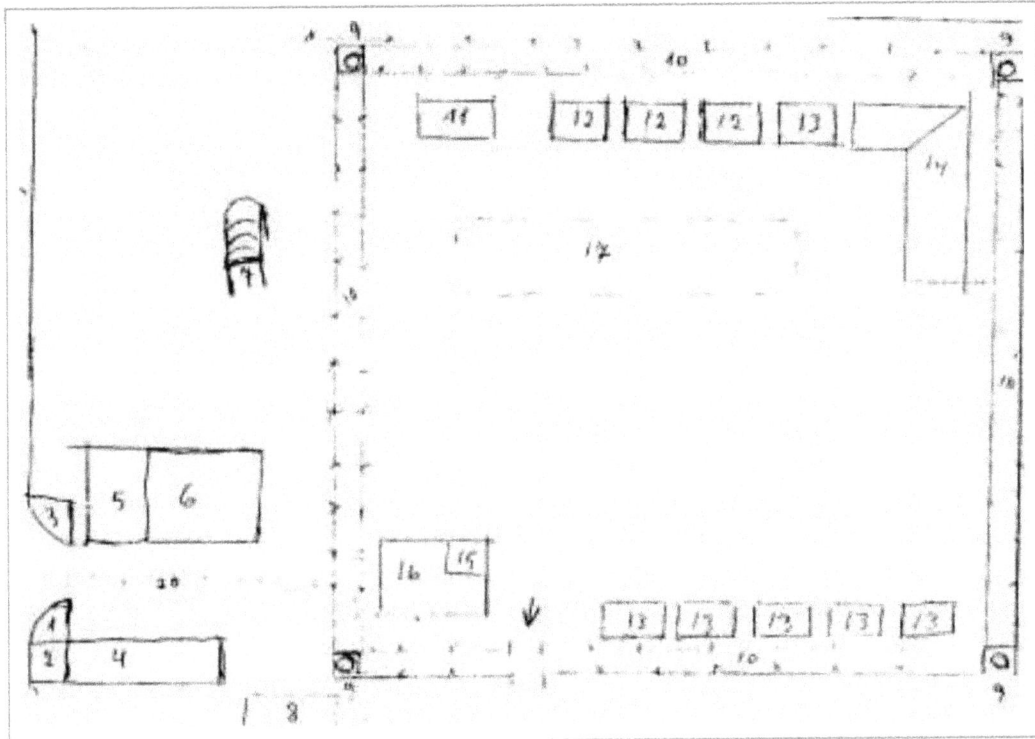

A sketch of the Schindler camp in Krakow as drawn by Mordechai Lustig in March of 1944. Below are the descriptions of the numbers

No.	Detail
1	The entrance to the camp
2	Schindler's residence
3	Camp guards
4	Hand grenade factory
5	Laboratory
6	Enamel factory
7	New factory being built
8	Coating factory
10	Watch towers

No.	Detail
11	Official residences
12	Women's barrack
13	Men's barrack
14	S.S. barrack, mostly Ukrainians
15	Camp offices
16	Warehouses
17	Roll Call place
18	Garbage and coal hips
19	Street adjuring entrance to the camp
20	Narrow gage railroad

The camp contained about 900 male Jewish Jews and 150 women in March 1944. Their quarters were separated.

The J.S.S. or the Jewish Self Help organization was created by the Polish Joint organization when Germany declared war against the United States. The Joint or JDC offices were closed in Poland December 21, 1941.The Joint foresaw these events and created the J.S.S. organization to step in when needed. With the closure of the Joint, the J.S.S. organization began to help the various Jewish social organizations. Most of the J.S.S. officials were former Joint officials, such as Dr.Michal Weichert. He worked under the watchful eyes of the S.S. and Gestapo. The J.S.S. helped many Jewish communities with money and food. Soon, the Germans forced Weichert to concentrate in the General Government areas of Poland or Galicia. He remained in Krakow and helped the remaining Jewish communities, and some concentration camps, notably Plaszów, with needed medical and nutritional foods that Lustig enjoyed.

Schindler treated us Jews like human beings. Prior to the war, he was a tractor salesman and, as such, the Germans sent him to Poland following the Sudetenland annexation to Germany. His official job was to sell tractors in Poland but his real job was to provide Germany with the military capabilities of the Polish army. He gave very good information and Poland was soon defeated. Schindler returned to Krakow and began to look for factories. The Germans gave him the enamel factory that produced pots and pans. Itzhak Stern helped Schindler to run the business. The factory was originally Jewish. Schindler was very shrewd. When he received the factory, he also began to produce hand grenades for the German army. The production of grenades gave him a perfect entrance to the German weapon industry. He also sold pots to the German army. A sizable part of his civilian production was sold on the black market that enabled him to buy the needed foodstuff for his workers. Schindler loved money, diamonds, alcohol, pretty women and cards. In Plaszow everybody knew that when one got a job at Schindler that meant a ticket to live.

At the Schindler factory I met former Sandzer Jews such as Nechemia Sheingot, Romek Gut Hollander, Motchie Bluzenstain, Baruch Hersh Unger, Benyamin Hausshtok. On several occasions Schindler himself came to the kitchen to inspect the food and spoke with some of the workers. Schindler was a close friend of the sadist Amon Goeth who killed forced laborers at the slightest pretext. Schindler and Goeth drank and played cards together and were very cordial to each other. Thanks to this relationship Schindler managed to save Jewish lives.

Schindler List of 1944

The list was compiled in March 1944, according to Mordechai Lustig, who is on the list under the name of Markus Lustig but was later removed and sent to Mauthausen with another group of Schindler workers. The list was taken from Krakow to Budapest and then to Turkey. It finally reached Palestine and was printed in the Hebrew newspaper "Davar" on September 9, 1944. The item was printed without a byline but apparently was reliable enough to be printed in an important daily. The list was divided into three sections that represented Schindler's enterprise:

A – main labor camp
B – women's camp
C – radiator plant

Last Name	First Name	Birth Year	Gender	Section
ADLER	Yossef	1906	M	A
AFTERGUT	Berta	1916	F	B
AMFANG	Peretz	1923	M	C
AMSTER	Isaac	1896	M	A
AMSTER	Ziegfried	1921	M	A
AMSTERDAM	Hirsh	1921	M	A
AMT	Rachel	1920	F	B
ANDER	Markus	1923	M	A
ANDER	Lazar	1896	M	A
APPFEL	Friedrich	1917	M	A
APPFEL	Gisella	1921	F	B
ARBETSMAN	Bruno	1928	M	A
ARMER	Yaakow	1903	M	A
ASPITETZ	Joseph	1908	M	C
AUERBACH	Henryk	1911	M	A
AUERBACH	Salomon	1925	M	A
AUERBACH	Sara	1919	F	B
AWRACHMER	Yossef	1922	M	A
AWRACHMER	Jacob	1918	M	C
AWRAMTCHIK	Yehoshua	1917	M	A
BADER	Ceasar	1897	M	C

BADER	Chaim	1921	M	C
BAGLEITER	Stefan	1925	M	A
BALSAM	Salmon	1903	M	A
BAMKIR	Meir	1917	M	A
BAMKIR	Awraham	1895	M	A
BAMKIR	Awraham	1910	M	A
BANACH	Lola	1908	F	B
BAUMAN	Jacob	1897	M	C
BAYAR	Yossef	1920	M	A
BEIN	Zisa	1928	M	A
BEIN	Solomon	1927	M	A
BEK	Kuba	1922	M	A
BENECH	Salomon	1922	M	A
BENECH	Shmuel	1927	M	A
BENET	Edward	1919	M	C
BERG	Awraham	1904	M	A
BERGER	Isidor	1909	M	A
BERGER	Moshe	1919	M	A
BERGER	Alter	1924	M	C
BERGILSON	Mendel	1922	M	C
BERGMAN	?	1911	M	A
BERHANG	Elka	1915	F	B
BERINAUM	Chaim	1914	M	C
BERINAUM	Isaac	1921	M	C
BERNSTEIN	Dawid	1922	M	A
BERNSTEIN	Chana Malk	1919	F	B
BERNSTEIN	Golda	1921	F	B
BET	Hersh	1912	M	A
BEWOT	Eliezar	1895	M	C
BEYER	Yossef	1909	M	A
BIATEWAROWA	?	1929	M	A
BIGEIER	Rachel	1918	F	B
BINTCH	Awraham	1898	M	A
BIRENBAUM	?	1904	F	B

BIRMAN	Itzhak	1906	M	A
BITERMAN	Meir	1912	M	A
BLASSBERG	Maximilia	1875	M	A
BLAT	Asher	1923	M	A
BLAT	Michael	1907	M	A
BLINDERMAN	Rudolph	1912	M	C
BLITZKI	Awraham	1903	M	A
BLUFIDER	Yaacow	1909	M	A
BLUMBERG	Melech	1895	M	A
BLUMBERG	Shimon	1927	M	A
BLUMENSTOCK	Meir	1923	M	A
BLUMENSTOCK	Shimon	1910	M	A
BLUSENSTEIN	Henryk	1925	M	A
BOGIR	Ester Reisel	1902	F	B
BORENSTEIN	Ozer	1907	M	A
BORENSTEIN	Basha	1926	F	B
BRAHANG	Slo	1916	M	A
BRAND	Meir	1924	M	A
BRAND	Awraham	1900	M	A
BRAND	Maximilian	1921	M	A
BRANDMAYER	?	1924	M	C
BRANDSTATER	Asher	1925	M	C
BRATKIWICZ	Hersh	1910	M	A
BRATKIWICZ	Natan	1911	M	A
BRECHNER	Rudolph	1901	M	A
BRECHNER	Gali	1908	F	B
BRENER	Adolph	1892	M	A
BRENER	Moshe	1923	M	A
BRENER	Raphael	1914	M	A
BRENER	Eta	1910	F	B
BRENGER	Baruch	1906	M	A
BRENGER	Yossef	1922	M	A
BRUDER	Henryk	1909	M	A
BRUDER	Mrkus	1921	M	A

BRUDERMAN	Chaim	1911	M	A
BRULARD	Adolph	1896	M	A
BRUNHEIM	Yechazkel	1921	M	A
BRUNNENBER	Helina	1926	F	B
BUKIT	Alter Simon	1918	M	C
BUKSBAUM	Yakow	1921	M	A
BUKSBAUM	Elma	1917	F	B
BURSTEIN	Fishel	1910	M	A
BZESKA	Cila	1924	F	B
CHMILEWSKI	Modik	1908	M	A
CHMILEWSKI	Feivel	1914	M	A
CHMILEWSKI	Yakow	1904	M	A
CINDER	Maritz	1907	M	A
COHEN	Beryl	1914	M	A
COHEN	Yochin	1897	M	C
CZERWOMIGDA	Chaim	1916	M	A
CZERWONIGOD	Dawid	1918	M	A
DANTZIG	Hersh	1909	M	A
DANTZIG	Berta	1915	F	B
DANTZIG	Chaya	1885	F	B
DANTZIG	Sara	1907	F	B
DANTZIGER	Jerzik	1907	M	A
DAWID	Salomon	1895	M	A
DEMBINSKI	Markus	1925	M	C
DEMBITZER	Theodoer	1897	M	A
DEMBITZER	Sara	1896	F	B
DIAMANT	Shaya	1902	M	A
DIAMANT	Oscar	1905	M	A
DIAMANT	Hendel	1893	M	A
DJUBAS	Dawid	1910	M	A
DOMINIK	Shimon	1925	M	A
DORENSTEIN	Leo	1919	M	C
DORTHEIMER	Awigdor	1918	M	A
DREIER	Seril	1925	F	C

DREKSLER	Elizsz	1905	M	A
DRENGER	Dawid	1910	M	A
DRESSLER	Shimon	1927	M	A
DRESSNER	Major	1918	M	C
DRUBIASZ	Shhlomo	1922	M	A
DUGAN	Leopold	1921	M	A
DULAUER	Anna	1922	F	B
EINSHITZ	Fishel	1920	M	A
EISENBERG	Awraham	1905	M	A
EISENBERG	Itzik	1909	M	C
EISENFELD	Chaim	1908	M	A
EISENFELD	Lemel	1913	M	A
EISENFELD	Moshe	1910	M	A
EISENFELD	Reuven	1918	M	A
EISENMAN	Itzhak	1895	M	A
ENGLANDER	Awraham	1927	M	A
ENGLANDER	Henoch	1915	M	C
ENOCH	Mairitz	1891	M	A
EPSTEIN	Israel	1896	M	A
EPSTEIN	Awraham	1921	M	C
EPSTEIN	Shabsi	1905	M	C
EPSTEIN	Israel	1896	M	C
ERLICH	Manashe	1919	M	A
ESSIG	Michael	1913	M	A
ESSIG	Moshe	1917	M	A
FACHNER	Suzman	1897	M	C
FACHNER	Wolf	1928	M	C
FARBER	Arieh	1876	M	A
FARBER	Julian	1893	M	A
FARBER	Yossef	1925	M	A
FARBER	Hirsh	1910	M	A
FARBER	Oskar	1905	M	A
FARBER	Irena	1922	F	B
FARBER	Mieczyslaw	1925	M	C

FARTIG	Gustawa	1921	F	B
FAUST	Joseph	1896	M	C
FEIGENBAUM	Simha	1911	M	A
FEIGENBAUM	Melech	1923	M	C
FEIGENBLAT	Kalman	1905	M	C
FELDMAN	Lola	1922	F	B
FELDMAN	Roza	1922	F	B
FELDSTEIN	Wolf	1923	M	A
FELDSTEIN	Joseph	1894	M	C
FELLER	Rina	1920	F	B
FELLER	Sara	1918	F	B
FELLER	Lisa	1912	F	C
FENNER	Chaim	1924	M	A
FEUEREISEN	Ludwig	1922	M	A
FEUERKRIZEN	Leonara	1924	F	B
FIDA	Eisisk	1921	M	A
FIDA	Salomon	1925	M	A
FILER	Salmon	1914	M	C
FILER	Melech	1925	M	C
FILER	Samuel	1921	M	C
FILLER	Hezkel	1926	M	A
FINGERLET	Itzik	1903	M	C
FINKELHAUSE	Monik	1923	M	A
FINKELHOLTZ	Eliyahu	1923	M	A
FIOLDICZ	Alter	1900	M	C
FIOLDICZ	Aaron	1926	M	C
FISHEL	Issachar	1914	M	A
FISHEL	Mendel	1923	M	A
FISHGROUND	Leopold	1901	M	A
FISHGRUND	Eliyahu	1907	M	A
FLEISHER	Natan	1915	M	A
FLICK	Markus	1900	M	A
FLINDER	Fela	1909	F	B
FLORENTZ	Ben Tzion	1914	M	A

FLRK	Norbert	1906	M	C
FORRER	Chaim Jjaco	1921	M	C
FORRESTER	Dawid	1914	M	C
FRANKEL	Moses	1911	M	C
FRANKEL	Eliasz	1905	M	C
FRANS	Israel	1915	M	C
FRANTZOIZ	Fishel	1923	M	C
FRAUDLICH	Hizik	1923	M	C
FRAUMAN	Joseph	1912	M	C
FREI	Moshe	1925	M	A
FREI	Wolf	1889	M	A
FREI	Cecilia	1921	F	B
FREUND	Yakow	1921	M	A
FREUNDER	Mordechai	1916	M	A
FRIDNER	Yoachim	1924	M	C
FRIED	Adolph	1899	M	A
FRIEDMAN	Bernard	1925	M	A
FRIEDMAN	Ignac	1917	M	A
FRIEDMAN	Leon Shmu	1909	M	A
FRIEDMAN	Shmuel	1899	M	A
FRIEDMAN	Libel	1897	M	A
FRIEDRICH	Awraham	1918	M	A
FRIEDRICH	Henoch	1893	M	A
FRIMAN	Leib	1906	M	A
FUCHS	Awraham	1926	M	A
FUCHS	Dawid	1924	M	A
FUHRER	Yakow	1922	M	A
GARDA	Adam	1913	M	A
GARDA	Mieczislaw	1921	M	A
GARDA	Itzhak	1897	M	A
GARDA	Mira	1898	F	B
GARFINKEL	Yakow	1909	M	A
GARTEL	Alexander	1920	M	A
GARTNER	Jonasz	1927	M	C

GASSNER	Yossef	1925	M	A
GELLER	Moti	1908	M	A
GELLER	Anna	1910	F	B
GEMINER	Ephraim	1898	M	C
GERBER	Leizer Chai	1904	M	A
GERDA		1918	F	B
GERSHENEWIT	Yossef	1902	M	A
GERSTENER	Leib	1912	M	A
GERSTENFELD	Reuven	1912	M	A
GESUNDHEIT	Leib	1919	M	C
GETZLER	Philip	1922	M	A
GETZLER	Ida	1913	F	B
GITMAN	Awraham	1896	M	C
GITMAN	Moses	1922	M	C
GITMAN	Natan	1925	M	C
GJIB	Salomon	1924	M	A
GLASS	Joseph	1890	M	C
GLAZER	Izhak	1918	M	A
GLITMAN	Osher	1905	M	C
GLITZENSTEIN	Avraham	1915	M	A
GOLDBERG	Herman	1895	M	A
GOLDBERG	Moshe	1924	M	A
GOLDBERG	Shmuel	1906	M	A
GOLDBERG	Joshua	1903	M	C
GOLDBERG	Kalman	1923	M	A
GOLDBLUM	Yehiel	1910	M	A
GOLDFINGER	Lazar	1921	M	A
GOLDFINGER	Bernard	1922	M	A
GOLDKORN	Chaim	1912	M	A
GOLDKORN	Mendel	1914	M	A
GOLDKORN	Moshe	1909	M	A
GOLDLUST	Maximalian	1923	M	A
GOLDSTEIN	Mauricy	1902	M	A
GOLDSTEIN	Bernard	1918	M	A

GOLDSTEIN	Ludwig	1926	M	A
GOLDSTEIN	Sami	1920	M	A
GOLDSTEIN	Shmuel	1898	M	A
GOLDWASSER	Michael	1911	M	A
GOTEL	Daniel	1916	M	A
GOTHERTZ	Henryk	1926	M	A
GOTHERTZ	Yossef	1921	M	A
GOTTLIEB	Maks	1924	M	A
GOTTLIEB	Naphtali	1927	M	C
GOWISH	Itzhak	1910	M	A
GRAUER	Wilhelm	1914	M	A
GRAUER	Yossef	1902	M	A
GREENBERG	Adolph	1912	M	A
GREINHAUT	Bernard	1927	M	A
GRENER	Idla	1893	F	B
GRENER	Pola	1921	F	B
GRINBAUM	Ben Tzion	1914	M	A
GRINBERG	Leonara	1919	F	B
GRINSHPAN	Henryk	1919	M	A
GRINSHPAN	Natan	1897	M	A
GRINSHPAN	Ziegfried	1906	M	A
GROS	Naphtali	1899	M	A
GROSSBART	Alexander	1911	M	A
GROSSBART	Yossef	1907	M	A
GROSSER	Moshe	1924	M	A
GROSSER	Benyamin	1893	M	A
GROSSFELD	Itzhak	1920	M	A
GRUBEL	Awraham	1900	M	A
GRUBEL	Naphtali	1910	M	A
GRUBEL	Lieibush	1923	M	A
GRUBNER	Yossef	1907	M	A
GRUNER	Gusta	1900	F	B
GRUNER	Hirsak Dawi	1905	M	C
GRUNER	Jacob	1928	M	C

GUT	Awraham	1924	M	A
GUTENBERG	Mendel	1913	M	C
GUTHERTZ	Augusta	1897	F	B
GUTMAN	Adolph	1919	M	A
HAAR	Isaak	1925	M	A
HABER	Israel	1900	M	A
HALBERSHTAM	Moses	1908	M	A
HALPERN	Edward	1925	M	A
HALPERN	Chaskel	1922	M	A
HARTMAN	Ferdinand	1917	M	A
HARTMAN	Salomon	1920	M	A
HEBESTOCK	Machmia	1898	F	C
HECHT	Zygmunt	1926	M	A
HEFTER	Ceasar	1926	M	C
HEILINGER	Julius	1922	M	A
HELFSTEIN	Joel	1907	M	C
HELLER	Salmon	1899	M	C
HENECH	Yakowherm	1920	M	A
HERBST	Yossef	1928	M	A
HERMAN	Bernard	1924	M	A
HERRENDORF	Elisa	1911	F	C
HERSCHLAG	Shmul	1905	M	A
HERSCHLAG	Israel	1923	M	A
HERSHKOWITZ	Yakow Itzik	1912	M	A
HERSHLOWITZ	Motek	1909	M	A
HERTHEIMER	Helena	1922	F	B
HERTZOG	Gershon	1912	M	C
HILFSTEIN	Chaim	1886	M	A
HILMAN	Henryk	1926	M	A
HIRSH	Ypssek	1922	M	A
HIRSHFELD	Shmuel	1919	M	A
HIRSHFELD	Pola	1921	F	B
HIRSHPRUNG	Itzik	1909	M	C
HIRSHPRUNG	Mauritz	1924	M	C

HIRSHPRUNG	Adolph	1923	M	C
HIRSHPRUNG	Awraham	1911	M	C
HIRSHPRUNG	Natan	1906	M	C
HITLINGER	Salomon	1912	M	A
HOFFMAN	Chaim Leib	1904	M	A
HOFFMAN	Yossef	1920	M	A
HOFSTATETR	Yossef	1909	M	A
HOLLANDER	Emanuel	1915	M	A
HONIG	Meir	1902	M	A
HONIG	Shmuel	1901	M	A
HONIG	Chana Malk	1902	F	B
HOROWITZ	Dawid	1906	M	A
HOROWITZ	Shachne	1888	M	A
HOROWITZ	Anshel	1925	M	A
HOROWITZ	Itzik	1911	M	A
HOROWITZ	Wolf	1898	M	A
HOROWITZ	Moses	1904	M	A
HOROWITZ	Nina	1911	F	B
HOROWITZ	Roma	1912	F	B
HOROWITZ	Lara	1888	F	B
HOSTOCK	Benyamin	1922	M	C
HOTZIG	Awraham	1920	M	A
HUGMAN	Shlomo	1912	M	A
HUPER	Marian	1925	M	A
IMERGLICK	Chana Malk	1902	F	B
INTIN	Joseph	1916	M	C
INTIN	Zolek	1915	M	C
ISRAELI	Hela	1910	F	B
IZOWITZ	Sala	1911	F	B
JAKUBOWITZ	Irene	1923	F	B
JESSKILL	Awraham	1908	M	C
JODA	Awraham	1910	M	C
KAN	Sacha	1914	M	C
KANAREK	Eliasz	1906	M	A

KAPLANER	Chaim	1925	M	A
KASHIBO	Shmuel	1914	M	A
KASSLER	Mauritz	1902	M	A
KATOLIC	Cila	1914	F	B
KATZ	Yehiel	1926	M	A
KATZ	Awraham	1906	M	C
KATZ	Moniek	1906	M	C
KAUFMAN	Adolph	1911	M	A
KAUFMAN	Shimon	1922	M	A
KAUFMAN	Helina	1919	F	B
KENIGSBER	Anna	1890	F	B
KEREN	Shiya	1906	M	A
KEREN	Sala	1904	F	B
KEZZ	Mauritz	1904	M	C
KIBTATZ	Fredel	1921	F	B
KIHAN	Helena	1922	F	B
KIRSCHNER	Shmuel	1908	M	A
KIRSCHNER	Artur	1915	M	C
KLAGBRUN	?	1918	M	C
KLASSNER	Joseph	1928	M	C
KLEIN	Salomon	1918	M	A
KLEIN	Meir	1924	M	A
KLEIN	Hillel	1928	M	C
KLEINER	Chaim	1907	M	C
KLEINER	Natan	1924	M	C
KLEINZELLER	Mendel	1910	M	A
KLIMAN	Zygmunt	1913	M	A
KLINGER	Henryk	1904	M	A
KLINGER	Sara	1911	F	B
KLOTZ	Slomon	1912	M	A
KLUGGER	Salomon	1901	M	A
KNOBLER	Moshe	1922	M	A
KONA	Monik	1922	M	A
KOPITU	Moses	1898	M	A

KORBER	Leker Lif	1907	M	C
KORN	Rachel	1906	F	B
KORNMEHL	Salomon	1911	M	A
KORNWASSER	Yehaskel	1911	M	A
KRAUSS	Sjomon	1909	M	A
KRAUSS	Jako	1904	M	C
KREBS	Henryk	1926	M	A
KREITZBERG	Dagobert	1896	M	A
KRESHER	Shiya	1918	M	A
KRIEG	Samuel	1911	M	A
KRIGER	Herman	1894	M	A
KRITZSTEIN	Marcel	1924	M	A
KRONFELD	Nuta	1912	M	C
KRUMHOLTZ	Richard	1916	M	A
KRUMHOLTZ	Lena	1917	F	B
KRUTESBERG	Dagobert	1896	M	C
KSINETZKI	Yossef	1903	M	A
KUKEIR	Mordke	1919	M	C
KUKEIR	Naphtali	1903	M	C
KUPETZ	Samuel	1911	M	A
KUPETZ	Zelig	1901	M	A
KUPPER	Shulem	1904	M	A
KUPTZIG	Leib	1926	M	A
KUTCHER	Ludwig	1921	M	A
LAKS	Mauricy	1914	M	A
LANDESHAT	Kofel	1917	M	A
LANDMAN	Yaakow	1901	M	A
LANDSBERG	Yankel	1908	M	A
LANDSDORFER	Ferdinand	1924	M	A
LAOS	Yaakow	1916	M	A
LASLOW	Yaakow	1901	M	A
LAST	Hersh	1915	M	A
LEBERTOW	Yaakow	1906	M	A
LEDEL	Duba	1893	F	B

LEDERMAN	Shmuel	1895	M	A
LEFEL	Sabina	1913	F	B
LEHRFELD	Simon	1922	M	C
LEHRFELD	William	1925	M	C
LEHRMAN	Herman	1910	M	A
LEIZER	Gerda	1911	F	B
LEIZEROWICZ	Isaac	1925	M	C
LEMBERGER	Moses	1925	M	A
LEMOUS	Yaakow	1903	M	A
LEMPEL	Anita	1923	F	B
LEOPOLHOLTZ	Haskel	1912	M	C
LERNER	Anna	1913	F	B
LERNER	Mieczyslaw	1905	M	C
LEWINGER	Joachim	1896	M	A
LEWINSKI	Dawid	1916	M	A
LEWINSTEIN	Israel	1912	M	A
LEWINSTEIN	Solomon	1915	M	A
LEWINSTEIN	?	1911	F	B
LEWISON	Chana Malk	1918	F	B
LEWITT	Moses	1914	M	C
LEWITT	Mordke	1920	M	C
LEWITTES	Wilhelm	1923	M	A
LEWITTES	Lazar	1907	M	A
LEWKOWITZ	Ethel	1906	F	B
LIBAN	Jan	1926	M	A
LIBLER	Awraham	1916	M	A
LIBLICH	Israel	1924	M	A
LICHTENSOHN	Henryk	1921	M	C
LICHTENSTEIN	Gershon	1905	M	C
LIEBENGOLD	Etka	1910	F	B
LINKOWSKI	Mauricy	1905	M	A
LIPA	Yaakow	1918	M	A
LIPNITZKI	Itzik	1925	M	A
LISSON	Dawid	1927	M	A

LISSON	Leib	1921	M	A
LISSON	Moses	1893	M	A
LITMAN	Stefan	1914	M	A
LITMANIWITZ	Leib	1915	M	A
LITMONOWITZ	Salomon	1915	M	C
LIZORK	Mendel	1927	M	A
LOEW	Philip	1909	M	A
LOWENTZER	Ludwiga	1921	F	B
LUBLINKER	Isaac	1910	M	A
LUFTENGLASS	Berl	1895	M	A
LUKS	Leonard	1921	M	A
LUNKER	Tchas	1913	M	A
LUPER	Sol	1920	M	C
LUSTGARTEN	Karol	1897	M	C
LUSTGARTEN	Richard	1924	M	C
LUSTIG	Markus	1925	M	A
MAHLER	Awraham	1902	M	A
MALINSKI	Yossef	1920	M	A
MANA	Tauba	1892	F	B
MANDELBAUM	Major	1920	M	C
MANDELBAUM	Mendel	1924	M	C
MANN	Shaya	1914	M	A
MARGOLIS	Mechel	1914	M	A
MARKIEL	Salomon	1905	M	A
MARKOWITZ	Awraham	1905	M	A
MARKOWITZ	Feivel	1920	M	A
MARKOWITZ	Israel	1909	M	C
MARMOR	Yossef	1888	M	A
MEHR	Jako	1916	M	C
MEKLER	Moses	1920	M	A
MELTZ	Eliasz	1923	M	A
MELTZ	Markus	1916	M	A
MELTZER	Eisik	1895	M	A
MENDEL	Naftali	1925	M	A

MENDEL	Wolf	1904	M	A
MERDER	Wilhelm	1905	M	A
METILANSKI	Leib	1925	M	A
MILER	Eugenia	1926	F	B
MILLER	Lipman	1918	M	C
MILNER	Mordke	1926	M	A
MINDER	Sela	1914	F	B
MITLER	Itzik	1908	M	A
MITLES	Hugo	1910	M	A
MITLES	Kalman	1920	M	A
MITLIS	Sender	1908	M	A
MITLIS	Shmul	1924	M	A
MITLUS	Alter	1906	M	A
MITTLES	Israel	1897	M	C
MITZNER	Wilhelm	1911	M	A
MOHLER	Shaul	1926	M	C
MONDRER	Nuchim	1923	M	A
MONHEIT	Mieczyslaw	1916	M	A
MONHEIT	Henryk	1926	M	A
MOTLETCH	Itzik	1922	M	C
MUNDSHEI	Binem	1918	M	C
MUNDSTEIN	Arnolf	1915	M	A
MUNDSTEIN	Yossef	1900	M	A
MUNDSTEIN	Moses	1923	M	A
MUNHOIT	Mozes	1892	M	A
MUNT	Hersh	1910	M	A
NACHMAN	Shiya	1894	M	C
NADEL	Leib	1906	M	A
NADEL	Felicia	1917	F	B
NADEL	Leon	1889	M	C
NADLER	Oskar Leize	1914	M	A
NAFKER	Israel	1904	M	A
NAFKER	Yakow	1911	M	A
NAFTALOWITCH	Itzik	1924	M	A

NAGEL	Markus	1924	M	A
NASS	Roza	1906	F	B
NATANSON	Yunes	1913	M	A
NEIGER	Markus	1902	M	A
NEIGER	Solomon	1908	M	A
NEIGER	Lea	1906	F	B
NESSEL	Baruch	1925	M	A
NEUBERT	Chaim	1924	M	A
NEUBURG	Wictor	1924	M	A
NEUDET	Mauritz	1917	M	A
NEUFELD	Alter	1906	M	A
NEUMAN	Zygmunt	1898	M	A
NEUMAN	Mona	1914	F	B
NEUMARK	Israel	1922	M	A
NEZEL	Salmon	1924	M	C
NIMETZ	Yossek	1925	M	A
NIWELEWSKI	Reuwen	1917	M	C
NIWLEWSKI	Leon	1917	M	A
NOWOTNI	Mordke	1904	M	A
NUSSBAUM	Eisisk	1905	M	A
NUSSBAUM	Otto	1923	M	A
NUSSBAUM	Henoch	1909	M	A
NUSSBAUM	Harta	1921	F	B
OFFMAN	Wolfi	1900	M	A
OFMAN	Henrika	1920	F	B
OFMAN	Herta	1929	F	B
OLNIK	Yaakow	1921	M	A
OPPENHEIM	Henryk	1923	M	A
OSTREICHER	Yakow	1917	M	A
OTZ—	Dawid	1909	M	A
PEARL	Salomon	1907	M	A
PEARLBERG	Naftali	1923	M	A
PEARLBERG	Samuel	1899	M	A
PEARLBERG	Dora	1907	F	B

PEARLMAN	Israel	1907	M	A
PEARLMAN	Naphtali	1891	M	C
PEARLMUTTER	Leon	1910	M	C
PEARLROT	Awraham	1925	M	A
PEARLROT	Nuchim	1893	M	A
PEARLROT	Awraham	1927	M	C
PELZMAN	Gusta	1912	F	B
PENIKEL	Leizer	1926	M	A
PINELESS	Maximilian	1921	M	C
PINKAS	Ester	1915	F	B
PINKASSOWITZKI	Zenkil	1912	M	C
POSNER	Israel	1904	M	A
PREISS	Emanuel	1924	M	A
PRESCHADECKI	Israel	1914	M	C
PRESSER	Bronislawa	1923	F	B
PRESSER	Fremia	1910	F	B
PRESSER	Roza	1919	F	B
PRESSLER	Bernard	1914	M	A
PRINA	Hermina	1900	F	B
PRINTZ	Eisisk	1893	M	A
PRINTZ	Yossef	1927	M	A
PROPKIR	Moses	1906	M	A
PSZEBORSKI	Kalman	1912	M	A
PSZECHATZKI	Alek	1920	M	A
PSZECHATZKI	Yakow	1925	M	A
PSZECHATZKI	Leibusz	1920	M	A
PULKA	Sculin	1898	M	C
RADZWILER	Adolph	1911	M	A
RAKOWSKI	Israel	1927	M	A
RAPPOPORT	Dawid	1917	M	A
RATH	Dora	1916	F	B
RATTAS	Chaim	1923	M	C
RATTAS	Paul	1920	M	C
RECHEN	Rihard	1921	M	A

RECHSBAUM	Stanislaw	1916	M	A
REDLICH	Wilhelm	1916	M	A
REICH	Awraham	1907	M	A
REICH	Emil	1894	M	A
REIF	Vicyor	1906	M	A
REWER	Pinka	1913	F	C
RIGER	Mendel	1927	M	C
RILES	Natan	1915	M	C
RINGELBLOOM	Arnold	1920	M	A
RITTER	Isidor	1911	M	C
RITTER	Simcha	1907	M	C
RIWA	Yeshayahu	1914	M	A
RIZMAN	Lola	1917	F	B
RIZMAN	Jacob	1915	M	C
RONZEK	Yaakow	1913	M	A
ROSEN	Moses	1917	M	A
ROSENBAUM	Eisik	1921	M	A
ROSENBAUM	Dawid	1926	M	C
ROSENBAUM	Hersh	1925	M	C
ROSENBERG	Meir	1906	M	A
ROSENBERG	Moshek	1925	M	A
ROSENBERG	Julius	1900	M	A
ROSENBERG	Motek	1911	M	A
ROSENBERG	Shlomo	1911	M	A
ROSENBERG	Shmuel	1913	M	A
ROSENBERG	Motek	1921	M	C
ROSENFELD	Natan	1925	M	A
ROSENFELD	Maurice	1924	M	C
ROSENHAHN	Samuel	1925	M	C
ROSENKRANTZ	Raphel	2906	M	A
ROSENKRANTZ	Raphael	1906	M	C
ROSENSTEIN	Henryk	1915	M	A
ROSENSTOCK	Benjamin	1928	M	A
ROSENTHAL	Chaim	1922	M	A

ROSENTZWEIG	Naphtali	1923	M	C
ROTHBERG	Erna	1915	F	B
ROTHBERG	Maurice	1908	M	C
ROTHEIM	Mozes	1906	M	A
ROTHENBERG	Aaron	1923	M	A
ROTHENBERG	Shmuel	1898	M	A
ROTHENBERG	Zygmunt	1923	M	A
ROTHER	Isaac	1923	M	A
ROTHER	Shaul	1919	M	A
ROTHER	Zygmunt	1920	M	A
ROZNER	Hirsh	1906	M	A
ROZNER	Helena	1909	F	B
RUBINSTEIN	Anshel	1918	M	A
RUBINSTEIN	Mauricy	1920	M	A
RUBINSTEIN	Shmuel	1914	M	A
RUDDER	Itzik	1900	M	A
SAFIER	Rita	1926	F	B
SAPHIR	Yehoshua	1885	M	A
SARNA	Jonka	1921	F	C
SCHANOWETTER	Dawid	1912	M	C
SCHARF	Dawid	1914	M	A
SCHARF	Tauba	1914	F	B
SCHEIN	Rita	1921	F	B
SCHEINHERTZ	Ester	1899	F	B
SCHEINHERTZ	Helena	1899	F	B
SCHEINHERTZ	Stefania	1906	F	B
SCHELLER	Awraham	1920	M	C
SCHENKER	Rebeca	1888	F	B
SCHICK	Irena	1921	F	B
SCHINTEL	Bela	1899	F	B
SCHINTEL	Regina	1917	F	B
SCHINTEL	Sara	1868	F	B
SCHISSER	Salmon	1912	M	C
SCHLAKCZIK	Israel	1921	M	C

SCHLUSSEL	Awraham	1914	M	C
SCHMALTZ	Aaron Yos	1897	M	C
SCHMIDT	Eliasz	1904	M	A
SCHMIDT	Naphtali	1902	M	A
SCHNIRER	Hela	1904	F	B
SCHNITZER	Dawid	1894	M	A
SCHNITZER	Dawid	1894	M	C
SCHNUFTBEK	Leon	1902	M	C
SCHNUR	Maurice	1907	M	C
SCHPIGEL	Chiel	1913	M	C
SCHTRENGST	Ester	1911	F	B
SCHTRENGST	Sara	1892	F	B
SCHUMACHER	Kalman	1912	M	C
SCHWARTZBAUM	Dawid	1912	M	C
SCHWARTZMAN	Bela	1909	F	B
SCHWARTZMAN	Solomia	1928	F	B
SCHWARTZMEHR	Lib	1921	M	C
SERBATKA	Feivel	1914	M	A
SEREBRANA	Giselle Stef	1918	F	B
SHADEL	Reuven	1888	M	A
SHAGRIN	Zacharias	1925	M	A
SHAK	Yerzi	1917	M	A
SHEIN	Chaim	1916	M	A
SHEINGUT	Nachmias	1921	M	A
SHEINHERTZ	Zygmunt	1914	M	A
SHEWSHOWSKI	Moshe	1924	M	A
SHIDLINGER	Markus	1918	M	A
SHIDLOWSKI	Yehiel	1919	M	A
SHIDLOWSKI	Meir	1922	M	A
SHIFF	Leizer	1925	M	A
SHIFF	Mitzsider	1924	M	A
SHIMEL	Aleksander	1927	M	C
SHINDEL	Samuel	1905	M	A
SHINOWITZ	Arian	1922	M	A

SHINRER	Solo	1927	M	C
SHLAGGER	Wilk	1916	M	A
SHLOMOWITZ	Chaim	1924	M	A
SHNITZKI	Yankil	1904	M	A
SHRAGER	Berish	1908	M	A
SHTAMLER	Yehazkel	1922	M	A
SHTAMLER	Chaim	1923	M	A
SHTAMLER	Shimon	1919	M	A
SHTAMLER	Zelig	1902	M	A
SHTERFELD	Yossef	1896	M	A
SHTERNBERG	Ephraim	1919	M	A
SHTERNER	Wolf	1919	M	A
SHTIL	Leon	1910	M	A
SHTIL	Norbert	1914	M	A
SHTRENGST	Awraham	1900	M	A
SHTRUZ	Wictor	1901	M	A
SHTRUZ	Wolf	1926	M	A
SHULKIND	Shmuel	1914	M	A
SKAMSKI	Jakob	1921	M	C
SMETANA	Ernest	1929	M	A
SOLANDER	Moses	1904	M	A
SOLANI	Leib	1921	M	A
SOLDINGER	Shmuel	1824	M	A
SPILER	Fritz	1922	M	A
SPINER	Chaim	1890	M	C
SPIRA	Yossef	1907	M	A
STAMPLER	Jakob	1912	M	C
STATEFELDT	Markus	1921	M	A
STEIN	Aaron	1920	M	A
STEIN	Henoch	1893	M	A
STEINHARDT	Rut	1922	F	B
STEINHAUS	Racia	1900	F	B
STEINPRES	Yossef	1895	M	A
STERN	Aaron	1908	M	A

STERN	Asher	1908	M	A
STIL	Sidonia	1922	F	B
STIL	Alice	1912	F	C
STOPNIKO	Solomon	1923	M	C
STRASSBERG	Mauricy	1903	M	A
SULTRANIK	Shlomo	1922	M	A
SWUSCHAKANTIL	Dawid	1909	M	C
TAG	Lazar	1924	M	A
TAWAS	Hersh	1911	M	C
TEITELBAUM	Awraham	1916	M	C
TEITELBAUM	Dawid	1917	M	C
TEITELBAUM	Dawid	1913	M	C
TEITELBAUM	Joseph	1920	M	C
TEITELBAUM	Menachem	1918	M	C
TELLER	Mendel	1923	M	A
TELLER	Maurice	1894	M	C
TENNENBAUM	Shimon	1928	M	A
TENNENBAUM	Marcel	1925	M	A
TENNENBAUM	Zuskind	1899	M	A
TENNENBAUM	Yakow	1919	M	A
TENNENBAUM	Hersh	1923	M	C
TEUIFEL	Ignacy	1917	M	A
TEUIFFEL	Beno	1925	M	A
THON	Tehila	1912	F	B
TIGER	Berl	1923	M	A
TOVIM	Herman	1905	M	A
TRAUNG	Stefania	1905	F	B
TRAURING	Ferdinand	1892	M	A
TUREK	Shmuel	1911	M	A
TURK	Lola	1916	F	B
TURK	Rosalia	1910	F	B
TZIPPS	Daniel	1905	M	A
TZNGER	Karolina	1909	F	B
TZUKER	Israel	1906	M	C

TZUKERMAN	Eliezer	1908	M	A
TZUKERMAN	Awraham	1924	M	A
TZUKERMAN	Herman	1912	M	A
TZUKERMAN	Chaim	1911	M	A
TZUKERMAN	Isaac	1916	M	A
TZUKERMAN	Yeti	1915	F	B
TZWEIG	Herman	1911	M	A
TZWIK	Yoachim	1916	M	A
UNDERMAN	Awraham	1933	M	C
UNGER	Meir	1898	M	C
UNGER	Moses	1928	M	C
WACHDLUBSKI	Baruch	1886	M	A
WACHDLUBSKI	Kalman	1922	M	A
WAGSHALL	Isidor	1908	M	A
WAGSHALL	Yakow	1920	M	A
WAHL	Mindel	1897	F	B
WANTZELBERG	Maurice	1919	M	C
WARENBERG	Leon	1929	M	A
WARSHAWSKI	Meir	1900	M	A
WASSERLAUFER	Nahum	1925	M	A
WASSERMAN	Baruch	1926	M	C
WASSERMAN	Jakob	1905	M	C
WASSERTEIL	Moses	1898	M	A
WASSERTIL	Cecilia	1922	F	B
WEIL	Naphtali	1914	M	A
WEINBERG	Adolph	1910	M	A
WEINBERG	Shiya	1902	M	A
WEINBERG	Markus	1909	M	A
WEINER	Yechiel	1919	M	C
WEINER	Natan	1903	M	C
WEINFELD	Israel	1904	M	A
WEINGARTEN	Shimon	1919	M	A
WEINGURT	Israel	1923	M	A
WEINRIB	Eda	1926	F	C

WEINROT	Israel	1923	M	A
WEINSTEIN	Moses	1918	M	A
WEINSTEIN	Daniel	1895	M	C
WEINSTEIN	Hersh	1919	M	C
WEINSTOCK	Hirsh	1915	M	A
WEINTRAUB	Moniek	1925	M	A
WEIS	Aaron	1918	M	C
WEISS	Yehuda	1913	M	A
WEISS	Wolf	1909	M	A
WEISS	Chaim	1915	M	C
WEISS	Joshua	1918	M	C
WEISSBERG	Kalman	1912	M	A
WEKSSLER	Chiel	1895	M	A
WEKSSLER	Adela	1900	F	B
WEKSSLER	Maria	1928	F	B
WELKES	Leib	1911	M	A
WERDIGER	Daaawid	1920	M	C
WERNER	Dawid	1923	M	A
WERTEL	Chaim	1928	M	A
WERTEL	Chaim	1892	M	A
WERTEL	Bernard	1922	M	C
WERTEL	Joseph	1927	M	C
WERTHEIM	Shmuel	1919	M	A
WERTHEIMER	Henryk	1906	M	C
WERTSTEIN	Chaim	1922	M	A
WIENER	Chaim	1904	M	A
WIENER	Israel	1921	M	A
WIENER	Shmuel	1907	M	A
WISENFELD	Rachmiel	1914	M	A
WOGEL	Maximilian	1914	M	C
WOHLBERG	Awraham	1921	M	A
WOHLBERG	Biner	1913	M	A
WOHLMUEL	Yakow	1894	M	A
WOLFEILER	Kalman	1896	M	A

WOLFEILER	Roman	1918	M	A
WOLFF	Dawid	1915	M	A
WOLFIELD	Alice	1912	M	C
WOLFILD	Chaya	1897	F	B
WOLFILER	Eliasz	1912	M	A
WOLFMAN	Adolph	1921	M	C
WOLFMAN	Jakob	1913	M	C
WOLFMAN	Salo	1935	M	C
WOLFOWITZ	Idek	1922	M	A
WULKAN	Ozish	1912	M	A
WULKAN	Reuven	1919	M	A
WURTHMAN	Sara Reisel	1890	F	B
WURTHMAN	Leon	1894	M	C
WURTHMAN	Maurice	1926	M	C
WURTZEL	Maurice	1926	M	C
WURTZEL	Stefan	1927	M	C
WURTZEL	Amsalem	1924	M	C
ZAHN	Leib	1908	M	A
ZAHN	Asher	1917	M	C
ZALTZBERG	Chaim	1925	M	A
ZALTZBERG	Emanuel	1919	M	A
ZALTZBERG	Hersh	1898	M	A
ZALTZBERG	Shmuel	1923	M	A
ZANGER	Moniek	1933	M	A
ZAUBERBRIN	Leon	1904	M	A
ZAUBERMAN	Dawid	1910	M	A
ZAUERBRUN	Rut	1913	F	B
ZEIBERSTEIN	Awraham	1909	M	C
ZELINGER	Emalia	1888	F	B
ZELLINGER	Chaim	1895	M	A
ZELNIK	Markus	1913	M	C
ZIDNUNG	Yerachmiel	1904	M	A
ZILBERBERG	Yoel	1900	M	A
ZILBERBERG	Yossef	1925	M	A

ZILBERBERG	Shlomo	1903	M	A
ZILBERBERG	Baruch	1924	M	A
ZILBERSTEIN	Hersh	1902	M	A
ZILBERSTEIN	Shimon	1912	M	A
ZILBIGER	Grad	1923	M	C
ZILENGUT	Lazar	1905	M	A
ZILLER	Dawid Yon	1904	M	A
ZIMBAR	Fishel	1918	M	A
ZINGER	Adolph	1911	M	A
ZINGER	Chaim	1922	M	A
ZINGER	Mendel	1925	M	A
ZINGER	Henryk	1903	M	C
ZIRLICH	Awraham	1922	M	A
ZLINGER	Ozrish	1917	M	A
ZLINGER	Shimon	1891	M	A
ZLINGER	Lazar	1924	M	A
ZOLLMAN	Maks	1923	M	C
ZOLLMAN	Moses	1911	M	C
ZOLMAN	Mechel	1907	M	A
ZONENSTEIN	Isaac	1905	M	A
ZONENSTEIN	Isaac	1923	M	A

This list would undergo numerous changes before the Schindler factory would leave Krakow. The Soviet armies were advancing rapidly in Poland and approaching Krakow. The Germans began to send concentration camp inmates to various places in the rear. In August 1944 a large transport of workers from Płaszów was assembled at the railway station. About 2,000 workers were there. Goeth insisted that Schindler contribute some people to the transport. Schindler negotiated with Goeth and they settled on about fifty workers that would have to leave the Schindler factory and join the transport. I was one of those selected workers. I felt like I was just condemned to death. I tried to intervene but did not have enough clout to change the decision. All the other workers selected for the transport tried to remain in the factory and used their connections. A great deal of pressure was applied on the camp leadership to change names. I did not succeed and resigned myself to my fate.

The morning of the departure, I was given jam and other foods from the camp warehouse and marched off to the railway station where I received a can of one kilo of meat and a military bread or the road that would last for about three days. We were squezeed into cattle cars at the rate of 140 people per car. I could not stand or sit and it was very hot. The train was standing in the blazing heat that became unbearable, when suddenly drops of cold water began to seep through the roof. As the water kept pouring into the car, it cooled the car. I saw Schindler directing the water hose holder to spray the cars. Finally we left Krakow and headed to the concentration camp of Mauthausen.

The following month, September 1944, Amon Goeth was arrested by the S.S. for stealing Jewish goods, a serious crime since the goods belonged to the state. The case never reached the S.S. court due to the continuous deterioration of the German military situation. However, Goeth was assigned to a mental hospital where the Americans found him and handed him over to the Polish authorities as a war criminal. He was condemned to death and executed on September 13, 1946 in Krakow, not far from the Płaszów concentration camp. Schindler managed to get the necessary papers to transfer his entire factory and personnel to Brunnitz in Czechoslovakia. He tried to enlist Madritsch to join him and move his factory to Brunnitz. Madritsch declined and closed his factory in Krakow. We have to remember the German military situation and yet Schindler managed to obtain cars and transport his workers to Czechoslovakia. In October 1944, the Schindler factory and the personnel left Krakow.One of his male transports wound up in the concentration camp of Gross Rosen. Schindler himself intervened and obtained their release. A female transport wound up in Auschwitz–Birkenau. Schindler persuaded the commandant to release his workers and paid for them. They were released and soon reached Brunnitz. Schindler maneuvered and negotiated until the Russians freed the camp and all the inmates were freed. On January 14, 1945, the last group of inmates left for Auschwitz. Shortly thereafter, Płaszów was liberated by the Soviets.

[Page 213]

Chapter IX
The Mauthausen–Gussen Concentration Camp Complex

The Mauthausen–Gusen concentration camp complex was a large group of German concentration camps that was built around the villages of Mauthausen and Gusen, roughly 20 kilometers east of the city of Linz in Upper Austria. The camp complex began with the German–Austrian unification in 1938 and lasted until the end of the war in 1945.

Initially, a single camp existed at Mauthausen; it expanded over time and by the summer of 1944, Mauthausen had become one of the largest complexes in the German–controlled part of Europe. Apart from the four main sub–camps, Mauthausen and nearby Gusen had more than 50 sub–camps, located throughout Austria and southern Germany. The complex was fueled by slave labor brought from all over occupied Europe. Tunnels were dug and military factories were brought and installed in these tunnels. The assembly plants produced munitions, rockets and armaments In January 1945 there were about 85,000 inmates in the complex. It is not known how many people died in the complex system of camps during its existence; estimates range between 122,766 and 320,000 people.

Sub–camp inmate counts Late 1944 – Early 1945

Gusen (I, II and III combined)	26,311
Ebensee	18,437
Gunskirchen	15,000
Melk	10,314
Linz	6,690
Amstetten	2,966
Wiener–Neudorf	2,954
Schwechat	2,568
Steyr–Münichholz	1,971
Schlier–Redl–Zipf	1,488

Some of the sub–camps of Mauthausen with the number of inmates.

The two main camps, Mauthausen and Gusen I, were labeled as "Grade III" or strict concentration camps. Mauthausen never lost this rating. Mauthausen specialized in killing inmates by sheer labor exhaustion, especially political inmates from across conquered Europe. The Mauthausen complex of camps began to go underground with the large-scale air offensive war across Germany. More and more tunnels were dug where entire factories were buried underground to protect them from Allied bombs. The inmates dug these tunnels, assembled the factories and began to produce the various military products. Thousands of inmates died in digging, building and maintaining the tunnels where the V–1 and V–2 rockets were being assembled and used against England. One of these places was the little town of Melk situated between Linz and Vienna.

We arrived at Mauthausen concentration camp and were immediately organized into groups and each group was led to the showers. We had to strip completely and each body was thoroughly examined. All body orifices were checked for valuables. We were then assigned barracks. Each barrack contained 1,000 people. Each barrack had a block chief. I was assigned to block number seven. The leader of the block was an Austrian communist. Shimon Wiesenthal was in our block. Following the war, Wiesenthal would remain in Austria and devote himself to hunting down Nazi criminals and help bring them to trial. We remained in this barrack seven days and were naked. The barrack was fenced and isolated from the rest of the camp. Once a day we received food. There were evening roll calls and then to bed. We slept like sardines since there was no room to move or turn. We slept as good as we could. Each day we received another piece of clothing. One day a striped shirt, the next day striped pants, shoes, then a box that contained numbers. I had to wrap the number around my left arm and tied it with a piece of wire. My number was "85366." All night I thought about this number. Then I remembered my yeshiva days and tried to figure out what the numbers represented. In the Hebrew alphabet each letter also has a number. The number 85366 symbolized the word " Koach " or power in Hebrew. I was hopeful that the number would bring me some luck. We also received a mess kit to receive our food. I was very lucky that I was not assigned to the quarry with all the steps. There were 186 steps in the quarry from the bottom to the top. The people assigned to the quarry lasted about a week.

Mordechai Lustig was recorded as Markus Lustig on all German documents. He was recorded as an inmate at the Mauthausen concentration camp on August 10, 1944. He had arrived from Plaszow concentration camp
(Yad Vashem archives)

Prisoners were forced to climb the 186 steps of the quarry with large blocks of granite on their backs. Kapos and S.S. men set a fast pace for the stone carriers. They used their whips and rifle butts to increase the speed of the inmates. Often the carrier and his stone would lose their footing and fall backwards. The "domino" effect would come into play whereby stone carriers would fall on top of each other backwards. When some of the stone carriers managed to reach the top, the S.S. men would then take them to the edge of the cliff and order them to jump to their death. The cliff edge was referred to as "the Parachute Jump" site. The senseless and bestial killing scene was a daily occurrence at the Mauthausen concentration camp. The camp specialized in other tortures with the aim of eventually killing the inmates.

As the war advanced, the extensive Allied bombing strategy affected the German war machine. Industrial plants were constantly bombed and the German air force could not stop the Allied planes. Factory after factory went up in smoke. The Germans decided to move their military plants further east and underground. Caves and tunnels were converted into industrial sites. New tunnels were ordered to be dug for the German war industry. Thousands of slave laborers were sent to these sites to dig and build factories underground, among them the concentration camp of Melk. The small town was best known as the site of a massive baroque Benedictine monastery named Melk Abbey.

Now Melk was also known as a concentration camp site. The camp was opened on January 11, 1944 and would operate until May 5, 1945.

**The infamous quarry of Mauthausen,
also called the "Stairs of Death."**

I was sent as a locksmith with a large transport of inmates from Mauthausen to Melk. The transport was divided into several sections. I went to Melk, other groups went to the concentration camp Gusen I and to the concentration camp Gussen II, and a fourth group was sent to Linz where they would be working for the Hermann Goering airplane factories. From a distance, the camp did not look bad. The Melk camp was established well within the bounds of a large Wehrmacht garrison; formerly it was an Austrian military base. Soldiers and civilians saw the concentration camp of Melk. In fact it was quite possible to look down on the camp and adjoining army barracks from the link roads which were on a higher level. The main purpose for the Melk concentration camp was to provide forced labor for the different tunneling projects in the surrounding hills. The hills consisted of fine sand and quartz. Due to this, a vast number of prisoners were buried alive beneath cave–ins while working inside. Melk also had its own crematorium. Its tall smoke stack, pointing like a finger to the sky, was an obvious landmark. It covered a large area and its design was an improvement on those of Mauthausen, Gusen and Ebensee. Adjoining the crematorium was a mortuary which was well ventilated and well tiled. In the summer months the crematorium accounted for eight to 16 deaths per day, while in the winter of 1944–1945, the number increased to between 20 to 30 a day. Nothing was done to conceal the stench and atrocities and consequently the inhabitants and soldiers were totally aware of what was going on.

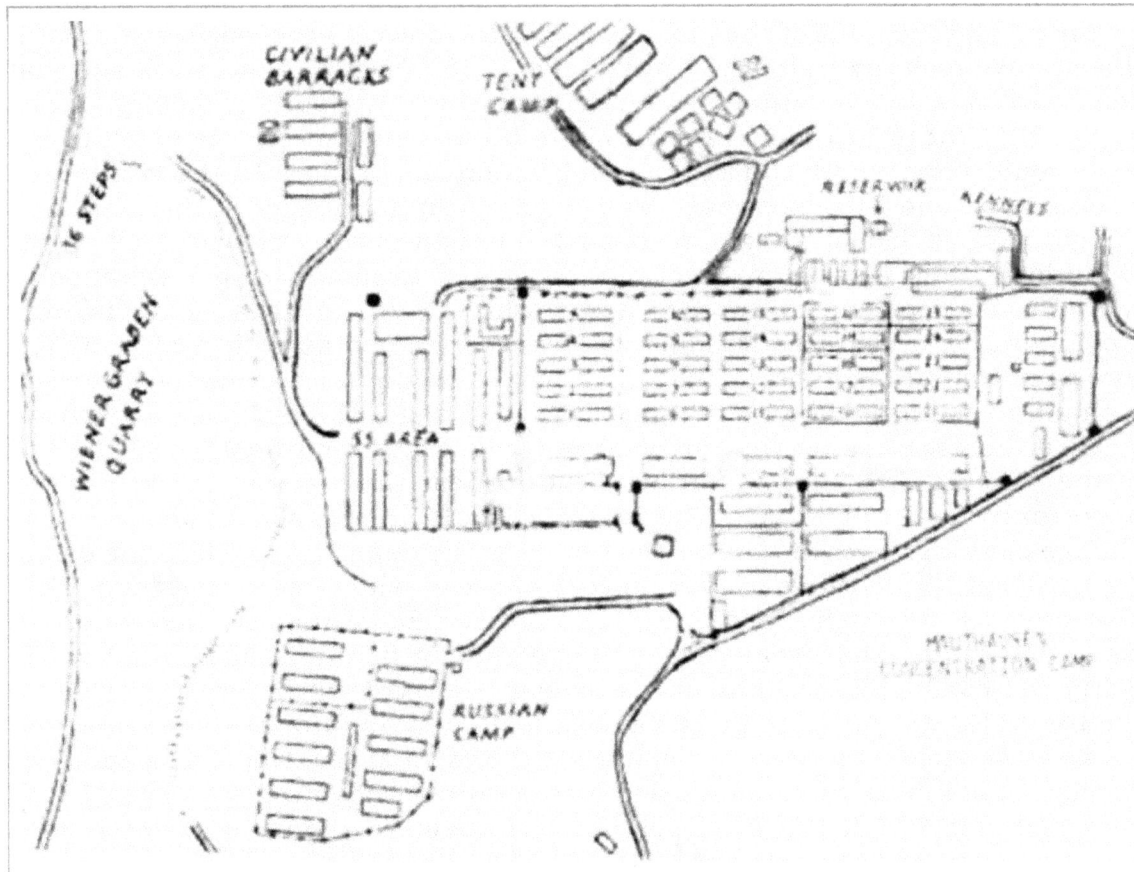

The Mauthausen concentration camp. On the top left side are the steps and the parachute jump site. Below are the quarries, the S.S. area, the civilian barracks, the Russian camp, the tent camp, the reservoir, the kennels.

We entered the camp of Melk and were immediately assigned to several blocks. There were also huge hangars. I was assigned to hangar number 16 headed by a Hungarian Jew named Harry who was formerly a musician.

He had several young assistants aged 14–16 who cleaned the place, distributed the bread and divided the food in the morning and the evening. We were 1,000 people in the hangar. The beds were three–layered beds. Each bed was assigned to two inmates. Each morning there was a bed inspection and then a full report. We then received our coffee and bread and headed out to the assembly ground where we were counted and recounted. The camp had about 20,000 inmates. It took quite some time to count all the inmates. We had to stand and wait until the count was finished. Then the commandant of the camp would arrive and receive the report from the reporting officer. We were constantly lifting our hats and putting them back on our heads, winter and summer. Then the order was given to march out of the camp. Group by group we marched out of the camp and headed down to the railway station in the city. We took the train and traveled about 15 minutes to our work site that consisted of a tall mountain hollowed out where we built a factory. I was assigned to the group that carried rails to build a railway for the small trains that would carry sand and other construction materials into the tunnels. A week passed and I realized that I would not last much longer at the job. I was the shortest worker in the group so the full weight of the rail would fall on my shoulders. I talked to the work group leader and explained to the situation to him. He assigned me to another group where I unloaded large ducts from trucks until two Viennese building workers took me on as their assistant. The Viennese workers connected the ducts to the ceiling and formed a structure with air holes in them below the real roof. They had a shower place where they washed themselves after they finished working. Fifteen minutes before the end of the working day, they would send me to heat the water. I would use the opportunity to wash myself. The workers would then wash themselves and change clothing. I went to the roll call prior to the departure back to the camp. On occasion, the workers gave me pieces of bread with cheese or salami. They also provided me each month with a bonus certificate that entitled me to 10 cigarettes that I could trade for 10 bread rations at my hangar number 16. Harry the block chief was the official trader. He received the bread supply for the block. He was supposed to slice each loaf of bread into 10 slices. However, he sliced the loaf into 12 slices. He traded the extra slices. Harry was an active homosexual and surrounded himself with a number of young boys aged 14–17 who also helped him run the block and the business. He worked closely with his assistant, aged 20, who was also his bed partner.

We all had to tie our mess kits and spoons to our bodies in order to retain them. If one lost his mess kit he had no utensil to receive food. I sharpened my spoon so that I could use it as a knife. I was caught and received 25 lashes on my backside. I was not the only one to be caught and punished. I was soon transferred to block number 10 headed by an Austrian political inmate who wore a red inverted triangle on his clothing. I spent a short time there and was sent to block number 13 that was situated above the kitchen. The kitchen head was a Russian. Every 10 days we were taken to the shower room. Ten people were given one showerhead. We washed as well as we could but were basically filthy. We worked long hours with all kinds of construction materials and needed more time. But this was not the case, so our hygiene was poor and the slightest scratch or cut of the skin resulted in infections and boils. I myself developed boils and could barely walk. I decided to admit myself to the hospital. This was a very dangerous decision, for the Germans injected many patients with deadly shots that resulted in their death. I had no choice and decided to go to the hospital. I was lucky and came out alive. I was always hungry. Some inmates pulled their gold teeth to sell the gold for bread or soup. The food rations were not so bad but insufficient for hard working people. We received in the morning 250 grams of bread, a slice of margarine and coffee. For lunch we received an unpeeled potato and a meat patty or soup. Every Thursday, the Red Cross distributed 250 grams of bread. On occasion I had diarrhea and abstained from eating all together.

Memorial to the victims of the Melk concentration camp erected by the Austrian government

On Sunday we did not work. We tended to the laundry and other chores. I went to the barber and shaved all the hair of my body except for a strip of hair along the head that identified us as inmates of the camp. This was the standing order of the camp. The head of block number 13 was a Jew from the vicinity of Sandz who helped Jews. In the winter of 1945, someone stole the shoes of an inmate in block 13 while he was sleeping. This puzzled everybody since all doors were locked at night and nobody could enter or leave the block. Yet, the shoes were gone. The inmate was punished for not guarding his shoes but it was wintertime and he needed shoes to survive. The block chief managed to procure for him a pair of shoes. I slept with my shoes under my head as did all the other inmates. So how did the shoes disappear? The block was above the kitchen that worked at night. Someone managed to climb up from the kitchen floor to the floor of our block, removed the shoes and dropped them to the kitchen floor and then lowered himself through the slight opening to the kitchen floor. The man was never caught but he sold the shoes for a full meal.

Soup in the tunnel of Melk
Sketch by Adrian Piquee–Audrain, a French inmate of the camp
The sketch was graciously donated by Michelle Piquee–Audrain

Our block consisted of inmates from different countries, such as Russians, Poles, Czechs, Yugoslavs, Greeks, Spaniards, Germans, Austrians, Hungarians, Frenchmen and others. We celebrated January 1, 1945 with a concert. We did not work that day and received a good meal. We sang songs and the day was pleasant. I was moved again to block number nine that was located on the road leading from the hospital to the crematoria. The porters who transported the dead bodies had extra portions of bread and I sold them my cigarettes for bread. A Jew worked at the crematoria who would survive the war and move to Ramat Gan in Israel. The Melk concentration camp was surrounded with electric fences. Some desperate and hopeless inmates decided to end their sufferings by sneaking up to the electric wires and ended their miseries. Each day the working groups brought back some dead bodies of inmates who were killed due to work incidents or beatings by kapos or were exhausted from work. There were also inmates who died of starvation for they had sold their bread rations for cigarettes.

After January 1945, Melk received many Polish inmates who had participated in the Warsaw revolt of August 1944 against the Germans. The Poles wanted to liberate the Polish capital but failed since the German forces were still strong enough to crush the revolt while the advancing Russian armies stood by and watched. Thousands of Poles were arrested and sent to the concentration camps. Melk also received transports from Auschwitz. Among them was my friend Moshe Hayes who looked well. He told me that he worked at the Canada camp in Auschwitz. This camp sorted the belongings of all the people who were gassed at Auschwitz. The Melk camp also received many Italian war prisoners toward the end of 1944 who were busy at assembling the factories underground. The Germans were in a rush to erect the factories and built rail lines into the tunnels so that trains could deliver machinery and supplies into the tunnels. The Germans had plans to force all the inmates into the tunnels and blow them up in case the Russians neared the site. The mayor of Melk used all his connections to defuse the plan for he feared that if the Germans blew up the camp, the Russians would exact revenge against him and his town. Apparently, he had powerful connections and the S.S. gave up the destruction plan.

In April 1945, we were told to assemble at the roll call place. Each group left the camp and headed down to the Danube River where we boarded a ferry that took us to the city of Linz where we disembarked and began our death march in a southwesterly direction. Many of the inmates were weak and sick and fell by the side of the road. The guards immediately shot them. As we marched, I constantly heard shots. The Germans hoped to kill us all by marching us to death. The first night we rested at a farm in Wels where we received coffee. Then we marched to the city of Gmunden where we slept in a brewery. Some inmates decided to make a break but the guards fired at them. We marched and marched. My feet walked automatically. The energy that I accumulated at the Schindler camp came in handy. I was determined to stay alive. As we marched, I saw a poster announcing that President Roosevelt had died. I kept walking and constantly heard rifle shots of inmates being killed. Whoever despaired and gave in was lost. You had to have hope and the will to persist. I survived. On Tuesday we entered the concentration camp of Ebensee under the banner of "Work Liberates."

Crematoria of the Mauthausen concentration camp

Production line in a tunnel near Melk
The picture was taken after World War II

The **Ebensee concentration camp** was established by the S.S. to build tunnels for armaments storage near the town of Ebensee, Austria, in 1943. It was part of the Mauthausen network complex. Due to the inhumane working and living conditions, Ebensee was one of the worst Nazi concentration camps for the death rates of its prisoners. The S.S used several code names – Kalk (English: limestone), Kalksteinbergwerk (English: limestone mine), Solvay and Zement (English: cement) – to conceal the true nature of the camp. The construction of the Ebensee sub–camp began late in 1943, and the first 1,000 prisoners arrived on November 18, 1943 from the main camp of Mauthausen and its sub–camps. The main purpose of Ebensee was to provide slave labor for the construction of enormous underground tunnels in which armament works were to be housed. These tunnels were planned for the evacuated Peenemande V–2 rocket development program that was bombed by the British bombers. Approximately 20,000 inmates were worked to death constructing giant tunnels in the surrounding mountains. Together with the Mauthausen subcamp of Gusen, Ebensee is considered one of the most horrific Nazi concentration camps. Jews formed about one–third of the inmates, the percentage increasing to 40% by the end of the war, and were the worst treated, though all inmates suffered great hardships.

As the Second World War in Europe came to an end, mass evacuations from other camps put tremendous pressure on the Mauthausen complex, the last remaining concentration camp in the area still controlled by the Nazis. The 25 Ebensee barracks had been designed to hold 100 prisoners each, but they eventually held as many as 750 each. To this number must be added the prisoners being kept in the tunnels or outdoors under the open sky. The crematorium was unable to keep pace with the deaths and naked bodies were stacked outside the barrack blocks and the crematorium itself. In the closing weeks of the war, the death rate exceeded 350 a day. To reduce congestion, a ditch was dug outside the camp and bodies were flung into quicklime. On a single day in April 1945, a record 80 bodies were removed from Block 23 alone; in this pile, feet were seen to be twitching. During this period, the inmate strength reached a high of about 20,000.

The concentration camp of Ebensee was located within a wooded area and the barracks were scattered between the trees. The first impression was one of a pleasant place. One could have mistaken the place for a health resort. The camp had a large assembly area and a crematorium that was located outside the camp entrance. The crematorium was surrounded with electric fences. This small compound also contained the S.S. living quarters, their kitchen and their offices. On entering the camp I was assigned to a barrack where I shared a bed with four inmates. The three–level bunk beds extended all along the barrack. The camp was located high in the Alp Mountains. The camp was above the city of Ebensee that was located in the valley. The camp was at a distance of a kilometer and a half from the city. The Ebensee area had many tunnels and some of them extended to seven kilometers in length. They produced tanks and other military machines. The English and American bombers began to bomb the area, especially the hamlets of Puchacha and Pucheim where there was a concentration of railroad cars that arrived from many places loaded with supplies. Following an Allied bombing raid, some of the inmates were taken to clear the area of the debris. They brought back in their coats, since it was still cold, some sugar, rice and other staples. They shared the goods with us. The food situation was very bad at Ebensee. In the morning, we received a slice of bread that weighed 120 grams and black coffee. For supper we received soup that consisted of potato peels. The soup distributor dished out the soup water and kept the thicker content for himself and friends. We were constantly hungry.

To reach the place of work, we descended many steps and then climbed steps. We loaded stones into small rail cars that were then pushed out of the tunnel and dumped in designated places. We found pieces of black charcoal that we chewed. The taste was similar to that of margarine. We also chewed pieces of tar as though it was chewing gum. We suffered from hunger and the bitter cold. The Germans killed many inmates daily. The crematoria could not handle all the dead bodies and some were left for the following days. At night, some Russian inmates and perhaps other inmates sliced pieces of meat from the corpses and roasted the pieces on fires and ate it. The Jewish inmates abstained from the practice.

In May 1945, we began to hear artillery shots fired in the distance. The shots were nearing. Our block decided to leave the barrack and to fall down on the steps going down. We were all over the place and claimed exhaustion. We were ordered back to the barrack where we remained for the day. The other barracks saw what we did and they followed. Before long, the entire camp refused to work. Three days we did not go to work. Then the Germans called all the inmates to a general assembly at the assembly square. They told us that they had to protect us from the American, English and Russian bombers and therefore we had to proceed to the tunnels for our safety. The assembled inmates responded in unison with a resounding "NO!" We shall not go. All the inmates had heard the rumors that circulated in the camp that the S.S. intended to blow up the tunnels with the workers and thus erase the traces of the inmates. An S.S. man relayed this information to an inmate who divulged the information throughout the camp. The Germans ordered all inmates to return to their barracks. The S.S. decided to abandon the camp. They brought some old military reservists from the nearby city and placed them in the watchtowers. The gates were locked. The S.S. vanished in the darkness. During the night, groups of inmates began to settle scores with the kapos and functionaries who had made their life miserable. Some were killed and others were seriously injured. These activities went on throughout the night. Chaos ensued in the camp. The next day, May 6, 1945, at about 10 o'clock in the morning, an American tank crashed its way into the camp. We were free at last. What a beautiful and sunny day it turned out to be. A day that I remember to this moment!

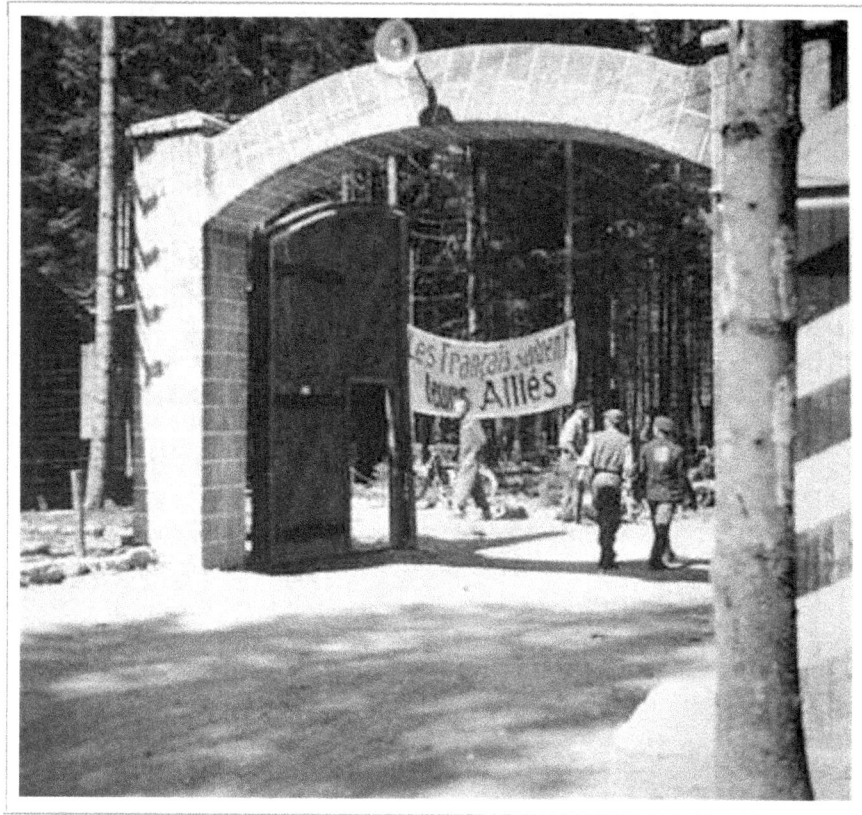

Entrance gate at the Ebensee concentration camp

On May 6, 1945, a banner was hung at the entrance gate by the French resistance fighters who survived the war. The banner read " Les Francais salutent les Allies" or the French greet the Allies. The camp was liberated by soldiers in the 80th Division of the US Third Army

[Page 253]

Chapter X
The Liberation

The inmates of the Ebensee concentration camp gather at roll call place following the liberation of the camp. An American soldier took the photo

At about 10 A.M. on May 6, 1945, the American army entered the Ebensee concentration camp and began to restore order. The night before and in the morning, serious disorders took place in the camp. The inmates rampaged throughout the camp and settled scores with the remaining staff of the camp. The Americans ordered all inmates to assemble at the square and to align according to nationalities. Each group, such as Jews, Poles, Frenchmen, Russians, Czechs, stood with their co-nationals. I now saw the Jewish survivors at the camp, particularly the Jews of Sandz. They were:

Chune Grinberg
Moshe Laor
Mendel Brown
Shimon Brown
Max Neuman
Itzik Goldberg
Shlomo Goldberg
Kuba Fuhrer
David Markus
Shmuel Salomon
Mendel Aftergut
Mosdhe Chayes

Nehemia Sheingit
Markus Fridenbach
Moshe Osteryoung
Romek Gut–Hollander
Asher Brandstern
Chune Elzner
Shimon Folkman
Shlomek Wolf
Mordechai Lustig
Benyamin Hausenshtock
Lulek Bittersfeld and father.

I later discovered that Lulek Bittersfeld and his father were also liberated but were at the hospital in Ebensee where they were treated for typhus.

Following the American roll call, we all ran to the S.S. warehouses looking for food. We found small quantities of sugar and imitation coffee. We returned to the main camp and American soldiers invited us to join them in the hunt for S.S. men that had run the camp. Indeed, some of the guards were caught. One S.S. man was brought to the gate of the camp despite the fact that he had already managed to change clothes. He was recognized by one of the camp inmates. The inmates decided to kill him on the spot by permitting the inmates to beat him. They stretched him out on a board near the gate and everybody began to hit him until he was killed. A sign was written that read "Heil Hitler." The sign was placed in his hand and a bayonet was placed in the other hand.

The Americans began to organize a kitchen to cook food for the inmates. The soup was loaded with solid foods and the inmates began to gorge themselves with the food. But they were no longer accustomed to such rich foods. Some inmates died since their intestines could not absorb the rich food. I was lucky that I took small portions and managed to digest them. I looked about and saw on top of the American tanks boxes of combat rations. I took some as did other inmates. We of course did not know what they contained. Romek Gut knew a bit of English and he read the content labels on the boxes and also the instructions on how to prepare the food. We organized a group that began to prepare our meals for the day. In the following days, we continued to live off the combat rations that we removed from the tanks.

The Americans forced the entire population of the township including the mayor and other important officials of the nearby Ebensee city to march to the concentration camp to witness the horrible scenes of masses of dead, naked bodies scattered all over the place. They started to dig mass graves and carried the bodies and buried them outside the camp. The Americans brought nurses from the hospital of the nearby city of Shteinkugel who began to care for the sick inmates. Some of the inmates that were afflicted with typhus or other serious diseases were taken to the hospital while others began to be treated on the spot.

A few of the Sandz survivors organized themselves into a small group that functioned as a unit. I took upon myself the position of cook and began to prepare the meals. Other members began to search the area for food. I cooked many soups and other items to help build the strength of the survivors. We then moved as a group to the Polish section of the camp. There were many civilian Polish citizens in the camp. They were brought to work mainly in agriculture. Of course there were also many Polish inmates who survived the war in the camp. We all began to travel in all directions to see the area. Once, my friend and I reached the city of Wels near Linz where the American military police arrested us. We had no papers or identification. We looked suspicious or perhaps they did not like us or our clothing. We wore "Hitler Jugend" or

Nazi youth clothing. We spent the night in jail and the next morning we were freed by the officer who might have been Jewish. We returned to the camp and I went to the office to get some identification papers. I was issued a temporary identification that stated that I was an inmate of the camp.

Identification paper stating that I was an inmate of the Mauthousen concentration camp

A short period of time elapsed and Jewish soldiers from the Palestinian Jewish Brigade arrived at the camp. We did not believe our eyes when we saw the shoulder pads with the word "Palestine" and the Star of David. They talked to us in Yiddish and urged us to register to go to Palestine. They promised to help us get to Palestine. They left the camp and soon those who had signed up to go to Palestine received packages from the Red Cross. I had signed my name and picked up my package. The Jewish soldiers returned to their base in Italy.

Most of Italy had been liberated by the British 8th Army under the leadership of Field Marshal Bernard Montgomery. Many of his soldiers were Palestinian Jews. The Jewish community in Palestine had volunteered to fight the Nazis as early as 1940. Over 5,000 Jewish volunteers from Palestine were organized into three infantry battalions. The "Jewish Brigade" was established in late 1944 and was officially named the Jewish Infantry Brigade Group, under the command of a career Jewish army officer, Brigadier Ernest F. Benjamin. The Haganah, the Jewish underground army in Palestine, ordered many Haganah men to volunteer for this brigade. These "volunteers" formed Haganah cells within the brigade, and took orders directly from the Haganah headquarters in Palestine.

The Jewish Brigade was deployed in Italy. One of the main Haganah officers in the Jewish Brigade was Captain Aaron Ishai Hooter; another was Sergeant Mordecai Surkiss. As the troops marched through Italy, these two men instructed their Haganah cells to be on the lookout for Italian Jewish survivors. These survivors, seeing the Star of David on the Jewish Brigade soldiers' shoulders, came out of hiding, ragged, hungry and desperate. Hooter and Surkiss helped organize support systems for these survivors, everything from small dispensaries to soup kitchens, all using British supplies and facilities. The Brichah movement was primarily interested in moving the Jews out of Europe to Palestine by any and all means. The Jewish Brigade and the Brichah began to work closely to get Jews to Palestine. These two organizations were soon joined by another organization called the "Mossad." This was a secret organization created by the Jewish Agency to smuggle Jews to Palestine illegally. The leader of the Mossad was Shaul Avigur. Shaul was born in Russia and brought as a child to Palestine. He devoted himself to military matters and joined the Haganah. He was appointed to head the Mossad. He personally selected his agents who were sent to Europe. He established an effective organization that worked closely with the Brichah, the America Joint Distribution Committee and the Jewish Brigade. All of the groups were very active and cooperated in Italy and throughout Europe.

Shaul Avigur

The head of the Mossad in Italy was Yehuda Arazi, a Polish Jew who arranged the movement of illegal Jewish refugees to Italy and then their transfer to Palestine. From the end of the war until 1947, nearly 50,000 Jewish refugees had entered Italy. Many of these refugees made it to Palestine while others were intercepted by the British navy on the way to Palestine and sent to British detention camps in Cyprus. These detentions did not deter Arazi from continuing to send Jewish refugees to Palestine. Arazi relied heavily on the Jewish Brigade and on Jewish soldiers in the British army such as Shimshon Lang, one of the 300 drivers in the 462nd General Transport Battalion of the British 8th Army. Lang's story was typical of the Palestinian Jews. He had escaped Poland for Palestine in 1939 on an illegal ship. The ship was stopped by the British navy and Lang was given a choice: spend the next few years in an internment camp or join the British army. He chose the latter and served until 1945. In an interview, Shimshon Lang said, "My unit delivered supplies to the army units from the coastal areas in Southern Italy, and on the return journey loaded the trucks with refugees. I spoke to the young skeletal survivors in Yiddish and saw myself as one of them who happened to have escaped Hitler's death squad nets just in time. They represented to me the survivors of my family who perished in the Shoah. No British army rule could stop me from extending help to my surviving brethren. I was not alone with these thoughts; others felt the same way. We translated the ideas into reality by transporting the surviving Jews from Austrian and German displaced persons camps to Italy and then to Palestine. We used empty shipping containers or extra military uniforms to hide the refugees at border crossings." According to Lang, not only trucking units were involved in this movement of Jewish refugees. Ambulances and maintenance vehicles were also used to smuggle survivors from the concentration camps in Austria and Germany into Italy. Most of the Jewish volunteers for the British forces in Palestine were similar to Shimon Lang: born in Europe and barely escaped to Palestine.

The war's end found many of these Jewish soldiers stationed at Treviso, near the triangle of Italy, Yugoslavia and Austria. As they received passes to travel through the surrounding countries, they encountered more survivors, and many were faced for the first time with the harsh truth of the Nazi horrors in the concentration camps. Some of the soldiers, if they could, smuggled individual survivors to the brigade camp. There, in Yiddish, these survivors told their tragic tales, shocking their fellow Jews with news of the Nazi atrocities. The details of the locations of the concentration camps were passed on to the Haganah. Captain Aaron Ishai Hooter and his staff then set out from the British camp in Treviso in search of the Jewish survivors in the concentration camps, in Austria and the British sector of Germany. Hooter and his men soon found Jewish survivors at Bergen Belsen, Mauthausen and other liberated concentration camps that were now displaced persons camps run by the United Nations Relief and Rehabilitation Administration (UNRRA).

Once Hooter and his associates reported back to Arazi that survivors existed in the concentration camps, Arazi notified his home office in Jerusalem. Arazi was then quickly ordered to remove any survivors he could and bring them to Italy. When the Jewish soldiers reported the existence of Jewish survivors at the Ebensee concentration camp, the order was given to bring them to Italy. This was easier said than done, since the Ebensee concentration camp was in the American military zone in Germany. The rescuers had to cross the British zone of occupation in Germany in order to get to the American zone. Many military forged papers had to be made before the rescue mission could start. The Jewish brigade made all the preparations and one day Jewish brigade soldiers appeared at the Ebensee concentration camp and told the Jewish survivors to board trucks that would take them to Italy and then to Palestine.

Jewish survivors of Ebensee concentration camp thank the local United Nations Relief and Rehabilitation Administration camp representative, Edward Crommelin, for the help and guidance he gave them after the war. He was assigned to the Ebensee concentration camp that later became the Ebensee displaced persons camp

I did not feel like going to Palestine and went to the men's room until the Jewish brigade left with some of the Jewish survivors. I was never a Zionist and I came from a very religious and Hasidic background that was opposed to Zionism. Palestine did not appeal to me. I wanted to live; I had suffered enough during the war. I was not going to a forsaken desert place to waste my life. I was not the only surviving Jew to remain in the camp although my name was recorded as wanting to go to Palestine.

Romek Gut, Kuba Furer, myself and two Poles from Warsaw, Poland decided to head back to Poland. There were no regular trains or buses. The few transportation lines were reserved for military personnel. So we decided to hitchhike through the villages and small towns of the area. Wherever we reached, we went to the local chief and presented our identifications and asked for sleeping accommodations and food coupons. Most of them obliged. I had two identity cards: one in the name of Markus Lustig and the other one in the name of Markus Kannengisser. In our wanderings, we reached the hamlet of Ried where we met some of the inmates of the Schindler camp. The latter took over a house that contained a restaurant. The place belonged to a Nazi. The survivors opened the restaurant and it soon became a center of lively encounters between the survivors and the local girls. The American military police soon closed the place for violating the non–fraternization order of the American military army. This order prohibited the mingling of the American soldiers with the local population. We spent one night at the place and continued our journey to Mitmach, then to Assbach. Finally we reached the town of Braunau where we stayed at the local school. There was a nearby restaurant where we ate, since we had food coupons. We remained a few says at the place. Romek Gut, Kuba Furer and the two Poles decided to head to Poland. I decided to return to the Ebensee camp. I had no wish to return to Poland at the time.

I returned to the Ebensee camp and rested for a while. I then decided to travel to Linz, Austria, where they opened a new camp for Jewish refugees called Hart, located in Leondik. There they provided rooms to every three refugees and also food. I was also informed that being a camp survivor I was entitled to replace my shoes and clothing. Indeed, my clothing needed replacement. I was given new shoes and new clothing; my appearance changed for the better. I also received a package with goodies from the Red Cross. Having time on my hands, I promenaded and walked about the city of Linz, which was very attractive. I encountered the two Austrian workers under whose supervision I worked at the Melk concentration camp. They helped me greatly by occasionally giving me bread, cheese or salami. We talked a bit and I invited them to a coffee shop. We sat and reminisced about the Melk days. The meeting was very pleasant and I was grateful to these people who helped me in my time of need. In my walks in the city I also encountered Awraham Friedman who was a native of Sandz. The latter showed me a building where I was given a bed and a mattress. I took the items to my assigned room and set the items. We had to stay in line to get our food and then we ate the contents standing since there were no seating arrangements. While in the room, I noticed that one of the room mates was a Jewish policeman at the Schindler camp. We did not want to share our room with him. He was constantly harassed and beaten. He located his wife and they left the camp. I also visited the local cemetery where Hitler's father Alois Schikelgrubber was buried.

85366

MAUTHAUSEN K.L.

Mordechai Lustig with his concentration cap following his liberation on May 6, 1945

In July of 1945, I was getting tired of doing nothing and standing on line to get food but I continued my excursions. I came across a huge parking area full of American tanks and saw the soldiers standing on line for their meals. The man standing behind the counter distributing the food was familiar. I suddenly remembered the face of the man who gave me some mashed potatos for the water that I was bringing to his restaurant in the ghetto of Rzeszow following my discharge from the local hospital. I waited until he distributed the food and approached him. He was glad to see me and likewise. He was dressed as an American soldier. I asked him to help me get a job, any job. He told me that he would speak with his supervisor. The supervisor was a sergeant. The American sergeant came over and brought a shirt and other clothing as well as a bar of soap. He told me in English to wash the clothing and to come the next day. I came as ordered. He gave me a military uniform that consisted of a shirt, pants, shoes and a hat. I started to work with my Jewish acquaintance and a young Polish fellow at distributing the food. They lived near the eating place and had a record player with many French records that they played. At the end of the day, I returned to my camp to sleep. The following week the tank regiment moved to permanent quarters in the city of Ablsberg near Klein Munich. I moved with the regiment and left the Jewish camp. At the new base I received a room and everything that the American soldiers received. I even received a footlocker. Everything was neat and arranged. The building also had a kitchen and dining rooms where officers ate. I assisted the cooks in preparing the meals for the next day. The kitchen prepared three meals a day that were served each day. We also had to clean the dining rooms. Every morning we served a slightly different breakfast. One morning we served scrambled eggs, or eggs with bacon, or cereals, or toast and the bread was like challa, juices, soft drinks and all kinds of desserts. Despite the abundance of food, I continued to receive packages from the Red Cross. At the end of August, the tank regiment left Austria and I was left alone in the barrack. An infantry company, number 259, soon arrived. It was in turn replaced by another infantry company, number 331 of the 83rd unit; that remained until February 1946 when the unit was replaced by a transport unit of trailers that distributed supplies through the occupied areas. I remained at the barrack until I left for Germany.

Near the barracks was a big stable with horses that Hungarian refugees tended. The farm belonged to a high-ranking Nazi and was now the property of the American army. Next to the farm stood many small houses where people from different countries lived. There were also barracks where Poles lived. The American army took some of the barracks and converted them to a social center where dances were held for the troops. Each evening a band played dance music and the soldiers entertained themselves. Drinks were served liberally. Among the inhabitants of the barracks were Hungarian gypsies who organized an excellent band that played beautiful music. Close to the base was a forest that contained military bunkers that contained weapons and ammunition. The American soldiers had to guard the forest and see to it that nobody entered it. They also guarded the bridges leading to the city.

As mentioned earlier, the tank unit left and was replaced by an infantry unit. I again worked in the kitchen. I then was assigned to care for four officers. I set their table in the dining room and brought them their food and removed their dishes. I also had to tend to their room. One of the officers had a girl friend and I had to bring her food. Units came and units went but I continued with my job of tending to officers. During my off duty hours, I promenaded in the city and saw a nice girl. We exchanged looks and smiles and approached each other. We started to exchange words and began to kiss. This was the first sweet kiss that I received after so many years. Her name was Helene and her family was Yugoslav. We continued to meet and talk. She told me that she lived near the barracks and that she had two sisters and parents.

She also told me that the family was practically starving. Yet we threw out large amounts of food at our military kitchen. I decided to bring some food like cooking oil or meat. Everything was accepted gracefully. I invited Helene and her sister Olga to the evening dances. Helene was sixteen and a half, Olga was eighteen and a half, and the youngest sister was twelve and a half.

At the evening dances, rum, Coke, whiskey and cognac were served to the servicemen. The two sisters took me to the dance floor but I never danced and did not know the dance steps. Following some liquor shots, I lost my inhibitions and began to move on the floor. The dance floor attracted many soldiers, among them a red–haired soldier who worked in the kitchen next to me. The latter became jealous that I was having a good time with the girls and he yelled at me and threw a knife at me. I ducked and missed the knife. I complained to the officer in charge and he was reprimanded. Then he and his two friends grabbed me and sat me do down on a chair. They poured half a bottle of whiskey down my throat and left. I was stewed drunk and did not know what happened. Eventually I managed to reach my barrack and I was given black coffee. The next morning everything was over.

Among the various American units there were some Jews; the tank outfit had a Jew and there were three Jews in the infantry unit but most of them only spoke English. I encountered one Jewish American soldier from Brooklyn who spoke Yiddish and I could converse with him. All soldiers spoke English. There were some soldiers from Chicago, Illinois, who knew a bit of Polish. I was picking up English fast but was still unable to converse in the language. In the Polish barracks I met Victor, a Pole from Warsaw. He had a motorcycle with a boat. He took me for a ride on his bike and we were almost involved in an accident. I spent some evenings with him and we spoke about Poland. I bought some cameras from the Poles. Within these barracks, some people opened a night club where there was dancing nightly. I visited the place, drank vodka and met lots of girls from different countries: Poles, Czechs, White Russians, Austrians and Yugoslavs. They taught me to dance. I had a fabulous time and tried to make up time for the years that I lost.

At the stable I used to take horses to ride, sometimes solo and sometimes with the military personnel. I went pheasant and rabbit hunting with some officers and in the winter we hunted deer. In the summer we went on picnics and carried on. In one of the barracks next to the officer's club lived a Polish woman with a baby. I met her on several occasions and we had a good time. Once I visited her and suddenly there was loud banging on the door. Apparently, the lady had another boyfriend and by his shouting voice I recognized him as an American soldier who served in our unit. I grabbed my belongings and left the place by jumping through the window while the woman kept shouting, "I am coming to open the door." She finally opened the door but I was no longer there. Outside it was dark and cloudy. The soldier was drunk, angry and shouting. He probably slapped her about.

Once, a Polish woman was hired by our company commander to work as a dishwasher. The officer asked me to arrange for her living quarters and whatever she needed. I took her to the stable house where there were rooms and fixed her room. She began to work in our unit. On occasion I visited her and we spent time. She later met an older Yugoslav man and married him. I still continued to visit her and spent time with her while her husband was cleaning the kitchen ovens. But the relationship waned with time since I had guilt feelings about spending time with a married woman. I began to rationalize that I did not need this relationship for I had other women. Besides, I started to think about myself and what I was doing and what I hoped to do.

I received many gifts from the American officers to whom I served meals or cleaned their rooms. Most of the gifts were items that had been confiscated from the Nazis. One officer gave me a gift of a bicycle that gave me mobility.

[Page 270]

Chapter XI
Going to Brazil

The bicycle gave me a great deal of freedom of movement. I went frequently to Linz where I soon located a Jewish D.P. camp called Binder–Michael. The camp consisted of several buildings that belonged to the Nazi party. Most of the inhabitants were camp inmates who survived the Shoah in the nearby concentration camps. They were soon joined by surviving relatives or friends from other camps. I visited the camp and met some Jews from Sandz like Romek Gut–Hollander, Berek Hirshtel, Benyamin Hausshtok, and some of the Friedman brothers. We reminisced and took pictures. Nobody had any plans but none of us wanted to stay in Austria in the camp. Meanwhile UNRRA provided food and shelter.

Following the war, there were hundreds of thousands of refugees in Germany and Austria that were forced laborers that Germany brought to keep the Germany economy going. Some of them were survivors of the concentration camps. Amongst them were about 50,000 Jewish concentration camp survivors. UNRRA repatriated most of the refugees to their native countries except for a hard core of refugees that refused to return home for fear of political retribution, religious persecution and past scores. Most of the Jewish surviving inmates refused to return to their native places, except the Jews from Western countries like France, Belgium and Holland. The few that ventured back home soon returned to their camps and described the terrible reception that they received from their neighbors upon arriving back home. The hostility and brutality that these survivors faced and the constant fear for their lives forced them to return to their camps where they lingered hoping to get to a Western country. Getting entrance visas to these countries was not easy, the HIAS (Hebrew Immigrant Aid Society) organization, an American Jewish society, helped with the necessary legal paper work but most countries did not want Jewish camp survivors. The medical tests that were administered to potential immigrants eliminated most camp survivors.

I soon discovered another Jewish camp in Linz. This was a transit camp for Jews that arrived illegally to Austria and continued to move to Italy and then to Palestine. The camp used to be a prison camp for SS men but they were relocated to another place. The "Brichah" or escape movement took over the place and transported Jews from Poland, Russia, Czechoslovakia and other countries illegally to Austria and Germany and then to Palestine. The Jewish refugees arrived by train to Klein Munchen and were transferred to the camp called Weg–Sheid where they rested and moved on. Once I went to the train station and witnessed the arrival of a transport of Jews from Poland. Amongst the transport passengers was a Jew from Sandz. We talked and then the "Bricha" guides moved the refugees aboard trucks and they left for their transit camp.

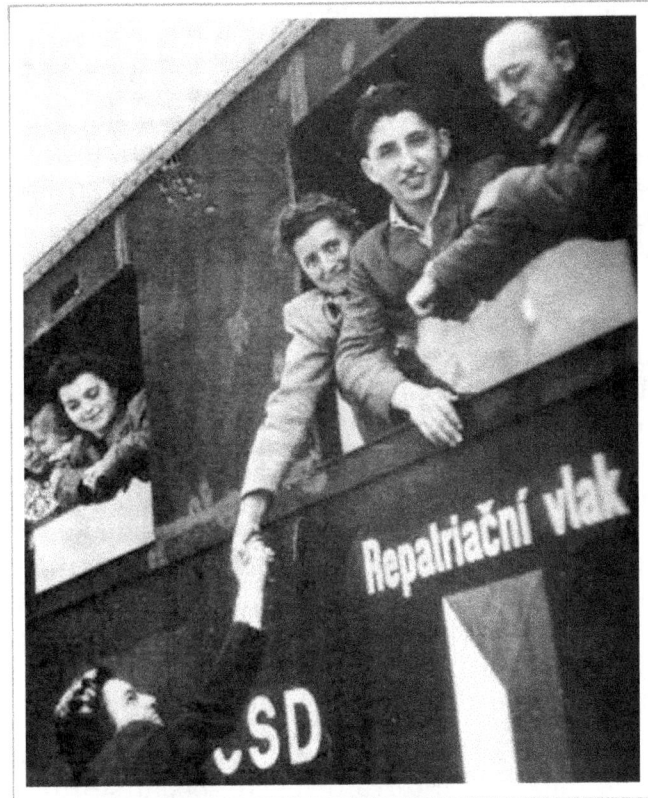

**Transport of Polish Jews leaving Nachod
(Czechoslovakia) camp on their way to the
Austrian or German D.P. camps.**

The "Bricha"–or escape movement organization started in Poland or prewar Polish areas and spread throughout liberated Eastern Europe.

The aim of the organization was to evacuate the surviving Jews from Europe and bring them all "home" to Palestine. Most of the Brichah members were young Zionists who had survived the Holocaust. Some were discharged Jewish soldiers from the Polish and Russian armies, others, partisans and concentration camp survivors. The Bricha founders and early leaders were Eliezer Lidowsky, Abba Kovner, Shmuel Amarant and Itzhak Tzuckerman. They were Zionist–oriented Shoah survivors who dreamt of heading to Palestine. But this was much easier said than done. In order to accomplish their goal, the Bricha leaders began to clandestinely organize in small groups, exploring safe southern routes to Romania, where they hoped to board ships and head to Palestine. The task was arduous and fraught with danger. The Russian security forces were on their trail. The Soviets were not interested in giving Jews the idea that they could leave the growing Soviet Union. Like theater owners the Soviets wanted to keep the theater full with the exit doors sealed.

The original Bricha group managed to reach Bucharest, the capital of Romania, where the Jewish emissaries recently arrived from Palestine to help them organize. The hope was that these homeless people would be brought to Palestine where they would find a safe home. These contacts between the Bricha and the Palestinian emissaries in Rumania resulted in the establishment of a regular route through some newly acquired Soviet areas as well as through Communist controlled Rumania. As the weeks and months went by the stops along this route became more defined and varied in order to elude the Russian police. The numbers of people joining the groups led by Bricha grew exponentially with the increased demand for passage to Palestine. To meet the demand for illegal passage, the Brichah expanded their operations westward into Poland. Krakow, Galicia became the center of operations. The transports left Krakow and headed south to Krosno, Dukla and Nowy Sacz, all located in Galicia, Poland, facing the Czechoslovakian border, according to Salomon or Salek Berger, a native of Krosno who survived the Shoah in Eastern Ukraine. Salekuwas liberated by the Russian army. He joined the Polish army and following the war was discharged. He returned to Krosno and joined the Brichah. He took Jewish transports across the border to Czechoslovakia. There other Bricha members took them to the next border until they reached the Rumanian Black Sea ports. This was a very demanding route that crossed the difficult Carpathian Mountains.

It wasn't long before Rumania stopped being a way station to Palestine, partly because of the impossible terrain, partly because Romanian authorities tightened the border crossings, partly because the Russian secret police took more control of the borders and in Czernowitz even managed to arrest several Bricha groups, and partly due to the shortage of ships. All Rumanian and Bulgarian ships were nationalized by the Communist governments. The most serious problem, however, was what to do with the refugees once they reached Romania? How to get them to Palestine? The Bricha had access to only a few ships willing to risk sailing to Palestine. British government agents had warned ship owners that their vessels would be confiscated and crews jailed if the ships were caught near Palestine. The Bricha began the search for other possible routes to get these Jewish refugees out of Eastern Europe. We already mentioned earlier that the Bricha worked hand in hand with the Mossad and the Jewish Brigade in Italy to transport Jews from the camps to Italy and then to Palestine. Jews to Palestine!

I often visited the Binder – Michael camp where I could converse with my friends at ease in Yiddish. We had similar fears, hopes and ambitions. We wanted to get out of Austria. Once, my friend Berek Hirshtal asked me to give him a ride on my bicycle to visit his girlfriend who was recuperating at the local hospital from war traumas. It so happened that I had some dry fruits and other goodies in my pockets so that I could give her something. Her name was Tushka and she was a beautiful girl. My friend was in love with her and shortly after her discharge from the hospital, they married.

Map of Eastern Europe drawn according to the borders established by the allied powers in 1945. Notice the Bricha route that starts in Wilno, Lithuania and reaches Czernowitz on the Romanian border and then the Black Sea. Illegal Bricha centers existed in Wilno, Rovno, Lwow and Czernowitz (Cernauti).

Meanwhile, the old American regiment moved out of the barracks and was replaced by a very big engineering unit. All refugees who lived near the barracks were moved to a refugee camp in Anas near the hamlet of Stayer Mark. Helena's family was also moved there. I went to visit them at times. Then at the end of 1945, the family was moved to a barrack in Eblsberg.

I was paid by the American military authorities for my work in scrips that were not really currency but could be exchanged at the military facilities. I traded a bit in dollars at the Binder–Michael camp and managed to save some money. When Austria devaluated the currency, my account was frozen with 6000 marks in it.

For the New Year celebration of 1946, I prepared a special celebration for my officers. The table was set and I (Mordechai Lustig) waited on them. They were very pleased and the next day we took some pictures with the officers. The unit left in February 1946 and was replaced by a big unit. The latter built a fuel station and established a big garage. They also installed an entrance gate and a guardhouse to check the flow of traffic to and from the station. I was moved to the farmhouse near the stable where there were many rooms. This new company assigned me to work at the gas station and then as a guard registering the licenses of the entering and leaving vehicles. I was issued a weapon and writing material. Once I took a military jeep for a ride and hit the corner of a building. The front of the vehicle was bent but the matter was dismissed. Some of the officers who lived near me decided to open a disco in the big room. Of course, they cleaned it, brought tables, chairs, light fixtures, installed taps for beverages, and a corner for playing records. They asked me to run the place and I accepted. I became a bartender.

I was now in charge of cleaning the hall and making all the necessary preparations for the nightly events. I had to see to it that all the tables had tablecloths and were neatly arranged. I had to check that there were ample supplies of beverages like beer, coke, whiskey, and cognac for the clients. Clean sheets had to be provided for the nearby empty rooms as well as contraceptives. The officers managed to bring a piano to the club. The club was a success and many girls visited the place. I had a very good time.

One day, I started to think seriously about my present situation. What would happen to me? What am I doing? I remembered that I had an uncle in Sao Paolo, Brazil who left Poland prior to World War Two. He lived at Sao Paulino Street. I later discovered the correct address was Jose Paulino. I told the officers about the situation and they sent a military cable to San Paulo. The civilian mail was still not organized in Austria. The cable was addressed to Chaim Lustig, Sao Paulino Street, Sao Paulo, Brazil. A few days later, I received a reply from my uncle with the exact address. I thanked the officers for their help. I was no longer alone. I had some family. My mother's brother was alive. We began to write to each other and he informed me that he wanted me to come to Brazil. He wrote me that he already contacted the agency in Brazil that handles these legal papers. Chaim also wrote me that my aunt Primet Mastebaum, her husband Yehuda and their daughter Sheindeleh survived the Shoah and are now in Italy. He also wrote me that my cousin Nathan Lustig who escaped to Russia was now in the British Army stationed in the British military zone in Germany. We began to write to each other. We kept in touch until I left the American military base and he was discharged from the army.

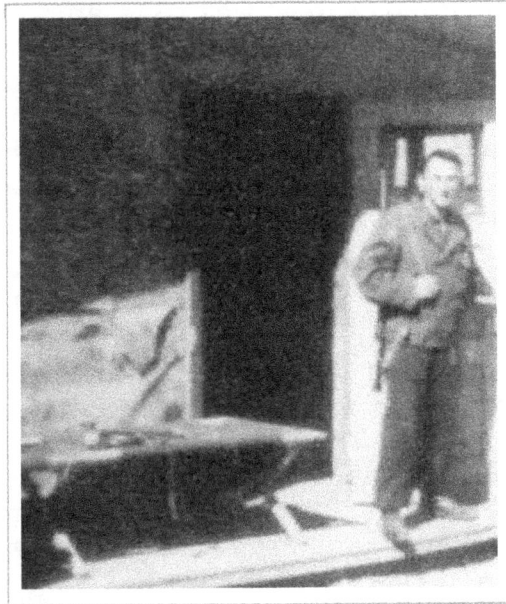

Mordechai Lustig on guard duty at the American military base

I continued to work at the base. With the arrival of the summer, the sergeant in charge of the kitchen gave me a new job that consisted in traveling through the countryside and exchanging coffee, cigarettes and chocolates for potatoes, apples, and apple cider. The exchanges were successful. I even took potatoes and apples to the parents of Helena at their barrack in Anas. Helena and Olga came to visit me at my base and once they overstayed their time. The curfew went into effect and they could not return back to their camp. They spent the night in my room where there was only one bed. We managed somehow to sleep all three in the bed. Olga continued to visit me until she found a Hungarian book and got involved with the book.

June 6, 1946, I took liberty from work. It was the anniversary of my liberation from the Ebensee concentration camp. I went to Bad–Ishel where some of my Jewish acquaintances from Sandz resided: Shimon and Mendel Braun, Max Neuman, and Chuna Grinberg. We toasted our luck that we had survived and continued to drink and reminisce. They asked me what are you doing and I answered I am having a ball. I have riding horses, a nightclub and women.

Shimon Braun had a gorgeous blond Austrian girlfriend. While riding one day to a picnic with American soldiers, I noticed Shimon and his girlfriend next to my farmhouse. I could not stop the jeep and get off. So I continued to ride with the soldiers until the picnic ground and then took the jeep and returned to my place where I met the couple waiting. I took them to my room where they spent an entire week and used all the available facilities of the base including the horses. Two weeks later, I was still in bed when someone knocked at the door. I asked who it was. She answered: " I am Shimon's girlfriend." I opened the door and let her in. She remained for one week with me. During the day we rode horses, in the evening I was at a club where my female companion played the piano and later we spent the night together. After the week she returned to Bad–Ischl. Benyamin Hausshtock and some Austrian friends from Eblsberg visited me at the base and spent time. I also saw quite a bit of Helena but she had to make the last tram home before the curfew set in.

In August of 1946, I received a postal card from the HIAS organization that I was to meet their representative on November 4, 1946 at the Linz railway station with all the papers that Chaim Lustig sent from Brazil. To get these papers was very difficult since most South American countries closed their doors to the Jewish survivors. There were so many obstacles placed for the entrance that it was almost impossible to get entrance visas. Chaim Lustig must have had good connections to get entrance papers. I was told that the train would transit Germany and France where it would continue to my destination. I began to prepare myself for the long trip. I requested the Austrian treasury to free my 6000 frozen marks since I was leaving the country. I bought a suitcase and a backpack. The day of the departure Helena came to see me. I gave her the key to my place and everything within. We said good–bye; she cried. The military jeep came and drove to the railway station where I boarded the train. The transport consisted of Jews heading to many places like Brazil, Argentina, Guatemala and other places.

The train started to roll towards Germany. In the morning we arrived in Munich, Germany. The HIAS representatives awaited us and took us by cars to a special camp called Funk–Kaserna that was once a communication base of the German army. The camp now belonged to UNRRA that provided food, lodgings and all other necessities. From this camp refugees went all over the globe. Each inhabited block had a manager and an assistant to accommodate the arrivals. There were also sport facilities at the camp as well as many offices. The camp was closed and there was a guard at the entrance to check papers. One had to have the necessary documents to enter the camp. On arrival we were assigned to quarters based on our destination. I was given a large room with three childless couples, who were heading to Brazil. We received beds, blankets and food from the main kitchen.

I left for Munich and went to the center of the city where the Jewish community had its office on Mehl Street. The place also contained the offices of HIAS and the American Joint. I soon discovered that near my camp there was another UNRRA camp called Neu Freiman where an old neighbor from Sandz lived. Celina or Cesia Goldberger was her name. I went to visit her and found her at home. In Sandz we called them Ferleiger. She was already married to Naphtali Goldman. I arrived just in time for the circumcision ceremony of her son. He was given a Hebrew name but was called Maxi. I have remained in touch with the couple until now. Two of her brothers, Shlomo and Itzi Goldberger were also in Germany.

The head of the Jewish community in Munich was Zvi Teler who survived the war in the Soviet Union. He was a Sandzer Jew. He was the one who gave my father the key to his apartment and warehouse when he left Sandz prior to the German arrival to the city. We were very glad to reminisce about our past. My lodging at the camp was soon changed to a smaller room with several lodgers: a Jew named Shtaier, a Spanish Christian, an Egyptian named Fuad, and a Moroccan named Eli, most of them non–Jews. We got along very well. Time passed and we already reached 1947. The winter of 1947 was a cold winter. We sat and played cards. The room was heated with wood provided by UNRRA. We had many visitors including girls and spent our time. One of the girls was from Belgium and she asked me whether I wanted to have my palm read. I replied in the affirmative. She then read my palm and said that I was supposed to cross a large ocean but this will not take place. My palm indicated that I would cross a small body of water. I was furious. I wanted to spit her in the face. I was determined to go to Brazil and so much effort was spent on the project and suddenly someone tells me that I am not going to Brazil where I planned to live. Of course, the girl read the cards and interpreted them for me. It was not her decision but what the cards indicated. She was on her way to meet her boyfriend in Belgium. Meanwhile we got acquainted and enjoyed each other's company. She even showed me her letters to her boyfriend. We met until she left for Belgium.

At the time Munich had two restaurants. One of them served camp inmates and students and the other one served business people. Of course the first restaurant was much cheaper; lunch was 20 marks and in the second restaurant the same meal cost 70 marks. At the first restaurant I met Aaron and Zvi Berliner from Sandz. We were very happy to meet and talked about old days. At the second restaurant named Piccadilly I met Moshe Dershewitz who changed his name to Max Berger. I studied with him in my youth. Each day I would travel to the Munich center where I went to the movies, to the theater, and to shows. The tickets were rather cheap. I also discovered that my friend Kuba Fuhrer who was liberated with me from the Ebensee concentration camp lived in Munich. I went to see him. At his place, I once met Oskar Schindler playing cards. Schindler loved cards. He was now dressed in simple clothing but it was Shindler my old boss who saved my life by giving me a job that helped to sustain myself during the war. I did not talk to him since he was busy playing cards but in my heart I thanked him for his deeds. In the room, someone pointed out that a group of refugees would be arriving to my camp heading to the USA. I went to see the visitors and met Yanka Kolber. Her brother was a friend of mine back in the days of Sandz. I visited her and saw that she was married and the mother of an infant. Her husband was not at home. She told me that she was a close friend of my uncle, Moshe Kannengisser in the ghetto of Tarnow until they separated. She told me that he was killed while trying to escape the Tarnow ghetto.

Oskar Schindler

On occasions I went to the Brazilian consulate in Munich to inquire about my status. I was supposed to get an entrance permit to Brazil for I had all the necessary papers. Every time I received the same laconic reply: it would take time until it arrived. Meanwhile UNRRA opened another camp near Geretstrid. The camp was beautiful and probably belonged to a German noble family. Some of the families that came from Austria moved to the camp. The old place was practically deserted. I moved to the new camp with three other Jews; two were brothers and the fellow named Shtayer. All three were on the road to Australia. They were hardly at the place. They were involved in commercial affairs. Next door to us moved in Katie Fersteig who was of Dutch origin. We started to socialize and went to Munich where we saw movies, theater performances and night shows. We led a very happy and careless life until I left Germany. I still maintained letter contact with Helena in Austria.

Zvi Teller the head of the Jewish community was also the head of the Sandzer Jewish landesmanschaft in Germany. He had collected a list of the Sandzer Jews in Germany and notified them that on May 28, 1947 there would be a memorial ceremony for the Jews killed in Sandz in Munich. About forty Sandzer Jews showed up. I took pictures of the event. In August of 1947, a fellow who was also going to Brazil showed up and told me that there was a camp where I could work and save some money. They do not pay in cash but they distribute goods like chocolate, cacao and cigarettes that can easily be sold on the market. The work was basically to move UNRRA supplies to the camp and distribute them amongst the designated places. We brought bread to the camp and unloaded coals from a train car. The work was hard but we were young and earned good money that we could save since UNRRA provided us with food and lodgings. At the camp I also had a room that I shared with two other fellows: a Pole and a Hungarian. The Pole was never there. He always traveled. The Hungarian fellow worked with us in the supplies. The camp was enclosed and a Jewish guardhouse was located at the entrance to the camp. The guards were Jewish policemen. Nearby was also a Jewish D.P. UNRRA camp. The camp was a training camp for young Jews who volunteered to fight in Palestine. The Bricha brought then from all over to undergo military training provided by the Haganah military emissaries.

Sandzer Jews attend memorial service held in 1947 in Munich for the murdered Jews of Sandz. Mordechai Lustig has his hand in his pocket. He is wearing white slacks and a grey jacket.

With the expanding agitation and fighting between the Palestinian Jews, the British soldiers and the Arabs, The Jewish Agency in Palestine decided to use the Jewish manpower reservoir bottled up in the refugee camps of Europe. All Jews D.P. camps were urged to conduct a campaign on behalf of joining the Haganah. Those who expressed interest were sent to draft board offices located in central points like Munich and Prague. Once they passed the physical and medical tests they were sent to special camps where they began military training. They would play an important military role in Israel's struggle for independence.

While in Munich I invited the girl that I had in Munich to come to my present camp. She came but could not enter the camp since she did not have the proper identification. I found a hole in the fence and we entered the camp and she came to my room. We lived together until one day, the chief of the Jewish police came and told me to get rid of my partner and to escort her out of the camp the same way I brought her in. The evidence pointed to the Hungarian fellow as having the informed the police about the presence of a female in the camp. I took my companion through the fence out of the camp and we slept the night in the forest. In the morning she left for Munich. She soon returned to the camp and managed to get official lodging within a barrack where the road maintenance crew lived. I decided to continue my relationship with Kathie and rode on my bicycle to a nearby village where I rented a room supposedly for my sister. The owner had a son in a prison of war camp in Belgium. He insisted on being paid in food. Evenings we ate at the family table and then went to Kathie's room that was right across the kitchen where we spent time in the nice room. Friday evenings we ate supper with the family and then we sat for a while whereupon I decided to act very sleepy and snuck into Kathie's room where I remained for the night. Saturday morning I climbed out of the room through the window and entered the house through the front door. I joined them at the table for breakfast. Saturday at four o'clock we also received cake and coffee. The rent that I paid for the room consisted of white bread, Quaker oats, and coffee.

November 27 1947, I heard that the United Nations granted the Jews a state. The radio also reported that bitter fighting was taking place in Palestine. The paper described the situation as grim. I suddenly had a change of heart. Maybe I should drop the idea of going to Brazil where I do not seem to be wanted and head to Palestine. Thoughts began to flow through my mind. On Chanukah we had a big party at our camp when Yanek Brawer shoed up unexpectedly. I was very pleased and kept in contact until he went to the USA. He then stopped the correspondence. Contact between us resumed when he came to Israel to participate in a memorial service for the Jews of Sandz. Near our camp was the D.P. camp of Fohrenwald where I met Beck who was related our landlord in Sandz. He told me that Itzi Sheinfeld, his son Zvi and his daughter Gusta survived the war in the Soviet Union and are presently in Berlin. In January, my landlord informed me that his son was coming home from the prison of war camp in Belgium and would therefore need the room. But he told me not to worry; he already made arrangements for an apartment in a two-storey house. The place was furnished and gave us privacy.

Katie had a friend named Reggi Tressler who lived in Frankfurt. She invited her friend to come to visit her. She came and remained with us. We only had one bed in the room but we managed to sleep in one bed. Next to our camp was a big mountain and when the sun was bright one could tan oneselve. Reggi insisted on climbing to the top and getting a tan. I escorted her to the top and started to fool around with her when in the distance I noticed Kathie approaching us. I stopped everything and received Kathie as though nothing happened. I later invited my friend Ezriel Poliwoda and introduced him to Reggi. Some days passed and I definitely decided to give up the idea of going to Brazil. I opted for Palestine where I felt I was needed. I traveled to Munich with Ezriel to report to the Haganah office where I was drafted. In May, I took Kathie back to the Funk–Kaserne D.P. camp and said goodbye.

**Kathie and
myself at a
picnic at the D.P.
camp in
Germany**

[Page 290]

Chapter XII
On the way to Israel

Mordechai Lustig with other Jewish volunteers heading to Israel

I was now a member of the military organization known as Haganah that was involved in heavy fighting in Palestine. I was ordered to proceed to a training camp in Holland that was not too far from our present camp in Germany. I began intensive military training at the base that consisted of physical and sport exercises, weapon handling and military drills. On May 14, 1948 the State of Israel was proclaimed and a big ceremony was held at our camp. All units attended the ceremony that was very impressive and was of a military nature. In June of 1948, we finished our military training and left the base. We headed to the railway station where we took the train to France. All the units boarded the train when the order came to descend from the train and to board military trucks covered with tarpaulin. The convoy was organized by the Brichah. We spent the night in a big hall and the next day we reached the French city of Strasbourg where we met the Brichah leader. We then boarded a train that headed in a southerly direction to the city of Lyon. There trucks took us to our Haganah camp of Sank. At the camp we continued to undergo training. On receiving a liberty pass, I went to meet Cesia who told me the story of the Exodus. This was her second visit to France. She originally joined a transport of Jewish immigrants that left Germany illegally and headed to Marseilles where she boarded the ship "Exodus" that headed to Palestine. The British intercepted the ship and sent her back to Germany, but she managed to get back to France and awaited the next ship to Palestine.

The Exodus 1947 ship
(Yad Vashem Archives)

The ship Exodus 1947 became a symbol of <u>Aliya Bet</u> or illegal <u>immigration</u>. With the end of the war in sight, the Jewish Agency of Palestine ordered the Haganah and especially the Mossad to bring to Palestine as many Jews as possible regardless of British objections. Britain was determined to continue its "White Paper " policy of no Jewish entry to Palestine. The Mossad and the Brichah began to ship boatloads of Jews to Palestine. Some ships made it while others were intercepted by the British navy and the illegal passengers were sent to camps in Cyprus. This did not prevent the ships from coming in ever–increasing numbers. Britain decided to stop the illegal ships by sending them back to Europe. Britain applied the new rule to the Exodus ship.

The ship sailed from the port of Sete, near Marseilles, on July 11, 1947, with 4,515 immigrants, including 655 children, on board. Most of the passengers came from the D.P.camps in Europe. The crew comprised a sizable number of American Jewish sailors who volunteered for the job. As soon as it left the territorial waters of France, British destroyers accompanied it. On July 18, near the coast of Palestine but outside territorial waters, the British rammed the ship and boarded it, while the immigrants put up a desperate defense. Two immigrants and a crewman were killed in the battle, and 30 were wounded. The ship was towed to Haifa, where the immigrants were forced onto deportation ships bound for France. At Port–de–Bouc, in southern France, the would–be immigrants remained in the ships' holds for 24 days during a heat wave, refusing to disembark despite the shortage of food, the crowding and the abominable sanitary conditions. The French government refused to force them off the boat. Eventually, the British decided to return the "would–be" immigrants to Germany, and on August 22 the ship left for the port of

Hamburg, then in the British occupation zone. The immigrants were forcibly taken off and transported to two camps near Lubeck. Journalists who covered the dramatic struggle described to the entire world the heartlessness and cruelty of the British. World public opinion was outraged and the British changed their policy. No more ships were sent to Europe. The majority of the passengers on the Exodus 1947were smuggled out of the British zone by the Brichah to the American zone in Germany and then onwards to Palestine.

I spent a nice time with Cesia and her mother. I reported back to my base where I was examined by a military doctor and underwent further military training. Then we were informed that we were shipping out to Marseilles. We reached the city and soon boarded the ship named " Mella Panama". We received false boarding cards. The entire ship was loaded with young men, mostly Shoah survivors. There were also non–military Jewish civilians, namely Cesia with her mother amongst the passengers.

The trip aboard the vessel took seven days. There was little food and water. We slept in three tiered bunks that run along the full length of the boat. But we did not care about the accommodations. After all we were young and inspired by the thought that we were going to fight for the Jewish state. Many youths were seasick but I managed to stay on my feet. I was busy taking pictures and meeting people. Finally, we saw Haifa from the sea, a very moving picture. July 11. 1948, we stepped ashore in Haifa. We were immediately moved to the reception camp named "Agrobank" near the city of Hadera. There we were assigned to tents that had beds with clean sheets and food. At the base there was a kiosk where I bought ices and took pictures of the place. In the morning, we were moved to the big military base named Beit Lid. I started on the wrong foot for I had no bed to sleep in at the new base. The next day, July 12, 1948, was extremely hot, my friend Eliezer and I spent the night in a forsaken hole in the ground but received food. The same day, the cities of Lod and Ramle were captured by the Israel Army. I saw for the first time Palestinian Arab and Sudanese soldiers. July 13, 1949, I finished all the military paper requirements and was issued the military number 77115. I was then sent with other soldiers to the base of Kfar Yona near the coastal city of Netanya. This was a Palmach base.

The **Palmach** (Hebrew: פלמ״ח, acronym for Plugot Maḥatz (Hebrew: פלוגות מחץ), literally "strike-forces") was the elite fighting force of the Haganah, the underground army of the Palestine Jewish community. The Palmach was established on 15 May 1941. By the outbreak of the Israeli War for Independence in 1948 it consisted of over 2,000 men and women in three fighting brigades and auxiliary units. Its members formed the backbone of the Israel Defense Forces. The Palmach leaders were Itzhak Sadeh, Yigal Allon, Moshe Dayan and Itzhak Rabin. The Palmach units were the elite forces of the Haganah and later of the Israel Army. The Palmach was later disbanded and integrated into the regular Israel army.

**Palmach badge
The badge worn
by the Palmach
soldiers)**

Women soldiers in the Palmach

Ezriel was assigned to the Negev Regiment and he was sent to Sodom near the Dead Sea. We were well received at the camp by the staff. We started battle training exercises, Hebrew lessons and various duties like guard duty and kitchen help and of course military roll calls. My unit consisted of soldiers that came from many places: Poland, Hungary Rumania, Germany, Holland, France and Belgium. I had my camera and made extensive use of it. Following four days of extensive training, we were given four days of liberty to tend to our various needs. I had to go to the warehouse of the Jewish Agency in Pardess Chanah to pick up my suitcase that was there since I arrived in the country. I located the suitcase and returned to Hadera. I entered a store with the suitcase and spoke to the owner in Yiddish. I told the owner that I just arrived in Israel and am in the Army. I have no friends or relatives in the country. I have no place to leave my suitcase. I asked him if he would care for my suitcase until I could make the proper arrangements since I have to return to my military unit. He accepted my suitcase for safekeeping. I sold him one of my cameras and also exchanged some foreign currency to Israel currency. I then left for Tel Aviv and reached the end of Allenby Street. I met some of the soldiers that arrived with me aboard the ship. I spent my liberty at a Tel Aviv hotel and returned to the base.

At the end of July, the Palmach took us in military trucks to the base of the 6th company of the Harel Brigade where I remained until the Palmach was dissolved. We traveled in the direction of Jerusalem via the old Burma Road. The road to Jerusalem was closed near Latrun by the Jordanian Legion. Jerusalem was starving, cut off from the Jewish hinterland. The Israel army tried to open the main road but failed. So they built an extensive by pass and called it the Burma Road. We traveled four hours until we reached Shaar Hagai at the entrance of the foot hills to Jerusalem. There was the military base called "Saris" later called Shoresh that was the home base of the 6th unit of the Harel Brigade. I was assigned to B-company. The base had two water wells surrounded by vegetation. The offices and supply units were located below in the older section of the base near the road. I was assigned to the top of the hill and issued bedding, weapons and ammunition. I made two trips to bring all my stuff to the barrack where I had my bed. I met some of the veterans of the unit that told me the battle history of the unit. They told me that in the battles for independence almost half the unit was killed. Slowly, I fell into line with the unit. I was assigned to squad number seven that was guarding a position. The squad consisted of 14 men. The commander of the position asked who would like to be in charge of food preparations and distributions. I volunteered for I had some experience with food distribution. I began to cook meals while the others were on guard duty. I was given a mule that carried every evening the food supplies that I received from the supply officer named Sinai along the main road. I also took many pictures of our position. The entire company was spread out in the hilly area of Shaar Hagai facing the Jordanian Legion.

We were constantly in training or resting or guarding. We were then moved to the post at Esthaol near Har Tuv opposite the Egyptian positions that were located in the hills. We were then moved to guard the Burma Road near Latrun that was held by the Jordanian forces. During one of liberty days that I received, I went to Haifa and reached Kings Street opposite the railway station. There was a two –story house and a huge queue of men that stretched from the street to the house. They were in line to meet Arab prostitutes. I was tempted to join the line when a sailor stopped me and gave me the address of a cleaner place and even told me the price that would be charged; 80 grush per visit.

Mordechai Lustig and his mule bringing supplies to his unit

I returned to the base and the entire unit was ordered to move to camp Israel, home base for the entire brigade for a period of rest. Indeed, the, 4th, 5th and 6th companies of the brigade assembled near the village of Wilhelma. We went to the Kol Nidrei Service on the eve of Yom Kippur to the synagogue of the village. Half way through the service, messengers arrived from the base and told us to report immediately to the base. At the base we were told to get our gear and were transported to the Har Tuv area where military clashes were taking place with the Egyptian forces. That night the 4th company attacked and conquered the high mountain named Dir El Hawa near Har Tuv. We supported the 4th company and went into direct action. By Sukkoth, we took Beit Jamal, Netiv Lamed Hey, and were on the outskirts of Beit Jala near the historical city of Beit Lechem. The British prevented us from occupying the city, so we set up our defense positions and began to patrol in the village of San and Allar. We even saw the famous tree of the Gush Etzion village.

We were again relieved and sent to the Israel camp to rest and recuperate. We also began to train. Towards Channukah of 1948, a big party was being planned with a performance of a big band headed by Yehuda Sharett, brother of Moshe Sharret formerly Shertok, the foreign minister. I was selected to participate in the chorale group of the evening with the daughter of Moshe Sharett who often entertained our unit. I had a real surprise at the party when the political adviser of the brigade showed up. His name was Ben Zeev Gantzweiich and he was from Sandz. He survived the war in Russia and was now a high ranking political officer in the Palmach. We began preparations for the sport day in the army. We set up sport places opposite the camp where the various units would compete with each other. Then the unit went to target practice, following which I was promoted and received my first stripes. Prior to Passover, I was sent for a month to study Hebrew and then was sent to various places to become familiar with the country like to Muchraka, Nahallal and Emek Israel.

I was given an extensive liberty pass for Passover and money to stay at a hotel in Tel Aviv. The army arranged for me to spend the seder night with the Kolski family in Tel Aviv. To celebrate with them in style, I went to Hadera and picket up my suitcase. I then bought a pair of pants and a shirt for myself. I had acquired a nice pair of brown shoes in a trading deal along the. Tel Aviv–Petach Tikvah road. I felt comfortable and clean in my presentation. The Kolski family received me warmly and we spent a nice evening. Back at the base preparations started for the Independence parade that would take place in Tel Aviv. We began drilling and marching. New uniforms were issued. Helmets from the USA were distributed to the unit. The day of the festivities we were brought to Tel Aviv and assembled at the main bus station. We began to march along Allenby Street and then detoured to King George Street while the main stage with the primeminister David Ben Gurion and chief of staff Yaakov Dori was located at the Mograbi Square. The members of the unit were very disappointed and returned to the base depressed. The next day, we were officially informed that the Palmach units were being being dismantled. The elder members of the unit were discharged and the rest of us were transferred to company 1212 of the Golani brigade.

I was already in Israel a full year and I did not know that I had an uncle here. My mother's brother Abish Lustig left Germany in 1933 and came to Palestine. Of course, I did not know this information. I visited often in Tel Aviv my Friend Berale Yakir who lived on Melchett Street. One day, I came to my friend and met his father, an elderly man. He asked about my family and I replied that my grandfather was Shalom Lustig. He told me that I have an uncle in Israel who lives in the city of Rehovot. I took the bus to the city and reached the center of town. I stepped into the first restaurant that I saw and asked whether they know where Abish Lustig lives. Someone told me that he lives in the Sha'araim section of the city. I went to the section and was told that they moved to Kibbutz Givat Brenner. I traveled to the kibbutz and found my family. I introduced myself that I am Mordechai Lustig, a grandson of Shalom Lustig and a nephew of Abish Lustig. I was very happy to discover another part of the family. My uncle was in a wheelchair; he suffered from Parkinson. His head was fine and he remembered things. He moved to the kibbutz where his daughter Rivka lived. She joined the "Habonim" Zionist group and made aliyah in 1933. She was one of the founders of Kibbutz Givat Brenner. She was married to Milan Oren and they had two sons and a daughter. I got to know the entire family including David Lustig who married in August of 1949 Ilana Baum. I would meet them often since I was now attached to a unit that was stationed at the Julis base that was near the kibbutz. They even showed me some pictures of my family.

Mordechai Lustig's unit preparing for the Independence parade

Mordechai Lustig with Rivkah's children at Kibbutz Givat Brenner

At the Kibbutz Givat Brenner, the family told me the story about my cousin Yehoshua Lustig who fell in Pessah of 1948, a few days after he was married. He was a soldier in company 52 of the Givati Brigade. He fell with 20 other soldiers in the battle of Tel Arish presently called Tel Giborim. The fight was intense and bloody, it took place on April 28, 1948. The British brought back the bodies of the killed soldiers and they were buried in brotherly grave since the bodies were badly mutilated by the Arabs. They were buried at the Nachlat Itzhak cemetery. Only in 2007 did the army unit to locate missing soldiers manage to identify the remains of the soldiers through the use of DNA equipment. They were officially reburied and Shlomo Lahat, former mayor of Tel Aviv, and someone who had participated in the actual battle, stated the dead soldiers had fought like lions.

At the Golani base there was a soccer field. I once attended the games when I heard a familiar voice in the background. I turned around and saw Peretz Peterzeil who was known in Sandz as Peretz Kacziki. We were students and knew each other well. During the war we played cards in Sandz. We shared our experiences and I was happy to meet another Sandzer Jew who survived the war. I think he was married and lived in Chalissa near Haifa.

Mordechai Lustig receives citation from the Israeli Defense Ministry for his military participation in combat.

My Golani unit was sent back into action facing the Gaza strip. My unit was positioned next to kibbutz Bari and Tel Dzema next to the sulphur pools. When we not on combat duty, we spent time training in the sands of Zikim under the leadership of our commander Ze'ev Yaki. In Golani I even managed to get sick due to boils and skin irritation that required hospitalization and transfer of blood. With the rank of corporal I was discharged from the army in August of 1949.

[Page 302]

Chapter XIII
Settling in the
New Old Homeland

I was discharged from the army late in 1949 and assigned to the reserve forces of the state. The army gave me 10 days paid vacation at a hotel in Tel Aviv to arrange my affairs. The vacation went very fast and now I had to make decisions. Kibbutz Brenner urged me to join the collective but I decided to make it on my own. I went to my friend Berale in Tel Aviv and extended my vacation by another 10 days. I then went to the office of discharged soldiers and was given a letter to the reception camp called Nevei Yehoshua in Ramat Gan. As I traveled to the camp I liked the small city of Ramat Gan. I shared a room with two other single soldiers. The camp was a distance from the center of the city and was serviced by busses three times a day. The main bus station was located opposite the Nussbaum restaurant. My room was in a barrack separated from other rooms by boards. I received beds, blankets and other items from the Jewish Agency. There was no charge but I signed that the items would have to be paid sometime in the future. The room had a shower, a hanging closet for clothing, a kitchen table with a washbasin. The outhouse was located outside the barrack. The local bus station was near the barrack.

During my leaves from the army I tried to get in touch with Jews from Sandz who had survived the war. I located some in Ness Tziona such as Awraham Neishtat,–Szpilman. There were also survivors in Tel Aviv and in Haifa and I tried to get in touch with everybody. In Haifa I contacted Chaim Yossef Hameltzar and the Kirshenboim family who I had met previously in Stuttgart, Germany. I slept in Shlomo Goldberger's flat. I met Yehuda Gertner, Dawid Einhorn and Awraham Schlachet. With the vacations finished, I had to start to look for a job and went to Ness Tziona where my acquaintance Awraham Szpilman lived. He was a foreman at the Solel Boneh company. He talked with his boss, Mr. Popper who consented to my employment.

The Solel Boneh company was the largest building conglomerate in Israel. It was founded by the Histadruth or workers union of Israel in the 1920s. The Histadruth was a union and also a job provider. It was founded in the 1920s and grew immensely with time.

Awraham took me on to work at the military airfield base of Tel Nof where they fixed the runways. Awraham also arranged lodging for me with another Sandzer Jew who lived near Ness Tziona at the village of Sarafand El Harab to avoid traveling from Ramat Gan to Ness Tziona each day. The place was an Arab house that stood near the main highway where I was picked up each morning by a truck and driven to the work site. The work was difficult under the beating sun. Then I tried to work at laying the foundations of a building but gave it up. I decided to learn a building trade. I gave notice and left the job in December.

I returned to Ramat Gan and went to the employment office where I saw Mr. Kurlander. I told him that I wanted to learn a building trade and he asked what trade I wanted to acquire. I consulted my friend Wolf Kempfner (Shwitzer) and he suggested tiling. I reported to Mr. Kurland and told him that I wanted to learn to lay down floors. He gave me all the tools and a letter of recommendation to a local office of the Solel Boneh. At the time there was a big project that was being built for new immigrants between Uziel and Fabrigat Streets. I presented myself at the site and started my training. The supervisor named Nahum was from Lodz, Poland. He was an excellent instructor and I acquired the trade. He was a patient man and taught us all the aspects of floor tiling, from mixing the cement to the exact tile measurements. While acquiring the trade, I was paid a lira a day in cash to keep me going.

In February of 1950, I started to work on a regular basis and I earned 2.50 lirot a day. I worked with a group of workers who took on jobs on the basis of units of work rather than the standard monthly payment. We worked with "Amidar Building Company." The latter was a joint government, Jewish Agency for Palestine and Keren Kayemet L'Israel (Jewish National Fund) company that built housing for new immigrants. We then worked on a big project at the Borochov section where we were paid by the day. I also worked for Solel Boneh, which was building housing for the old timers in Israel. I also took Hebrew courses at the reception center that were offered by the Histadruth in one of the barracks. I also attended English courses given at the Borochov center.

I renewed my communications with my uncle Chaim Lustig in Brazil that had suffered greatly while I was in the service. I also renewed contact with the Shtapler family in Geretstrid, Germany, and with Katie Freitlieg in Frankfurt, Germany. At the end of the barrack lived a fellow named Mishke who used to entertain us with his accordion. Awraham Wallach lived in our barrack but in name only. He worked with Solel Boneh as a scaffold builder.

He had a sister and brothers who lived in Salama in an Arab house. Wallach lived there and on occasion came to the reception camp and insisted that I join him socially. He wanted to introduce me to a friend of his from Sanok, Poland. She was married and had a daughter but left her husband in Germany. She lived in the Agemia section of Jaffa. I met her and we enjoyed each other's company. We went to dance, to the movies and enjoyed life.

In 1950 I met Zvi Sheinfeld who owned the house in which we lived in Sandz. He told me that that he was married and had a small daughter. They lived in an Arab house in Lod. His father and sister also lived in Israel. His sister Gusta was married and lived in Kfar Saba. His father lived with his sister. Zvi invited me to visit him in Lod, which I did. I also visited his sister in Kfar Saba.

At Solel Boneh there was a kitchen that provided breakfast and lunch at reduced prices until 1952. I then started to work on a project along the "Flyers

Road Street" where Solel Boneh was building popular–priced apartments. We worked as a group and were paid by the section. We finished our assignments quickly and took off. At the time I ate at various restaurants. One in particular served meals that replaced meat with broccoli and eggs or filet of fish. In the evenings I would travel to Tel Aviv where I attended Hebrew classes to improve my Hebrew at the Balfour school. On Friday nights, some fellow brought girls from Tel Aviv who solicited business. There were several dance places in Ramat Gan and also a movie house. The same year I was also called for reserve duty in the Israeli Army. I was sent to several courses and was promoted to the rank of corporal in the reserves. My home base was in Kfar Yona, the training courses in Caesarea and the shooting ranges in Givat Olga.

I visited my uncle Abish in Kibbutz Brenner. He was later moved to a special old age home in Tel Aviv. I visited him on occasion and he always had the same question: When would I get married? During one of these visits, I met my grandmother Esther's sister Sarah, my father's aunt. She spoke only Yiddish and we discussed the old homestead. In November my uncle Abish passed away. I attended the funeral that took place at Kibbutz Brenner where he was buried.

The days were difficult and shortages were everywhere. The government introduced rationing and everything was sold through coupons that were distributed by the government. Of course, a black market developed for everything, especially meat. The national treasury was empty and the small amount of foreign currency that the state received had to be saved for vital expenses such as fuel, weapons, medicine and industrial machinery to develop the country and provide jobs to the thousands of immigrants who needed everything from housing to food.

I managed to survive but had to do a lot of combinations to obtain the food that I needed. The most difficult item was meat. I bought a record player in partnership with my friend Ezriel. I bought many cantorial and romantic records, Yiddish comedies and light operas. Saving some money I bought a bicycle to give me some mobility. The record player attracted many people who came to listen to the recordings and frequently dances were held in our barrack. I received letters from my uncle in Brazil that I replied to. He also sent a package of clothing that included nice shirts, socks and other clothing items. By chance I also discovered that a nephew of my mother's named Chaim Brandstater lived in Ramat Gan. I established contact and visited him. He was an elderly bachelor who had left Poland prior to the war and had recently visited Poland. He showed me some family pictures that I had never seen before. I also came in contact with my father's niece Mania Ebershtark. She was the daughter of Liebe Jakubowicz, lived in Nevei Ne'eman and was married to Awraham Perlberger. They had a son named Moshe. I also established contact with the daughters of my father's brother in Tel Aviv such as Mari, the daughter of Sara, married to Alfred Rimler and their son Menachem. They provided me with a picture of my father's brother Zvi Kannengisser with his wife; they were married before 1938.

While walking along Bialik Street in Ramat Gan, I heard a voice calling me. I turned about and it was Shoshana Kaufman who had served with me in the Palmach forces. She was the one responsible for my nickname in the Palmach days. Shoshana had been distributing fruit soup to the soldiers. When I approached the distribution table I asked for a half portion of soup. She granted my request but I became known as "Hatzi Manah" or half portion. We reminisced about the old days and the present days. She lived with her parents and young sister Zina in Givat Bracha near Kfar Onu. They had a farm with cows, turkeys, a large house and a large garden around it. Shoshana invited me to visit her and I took her up on it. I visited the farm and met her family, including her married sister Chaya who had a baby. We arranged several social parties at her house. On Saturdays, we went to the pool named "Gali Gil" where we all met and then went to Shoshana's home to continue the parties. I had a very nice time at these social gatherings. I made many friends at these parties. I also organized some social dance meetings that were attended by many girls and fellows from the area.

At the time I became a member of the Sandzer society in Israel. Yehuda Knabel was the presiding officer. The society organized a social evening for the Sandzer Jews in Israel that was very successful. I helped with the selling of the tickets. At the gatherings in Shoshana's house I met a girl named Esther and started to date her. One day she opened her picture album and I saw her with a beautiful friend. I asked Esther, Why don't you invite your friend to your house for a Shabbat? She decided to invite her friend Rivkah. I was instantly attracted to her but she was rather cool. She was very pretty, short, had two braids. She was from Poland. I did not accept her coolness toward me and persisted in my interest in her. I guess I was in love at first sight. I asked her where she lived but she refused to disclose it. There were few telephones and fewer telephone books in those days to look up addresses. After a while I asked Esther for Rivkah's address. I had some acquaintances in the Salama reception center and on occasion I went to dances at the camp. One day I decided to present myself at the house of Rivkah without any announcement or invitation. I looked up Rivkah's address and went directly to her place. She lived with her father Yaacov Tenenbaum from Janow Podlaski who had lived in Biala Podolsk in Poland, her brother Asher and her stepmother Rachel, a native of Lithuania. I started to visit her place and slowly I started to date her.

The entire year of 1953 we spent seeing each other. The relationship stopped and started. Maybe Rivkah had higher aspirations. Perhaps she was hoping to marry a doctor or an engineer. I continued to visit the family and also bought myself a DKW motorcycle.

In 1954, I was called to reserve duty during the summer. I reported to company 106 of the Harel Brigade as in previous years. But presently the situation was tense and our brigade was posted along a line stretching from Abu-Gosh to Jerusalem proper at the Mandelbaum gate and Abu Tor. We were positioned in defensive positions. I took along my motorcycle to the army and used it frequently. One day I gave my sergeant a lift and the chain snapped on the bike. I tried to repair it but it was never the same. I tried to sell it but it proved very difficult. Eventually I sold the bike. Upon my discharge, I resumed working for Solel Boneh and was building flats at Ramat Aviv in Tel Aviv. That year my niece Laura from Brazil, the daughter of Chaim Lustig, and her husband came to visit me. I introduced them to Rivkah. Then Rivkah and I broke up.

As mentioned earlier, the Israel government introduced an austerity program to cope with the serious economic situation in the country. Unemployment was very high, especially in the *"ma'abarot"* or reception camps, and foreign currency reserves were scarce. Ben Gurion decided to negotiate an agreement with Germany whereby West Germany was to pay Israel for the slave labor and persecution of Jews during the Holocaust and to compensate for Jewish property that was stolen by the Nazis. The Reparations Agreement between Israel and West Germany was signed on September 10, 1952, and entered in force on March 27, 1953. According to the agreement, Germany would pay to Israel a sum of 3 billion marks over the next 14 years; 450 million marks were paid to the World Jewish Congress. The payments were made to the State of Israel as the heir to those victims who had no surviving family. The money was invested in the country's infrastructure and played an important role in establishing the economy of the new state. The reparations would be paid directly to the headquarters of the Israeli purchase delegation in the city of Cologne, Germany, which would receive the money from the German government in annual installments. The delegation would then buy goods and ship them to Israel, according to the requests from a Tel Aviv–based company that had been set up to decide what to purchase and for whom. A great part of the reparations money would go into purchasing equipment and raw materials for companies that were owned by the government, the Jewish Agency and the Histadrut labor union. The Israeli government also decided to establish an office to begin to pay survivors for their hardships during the war. All these decisions were made despite large protests against dealing with Germans. The opposition parties had a heyday in campaigning against the agreements but the government decided to implement the programs.

I received payment for my hard work in the camps in Israeli money. Now I could begin to think of getting a small place of my own and began to make inquiries. Meanwhile I met Ella who had served in my unit of the Palmach. I started dating her and once brought her to my reception center. I suggested that she move in with me but she refused. She wanted me but did not like the place and we started to drift apart. Near the reception camp lived a Sandzer Jew named Samek Teitelbaum, now Bar–Ilan, with his wife and three children. He worked at the police garage and always dressed in a police uniform. He lived in a nice two–family house. Menashe Wolf and his wife Lucia and small child also lived in a nice two–family house on Eilat Street. The entire development was built by the Progressive Building Company. I visited them and even participated at their Passover Seder. I met his brother Shlomo who was still a bachelor. We spent time together. These two families were pleased with their flats and I decided to purchase an apartment in this area. In 1955 I finalized the purchase of my apartment that consisted of a room and a half. The price of the place was 5,000 Israeli pounds (the exchange rate of the pound was U.S.$1=1.80 Israeli pounds) or about U.S.$2,800. I took all the money that I received from the Germans and paid toward the apartment but it was not enough. I also took a loan from Bank Hapoalim. Still I was short. I took all my savings and still needed 500 pounds to finish the deal. I asked my friend Arnold Remer to loan me the money, which he did. Thus, I acquired my flat located at the Progressive Street 28. The street name would be later changed to Haroe Street 246, Ramat Gan. I fixed up the place and left the reception center.

I was then introduced to a girl named Malka whose parents were originally from Austria. The family was well to do and had a store in Tel Aviv and lived in a nice house in Ramat Gan. She was rather young and I began to visit the family where I was invited almost every Saturday. I even took her to Tel Aviv to celebrate Purim in 1956. Her parents were very anxious to marry their daughter. I bought her a golden watch but my heart was not in it. Something told me to stop. Meanwhile, in May I received an order to present myself for reserve duty. I decided to stop the relationship and stopped visiting the family. The moment was very propitious since I was going to be away for some time. Prior to my departure, her father showed up and inquired why I had stopped the relationship. I told him that he knows his daughter better than anyone.

I reported for military duty at the Naballah base where new weapons were presented to us. The army was getting ready for the Sinai action of the 1956 war. I started to renew my contact with Rivkah whom I loved. We went to the movies, to shows and I even took her to my place. In September 1956, Solel Boneh sent me to Eilat by plane. This was the first time that I flew in a Dakota. The flight took one hour and fifteen minutes and I was in the Solel Boneh barrack in Eilat. Solel Boneh was building the first hotel in Eilat, which was called the Queen Sheba Hotel. The barrack was extremely hot. To cool the place, pipes were placed in the windows through which cold water was running. This refreshed the room. The working day started at five o'clock in the morning when it was still cool. Later, a tender came to take us to eat breakfast and we returned to work. For lunch we were also driven. I ate supper at the restaurant. I also tiled the floors of several warehouses at the Timna mines. Then the Sinai action started.

From 1949 to 1956 the truce between Israel and the Arabs, enforced in part by the U.N. forces, was punctuated by raids and reprisals. Among the world powers, the United States, Great Britain and France sided with Israel, while the Soviet Union supported Arab demands. Tensions mounted during 1956 as Israel became convinced that the Arabs were preparing for war. The nationalization of the Suez Canal by Egypt's Gamal Abdel Nasser in July,

1956, resulted in the further alienation of Great Britain and France from Egypt. Both countries signed secret military agreements with Israel.

On October 29, 1956, Israeli forces led by Moshe Dayan attacked Egyptian forces in the Sinai Peninsula. Early Israeli successes were reinforced by an Anglo–French invasion along the canal. Although the action against Egypt was severely condemned by the nations of the world, the ceasefire of November 6, which was promoted by the United Nations with U.S. and Soviet support, came only after Israel had captured several key objectives, including the Gaza Strip and Sharm el Sheikh, which commanded the approaches to the Gulf of Aqaba. Israel withdrew from these positions in 1957, turning them over to the U.N. emergency force after access to the Gulf of Aqaba, without which Israel was cut off from the Indian Ocean, had been guaranteed.

I was immediately called up and ordered to report to a base in Eilat where I was to instruct soldiers in the use of new weapons. A special unit was created to protect Eilat and vicinity. Many of the construction workers were also in the reserve unit. Our job was to defend this strategic post. I was also instructed in the use of new weapons. We patrolled the area, especially the airfield of Eilat. The commander of the region, named Dani, had his headquarters near the airport. With the end of military operations, I was granted a liberty pass to fly north and spent time to recuperate. In December I was back in Eilat to finish the job. I returned north in January to my place and started to see Rivkah on a steady basis. In April 1957, I was sent by Solel Boneh to build houses in Beer Sheva for new immigrants. (They were part of the "Gomulka Aliyah.")

The Gomulka Aliyah refers to the Polish Jewish aliyah that started in 1955. Wladyslaw Gomulka was one of the leaders of the Polish Communist Party. He was the de facto leader of Poland from 1945 to 1948, and again from 1956 to 1970. Between 1945 and 1947, thousands of Polish Jews left Poland illegally and headed to Czechoslovakia and then to German, Austrian and Italian D.P. camps. Then, in the spring of 1947, the Polish borders were hermetically closed. Jews who wanted to leave Poland for Palestine had to obtain exit papers based on admission requests from the British Mandatory Administration in Palestine. Few Jews left Poland. Then a gradual increase in the number of applications and exit papers began. In 1955 2,500 Polish Jews were permitted to leave Poland and in 1956 19,000 Jews were permitted to leave. Overall in the late 1950s another 40,000 Jews left Poland.

I worked from Sunday to Friday in Beer Sheva and then went home for Shabbat where I met Rivkah. This continued for some time. During the week, we stayed at a rented room of Solel Boneh that paid premium payments and extra payments for food. I managed to save some money to pay back the loan that I took from Remler. I was then sent to work at Ashdod in the power plant. Other housing projects followed, namely in Rishon LeTzion and in Holon. Toward the end of 1957, we started to think of marriage. Rivkah worked for a textile company called "Hanko." She did not earn much but she managed to save.

[Page 315]

Chapter XIV
Building a Family

Rivkah Tenenbaum and Mordechai Lustig on their wedding day

Rivkah and I decided to concretize our relationship by establishing a family in spite of Hitler's plans for us. In 1958 we decided to get married and preparations began immediately. Rivkah rented a wedding dress that would have to be adjusted, and we selected invitation cards and ordered them printed. We took pictures on Tel Aviv's long Allenby Street. The wedding was scheduled to take place on February 28, 1958, at a wedding hall along Nachlat Benyamin Street. Relatives prepared and baked cakes and we prepared sandwiches and bought fruit. We invited family, friends from Sandz, from the Palmach, from the army, from my work place and from Rivkah's work place. The wedding went off smoothly and I was very happy to marry and settle down. We went on our honeymoon to Eilat. We then decided to travel to the community of Nahalal where my maternal niece Hannah lived. We spent the night at her place and then left to explore the city of Tiberias and Lake Kinneret. We continued our journey to Kibbutz Dafna where I met Rivkah's family. Esther and Mendel Nachshoni received us as well and we remained two days at the lovely kibbutz. We returned home and started to live the family life.

In April 1958, my uncle, Chaim Lustig from Brazil, and his wife traveled by boat to Israel. They stayed with a family from Sandz in Tel Aviv since our place was very small. The Lustigs brought us very nice gifts and bought a nice refrigerator for us. We visited our friends and had a good time with the Brazilian Lustigs. We really bonded with them.

November 30, 1959, was a very moving day for both me and my wife. We gave birth to our first child. I could not believe my eyes. I, the Shoah survivor, had a son. What a wonderful gift to us. A few months prior to this event, I bought a Vespa scooter to give us a bit of mobility. I also made arrangements with a cab driver to be on call when the moment arrived. Soon enough, when Rivkah said that she wanted to go to the hospital, the taxi arrived and took her to the hospital where she gave birth to our first child. On the eighth day, our son was circumcised at the hospital and was given the name of Moshe Lustig. We had a small party at the ceremony. Later in the day, I took a taxi and brought home the entire family. Rivkah from Kibbutz Brenner came to help the new mother. Of course, we had made many preparations for the baby. It was a bit crowded but the joy of having a child offset all difficulties.

I urged Rivkah to stop working and to stay at home to care for the baby. I resumed my flooring work. I bought an attachment to the Vespa so that I could take the baby and my wife for rides in the area or to visit family. I used my Vespa to get to work at Holon and even gave rides to my supervisor, Itzhak Klein.

In 1960, the mass murderer Adolf Eichmann was kidnapped in Argentina and flown to Israel aboard an El Al plane. He faced Israeli judges in Jerusalem where he had to defend himself, for his life was at stake. He faced serious charges of atrocities against the Jewish people. The Israeli police and Justice Department began to prepare the case against Eichmann. Ads appeared everywhere asking people to step forward and give testimony against Eichmann. Witnesses stepped forward who had personally seen his heinous activities. Masses of documents were accumulated and translated into Hebrew for the trial. Extreme precautions had to be installed at the prison to protect the prisoner from any harm. When all the preparations were finished, the trial began in Jerusalem. The prosecutor was Gideon Hausner and the defense lawyer was Robert Servatius, a German lawyer. Exception was granted to Eichmann to use a German lawyer who was not a member of the Israeli association of lawyers. Ironically, all judges understood and spoke German; some of them had even practiced law in Germany before they were dismissed from their jobs. The entire country was glued to the televised trial proceedings. The local and international press was in full attendance. The Shoah was presented in full force. Survivors and Jews in general saw for the first time what had taken place in Europe. Eichmann was found guilty and condemned to death. Of course he claimed that he was a mere small clerk but in reality had the power to send trains of people to their death. Eichmann appealed his verdict but the appeal was rejected. He was hung, cremated, and his ashes were scattered outside the territorial waters of the State of Israel.

Adolf Eichmann on trial in 1961 in Jerusalem, Israel

The trial brought back sad memories of my past. I had a friend from Sandz who worked at the police prison where Eichmann was kept and he told us that all the policeman had to restrain themselves from harming the prisoner. I watched the proceedings and saw my past in front of my eyes. I kept reminding myself that I was there and managed by some chance or miracle to survive. I also found some satisfaction that the man was brought to justice.

Prior to the capture of Eichmann, I had filed the necessary legal papers that were prepared by attorney Appelbaum against the German state. I sued for health damages that occurred to me during the period when I worked for the German authorities. The preparation of the papers took a long time and finally in 1961 I appeared before a medical commission that the German government had established in Israel. The commission established that I had a 40% disability as a result of the forced labor imposed on me during the war years. In 1962, the German government started to pay a monthly payment as well as a retroactive sum for the years past. Rivkah was again expecting and our place was very small. I began to think of expanding our flat by another room. My neighbor Witkowski added a room, a hallway and a balcony. I was thinking of doing the same thing and began implementing the idea of enlarging my apartment. I was short of cash so I took a bank loan and started my project. Work soon stopped since I was called to the reserves. I was now assigned to the armored corps instead of the infantry unit to which I used to belong. I was sent to special courses and had to undergo training. I was then stationed at the Hatzerim military base. My stay did not last long for I was soon transferred to the signal corps that would be my permanent reserve assignment.

On August 17, 1962, Rivkah gave birth to our second child, a daughter. We named her Yehudit. We were very happy with our children. We felt that they were the answer to those who had tried to eliminate us from the face of the earth. The children brought us great joy but we were crowded. I continued to build my extension since I received German reparation money that helped cover the cost of my expansion. I added a room that became the children's room. Rivkah was busy with the children and I devoted myself to the outside of the house. I planted several fruit trees and two Canadian pines. I seeded some grass and fenced in the entire garden. Later, I had to redo the entire garden when the city widened the road and took some of my garden and my pines.

Part of the German compensation consisted of sending me to a health spa each year. Rivkah, the children and I went usually to the Kibbutz Maaleh Hamisha near Jerusalem. I took the family on my Vespa and traveled to the resort. We traveled all over the country with the Vespa and even reached Kibbutz Dafna in the north of Israel. From 1964–1967 I continued to work at a big housing project in Holon. I worked on the basis of piecework. I started to work very early and returned home early. On one occasion I ran into Mordechai Goldfinger from Sandz who lived in London but was visiting Israel. I started to talk to him and mentioned that I had family in London. I mentioned the name of Nathan Lustig with whom I was once in contact. Goldfinger immediately replied that he knew him and gave me his address. I wrote Nathan a letter and he replied. We renewed our mail contacts.

With the tension rising in the Middle East, I was called up for reserve duty and reported to the Hatzerim base. I was assigned to guard the large military base. I was promoted to sergeant of the section and served in this capacity until the end of the Six Day War in 1967. Following the war, my uncle, Chaim Lustig, came to Israel. He stayed with us and we toured the country and saw many Sandzer friends in Israel. He helped me buy a Fiat car and we used the car extensively. We visited Jerusalem, Rehovot, Majdal Shams, and the Golan Heights. On our return home, the gearbox went near Ramat Gan and we came back home by taxi. The following year, I was called for reserve duty and the entire unit was sent to guard the military base in Rafidim in the Sinai desert. When not on guard duty, I toured the desert and saw the remnants of the Egyptian armor all over the place. I finished the tour of duty and returned home. I began to work on a housing project at Kiriat Bavli in Tel Aviv and later along Bari Street in 1971.

Rivkah Lustig, her son Moshe Lustig and Mordechai Lustig celebrating the Bar Mitzvah of Moshe

In December 1971, we celebrated the bar mitzvah of our son Moshe at the hall named "Oasis" in Ramat Gan. For us it was a very festive occasion and we invited family and friends. In 1973, my Uncle Chaim arrived from Brazil with his wife Ruth. They stayed with us. Chaim helped me financially to purchase a car that served us well during the family stay in Israel. We traveled and visited many friends and relatives. Then I was called up for reserve duty with the civil defense forces. The Yom Kippur War began and I used my car extensively during the war. I patrolled large areas in Tel Aviv with other reserve soldiers. The following year, Rivkah and I went to Tiberias for our annual vacation paid by the German government.

Mordechai Lustig and son Moshe Lustig in the Israeli armed forces

In 1976, Moshe Lustig was drafted and I was called up for reserve duty. I was in uniform and so was my son. With the end of reserve duty, I started working on a big project in Ramat Aviv that was finished in 1979. I then started to work for the "Azorim" building company that built expensive apartments with different color tiles. The company insisted on high building standards and I had to work very carefully, especially with the ceramics that contained pictures. In 1980, we joined an organized tour of Europe. We landed in Rome, Italy, travelled extensively through the country, entered Switzerland and continued to Paris, France. We continued to Belgium and Holland, and then returned to Calais in France where we took the ferry to England and reached London. Nathan Lustig and his wife received us nicely. We stayed with them for three days and enjoyed our stay. We then left for Israel.

From left to right; **Mordechai Lustig, Rivkah Lustig and Nathan Lustig**

In 1981, I was officially informed by the Israeli Ministry of Defense that I was hereby discharged from the reserve forces and from all other military obligations. I was sent an official form that informed me of my termination of military service. I continued to work for Solel Boneh, which was building a big and expensive project along King David Street in Tel Aviv. I worked at this project until 1985. Seven months prior to my retirement, I was promoted to foreman in charge of inspecting the finished apartments, especially the tiling of floors and ceramic walls. I had a crew of about 20 workers, mostly Arabs. The apartments were very expensive and some famous people moved in such as attorney Ram Caspi, Rafi Arzi, Professor Gur, Professor Laniado and others.

In March1985, our daughter Yehudit Lustig married her boyfriend Ilan Kaufman. We were in ecstasy. Our Lustig family continued to expand despite all the plans to destroy us. The wedding was held in a nice hall with many guests. It was a festive and happy occasion.

Yehudit Lustig and Eitan Kaufman on their wedding day

Following the marriage of my daughter, I retired from work at the age of 60. I devoted myself to my father–in–law who needed extensive medical help. I also began to develop my old hobbies that I never had time to tend to, namely woodcarving, playing the harmonica and the piano. Our first grandchild was born on April 1, 1981. He was named Alon. We catered a very nice affair for the occasion. Several years later, I was in Poland when our daughter gave birth to another grandchild who was named Lital. I had organized a party in Sandz, the place where my family was wiped out, to celebrate the rejuvenation of our family. My daughter's family continued to grow as she gave birth to Sivan June 13,1998. The following year, we celebrated the bar mitzvah of our grandson Alon.

I was now fully retired and busy with my hobbies. While sitting in the park, I began to talk to a retired electrical worker. We talked about everything and then he told me that he has been several times to the studios of Golan Globus in Nevei Ilan near Jerusalem where he was used in pictures. He asked me if I was interested in working for the movies and, if so, would I come along with him. I replied in the affirmative. We went to the company office in Tel Aviv and registered. The next day, we were already driven by bus to Nevei Ilan. Since that day, I have been called to the studio to appear in movies and advertisements. I participated in many movies and ads starting in 1984. A full list of the movies in which I took part appears in the appendix chapter where there is also a partial list of the famous actors with whom I worked.

In 1981, I received from the Israeli Defense Ministry a form that informed me that I was hereby discharged from all future military formations

I also became a member of the board of the retired Solel Boneh construction workers. I helped with the administrative chores and attended the various executive meetings. I became the chairman of the Sandzer landsmanschaft in Israel where I prepare the annual memorial ceremony for the Jews who were killed in Sandz by the Germans and their helpers. To keep myself physically fit, I joined a swimming pool to do exercises.

From left to right: **Mordechai Lustig, Aviva Kaduri, Moshe Lustig and Rivkah Lustig**

In 1989, Rivkah and I joined an organized trip to Poland. My first visit to the old homestead. When the group reached Krakow, we rented a car with a chauffeur who drove us to Sandz. On the way we stopped at the hamlet of Mszane Dolne and in our village of Slomka where my grandfather had lived. The house was gone; according to a neighbor, Franciszek Antusz, the house burned down during the war. The place is still empty. Franciszek remembered me as a child who had spent his summer vacations at the village. The neighbors received us very nicely. I spoke Polish with them. We established and maintain contact to this day. We then headed to Sandz where I visited the cemetery and the memorial for the killed Jews. I did not think, I just stood and cried; tears were flowing. We left Sandz and headed to Krynica, Fibnicza and Ritro where I worked after the liquidation of the Jewish community of Sandz. We continued our trip to Stary Sacz, Roznow where we built the dam on the river, and returned to our hotel in Krakow. I paid the driver 40 American dollars. I took pictures all along the trip. I was sadly disappointed in Sandz by the area of the former Jewish ghetto. Some houses were gone, others were changed. I did not get the feeling of being in the ghetto area.

At last, Moshe met and married Avivva Kaduri. They were married in August 2002. The wedding took place at the "Recital" hall in Ramat Gan. The Israeli television and radio personality Judy Moses photographed the entire wedding and then used parts of it in her television programs dealing with young couples. Of course, we also took our own pictures of the wedding. We were very happy that both of our children were happily married.

Rivkah and Mordechai Lustig in Brazil

In April 2003, I received an invitation from Luis Lustig, the son of Chaim Lustig, to attend the bar mitzvah of his son Daniel Lustig. He sent us tickets and insisted that everything was paid for and we only had to show up. Rivkah and I flew to Frankfurt and then took a Brazilian plane to Sao Paulo. The plane could not land since there was a heavy fog. We were diverted to Rio de Janeiro where we waited for four hours on the tarmac. Finally, the plane left for San Paulo where Luis and his son were waiting for us. He drove us to our hotel named "Harmonia," situated along Harmonia Street. Daniel put on tefilim or phylacteries on Friday at the reform synagogue in San Paulo. We missed the opening session due to a heavy fog and arrived late. Saturday afternoon we prayed at the synagogue, the early afternoon and evening prayers, then we lit candles to signify the end of the sabbath. The regal party then started: dancing, singing, beverages were flowing and food was unlimited. The next day, Luis then took us to Rio de Janeiro and we spent three lovely days in the city. I visited a friend from Israel, Ben Zion Katz, who was already in a wheel chair but his family was happy to receive us. In San Paulo I met Hillel Landau and his wife Eva from Sandz.

Luis took us to his farm, about an hour and a half drive from his residence in Sao Paulo. The place is located on top of an elevated plateau. There are two buildings there: one is for the caretaker family. The place grows vegetables, fruit and various trees. The main house has two bedrooms with toilet facilities, a kitchen, a sauna, a rest room and a swimming pool and a piano. In the city of Sao Paulo he has a building where his office is located. He also grows coffee plants. In San Magdelena he has a house where the apartments are rented to residents. The place is guarded. The family also has a summer home facing the sea. There we met his maternal uncle, Samuel Frukesh. Rivkah and I were also invited to a Friday night dinner at Ismael Kalpatz's home. The entire family was there. He has been recently widowed. We visited the cosmetic plant of Neta and Markus Silva. We also met Dvorah, daughter of the late Stabskis from the Palmach. We had a very nice time and spent 25 days in Brazil. We left for Switzerland but had small delays and continued to Israel. Our luggage arrived a day late.

Rivkah and Mordechai Lustig with their grandchildren Ed and Omri

Aviva and Moshe gave birth to their first son Ed, December 20, 2004. He was soon joined by a younger brother, Omri, who was born June 7, 2006.

In between the births of Moshe's sons, our oldest grandchild Alon was drafted in 2005 into the army, the third generation soldier of the State of Israel.

Alon Kaufman drafted into the Israeli army

[Page 335]

Chapter XV
Active Retirement

In 1990, the Association of Sandzer Jews in Israel organized a tour to Sandz in Poland. The delegation was large and was headed by the president of the group, Chaim Bromfeld. The late Rabbi Pinchas Rosengarten, a native of Sandz and former chaplain of the Jewish soldiers in the Polish Army under the command of General Wladyslaw Anders, escorted us and provided excellent explanations regarding the Jews of Sandz. He knew his Jewish history Rabbi Rosengarten survived the war in the Soviet Union. When the Polish government and the Soviet government decided to establish a Polish Army in Russia he was invited to assume the post of Jewish military chaplain of the Polish army. The army headed by Anders eventually left Russia and reached Palestine where it began to train and later joined the British 8th Army in Africa.

The late Rabbi Pinchas Rosengarten in Polish uniform, rabbi in the Anders Army and was able to coherently explain historical facts

The group was also escorted by the Israeli television personality Zvi Slepon and scriptwriter Israel Winer. They extensively filmed the city and later produced a historical documentary entitled "There Were Once Jews in Sandz." The movie was also shown on Israeli television. In Sandz, I met the sons of the late righteous Krol who saved six members of the Steilauf family during the war. They took the entire delegation to the actual site where the family was hidden. We visited a few concentration camps. We then saw a movie that portrayed the suffering of the Jews during the war. I appeared in several scenes in the movie. The Polish press took an interest in our visit and published items about our visit. We were also invited to the mayor's office where Rabbi Rosengarten delivered a lengthy historical lecture in flawless Polish on Jewish contributions to the city of Sandz. The entire event was filmed and presented on Israeli television. While in Poland I met members of the Karol family. We returned back to Israel where the documentary film about Sandzer Jews was being finished. On completing the film, the Sandzer Jews in Israel were invited to attend the official screening of the film about Jews in Sandz at the Museum of the Diaspora in Tel Aviv.

With the end of the war with Iran, Iraq invaded Kuwait and took control of the oil fields. The United States and other countries could not let this situation continue and declared war on Iraq. Saddam Hussein warned the allies that he would "burn half of Israel" if they attacked Iraq. The threat had to be taken seriously. The IDF was concerned at the availability to Saddam Hussein of considerable quantities of Russian–made Scud missiles with a range of 600 kms., against which no effective countermeasure was as yet in Israel's arsenal; particularly if those missiles were to be equipped with chemical warheads, which Saddam was reputed to have perfected with the help of German companies.

On the night of January 17/18, 1991, coalition air forces attacked Iraq. In response, Iraq fired salvos of ground–to–ground missiles into Israel. Over a period of more than one month, approximately 38 Iraqi versions of Scud missiles fell (33 El Hussein missiles and 5 El Tijara missiles) in 19 missile attacks. These missiles mainly hit the greater Tel Aviv region, mainly Ramat Gan and Haifa, although Western Samaria and the Dimona area were also hit by missiles. Directly, these attacks caused two civilian deaths, although indirectly, they caused heavy damages.

I lived in one of the targeted areas but we escaped without harm from the missiles that hit our area. On September 28, 1993, I met the famous producer Steven Spielberg who was finishing the last shots of his movie entitled "Schindler's List." He invited my wife and myself to participate in the movie and asked us to come to Jerusalem where we spent the night at the Zion Hotel overlooking the walls of the old city. We were also invited to supper at the King David Hotel where we met some of the main actors such as Ben Kingsley who participated in the film. The event was very impressive and memorable. Some other Sanzder survivors were also there such as Samek Teitelbaum, Mordchai Blauzenstein and Basha Hendler. The next morning we had breakfast at the hotel, and then the entire group went to the Christian cemetery of Jerusalem where Oskar Schindler is buried. Spielberg ordered the film crew to film the entire event as we approached the grave arm in arm.

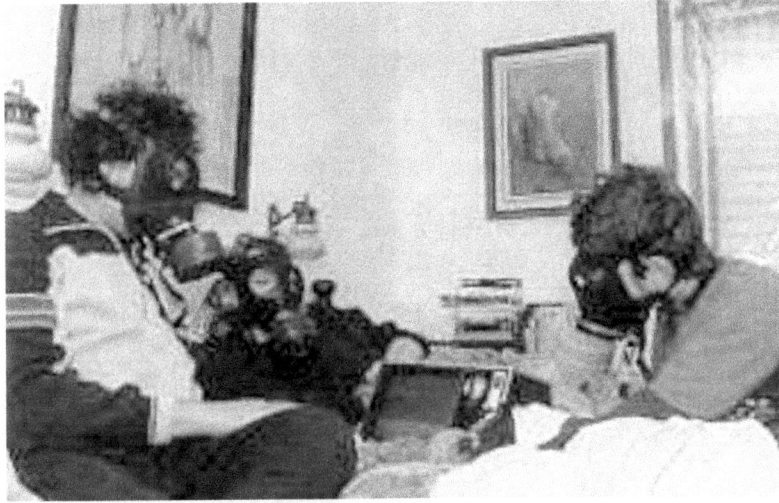

People sitting in a so–called safe room with gas masks on their face during the missile attacks

On July 20, 1995, Rivkah and I joined a tour that went to Austria, Hungary, Czechoslovakia and Munich, Germany. I was familiar with Munich, having spent some time following the war in the city. We left Munich by ourselves and headed to Salzburg, Bad Ischl, Linz, Edelsberg and Ebensee. Places where I suffered and starved daily. The places brought back sad and tragic memories, especially the last place where I was liberated in May 6, 1945. While traveling to the Ebensee concentration camp I ran into an old buddy from the Palmach days, Alex Sral and his wife Sara. We exchanged small talk and then headed to the memorial. I recorded the place on video. We then headed to Vienna where we spent the night and then headed to the Melk concentration camp where I had endured hell. We visited the place and recorded the visit. I even bought a book about the camp in German. We then left for Israel.

I returned to Poland in 1994 with the committee of Sandzer Jews in Israel to bring special inscribed panels that were attached to the entrance of the famous synagogue in Sandz. At the ceremony, the mayor of Sandz and other important Polish officials participated and the Polish press described the entire event. Rivkah and I then extensively toured Sandz, Krynica, Lublin, Biala Podlaski, Janow Podlaska and Warsaw. We returned home and began to renovate our house, especially the kitchen.

**Rivkah Lustig, Steven Spielberg and Mordechai
Lustig at the King David Hotel**

In 1996 we joined an organized tour of the United States and Canada. We landed in New York, headed to Washington, D.C., then to Philadelphia, Boston and Toronto. We flew from Toronto to Buffalo, then to the Grand Canyon and Las Vegas. We reached Los Angeles by plane and headed to San Francisco. We then flew to Orlando, Palm Beach, Miami and New York. Exhausted, we flew back home. The next year we took a small tour to Turkey that included Anatolia, Istanbul, Izmir, Kusha and Dashi. The same year, 1997, we were invited to participate in a special reception for the famous righteous Pole, Jerzy Bielecki, who came to Israel. The reception received headlines, for Bielecki was a great hero but never pushed himself to the forefront.

**From right to left: Rivka Lustig, Mordechai Lustig, at the memorial.
Alex Sral and the guide at Ebensee concentration camp**

Mordechai Lustig with Jerzy Bielecki

Jerzy Bielecki   **Cyla Cybulska**

Jerzy Bielecki and Cyla Cybulska during the war

Jerzy Bielecki was arrested by the Gestapo on suspicion of belonging to the Polish resistance. He was sent to the Auschwitz concentration camp. He spoke German and slowly reached a position that enabled him to plan his daring escape. Dressed as an S.S. officer he supposedly took his friend Cyla Cybulska to be interrogated. They escaped from the camp in 1944. They walked at night until they reached a relative's home who took them to Krakow. Here they were separated for safety reasons. He remained in Krakow and she was sent to a farm. Both survived the war but did not meet again until 1993. He went to live in Nowy Targ, Poland. She met and married David Zacharowicz. They moved to Sweden and then to the United States.

The next year, the association of Palmach veterans organized a parade in the streets of Jerusalem. I took part in the parade in Jerusalem of the veterans of the Palmach headed by Zvi Zamir in 1998. Prior to the parade, I met former comrades in arms who brought back many pleasant and unpleasant memories. I met a number of people who I had not seen for a long time. The next year we went to Scandinavia and sailed on a ferry along the coast to Finland. Helsinki was a nice city and we continued our trip to Norway and Denmark.

On May 9, 2000, I was invited to participate in the celebration of the defeat of Germany at Yad Vashem in Jerusalem under the auspices of the Prime Minister of the State of Israel, Ehud Barak. The ceremony was very impressive and I saw many veterans who participated in the fight against

Germany. The prime minister was kind enough to permit me to have my picture taken with him. We returned to Poland the next year where we erected tombstones for my dear family that was murdered by the Nazis. They were buried in a mass grave at the Jewish cemetery in Sandz. I ordered the erection of a white marble headstone to be executed while I was in Israel. I continued my trip in Poland to Krynica and Lublin where I met the righteous gentile Stefan Mazor who saved the Jewish girl, Berta Kornman, in the clock tower of the municipal building of Sandz. She was no longer alive. I was in contact with him until he died.

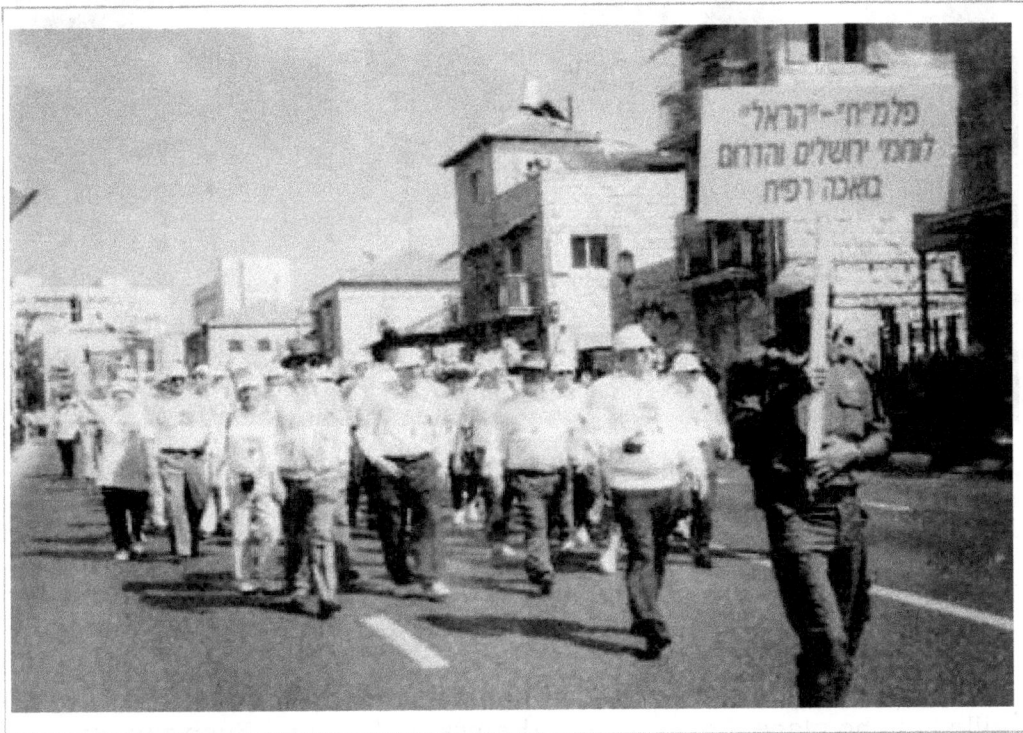

Palmach veterans parading under the leadership of Zvi Zamir

In July 2007 we left again for Poland and landed in Warsaw where we had a reservation at the Halupa Hotel. We stayed three days in the capital and proceeded to the resort place called Czehocinek located in the northwest of Poland. We remained one week at the resort where we had a nice time. We then left for the Victoria Hotel in Lublin where we met some friends. Roman took us to Lanalczow where we spent a nice day and ended by inviting everybody to supper at the Shalom restaurant. The next day we left for Rzeszow and lodged at the "Hatman" Hotel. There we met some of the people who had worked very hard to erect a Jewish memorial at the death camp of Pustkow near the city of Debice. The Polish government had erected Polish and Russian monuments right after the war but no Jewish monument despite the fact that the number of Jewish killed at the camp was the largest.

Prime Minister of Israel and Mordechai Lustig at Yad Vashem in Jerusalem

I first met Marek Kszenzor and Janusz Korbacki and his wife Annia. She immediately called Waclaw Wiezibienec, a Judaica professor. The latter arrived the next morning, escorted by two students and he interviewed me along the road to the site. From the road to the memorial of Pustkow were many stairs. I lit a memorial candle and recited the Kaddish for the thousands of Jews who were killed at the place. I also recited the prayer El Malei Rachmim or merciful God. About 10 days prior to my arrival at Pustkow, the Jewish memorial was dedicated in a very impressive official ceremony that included the planting of trees for Moshe Oyster, Asher Laor Lamansdorf and myself. We spent some time with our friends and then went to visit the city of Lancut where we visited the castle of Graf Potocki. We returned to the city of Rzeszow and spent time with our friend Tadeusz Pienta and his wife who were the main pushers of the Jewish memorial at Pustkow. We took pictures and they presented me with a pine sapling that they would plant in my honor at the Pustkow memorial. We said goodbye and left for Sandz where municipal officials were waiting with a proposal. They wanted to send a delegation of three officials to Israel to interview Sandzer Jews in order to publish a book on Jews in Sandz. There was only one problem: there was no money for the project. I even met the deputy city mayor regarding the money problem but the subject was dropped. I gave several interviews, notably to "Gazeta Wyborcza", "Nasz Beskid" and the local paper. I again met with the righteous Poles in the city, namely the Karol family and the Jewish woman Anna Kriegel and her husband Eduard Leszinski.We left Sandz and headed to the spa of Krynica to rest for 10 days at the "Levigrad" Hotel. As we were leaving, Yehuda, the son of Samek bar Ilan, showed up with his wife and mother–in–law and the driver Wacek. We all piled into the car and headed to Krakow where we had ice cream and promenaded in the city. We then left for our hotel, packed and headed to the airport. We passed the customs office and boarded a plane for Warsaw where we took the flight to Israel.

Meeting old friends from Sandz at Yad Vashem in Jerusalem

On June 1, 2008, the Israeli Ministry of Defense invited all soldiers who participated in the War of Independence of 1948 to be honored by their presence at the artistic ceremony dedicated to them. Following the ceremony, certificates were distributed to each of the participating soldiers in the war. I met many former Palmach soldiers, members of the 6th Battalion and other soldiers who I knew. We reminisced about the past. In July we again left Israel for Poland. We landed in Warsaw and proceeded to a well–known spa called Srodborowianka, near Otwock. The trip lasted about one hour. The Jewish–owned place was renowned as a Jewish rest home prior to the war. Presently there was a Jewish organization named Shalom in Warsaw that tended to Jewish war veterans. The head of the organization was Albert Herman who was also in charge of the spa. About 90 percent of the visitors were Jews. The prices were very reasonable, 150 zlotys per day for full pension. We remained at the resort two weeks. Occasionally we visited Warsaw or Otwock. We walked a great deal at the resort that is located in a forest. With us was the Fuchs

family and a few other families from Ramat Gan. Most of the visitors were
Jews from all over Europe. There were also non–Jews. Each Friday night,
candles were lit, the blessing over the wine was made. Traditional Jewish
meals were served that included carp, chicken soup, Challah. Songs were
sung at the tables and once there was even a Jewish singer from the Warsaw
Jewish Theater. We spent 11 days at the resort and left for Ciechocinek pod
Teurzeniami, which we had already visited in the past. The place served three
full meals each day, and provided daily entertainment and dances. We walked
about in the place. After a week we left the place. We took a taxi and headed
for Warsaw and checked in at the Chalupa Hotel. On Saturday we went to the
famous Nozyk Synagogue.

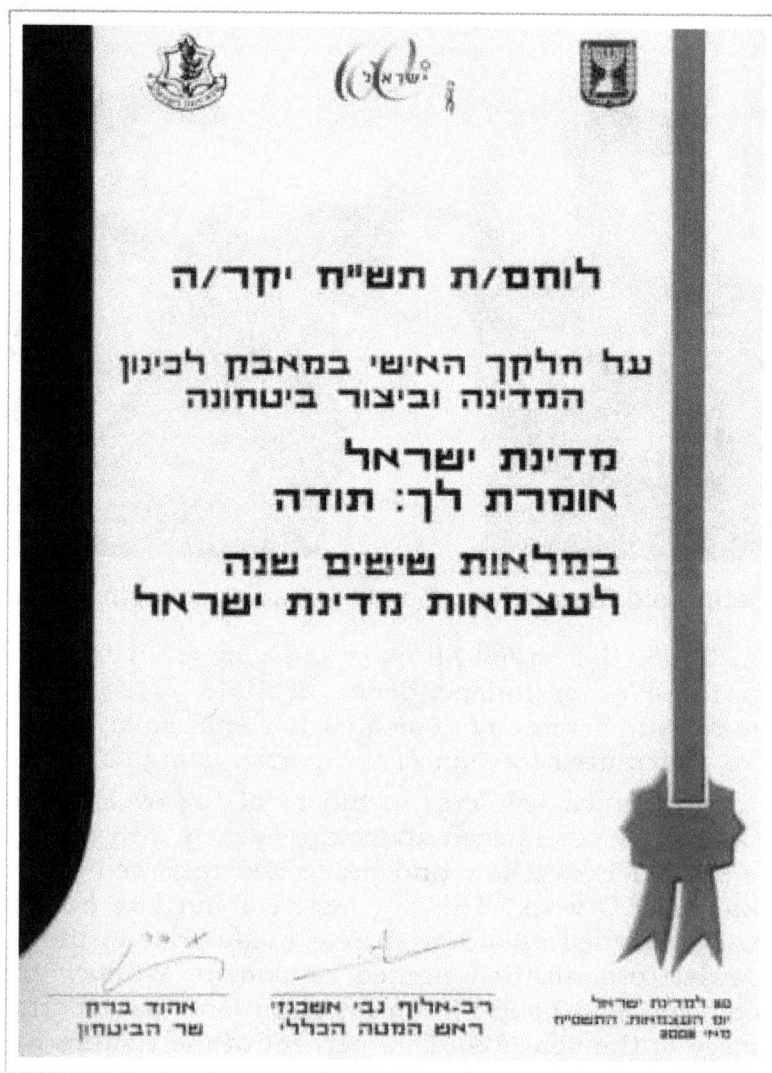

**Certificate issued by the Defense Ministry to all participants
in the War of Independence**

Nozyk Synagogue in Warsaw Poland
(Yad Vashem Archives)

The Nożyk Synagogue is the only surviving prewar Jewish synagogue in Warsaw, Poland. There were about 400 synagogues in 1939. It was built in 1898–1902 and was restored after World War II. It is still operational and currently houses the Warsaw Jewish Commune, as well as other Jewish organizations.

While we attended services, there was a bar mitzvah party. The official Jewish ritual slaughterer of Warsaw, a converted Christian, dressed as a Hasid in Bnei Brak was celebrating his son's bar mitzvah. There were about 40 people in the synagogue. Following the services, the congregants were offered wine and cakes. Then everybody was invited to go to the nearby restaurant where a traditional meal was served on paper plates. Cold and hot dishes were available as well as beer, vodka and cola. We also visited Stalin's building in Warsaw. He gave the building as a gift to Poland. We also saw the international dance festival held in Warsaw. We then flew home.

Mordechai Lustig with the honorable Polish Ambassador Agniedzka Magdzach at Yad Vashem in 2009

Mordechai Lustig with Judge Bach and Roman Jagiello at Yad Vashem

Yad Vashem in Jerusalem invited us to the official ceremony in 2009 that celebrated the defeat of Germany by the Allies. Many surviving veterans who participated in the war were present as were members of the diplomatic corps, including the Polish ambassador to Israel, the honorable Agnieszka Magdzach. She was kind enough to consent to have her picture taken with me. She placed a wreath of flowers at the memorial.

Later the same year we flew to Poland for the eighth time. We landed in Krakow and headed for Sandz. We prepared an exact plan for this trip. On Friday evening we would meet Anna, on Saturday morning we would meet Lesniak and Koltz. For lunch we made a reservation with Koltz. On Sunday we would visit the cemetery where 400 Jews are buried, including my parents, sister and brother. I planned to light candles in their memory and recite Kaddish for them. I also intended to visit the grave of the late rabbi Chaim Halberstam. I planned to visit the Meleck family. For lunch, I wanted to meet the Tokaz family and for supper the righteous Laura Kozik and her brother Artur Karol. Everything went according to plan in Sandz. We then left for Mszana Dolna and from there to Slomka where my grandfather had lived. We had a good time with the grandchildren of my grandfather's neighbors' children. On Tuesday we met the mayor of Sandz and thanked him for placing a memorial plaque for the Jews of Sandz who were killed in the action of April 29, 1942. The plaque was placed in the center of the Jewish ghetto. The meeting and the event were publicized in the local press. On Wednesday we were invited to the Lewowska museum. We were escorted by the daughter of Rutenberg who is married to a Russian woman. The latter was very active in cultural activities in the city. She also lectures on art and was writing a book. The next day Koltz took us to breakfast. We left for Krynica later in the day. We remained at the spa for 15 days and enjoyed ourselves. One day I received a telephone call from Marcin Kowalski that I was needed in Sandz where they were shooting a movie and they wanted to take shots with me in the special places like the ghetto of Sandz, the place where I lived in Sandz. When the shooting was done, we went to eat and they drove me back to Krynica. We left the place and headed to Zakopane where the movie crew continued to shoot our movements throughout the city. The filming continued at the hotel in Krakow, at the Plaszow concentration camp site and at the Schindler place. We were then returned to the Schindler place where a ceremony was conducted by the famous Jagielonski University prior to the opening of the Schindler Museum in Krakow. The university wanted to create authenticity by presenting me at the ceremony as having survived the place. The film crew also included this event and asked me to describe the conditions in Plaszow and at Schindler's place. Following the interview they drove us to the Eden Hotel. The crew presented us with a book entitled "The Legends of Krakow." We then left for home. Shortly thereafter, the Polish film crew came to Israel to continue shooting scenes of us in Israel. In 2010, we were notified that the documentary was finished. It runs for about a half an hour. I was presented with a copy of the film. The film was sold to the city of Sandz.

In March 2010, I received an invitation from the city of Krakow asking me to attend the official opening of the Oskar Schindler Museum in Krakow. The event would take place June 10, 2010 and all expenses would be paid by the municipality of Krakow. We flew to Warsaw and then took a plane to Krakow where a car awaited us. We were driven to the Krakowia Hotel. We dressed and went to the restaurant where we were invited to join the assistant mayor of the city. We ate and then proceeded to the opening of the museum. About a thousand guests arrived to partake in the event. Many Jewish delegations from Israel and other countries arrived. Yad Vashem in Jerusalem was represented by Avner Shalev, head of the institution. Speeches were made by several people, while a film describing Jewish life in Krakow under the German occupation was shown. Then the mayor and the director of the museum removed the veil at the entrance to the museum and a group of us were directed to be the first visitors of the museum. The mayor professor Jacek Maichrowski and the director of the museum, Magister Michael Neizabitowski, received us. The audience applauded us and then the crowd entered the museum. Following the visit, we were invited to a very nice reception where there was an abundance of food and beverages. On the way out, I gave some interviews to the press and was driven to the hotel. The next day, we had breakfast and then were driven back to the museum where they screened a film that I participated in. The film dealt with Schindler and Jewish life in Krakow under the occupation. We had lunch at a famous restaurant in the center of the city with the mayor and his assistant, Krzysztow Gruner. We were driven back to the hotel. We also had supper with a municipal official. The next day was very hot and we spent it resting. In the afternoon we were driven to the airport and left the city for Frankfurt and then Tel Aviv.

Later this year, we returned to Poland and headed to Sandz where we visited the Jewish cemetery and lit a candle. I recited the Kaddish for the death souls. We then met the mayor, Riszard Nowak, and his deputy, Jerzy Gwizdz, newspapermen, the head of the local college and some righteous people. We then left for the village of Slomka near Mszana Dolna. We continued our trip to Krynica, Lublin, Biala–Podolska, Zamosc, Tomaszow Lubelski and Bełżec.

The Lustigs at the opening of the Oskar Schindler Museum in Krakow

Belzec extermination camp

Memorial at the site of the extermination camp at Bełżec

Belzec in the district of Lublin started out as a slave labor camp in 1940. It was then converted into a massive extermination camp. It is estimated that 500,000 to 600,000 people were killed in the camp, mostly Galician Jews including the Jews of Sandz and vicinity. The extermination camp operated from March 17, 1942, to the end of December 1942. With the German military defeats in the east, the S.S. decided to dig up the buried corpses and disposed of them. They exhumed the bodies and burned them on five open–air grids and bone crushing continued until March 1943 and back to Lublin. We then left for the spa of Srodborowianka near Otwock. Marcin Kowalski, who made a film about us a year ago, arrived there. The movie, entitled in Polish Statista or "silent actor," was awarded third place at the international documentary festival in 2011. He took us to his estate in Kruszwica, a distance of about 250 kilometers from the spa. He insisted that we should be his guests at a party in honor of his marriage of 10 years. The party was impressive with many family guests and his two children. He gave original films that he made of me and some nice individual shots. The next day, he and his small son took us sightseeing. Indeed a beautiful place. We ate lunch and then Krzystow Smith took us back to the Srodborowianka spa. There we met some acquaintances from two years earlier. On Friday night, candles were lit, Kiddush over the wine was made, followed by a traditional Jewish meal that included fish, chicken soup with noodles, chicken, tea and cake. Songs were sung. We had a very nice time. The vacation ended, we flew back home where our children awaited us. We were exhausted but felt good. I decided to stop working in the movies. I now decided to retire at last.

This is my story of a Jewish individual who was lucky to survive and tell his story. I cannot give advice or direction of how I survived for I do not know. I was not the smartest or the bravest or the strongest, yet I managed to survive all the hardships and resume life and build a family in Israel that would continue Jewish history.

The Lustigs at their granddaughter Sivan's bat mitzvah

Mordechai Lustig with his son's family

[Page 376]

Chapter XVI
Pictorial Chapter of Sandz

Mordechai Lustig returns to Sandz

Mordechai Lustig, center, escorted by his grandson Alon on the right visit the farm of Mszana Dolne where he spent his summers with his grandfather

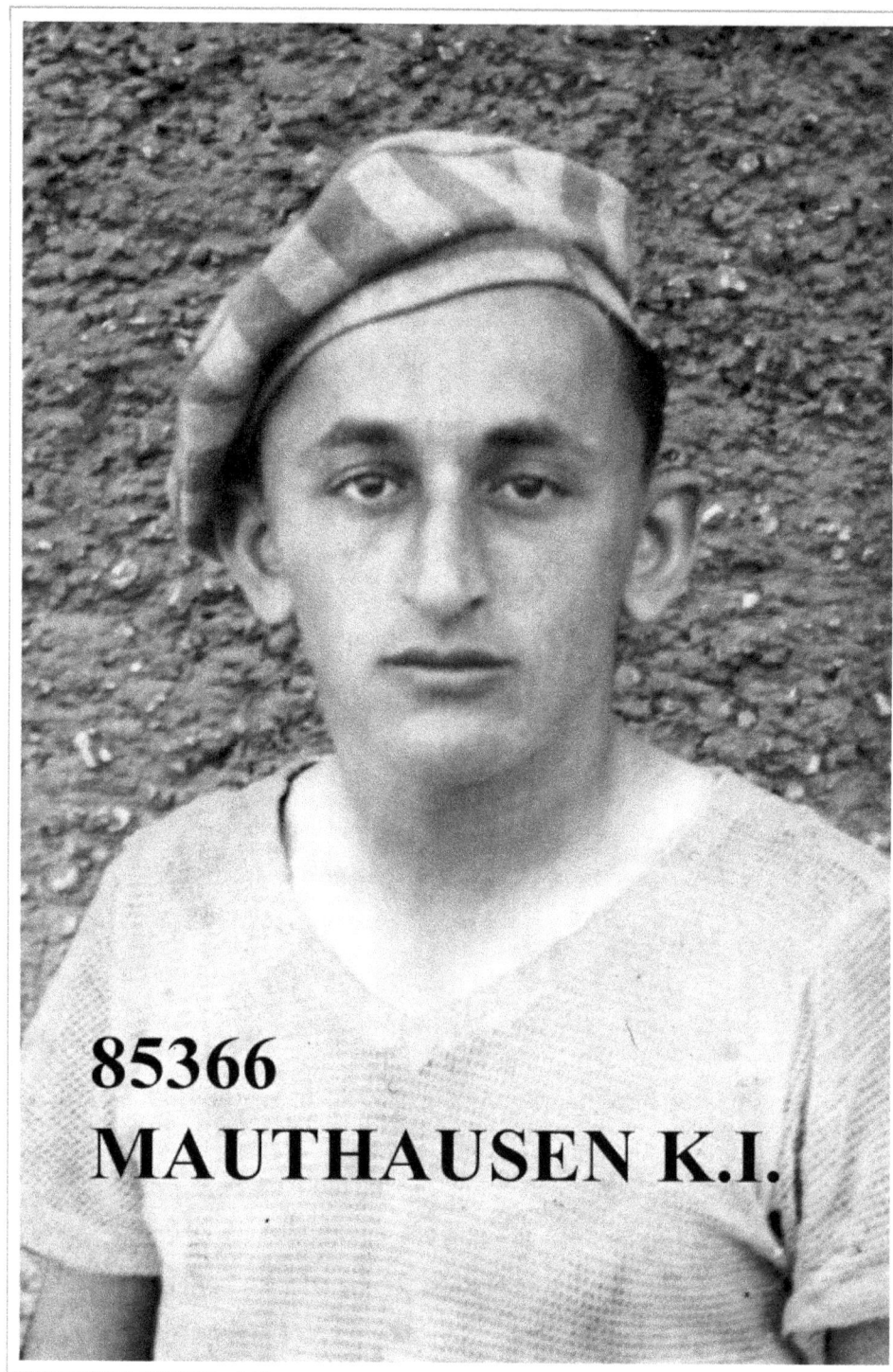

Mordechai Lustig liberated in 1945

The great synagogue still stands
(Photograph donated by Jean Krieser of Paris, France)

The Great Synagogue in Nowy Sacz was built around 1780, near the Royal Castle. It was commonly referred to as a Magistrate synagogue (Grodzka synagogue). It burned down in 1894 but fortunately it was restored through great efforts. During World War II it was transferred by Germans into a warehouse. When the war ended, the building returned to the Kraków municipality. In 1974 it was passed on to the city. The art gallery exhibiting the objects of Jewish culture (judaica) was created after the major renovation and adaptation of the building in 1982. There is a memorial tablet in memory of 25,000 exterminated Jews, founded by Ziomkowstwo Sądeczan in Israel. Nowadays the old synagogue is the seat of the branch of the Regional Museum in Nowy Sacz. It houses the old and modern art and is also used as a concert hall because of its excellent acoustics. Moreover, it contains a permanent exhibition concerning the history of Jews in Nowy Sącz entitled 'They were here among us'. The synagogue, which long housed a museum, is being used once again for religious Jewish services by Hassidim visiting the tombs of the Tzaddik Haim Halberstam and his descendants in the Jewish cemetery.

Main entrance to the Great Synagogue
(Photograph donated by Jean Krieser of Paris, France)

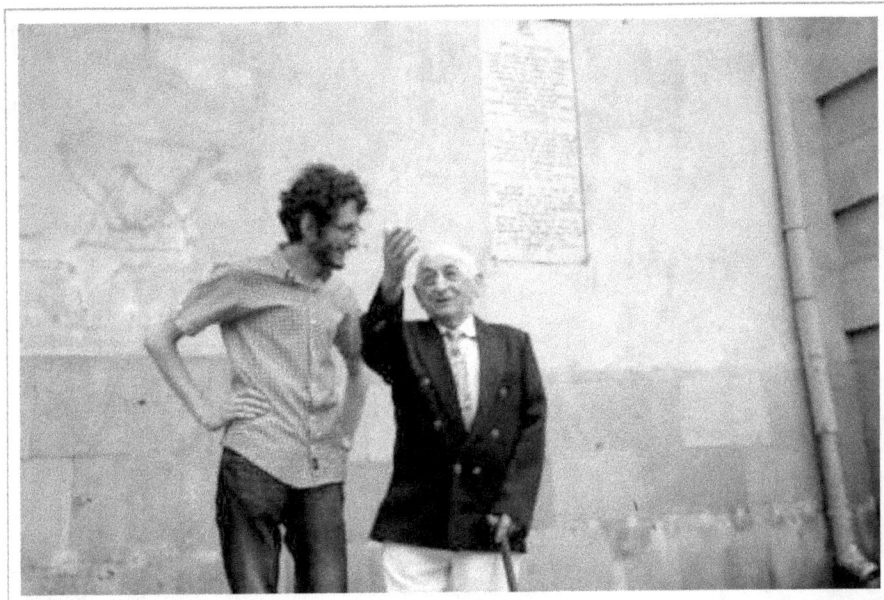

Mordechai Lustig with Lukadz Polonski local historian in front of memorial plaque honoring the Jews of Sandz. The Plaque is written in Polish, Hebrew and Yiddish, and dedicated to the 25,000 Jews that lived in Sandz and vicinity and were murdered by the Germans.
(Photograph donated by Edita Zajac of Nowy Sacz)

The Hassidic court of Bobow is an offshoot of the main Hassidic dynasty established by Rabbi Haim Halberstam in Sandz. The city became a center of Hassidism in Poland and provided the city with a sizable income for the Hassidim visited their rabbi and spent time and money in Sandz. Rabbi Halberstam had many sons who became rabbis in their turn and formed Hassidic courts. The Sandzer Hassidic movement expanded with time and became a mass movement mainly in Galicia, Poland. Most of the Hassidic movement and their rabbis were exterminated by the Germans during the war. Some Hassidic disciples survived the war and re–established the Bobower Hassidic movement namely in the United States, Israel and in Belgium.

The Bobower rabbi is related to the Sandzer hassidut, at the entrance to the Great Synagogue where memorial services would be held in memory of the Jewish victims of Sandz who the Germans and their helpers killed during World War II.

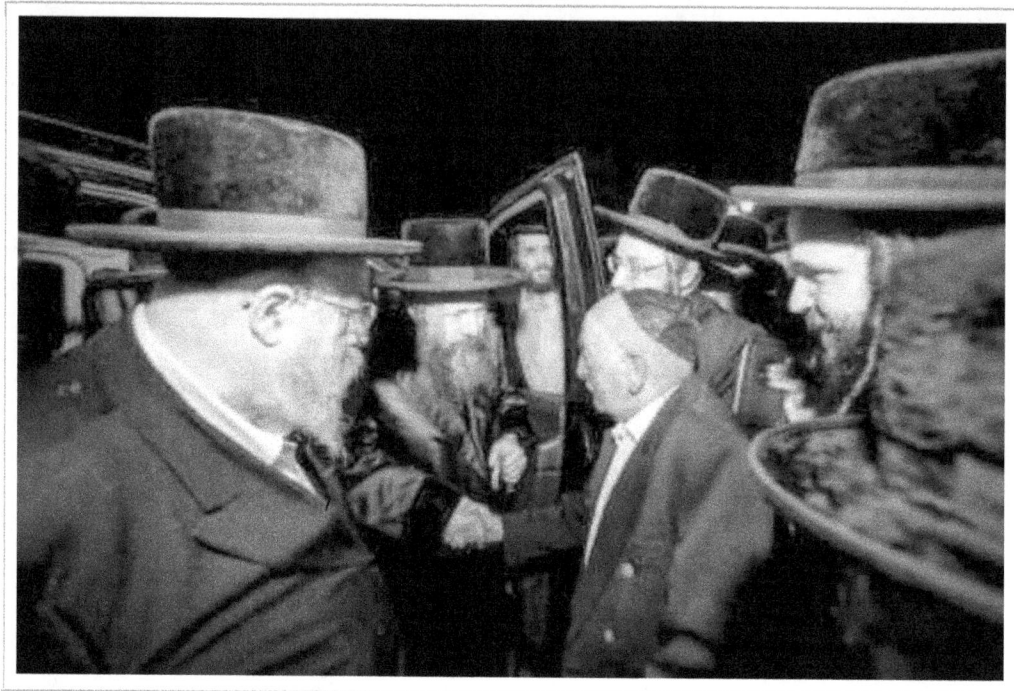

Mordechai Lustig greets the Bobower Rabbi, spiritual leader of the Bobower Hasidim who came to participate in the memorial services for the Jews of Sandz who were killed during World War Two by the Germans and their helpers. The memorial ceremony would take place at the Great Synagogue.

Rabbi Haim Halberstam

Rabbi Haim Halberstam was born in 1793, in Tarnogród, Poland. His father was Aryeh Leib Halberstam who was the head of the religious court of Tarnograd. He was a pupil of Rabbi Moshe Yehoshua Heshl Orenstein and the Rebbe, Rabbi Naftali Zvi of Ropshitz. His first rabbinical position was in the hamlet of Rudnik. In 1830 he was appointed as the town rabbi of Sandz, (Polish; *Nowy Sącz*) where he founded the Sandzer Hassidic dynasty. He attracted many followers and students, due to his piety and great Talmudic knowledge. His great work was "The *Divrei Haim*" or words of Haim was published in Sandz. He remained in the city for the rest of his life and passed on April 19, 1876. He was succeeded by his son Awraham Halberstam. The Hassidut of Sandz has been succeeded nowadays by the Sandz–Klausenberg, Sandz–Zmigrod and Bobov Hassidic dynasties.

Mordechai Lustig proceeds to the prayer hall surrounded by Bobower Hassidim

Mordechai Lustig seated at the memorial service in the synagogue

Mordechai Lustig describes the liquidation of the Jewish population of Sandz

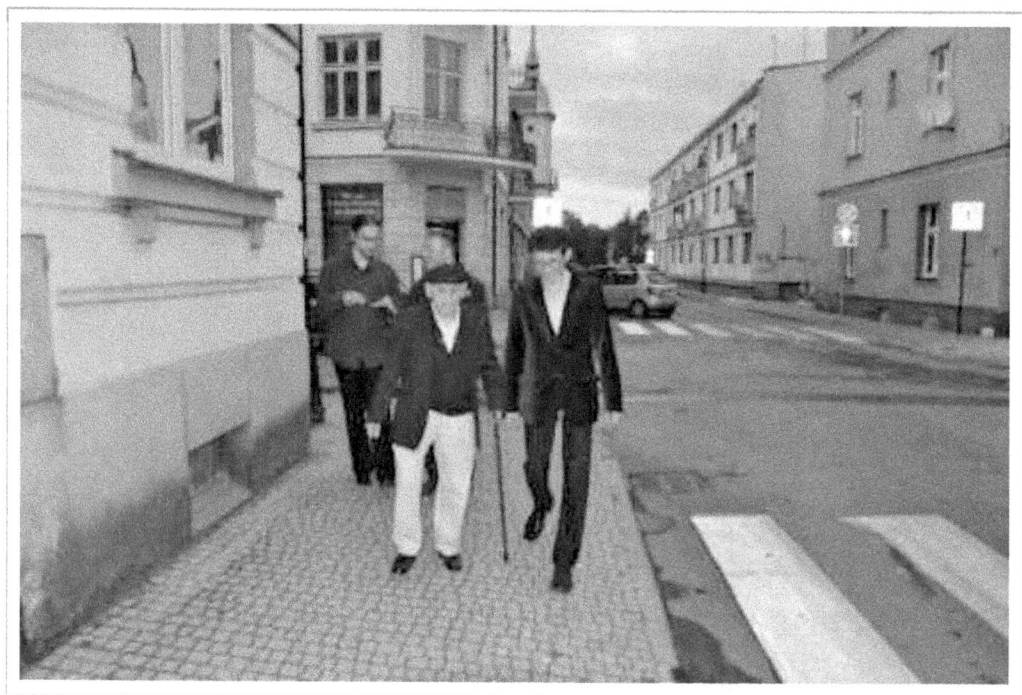

Mordechai Lustig walks the familiar streets of his native Sandz

The Lustigs promenade in Sandz
(Photograph donated by Edita Zajac of Nowy Sacz)

To the Cemetery of Sandz

The cemetery of Sandz was almost destroyed by the Germans who removed the tombstones for construction purposes. There are some stones that remained or were restored following the war. But we can see the emptiness of the field. Mordechai Lustig describes to his grandson Alon the cemetery prior to the war.

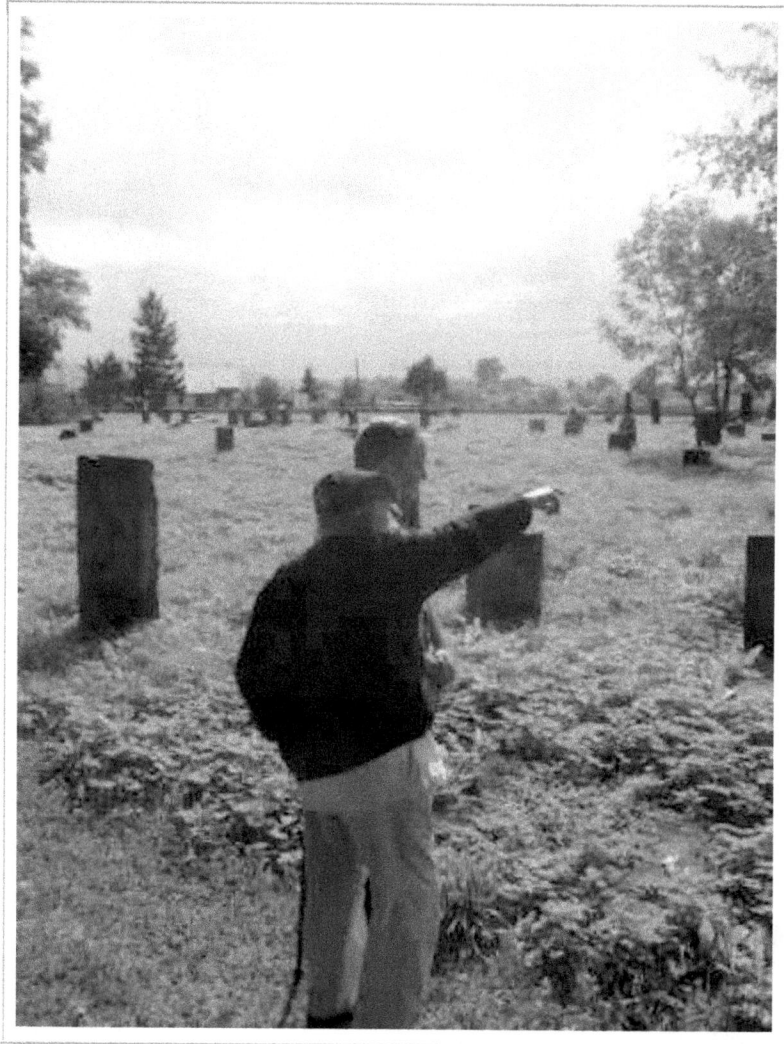

Mordechai Lustig describes the cemetery to his grandson

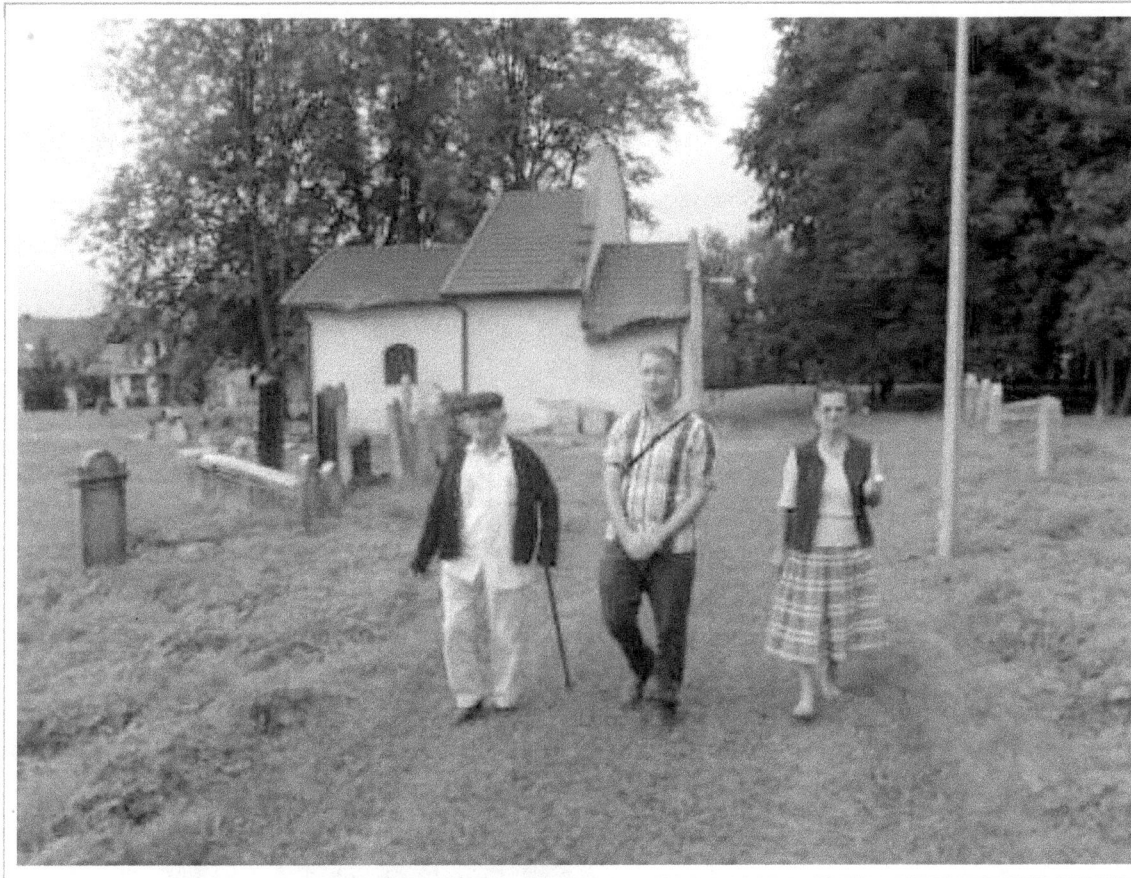

Mordechai Lustig and his grandson Alon walking amongst the graves

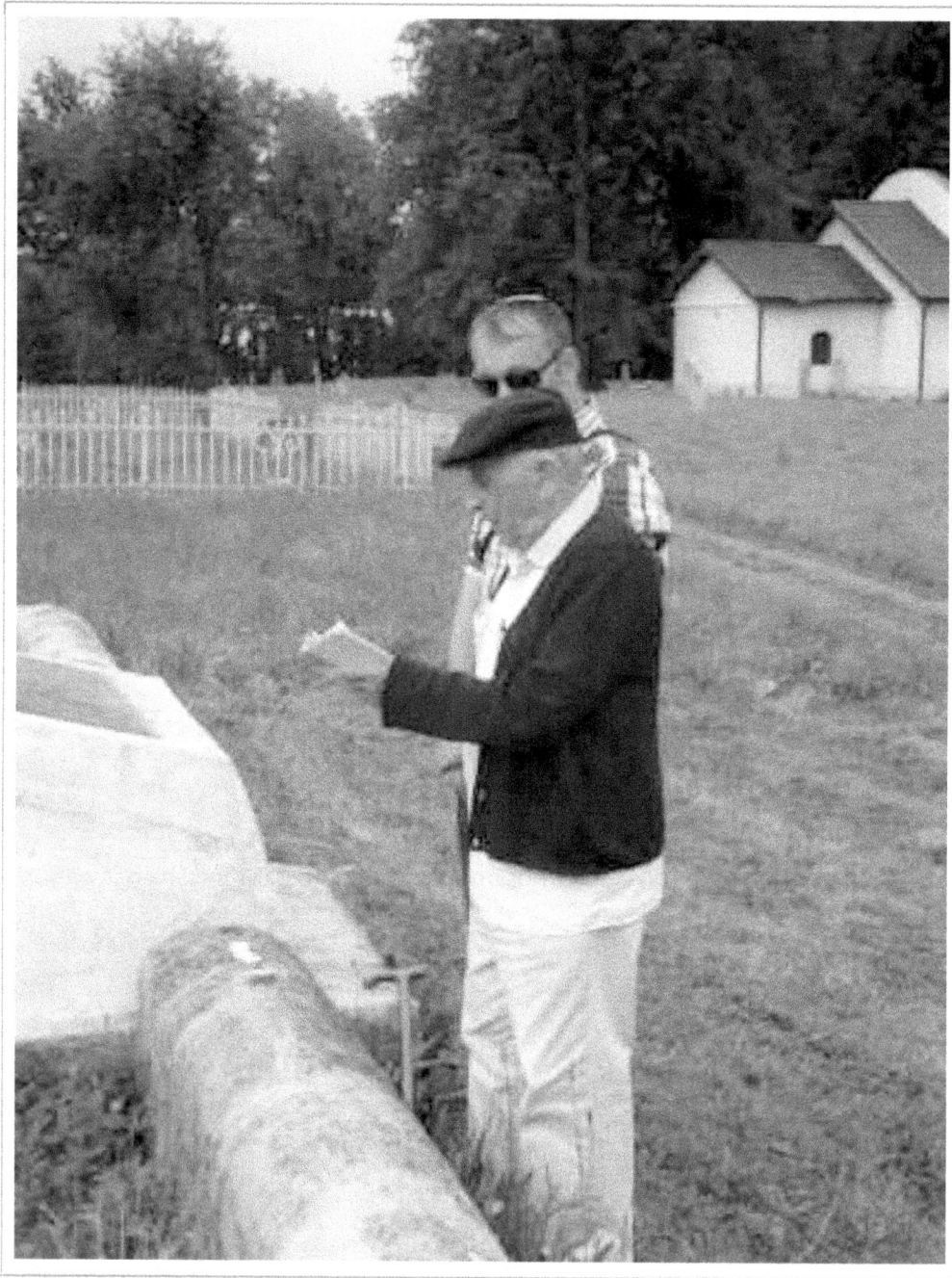

Mordechai Lustig and his grandson Alon recite the memorial kaddish for the members of their family who were killed the night of the slaughter and were buried in a mass grave at the Jewish cemetery of Sandz. In the background is the burial ground of Rabbi Haim Halberstam that remained untouched during the war.

Lighting candles in memory of the family buried at the cemetery

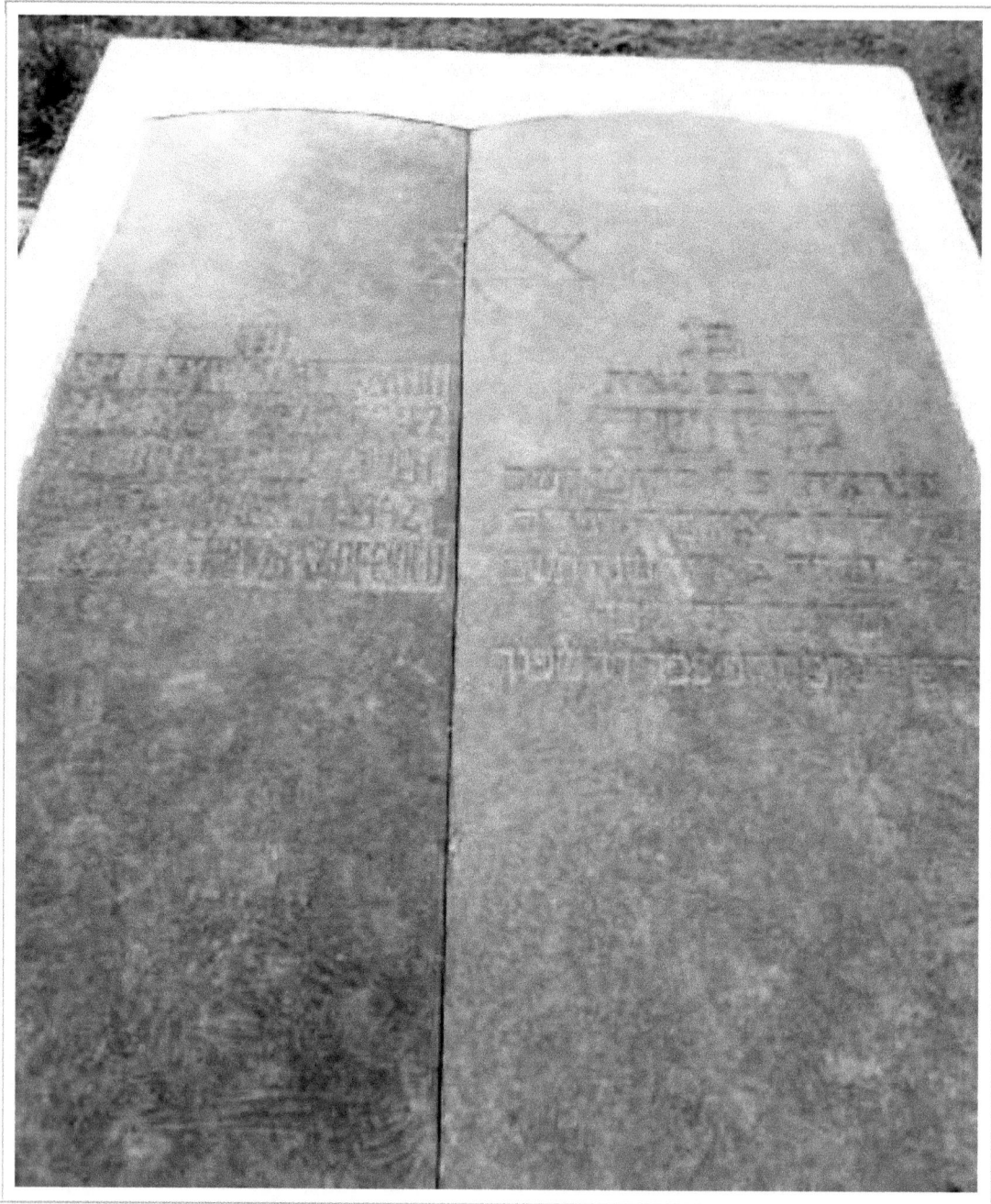

Memorial to the Jews in Sandz at the cemetery

אלה אזכרה ונפשי עלי אשפכה

על קהלה קדושה צאנז וגלילותיה החריבה

החסידים קדושים וטהורים צדיקים אשר הלכו בגולה
וחשכו המאורות ובטלו משמורות בבתי מדרשיה,

ועל ראשי חישיבה ומרביצי תורה בישיבת הק' המפורסמת בני תורה בבית המדרש הגדול של
רבוה"ק מהרא"ל מצאנז וזוק"ר בחדריה הנחמדים, אהובים ויקרים,
ועל רבנים ובעלי הוראה, אנשי מעשה ואדמו"ר, צבעי חוט ועדיקם, זקנים ונערים, ועבדים יהדים, בכל מקומות
מושבותם שרסחותם בגולם על רבותינו הקדושים שלשלתא לבית צאנז ורבנן בם בכל נשי וטפם ומאירים,

בראש וראשון אצל אביר הרועים ראש השלשלת

רשכבה"ג מרן קודש הקדשים צי"ע

מורה מורינו רבי חיים מצאנז זצוק"ל

ואצל בנו מ"מ

מרן הקוה"ט טמיר ונעלם צי"ע

מורה מורינו רבי אהרן מצאנז זצוק"ל

ואצל בנו מ"מ

מרן הקו"ט מופת הדור צי"ע

מורה מורינו רבי ארי' ליבוש מצאנז זצוק"ל

ואצל בנו מ"מ, אדמו"ר האחרון מצאנז

מרן הקו"ט גאון הגאונים צי"ע

מורה מורינו רבי מרדכי זאב מצאנז זצוק"ל הי"ד

הנאהבים והנעימים בחייהם ובמותם לא נפרדו
שעלהדינו ונרצחו על קידה"ש בשנות ת"ש ת"ש על ע' ד' על הרשעים האוכרים יש ס
יזכרם אלקינו לטובה לעובה עם שאר צדיקי עולם ויקום דם עבדיו השפוך

ת.נ.צ.ב.ה.

על אלה עיני זכיות יזכרם לא יחוש מאתנו לעולמים

בשם תלמידי בני תורה וחסידי צאנז

משה דוד בן רחל ושטראם טיאנא לינדאן
שלמה זלמן בן יוטא ולערהרער נחנ אנטווערפן
ראש הקהל קהלה החדשים פתורי ודת אקטוערען
בן הרה"ג רבי נתן ונתן בוקפמים זע ל ח בישי מד בני תורה צאנז
יהושע פנחס בן עלא ווואלף ותלא אוסטראליא

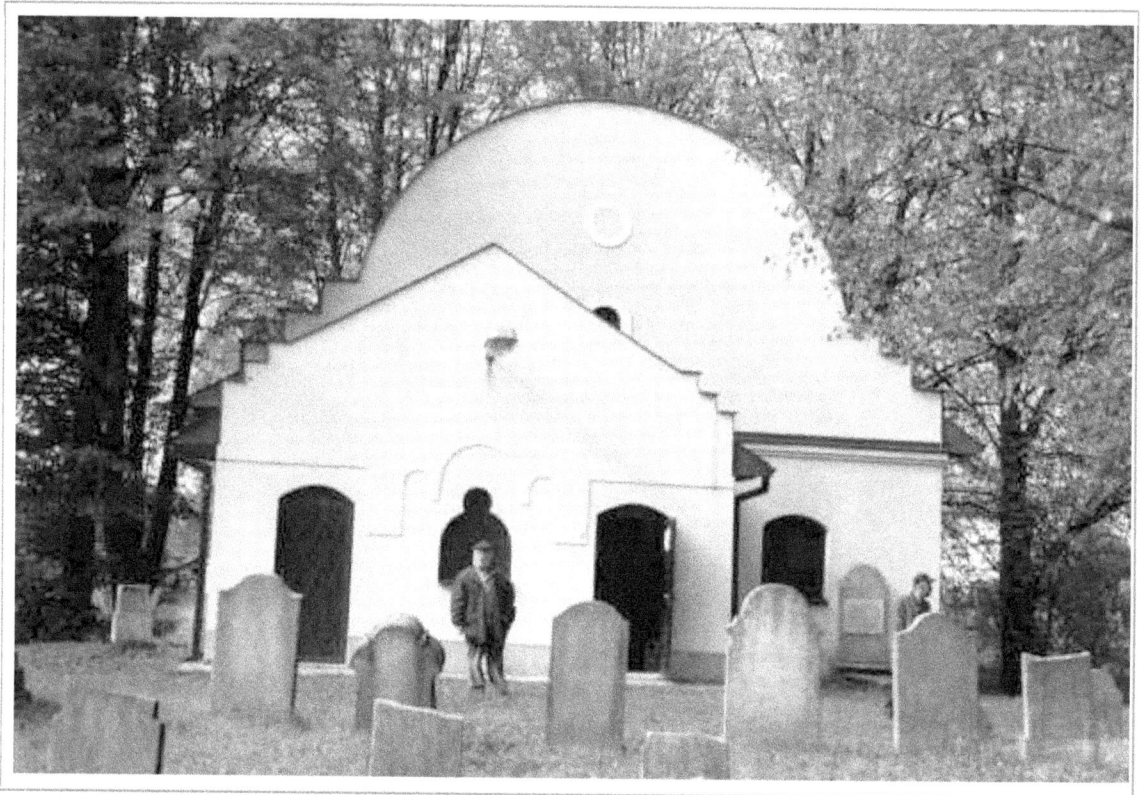

The renovated memorial building of the Halberstam family in Sandz that contained the tombstone of Rabbi Haim Halberstam and those of some family members
(Photograph donated by Jean Krieser of Paris, France)

**The memorial gravestone of Rabbi Haim Halberstam inside the
pantheon of the Halberstam rabbinical family in Sandz**
(Photograph donated by Jean Krieser of Paris, France)

City of Nowy Sacz honors the Shoah victims of the city
(Photograph donated by Edita Zajac of Nowy Sacz)

Mordechai Lustig talks to city youngsters

(Photograph donated by Edita Zajac of Nowy Sacz)

Mordechai Lustig tells his life story and explains Jewish items on the table
(Photograph donated by Edita Zajac of Nowy Sacz)

Going Home

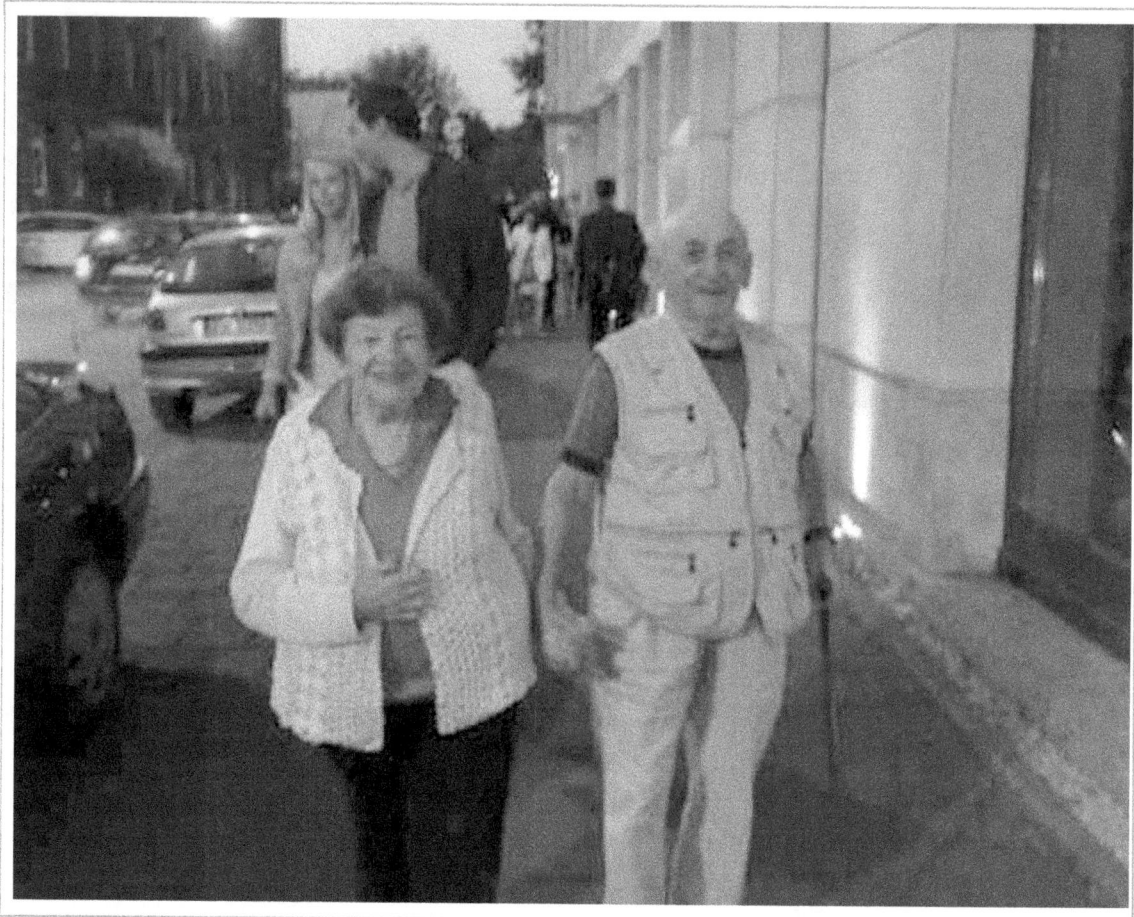

Mordechai and Rivkah Lustig promenading in Krakow before heading home to Israel

Nowy Sącz was established on November 8 1292 by the Bohemian king Wenceslaus II, on the site of an earlier village named Kamienica. The foundation of Nowy Sącz took place due to the efforts of Bishop of Kraków, Pawel z Przemankowa, who owned Kamienica. The city is one of the oldest in the Lesser Poland region. The town has been known in German as *Neu Sandez* and in Hungarian as *Újszandec*. The Rusyn (Galician) name was Novyj Sanc. Its Yiddish names include צאנז (*Tsan, or Sandz*) and נײ סאנץ (*Nay–Sants*).

In the 14th and 15th century Nowy Sącz emerged as one of the most important economic and cultural centers of this part of the Kingdom of Poland. The town benefited from its proximity on the trade route to Hungary and also due to royal privileges. During these times, the majority of the town's inhabitants were German colonists. In the 15th century it produced steel and woolen products, and nearly rivaled Kraków in visual arts. In 1329, In the mid–14th century, King Casimir the Great built a royal castle here and surrounded the town with a defensive wall. Nowy Sącz was the seat of a castellan and a starosta, becoming an important point in the system of defense of the southern border of Poland. The town was further elevated in

1448 when Bishop Zbigniew Oleanicki promoted a local church to the status of a Collegiate.Nowy Sącz prospered in the Polish Golden Age (16th century). It was an important center of the Protestant Reformation. Good times ended in the 17th century. In 1611 a great fire destroyed much of the town, and during the Swedish invasion of Poland, the town was captured by the Swedes who burned and looted it. Nowy Sacz continued to decline. The city then decided to invite the Jews to settle in Nowy Sacz proper. We do not have specific information about the origin of the Jews of the Nowy Sacz district or where they lived. But we have two records of Jews; one in 1469 dealing with Awraham from Krakow and another one named Abraham, an eye doctor of New Sandec in 1503.

Nowy Sacz was an important trade center with Hungary, and Jewish merchants passed it. The Luborski family who ruled the city were favorably disposed to Jews and hoped to revive the economic life in the city. They managed to obtain a royal permit that permitted Jews to settle in the city. The royal privilege of 1676 (ratified in 1682 by King John III Sobieski) accorded the Jews the right to build their houses on the town's empty lots and to engage in commerce (mainly with Hungary) and weaving. The Great Synagogue, renowned for its beautiful frescoes, was completed in 1746. In 1765 there were 609 Jews (154 families) in Nowy Sacz paying the poll tax and owning 70 houses (595 additional Jewish poll tax payers lived in 103 surrounding villages). At the beginning of the 19th century Austrian authorities compelled the Jews to live in a special quarter. During the first half of the 19th century the Hassidic dynasty of the Zanzer Hassidim was established by Rabbi Haim Halberstam In 1880 there were 5,163 Jews (46% of the total population) living in the town, earning their livelihoods from the sale of wood, agricultural produce, and clothing, or engaging in such trades as tailoring, carpentry, shoemaking, and engraving. By 1890 the number of Jews had decreased to 4,120 (32%), to rise again to 7,990 (32%) in 1910. Between 1900 and 1914 a Jewish school was established by the Baron de Hirsch fund, which in 1907 was attended by 204 pupils. In 1921 the Jewish community numbered 9,009 (34%). Tarbut and Beth Jacob schools, a yeshivah, and sport clubs were supported by the community. Over 10,000 Jews lived in Nowy Sacz before the outbreak of World War II, with another 5,000 living in smaller towns of the county.

The German army entered the town on Sept. 5, 1939, and the anti–Jewish terror began. In March 1940 about 700 Jews from Lodz were forced to settle there; in August 1941 a ghetto was established. Two forced labor camps for Jews were built by the Germans near the town: one, in Roznow, existed from the spring of 1940 until December 1942, and the second, in Lipie, from the autumn of 1942 until July 1943. Over 1,000 Jewish prisoners perished in these camps. In April 1942 the Germans arrested all Poalei Zion members in the city and murdered them at the Jewish cemetery. On April 29, 1942, the Germans went on a killing spree and killed many Jews in the city including

Mordechai Lustig's entire family. He managed to hide under the blankets and survived. The victims were buried in a mass grave at the Jewish cemetery.

In Aug. 24-28, 1942, the entire Jewish population was deported to the Belzec death camp and killed there. A few Jews survived the deportations and were Red Army fought its way into the city on 20 January 1945. The city was greatly damaged. There were hardly any Jewish survivors in the city. Some Jewish from the city survived in the Soviet Union or in hiding places or still in the concentration camps, amongst them Mordechai Lustig. Alone, a total orphan devoid of relatives or friends. He began to make his first steps in reality. Slowly he gained his self confidence and direction in life. He began to relate to people and to situations. He started to live, hungry for life experiences that he was deprived off while sitting behind barbed wires not knowing what the next day will bring. Slowly he returned being a free person and making decisions. He established contacts with distant relatives and friends. He began to make plans, meanwhile he worked at various jobs He even toyed with theidea of settling in Brazil where he had family but abandoned the idea and decided to head to Palestine. He enlisted in Palestinian para-military groups in Euriope and sailed witrh them to Palestine to fight for a Jewish state. He landed in the country and went into military action. Following the army service, he began to work and married Rivkah. They had two children; Moshe and Yehudit. Mordechai retured from work and began to work in the Israeli movie industry while his family expanded and grew. He was proud of having survived Hitler. He of course enjoys greatly his grandchildren that will assure the continuation of the of the family and the Jewish people.

Chanuka 2016, the Lustig family celebrates

The Lustig family celebrates Chanukah in 2016. From right; Rivkah Lustig wife of Mordechai Lustig. Yehudit Lustig-Kaufman daughter of Mordechai and Rivkah Lustig. Mordechai Lustig. Moshe Lustig son of Mordechai and Rivkah Lustig, husband of Aviva Kaduri. Omri Lustig son of Moshe and Aviva Lustig. Edward Lustig son of Moshe and Aviva Lustig. Eitan Kaufman husband of Yehudit Lustig-Kaufman. Sivan Kaufman, Lital Kaufman children of Eitan and Yehudit Kaufman. Yehudit Lustig Kauman married to Eitan Kaufman and Alon Kaufman son of of Eitan amd Yehudit Kaufman.

[Page 357]

Chapter XVII
My Work in the Movie Industry

I worked for many years in the movie industry and participated in many movies, commercials, and documentaries. Below is a list of the productions I took part in.

1986

Hansel and Gretel, Snow White, The Beauty and the Beast, The Frog Prince, Little Red Riding Hood, Puss in Boots, and New Royal Clothes

1987

Eli Cohen, Stalin's Children, Jabotinsky, The Unemployed Batito, The War Shepherd, Meeting Death, The Laughing Owl, The Stolen Father, Rambo 3, Above the Abyss, and Her Father's summer

1988

Eskimo Limon, The Green Fields, and The Intended

1989

The Victory of the Spirit, and Not Without my Daughter

1990

A Kiss on the Forehead, The Flight of the Eagle, The Cover Up, The Closing Door, The Killing Streets, For Sacha, Their Beautiful House, Human Protector and Tel Aviv Stories

1991

A Bit of Luck, Mercy, and The Big Fight

1992

The Black Box, Tropical Heat, Misses Kerry, Night Nightmares, Cold Contact, The story at the Snakes Funeral, Hospital Emergency Room–TV

1993

Apostrophe for Students, Bezek Commercial, The Duel, Uncle Peretz Takes off, Toto Commercial, The Schindler List,Painful Love, Looking for an Animal, and Kofico Max and Moritz, The Flying Camel, The new Country, Oskar killed at the Dead Sea ,The Lost Treasure, Electric Blanket, The Scar, and Imaginary Biography.

1994

The Uri Geller Show, Toto Commercial, With the Gshashim, The Kastner Trial, The Actors, Searching for Love from the 3rd District, Insurance

Commercial, Martzipan, Jerusalem Commercial, American Tourism, and The Tzvika Pik Show.

1995

Ephraim's Piano, No Responsibility, The Kamerit Theater Group, Mr. Many, Lentour Commercial, Co–Op Commercial and Marko Polo

1996

The Unmarked Door, Watching TV, Robbery in the Bus, The Revolutionary, Summer Love, Rubi's Program, The Comedian Yatzpan, Tnuva Commercial, Pick a Card, and Death of a Dancing Girl

1997

Forbidden Love, Hello Germany, Family secret, Theater games With Budo, The Little One and Fruma with Yael

1998

Bruno, The Legend of the Silent Man, Tzur Hadassim, Dangerous, Roza Roth, Sirens, The Israeli Railway, Ennemy's Area and The Lover Linski

1998

The Children Seder, Pilot Project with Kushnir, Election Commercial, Vulcan Intersection and Teaching Documentary

2000

The Body, From the Beginning, Life is not Everything, The Middle Class, To Grab the Sky, Bezek Commercial, The Schrimp, The Georgian Wedding, Duty Free Commercial,I want to be a Millionaire, Zirpa, Lottery Commercial, 6 Million Splints, Clip with Michael Yanai, My First Sony, and Chicken Soup Commercial

2001

Mercantile Bank Commercial, Teenage Channel Show with Greinik, Sefi Rivlin's Show, Barak Commercial and Return from India

2002

He and She, Attorneys, Show with Didi Harari, He and She, Saturdays and Holidays, Start Up, Weitzman Institute, Oral Torah Contest Winners, Policewoman and Nava's Disasters

2003

With Dudu Topaz, Father Remained in Sderot, Found a Woman Shoshana Schwartz, The Neighborhood Stars and The Zero Year

2004

With Berkovitz, You Will Have Hope, No Benyamin, With Dan Zalman, Lod Terminal 3 and Close to Home

2005

Har Hazeitim, Music Clip, Mishaan and 3 Mothers

2006

Teva Commercial, I never Promised You, The Debt and Elite Commercial

2007

On the Way to the Sick One, What's the Connection, The Man is like a Dog and Movie with Dan Zalman

I worked with and met the following actors, directors and producers in the Israeli movie and television industry;

ABUKSIS Yael. ALBIN Galia.	DAYAN Assi.
ALEXANDER Sharon.	DIPO William.
ALMAGOR Gila.	DOUGLAS Arik.
ALTERMAN Ido.	DRYFUSS Richard.
AMARNI Avi.	ELIAN Yona.
ARCADI Alexander.	FARD Myycki.
ATZMAN Anat.	FIELD Sally.
ATZMON Shmuel.	FIRSTENBERG Hni.
AVAVI Shay.	FORST Ted.
AVNI Aki.	GABBAI Sasson.
BANDERES Antonio.	GERBER Yossi.
BAR Sandi.	GLICKMAN Dovale.
BARABASH Uri.	GOLDSTEIN Limor.
BARKAN Yehda.	GREINIK Avi.
BAT Michal. A	HADAR Yael.
DAM BASSAR Sdalia.	HALPERN Yaacov.
BEN ARI Shmil,	HALPERN Emanuel.
BEN SIRA Yaacov.	HATAV Yoram.
BODO Yaacov.	NEUBERGER Rami.
DORON Caspi.	IVGI Moshe.
DORON Mati.	KAMBOS Rozina.
CYR Myriam.	KEONIG Lea.
DANON Rami.	KIDDER Dworah.

KINGSLEY Ben.

LAVIE Amos.

MARSO Sofi.

MILSHTEIN Shifra.

MORRIS Robert.

MOSHIKO Alkalai.

MOSHONOV Moni.

NAVON Dovale.

NESHER Doron.

NEUHI Tzhahi.

NORRIS Chuck.

NORRIS Mick.

PICK Tzvi.

POLI.

SHAIKE.

GAVRI.

REEG Diana.

REVAH Zeev.

RIVLIN Leora.

RIVLIN Sefi.

ROSSELINI Isabella.

SAXON Ralk

SCHWARTZ Anat.

SELPHON Tzvi.

SHAGRAN Julian.

SHAIKE John.

SHILA Samuel.

SPIELBERG Steven.

STALON Sylvester.

STEWARD Gavriel.

TEIB Ninette.

TOPAZ David.

TZAFIR Tuvia.

TZAFIR Yoav.

TZARFATI Tzadi.

WAKSMAN Anat.

WALLACH Eli.

WEINER Amnon.

WOLMAN Dan.

YANAI Michael.

YOUNG Roger.

ZAMIR Anat.

ZOHAR Ayelet.

Appendix - List of Jews in Sandz

List of Jews that lived in Nowy Sacz or Sandz prior to and during World War Two.

MAY THEY ALL REST IN PEACE

*Legend for Sources:

1. The Holy City that vanished - Lehrer, 1995
2. Research letters & interviews
3. Death book of Auschwitz
4. Galician business directory of 1891 (Nowy Sacz)
5. Gad Neuman
6. Road of ordeals to Israel - Written by Chaim Bronfeld
7. Irit Laufer - Nowy Sacz researcher
8. JewishGen
9. Zans cemetery list submitted by Debbie Raff
10. Markus (Morde) Lustig collected the names
11. Nowy Sacz Society in New York
12. Sefer Sandz edited by Raphael Mahler
13. Roman Catholic records
14. Nowy Sacz municipal records
15. Yad Vashem testimony pages

In the Remarks Column "Died" means "Died in the Shoah"

Surname	First Name	Maiden Name	Birth Date	Residence	Father	Mother	Gender	Spouse	*Source	Remarks
AARONI	Deworah	BLASENSTEIN			Beny	Shewa	F		[2]	Survived
ABEK	Mosze						M		[15]	Died
ABEK	Naphtali						M		[11]	Died
ABEK	Hillel				Naphtali		M		[11]	Survived
ABELES	Josef						M		[15]	Died
ABELOWICZ	Chaim		1921				M		[7]	Survived
ABLEZER	Leon						M		[11]	Survived
ABLEZER	Itzhak						M		[11]	Died
ABLEZER	Shmuel Zwi						M		[11]	Died
ABLEZER	Zelda	KAUFER					F		[11]	Died
ABLEZER	Sara	KAUFER					F		[11]	Died
ABLEZER	Esther	KAUFER					F		[11]	Died
ABLEZER	Pesia	KAUFER					F		[11]	Died
ABLEZER	Moshe Dow	KAUFER					M		[11]	Died
ABLEZER	Aaron	KAUFER					M		[11]	Died
ABLEZER	Feige	HOROWIC					F		[11]	Died
ABLEZER	Zelda	HOROWIC					F		[11]	Died
ABLEZER	Sara	HOROWIC					F		[11]	Died
ABLEZER	Moshe Shmuel	HOROWIC					M		[11]	Died
ABLEZER	Chaya Feig	SCHAPIRO					F		[11]	Died
ABLEZER	Shulem Shaja	BRAUNFELD					M		[11]	Died
ABLEZER	Tobiasz I.		1890				M		[3]	Died
ABLEZER	Leon						M		[12]	Survived
ABLEZER	Mania	KORNREICH					F	Leon	[12]	Survived
ABLEZER	Herman Israel						M		[2]	Died
ABRAHAM	Elkhanan						M		[15]	Died
ABRAMOWITZ	Berish						M		[12]	Died
ABRAMOWITZ	Franco						M		[12]	Died
ABRAMOWITZ	Moniek						M		[12]	Died
ABRAMOWITZ	Markus						M		[10]	Survived
ABRAMOWITZ	Mathilde						F		[10]	Survived
ABRAMOWITZ	Shmuel						M		[10]	Survived
ABRAMOWITZ	Emalia						F		[10]	Survived

List of Jews in Sandz   APP-1

Surname	First Name	Maiden Name	Birth Date	Residence	Father	Mother	Gender	Spouse	*Source	Remarks
ABRAMOWITZ	Jakob Dow						M		[9]	Died
ABRAMOWSKI	Chaja						F		[15]	Died
ABUSZ	Mania						F		[15]	Died
ABUSZ	Chaja						F		[15]	Died
AFTERGUT	Bernard						M		[7]	
AFTERGUT	Koiftche						M		[11]	Died
AFTERGUT	wife						F	Koiftche	[11]	Died
AFTERGUT	Meir						M		[11]	Died
AFTERGUT	Helena						F		[11]	Died
AFTERGUT	Dwora						F		[11]	Died
AFTERGUT	Feiga						F		[11]	Died
AFTERGUT	Mania						F		[11]	Died
AFTERGUT	Benyamin						M		[11]	Died
AFTERGUT	Melech						M		[12]	
AFTERGUT	Mendel						M		[12]	Died
AFTERGUT	Abraham						M		[15]	Died
AFTERGUT	Emanuel						M		[15]	Died
AFTERGUT	Lewy						M		[15]	Died
AFTERGUT	Symche						M		[15]	Died
AFTERGUT	Eidel						F		[15]	Died
AFTERJUNG	Moshe						M		[10]	Survived
AKERMAN	Yossef						M		[15]	Died
ALTMAN	Melech						M		[14]	Died
ALTMAN	Elimelech						M		[15]	Died
ALTMAN	Tola	KORAL	1917		Dow Ber	Breine	F		[2]	Survived
ALTSCHILLER	Natalia						F		[15]	Died
ALTSCHILLER	Tina						F		[15]	Died
ALTSHULER							M		[12]	
AMATUR	Izak		1901				M		[7]	
AMEIZEN	Maurycy		1872				M		[11]	Died
AMEIZEN	Jadwiga						F		[11]	Died
AMEIZEN	Zoska						F		[12]	Survived
AMKROUT	Heshek						M		[12]	

List of Jews in Sandz   APP-2

Surname	First Name	Maiden Name	Birth Date	Residence	Father	Mother	Gender	Spouse	*Source	Remarks
AMKROUT	Itke						F		[12]	Died
AMKROUT	Leibek						M		[12]	Died
AMKROUT	Leib						M		[12]	
AMKROUT	Haimel						M		[12]	
AMSTER	Moshe Yoss						M		[11]	Died
AMSTER	Faya						F		[11]	Died
AMSTER	Hershe						M		[12]	
AMSTER	Moshke						M		[12]	
AMSTER	Awraham						M		[12]	Died
AMSTER	Uria						M		[15]	Died
AMSTER	Yehuda						M		[15]	Died
AMSTER	Malka						F		[15]	Died
AMSTER	Simka						F		[15]	Died
AMSTER	Pinkas						M		[15]	Died
AMSTER	Sara						F		[15]	Died
AMSTER	Lezer						M		[15]	Died
AMSTER	Herman						M		[15]	Died
AMSTER	Chune						M		[15]	Died
AMSTER	Chana						F		[15]	Died
AMSTER	Anna						F		[15]	Died
AMSTER	Isachar						M		[15]	Died
AMSTER	Leizer						M		[15]	Died
AMSTER	Zotka						F		[10]	Survived
AMSTERDAM	Sheindel						F		[12]	
AMSTERDAM	Bluma						F		[12]	
AMSTERDAM	Shaul				Shmuel		M		[12]	brother. Survived
AMSTERDAM	Awraham	WRUMEK			Shmuel		M		[12]	Died
AMSTERDAM	Shmuel						M		[12]	Died
AMSTERDAM	Heshek						M		[12]	Died
AMSTERDAMER	Karolina						F		[15]	Died
AMSTERDAMER	Sara						F		[15]	Died
ANGER				Lwowska			M		[10]	Died

Surname	First Name	Maiden Name	Birth Date	Residence	Father	Mother	Gender	Spouse	*Source	Remarks
ANISFELD	Pnina-Pearl						F		[11]	Died
ANISFELD	Yehoshua						M		[11]	Survived
ANISFELD	Moshe						M		[10]	Survived
ANISFELD		ROSENFELD					M		[12]	
ANISFELD	Matchek						M		[12]	
ANISFELD	Shiek						M		[12]	Died
ANISFELD	Brek						M		[12]	
ANISFELD	Yossel				Moshe		M		[12]	Died
ANISFELD	Haike				Moshe		M		[12]	Died
ANZIG	Lena						F		[15]	Died
APFEL	Pinie						M		[12]	shot
APFEL	Dawid						M		[14]	
APFEL	Natan						M		[15]	Died
APFEL	Sima						F		[15]	Died
APFEL	Pesha						F		[15]	Died
APFEL	Pinchas						M		[15]	Died
APFEL	Chawa						F		[15]	Died
APFEL	Siskind						M		[15]	Died
APFEL	Blima						F		[15]	Died
APFEL	Leah						F		[15]	Died
APFEL	Leib						M		[15]	Died
APFEL	Shaya						M		[15]	Died
APFEL	Shlomy						M		[15]	Died
APFEL	Izaak						M		[15]	Died
APFEL	Shulek						M		[15]	Died
APFEL	Pessah						M		[15]	Died
APFEL	Cesia						F		[15]	Died
APFEL	HENryk						M		[10]	Survived
APOTHEKER	Augustine		1888				M		[3]	Died
APOTHEKER	Leibish						M		[15]	Died
APOTHEKER	Lazar						M		[15]	Died
APOTHEKER	Saul						M		[15]	Died

List of Jews in Sandz   APP-4

Surname	First Name	Maiden Name	Birth Date	Residence	Father	Mother	Gender	Spouse	*Source	Remarks
APTELON	Basha						F		[15]	Died
ARBEITSMAN	Yaakow						M		[12]	
AREM	Aaron						M		[12]	
ARENT	Edmund						M		[15]	Died
ARENT	Ludwig						M		[15]	Died
ARENT	Helena						F		[15]	Died
ARENT	Paul						M		[15]	Died
ASHER	Ita						F		[15]	Died
ASHER	Selig						M		[15]	Died
ASHER	Mali						F		[15]	Died
ASHER	Selig						M		[15]	Died
ASHER	Mirl						F		[15]	Died
ASHER	Malka						F		[15]	Died
AUDIZER	Moshe						M		[11]	Died
AUSTRING	Moshe						M		[10]	Survived
BACHNER	Sol						M		[11]	
BACHNER	Mania						F	Sol	[11]	Survived
BACHNER	Mayer						M		[11]	Survived
BACHNER	Esther						F	Mayer	[11]	Survived
BACKNROTH	Estera		1920				F		[7]	
BADNER	Menachem						M			
BADNER	Yehoshua				Menachem		M		[9]	
BAKON	Leib						M		[14]	
BAKON	Abraham						M		[15]	Died
BALAGULA	Pesach						F		[15]	Died
BALDENGRIN	Baruch						M		[14]	
BALDENGRIN	Hersh			Romanowskiego 4			M		[10]	Died
BALDINGER	Chaim						M		[2]	shot
BALDINGER	Gotlob I.		1904				M		[3]	Died
BALDINGER	Regina						F		[15]	Died
BALKAN	Moshe Leib						M		[15]	Died
BALKAN	Lejbis						M		[15]	Died
BAR	Sima	BERGMAN					F		[12]	

List of Jews in Sandz   APP-5

Surname	First Name	Maiden Name	Birth Date	Residence	Father	Mother	Gender	Spouse	*Source	Remarks
BARCHASH	M.						M		[12]	
BARON	Michael						M		[15]	Died
BARON	Eliezer Jeruchim						M		[7]	
BARON	Menachem M				Eliezer Jeruchim	Yetta	M		[7]	
BART	Chana						F		[15]	Died
BARUCH	Awraham						M		[11]	Died
BATIST	Moshe						M		[2]	Died
BATIST	Rachel	LEHRER	1917		Meir	Frida	F	Moshe	[2]	Died
BAUERNFREUND	Taube						F		[15]	Died
BAUERNFREUND	Josef						M		[15]	Died
BAUERNFREUND	Matel						F		[15]	Died
BAUERNFREUND	Gershon						M		[15]	Died
BAUERNFREUND	Kalman						M		[15]	Died
BAUMAN	A.K.						M		[2]	Died
BAUMAN	Shmuel						M		[15]	Died
BAUMAN	Zwi						M		[15]	Died
BAUMAN	Izaak						M		[15]	Died
BAUMAN	Zeew						M		[10]	Survived
BAUMOL	Emma						F		[15]	Died
BAUMOL	Chaim						M		[15]	Died
BAUMOL	Meir						M		[15]	Died
BECHNER	Eidel						M		[12]	
BECKER	Jozef I.		1917				M		[3]	Died
BECKER	Chaim						M		[15]	Died
BECKER	Tova						F		[15]	Died
BECKER	Rachel						F		[15]	Died
BECKMAN	Hinda						F		[15]	Died
BEER	Yehezkel						M		[12]	
BEER	Simcha						M		[10]	Survived
BEK				34 Pijarska st					[10]	Family. Died
BEKERMAN							M		[12]	

Surname	First Name	Maiden Name	Birth Date	Residence	Father	Mother	Gender	Spouse	*Source	Remarks
BER	Simcha						M		[10]	Survived
BEREL	Eliezer						M		[12]	
BEREL	Sarah						F		[12]	
BEREL	Mordechai D						M		[12]	
BERGER	Jozef		1909				M		[7]	
BERGER	Maria		1916				F		[7]	
BERGER	Leon						M		[11]	Died
BERGER	Aaron						M		[11]	Died
BERGER	Hawa						F		[12]	
BERGER	Dudek						F		[12]	Died
BERGER	Moshe						M		[12]	
BERGER	Mala	ABRAMOWICZ					F	Dawid	[12]	
BERGER	Dawid						M		[12]	Survived
BERGER	Haim R.						M		[12]	
BERGER	Benjamin						M		[12]	
BERGER	Lonek				Haim R.		M		[12]	Died
BERGER	Esther				Haim R.		F		[12]	Died
BERGER	Eva				Haim R.		F		[12]	Survived
BERGER	Aaron						M		[15]	Died
BERGER	Liber						M		[15]	Died
BERGER	Naftali						M		[15]	Died
BERGER	Tzwi						M		[10]	Survived
BERGER	Moniek						M		[10]	Survived
BERGER	Zofia						F		[9]	Died
BERGLASS	Leon						M		[12]	
BERGMAN	Itzhak						M		[11]	Died
BERGMAN	Hindel						F		[11]	Died
BERGMAN	Hela						F		[11]	Died
BERGMAN	Yehezkel						M		[11]	Died
BERGMAN	Mendel						M		[11]	Died
BERGMAN	Roza						F		[11]	Died
BERGMAN	Itzhak						M		[11]	Died
BERGMAN	Hinde						F		[11]	Died

List of Jews in Sandz   APP-7

Surname	First Name	Maiden Name	Birth Date	Residence	Father	Mother	Gender	Spouse	*Source	Remarks
BERGMAN	Shmuel						M		[11]	Died
BERGMAN	Yossef						M		[9]	
BERGMAN	Mendel				Yossef		M		[9]	Died
BERGMAN	Hela						F		[11]	Died
BERGMAN	Reisel						F		[11]	Died
BERGMAN	Gitel						M		[12]	
BERGMAN	Eli			Romanowskiego 4			M		[10]	Died
BERGMAN	Mirla						F		[15]	Died
BERGMAN	Riwka						F		[15]	Died
BERGMAN	Itzhak						M		[15]	Died
BERGMAN	Yaakow						M		[15]	Died
BERGMAN	Hawa						F		[15]	Died
BERGMAN	Itzhak						M		[15]	Died
BERGMAN	Mirla						F		[15]	Died
BERGMAN	Yeshayahu						M		[10]	Survived
BERGMAN	Tzila						F		[10]	Survived
BERGMAN	Moshe						M		[10]	Survived
BERGMAN	Yehoshua						M		[10]	Survived
BERL	Anna						F		[15]	Died
BERL	Bronek						M		[15]	Died
BERLINER	Reisel						F		[11]	Died
BERLINER	Tzirel				Avraham		F		[11]	Died
BERLINER	Baruch Tz.				Eliezar		M		[11]	Died
BERLINER	Shoshana						F		[11]	Died
BERLINER	Elisheva						F		[11]	Died
BERLINER	Liber						M		[11]	Died
BERLINER	Baruch						M		[12]	shot
BERLINER	Yosek						M		[12]	Survived
BERLINER	Haya						F		[12]	Survived
BERLINER	Haim			Piotrskargi St			M		[10]	Died
BERLINER	Helena						F		[15]	Died
BERLINER	Riwke						F		[15]	Died
BERLINER	Shlomo						M		[15]	Died

Surname	First Name	Maiden Name	Birth Date	Residence	Father	Mother	Gender	Spouse	*Source	Remarks
BERLINER	Aaron						M		[10]	Survived
BERLINER	Tzwi						M		[10]	Survived
BERLINER	Nehemia						M		[10]	Survived
BERLINER	Menachem						M		[10]	Survived
BERLINER	Berish						M		[10]	Survived
BERMAN	Frida						F		[15]	Died
BERMAN	Abraham						M		[15]	Died
BERMAN	Sara						F		[15]	Died
BERNFELD	Nataniel						M		[15]	Died
BERNFELD	Chana						F		[15]	Died
BERNKNOPF	Tzirla						F		[15]	Died
BERS	Chawa-Eva	BIRNBAUM	1910		Itzhak	Liba Ahuva	F		[2]	
BESLER	Samuel						M		[9]	
BEST	Joseph						M		[11]	Survived
BESTER	Samuel						M		[15]	Died
BEZONDER	Gershon						M		[10]	Survived
BIKULES	Charlotta		1920				F		[7]	
BIKULES	Ryszard		1921				M		[7]	
BILDER	Freidil						F		[15]	Died
BILDER	Nahum						M		[12]	
BILDER	Nathan						M		[12]	
BILDER							M		[12]	
BINDER	Yona						M		[11]	Survived
BINDER	Mojszecz		1900				M		[2]	Died
BINDER	Tunka						F		[12]	
BINDER	Gidia						F		[12]	Survived
BINDER	Yosh						M		[12]	shot
BINDER	Yehoshua						M		[15]	Died
BINDER	Sheftel						M		[15]	Died
BIRAN	Tzwi						M		[11]	Died
BIRENBAUM	Pinhas						M		[14]	
BIRENBAUM	Chaim						M		[15]	Died

List of Jews in Sandz APP-9

Surname	First Name	Maiden Name	Birth Date	Residence	Father	Mother	Gender	Spouse	*Source	Remarks
BIRENBAUM	Tzudik						M		[15]	Died
BIRENBAUM	Shalom						M		[15]	Died
BIRENBAUM	Naftule						M		[15]	Died
BIRENBAUM	Chana						F		[15]	Died
BIRENBAUM	Dawid						M		[2]	Died
BIRENBAUM	Rosa						F		[2]	Died
BIRENBAUM	Beile						F		[15]	Died
BIRENBAUM	Tobias						M		[11]	Survived
BIRENBAUM	Tovia						M		[10]	Survived
BIRENFRUEIND	Gershon						M		[12]	
BIRKENBAUM	Haim						M		[12]	
BIRKENFELD	Yossef						M		[12]	
BIRKENFELD	Haim						M		[12]	
BIRKENFELD	Yehoshua				Gad		M		[9]	
BIRN	Turel						M		[12]	
BIRN	Natan						M		[15]	Died
BIRN	Lea						F		[15]	Died
BIRN	Leibusz						M		[15]	Died
BIRN	Berta						F		[15]	Died
BIRNBAUM	Pinhas						M		[15]	Died
BIRNBAUM	Chaim						M		[15]	Died
BIRNBAUM	Tzudik						M		[15]	Died
BIRNBAUM	Shalom						M		[15]	Died
BIRNBAUM	Naftule						M		[15]	Died
BIRNBAUM	Chana						F		[15]	Died
BIRNBAUM	Dawid		1927				M		[3]	Died
BIRNBAUM	Rosa		1897				F		[3]	Died
BIRNBAUM	Israel						M		[12]	Survived
BIRNBAUM	Tobias						M		[2]	Survived
BIRNBAUM	Beile						F		[12]	
BIRNBAUM	Itzhak		1882		Shmuel Isra	Shosie	M		[2]	Survived
BIRNBAUM	Liba Ahuva	BUKSBAUM	1884		Avraham	Pearl	F	Itzhak	[2]	Survived

List of Jews in Sandz   APP-10

Surname	First Name	Maiden Name	Birth Date	Residence	Father	Mother	Gender	Spouse	*Source	Remarks
BITNER	Itzhak						M		[11]	Survived
BITNER	Miriam	HALBERSHTAM					F		[11]	Died
BITNER	Tzila						F		[11]	Died
BITNER	Israel						M		[12]	Survived
BITNER	Moniek						M		[10]	Survived
BITTERSFELD	Hirsh Dawid		1921				M		[3]	Died
BITTERFELD	Naftali						M		[2]	Survived
BITTERFELD	Lina						F	Naftali	[15]	Died
BITTERFELD	Leib		1922		Naftali	Lina	M		[2]	Survived
BITTERFELD	Rozia		1924		Naftali	Lina	F		[15]	Died
BITTERFELD	Irka		1929		Naftali	Lina	F		[15]	Died
BITTERFELD	Lusia		1934		Naftali	Lina	F		[15]	Died
BITTERFELD	Leon		1909				M		[7]	Died
BITTNER	Miriam						F		[15]	Died
BITTNER	Rywka						F		[15]	Died
BITTNER	Sonia						F		[15]	Died
BLAS	Mayer						M		[15]	Died
BLAUSNSTEIN	Benyamin									
BLAUSNSTEIN	Shewa	BUKSBAUM			Avraham	Pearl	F	Benyamin	[2]	Survived
BLAUSNSTEIN	Markus		1912				M		[15]	Died
BLATT	Taube						F		[15]	Died
BLAU	Moshe						M		[12]	Died
BLAU	Leib						M		[15]	Died
BLAUFUCHS	Awraham		1920				M		[7]	Died
BLAUGROUND	Ida		1912				F		[7]	Died
BLAUGROUND	Ryfka						F		[15]	Died
BLAUGROUND	Rachela						F		[15]	Died
BLAUGROUND	Salomon						M		[15]	Died
BLAUGRUND	Yehezkel Me						M		[11]	Died
BLAUGRUND	Zalke						M		[11]	Died
BLAUGRUND	Yaakow						M		[11]	Died
BLAUGRUND	Esther						F		[15]	Died
BLAUGRUND	Hinda						F		[12]	

List of Jews in Sandz   APP-11

Surname	First Name	Maiden Name	Birth Date	Residence	Father	Mother	Gender	Spouse	*Source	Remarks
BLAUGRUND	Rywka						F		[15]	Died
BLAUGRUND	Menashe			Rynek			M		[10]	Died
BLAUGRUND	Eliezer			Rynek			M		[10]	Died
BLAUGRUND	Shila						F		[10]	Died
BLAUSTEIN	Bronka	LUSTGARTEN					F		[11]	Died
BLAUSTEIN	Melech						M		[12]	
BLAUSTEIN	Melech						M		[15]	Died
BLAUSTEIN	Melech						M		[15]	Died
BLAZENSHTEIN	Meir				Benyamin	Shewa	M		[15]	Died
BLAZENSHTEIN	Mendel				Benyamin	Shewa	M		[15]	Died
BLAZENSTEIN	Zinwel						M		[15]	Died
BLAZENSTEIN	Ida	LINDEN					F		[11]	
BLAZENSTEIN	Mordechai						M		[10]	Survived
BLECHEISEN							M		[15]	Died
BLIMAN	Yossef						M		[15]	Died
BLITZ	Sala		1919				M		[3]	Died
BLOCH	Mendel		1904				M		[2]	Died
BLOCH	Hershel						M		[12]	
BLOCH	Aron						M		[15]	Died
BLOCH	Dora						F		[15]	Died
BLONDER	Aron						M		[15]	Died
BLONDER	Isaac						M		[15]	Died
BLONDER	Gershon						M		[10]	Survived
BLJUBSTEIN	Zeidel						M		[13]	Survived
BLUM	Yehezkel						M		[12]	died
BLUM	Haim						M		[14]	
BLUM	Sheina						F		[15]	
BLUM	Awraham						M		[15]	Died
BLUM	Mirjam						F		[15]	Died
BLUM	Moshe						M		[15]	Died
BLUMBERG	Chana						F		[15]	Died
BLUMENFELD	Leibush						M		[14]	
BLUMENFELD	Tzwi						M		[15]	Died

List of Jews in Sandz   APP-12

Surname	First Name	Maiden Name	Birth Date	Residence	Father	Mother	Gender	Spouse	*Source	Remarks
BLUMENFELD	Kreindel						F		[15]	Died
BLUMENFELD	Itzhak						M		[15]	Died
BLUMENFELD	Ester						F		[15]	Died
BLUMENFELD	Yossef						M		[10]	
BLUMENFELT							M		[12]	
BLUMENFRUCHT	Yehezkel						M		[14]	
BLUMENSTOCK	Elisza						M		[11]	Died
BLUMENSTOCK	Henia	MEHL					F		[11]	Died
BLUMENSTOCK	Feige	STERN					F		[11]	Died
BLUMENSTOCK	Eliezar						M		[11]	Died
BLUMENSTOCK	Eidel						M		[11]	Died
BLUMENSTOCK	Awraham						M		[10]	Survived
BLUZENSHTEIN	Mordechai D						M		[10]	Survived
BLUZENSHTEIN	Sonia						F		[10]	Survived
BLUZENSTEIN	Benjamin						M		[15]	Died
BLUZENSTEIN	Dawid						M		[15]	Died
BOBER	Itzhak			Kazimierz St			M		[10]	Died
BOCHNER	Yidel						M		[12]	Died
BOCHNER	Hindel						F		[12]	Died
BOCHNER	Abale						M		[14]	
BOCHNER	Eliezer						M	Abale	[14]	
BOCHNER	Zelig						M		[15]	Died
BOCHNER	Taibela						F		[15]	Died
BOCHNER	Jakob						M		[15]	Died
BOCHNER	Chaim				Yossef		M		[9]	
BODENSTEIN	Reisl						F		[15]	Died
BODENSTEIN	Leibusz						M		[15]	Died
BODENSTEIN	Jakob						M		[15]	Died
BODNER	Mendel						M		[15]	Died
BODNER	Pinhas						M		[15]	Died
BODNER	Riwka						M		[15]	Died
BODNER	Israel						M		[15]	Died
BODNER	Frymet						F		[15]	Died

List of Jews in Sandz   APP-13

Surname	First Name	Maiden Name	Birth Date	Residence	Father	Mother	Gender	Spouse	*Source	Remarks
BODNER	Sulamit						F		[15]	Died
BODNER	Wolf						M		[15]	Died
BODNER	Ephraim						M		[15]	Died
BODNER	Dawid						M		[15]	Died
BODNER	Judit						F		[15]	Died
BODNER	Mosze						M		[15]	Died
BODNER	Lea						F		[15]	Died
BODNER	Eisig						M		[15]	Died
BODNER	Hershel						M		[15]	Died
BODNER	Shlomom						M		[15]	Died
BODNER	Hershel						M		[15]	Died
BODNER	Rywka						F		[15]	Died
BODNER	Menachem						M		[15]	Died
BOGLER	Adolf						M		[15]	Died
BOGUCHWAL				Romanowskiego 4			M		[10]	With family. Died
BOK	Yehuda						M		[15]	Died
BOLDERGRIN	Regina						F		[15]	Died
BOLDERGRIN	Harry						M		[11]	Survived
BONDER	Sheva	BUKSBAUM			Yerachmiel	Rachel	F	Shmuel	[14]	Died
BONDER	Shmuel						M			
BORENFREUND	Leibisz						M		[11]	Died
BORENFREUND	Yehudit						F		[11]	Died
BORENFREUND	Pessia						F		[11]	Died
BORENFREUND	Israel						M		[11]	Died
BORENFREUND	Yossef						M		[11]	Died
BORENFREUND	Gerszon						M		[11]	Died
BORENFREUND	Kalman						M		[11]	Died
BORENFREUND	Tania						F		[11]	Died
BORENSTEIN	Malka						F		[15]	Died
BORENSTEIN	Salomon						M		[15]	Died
BORGENICHT	Mira						F		[15]	Died
BORGENICHT	Sheinedel						F		[15]	Died

List of Jews in Sandz   APP-14

Surname	First Name	Maiden Name	Birth Date	Residence	Father	Mother	Gender	Spouse	*Source	Remarks
BORGERNICHT	Pela						F		[15]	Died
BORGERNICHT	Mordechai						M		[12]	
BORGERNICHT	Rachel						F		[12]	
BORGERNICHT	Berta						F		[15]	Died
BORGERNICHT	Pnina						F		[15]	Died
BORGERNICHT	Sara						F		[15]	Died
BORGERNICHT	Mozes						M		[4]	
BOROWKA	Tzila						F		[15]	Died
BOSLIK	Golda						F		[15]	Died
BRAND	husband						M		[11]	Died
BRAND	Blima						F		[11]	Died
BRAND	Zigmund						M		[11]	Died
BRAND	wife						F	Zigmund	[11]	Died
BRAND	Henoch						M		[11]	Died
BRAND	Wilek-Zew						M		[11]	Died
BRANDER	Sheine						F		[11]	Died
BRANDER	Amalia						F		[11]	Died
BRANDER	Peretz						M		[11]	Died
BRANDER	Sarah						F		[11]	Died
BRANDER	Avraham						M		[11]	Died
BRANDER	Hinde						F		[15]	Died
BRANDSTATER	Guta						F		[15]	Died
BRANDSTATER	Moshe						M		[15]	Died
BRANDSTATER	Chaim						M		[15]	Died
BRANDSTATER	Jehuda						M		[15]	Died
BRANDSTATER	Gitel						F		[15]	Died
BRANDSTATTER	Rozia						F		[15]	Died
BRANDSTATTER	Bronnia						F		[15]	Died
BRANDSTATTER	Asher						M		[10]	Survived
BRANSDORFER	Abish Meir						M		[14]	
BRANSDORFER	Rajsel						F		[15]	Died
BRANSDORFER	Bracha						F		[15]	Died
BRANSDORFER	Zina						F		[15]	Died

List of Jews in Sandz   APP-15

Surname	First Name	Maiden Name	Birth Date	Residence	Father	Mother	Gender	Spouse	*Source	Remarks
BRANSDORFER	Reisel						F		[15]	Died
BRANSTADTER							M		[12]	
BRANSTADTER	Asher						M		[10]	Survived
BRATER							M		[12]	
BRAUN	Aaron						M		[11]	Died
BRAUN	Esther	HOLLANDER					F		[11]	Died
BRAUN	Pessel						F		[11]	Died
BRAUN	Henoch						M		[2]	Died
BRAUN	Hanine						M		[12]	
BRAUN	Ephraim						M		[12]	
BRAUN	Shimon M.						M		[10]	Survived
BRAUN	Awraham						M		[12]	
BRAUN	Yehezkel						M		[12]	
BRAUN	Mendel						M		[10]	Survived
BRAUN	Abisch						M		[15]	Died
BRAUN	Miriam						F		[15]	Died
BRAUN	Gershon						M		[15]	Died
BRAUN	Wolf						M		[15]	Died
BRAUN	Ester						F		[15]	Died
BRAUN	Aron						M		[15]	Died
BRAUN	Shmuel						M		[15]	Died
BRAUN	Miriam						F		[15]	Died
BRAUN	Mendel						M		[11]	Survived
BRAUN	Henry						M		[11]	Survived
BRAULEL	Helena		1919				M		[7]	
BRAULEL	Oscar		1916				F		[7]	
BRAUNFELD	Mayer		1904				M		[3]	Died
BRAUNFELD	Israel						M		[12]	Died
BRAUNFELD	Shmuel						M		[14]	
BRAUNFELD	Samuel						M		[15]	Died
BRAUNFELD	Chana						F		[15]	Died
BRAUNFELD	Neche						F		[15]	Died
BRAWER	Max						M		[12]	

Surname	First Name	Maiden Name	Birth Date	Residence	Father	Mother	Gender	Spouse	*Source	Remarks
BRAWER	Roza						F		[15]	Died
BRAWER	Oscar						M		[15]	Died
BRAWER	Yaakow						M		[10]	Survived
BRETT	Eugenius		1919				M		[7]	
BREINFELD	Kapel						M		[12]	
BREINFELD	Meir						M		[12]	
BRENNER	Riwka						F		[15]	Died
BRIKMAN	Hinde						F		[15]	Died
BRINER	Sarah						F		[12]	
BRINGER	Mina						F		[12]	
BRINGER							M		[12]	
BROCHMAN	Dawid						M		[11]	
BRODMAN	Eliasz						M		[15]	Died
BRONER	Dora						F		[15]	Died
BRONFELD	Reisel	ZIBNER					F		[11]	Died
BRONFELD	Lipke	ZIBNER					F		[11]	Died
BRONFELD	Mania	ZIBNER					F		[11]	Died
BRONFELD	Leibish	ZIBNER					M		[11]	Died
BRONFELD	Yossef						M		[11]	Died
BRONFELD	Mina						F		[11]	Died
BRONFELD	Chaim						M		[11]	Survived
BRONFELD	wife						F	Chaim	[11]	Died
BRONFELD	Yehiel						M		[11]	Died
BRONFELD	Israel						M		[11]	Died
BRONFELD	Riwka Lea						F		[11]	Died
BRONFELD	Neche						F		[11]	Died
BRONFELD	Kopel						M		[11]	Died
BRONFELD	Yehuda Meir						M		[11]	Died
BRONFELD	Hersz						M		[11]	Died
BRONFELD	Lea	KLEIN					F	Yossef	[6]	Died
BRONFELD	Reitzel				Yossef	Lea	F		[6]	Died
BRONFELD							F		[6]	Survived
BRONFELD	Libke	AHUVA				Reitzel	F		[6]	Died

List of Jews in Sandz   APP-17

Surname	First Name	Maiden Name	Birth Date	Residence	Father	Mother	Gender	Spouse	*Source	Remarks
BRONFELD	Mania	MIRIAM				Reitzel	F		[6]	Died
BRONFELD	Leibish	ARIE				Reitzel	M		[6]	Survived
BRONFELD	Haim					Reitzel	M		[6]	Survived
BRONFELD	Dawid				Yossef	Lea	M		[6]	
BRONFELD	Nehema						F	Dawid	[6]	
BRONFELD	Yossef						M		[13]	Died
BRONFELD	Isak						M		[15]	Died
BRONFELD	Haim						M		[15]	Died
BRONFELD	Dworah	TAUBTSCHE			Yossef		F	Dawid Berish	[15]	With family. Died
BROTMAN	Heniek						M		[12]	Died
BROTMAN	Lippe						M		[12]	Died
BRUDER	Hena						F		[15]	Died
BRUN	Bluma						F		[15]	Died
BRUN	Shimon						M		[10]	Survived
BUBER	Itzhak						M		[11]	Died
BUBER	Minka	HOROWICZ					F		[11]	Died
BUBER	Benyamin						M		[11]	Died
BUBER	Aaron-Olek						M		[11]	Died
BUBER	Chawa	FREILICH					F		[11]	Died
BUBER	Samuel						M		[15]	Died
BUBER	Gua						M		[15]	Died
BUCHBINDER	Mojzes		1911				M		[7]	
BUCHBINDER	Ester						F		[15]	Died
BUCHBINDER	Pearl						F		[15]	Died
BUCHNER	Shulem						M		[10]	Survived
BUKSBAUM	Natan Mordechai		1863		Moshe	Chawa	M		[2]	Died
BUKSBAUM	Hinda Lea						F	Natan Mordechai	[2]	Died
BUKSBAUM	Markus I.		1910				M		[3]	Died
BUKSBAUM	D.						M		[12]	
BUKSBAUM	Jakub						M		[12]	
BUKSBAUM	Natan						M		[2]	died

List of Jews in Sandz   APP-18

Surname	First Name	Maiden Name	Birth Date	Residence	Father	Mother	Gender	Spouse	*Source	Remarks
BUKSBAUM	Golda		1797				F	Natan	[2]	died
BUKSBAUM	Moshe		1824		Natan	Golda	M		[2]	died
BUKSBAUM	Chawa						F	Moshe	[2]	died
BUKSBAUM	Dow Ber		1846		Moshe	Chawa	M		[2]	
BUKSBAUM	Breine						F	Dow Ber	[2]	
BUKSBAUM	Itzhak				Moshe	Chawa	F		[2]	
BUKSBAUM	Rachel		1859				F	Itzhak	[2]	
BUKSBAUM	Tuvia				Moshe	Chawa	M		[2]	died
BUKSBAUM	Awraham				Moshe	Chawa	M		[12]	
BUKSBAUM	Pearl	SCHAPIRA					F	Awraham	[2]	
BUKSBAUM	Chaim		1886		Avraham	Pearl	M		[2]	Died
BUKSBAUM	Blume Sheindel	BUKSBAUM			Itzhak	Riwka	F	Chaim	[2]	Died
BUKSBAUM	Netti	BUKSBAUM	1916		Chaim	Blume Sheindel	F		[2]	Died
BUKSBAUM	Atar Chawa	BUKSBAUM			Chaim	Blume Sheindel	F		[2]	Died
BUKSBAUM	Moshe (Max)				Chaim	Blume Sheindel	M		[2]	Survived
BUKSBAUM	Yerachmiel				Moshe	Chawa	M		[14]	died
BUKSBAUM	Rachel		1859				F	Yerachmiel	[2]	
BUKSBAUM	Berish				Yerachmiel	Rachel	M		[14]	
BUKSBAUM	Awraham				Yerachmiel	Rachel	M		[14]	
BUKSBAUM	Nathan				Yerachmiel	Rachel	M		[14]	
BUKSBAUM	Itzhak				Yerachmiel	Rachel	M		[14]	
BUKSBAUM	Tovia				Yerachmiel	Rachel	F		[14]	
BUKSBAUM	Shifra				Yerachmiel	Rachel	F		[14]	
BUKSBAUM	Natan			Kazimeirz			M		[10]	Died
BUKSBAUM	Mina						F		[15]	Died
BUKSBAUM	Yetta						F		[15]	Died
BUKSBAUM	Jakob						M		[15]	Died
BUKSBAUM	Etel						F		[15]	Died
BUKSBAUM	Mordechai						M		[15]	Died

Surname	First Name	Maiden Name	Birth Date	Residence	Father	Mother	Gender	Spouse	*Source	Remarks
BUKSBAUM	Nathan Mordechai		1890				M		[2]	Died
BUKSBAUM	Jetti	LEHRER	1890				F	Yaakow	[2]	Died
BUKSBAUM	Tovia				Yerachmiel	Rachel	F		[14]	
BUKSBAUM	Awraham Chaim				Dow Ber	Breine	M		[2]	
BUKSBAUM (LEHR	Schlomo Zalman						M		[2]	Survived
BURSZTYN	Pinhas-Marian						M		[10]	Survived
CHAJAT	Bluma						F		[15]	Died
CHAJES	Chaja						F		[15]	Died
CHAJES	Murray						M		[11]	
CHAYES	Yaffa						F		[15]	Died
CHILOWICZ	Janina		1902				F		[7]	Survived
CHORON	Elimelech						M		[12]	
CIGEL	Haim						M		[15]	Died
CIMER				Joselowicza			M		[10]	Died
CIMETBAUM	Matayew						M		[15]	Died
COHEN	Pella	KORAL	1919		Dow Ber	Breine	F		[2]	Survived
CZERNOTA	Elik						M		[15]	Died
CZERNOTA	Rachela						M		[15]	Died
CZESZNOWER	Berisz						M		[11]	Died
CZESZNOWER	Chaim						M		[11]	Died
CZESZNOWER	Perl	HIRSZ					F		[11]	Died
CZESZNOWER	Mendel						M		[11]	Died
CZESZNOWER	Gerszon						M		[11]	Died
CZESZNOWER	Chaim Itz						M		[11]	Died
CZESZNOWER	Chana						F		[11]	Died
CZESZNOWER	Zelig						M		[11]	Died
CZESZNOWER	Moshe						M		[11]	Died
CZESZNOWER	Taube						F		[11]	Died
CZESZNOWER	Sima						F		[11]	Died
CZESZNOWER	Mordechai D						M		[11]	Died
CZESZNOWER	Breindel						F		[11]	Died

List of Jews in Sandz   APP-20

Surname	First Name	Maiden Name	Birth Date	Residence	Father	Mother	Gender	Spouse	*Source	Remarks
CZESZNOWER	Yossef						M		[11]	Died
CZESZNOWER	Aaron Meir						M		[11]	Died
CZESZNOWER	Feige						F		[11]	Died
CZESZNOWER	Itzhak						M		[11]	Died
CZESZNOWER	Dawid						M		[15]	Died
CZESZNOWER	Mordechai						F		[15]	Died
CZESZNOWER	Moses						M		[15]	Died
CZESZNOWER	Breindel						F		[15]	Died
CZESZNOWER	Chaja						F		[15]	Died
CZESZNOWER	Chana						F		[15]	Died
CZESZNOWER	Miriam						F		[15]	Died
CZESZNOWER	Sima						F		[15]	Died
CZESZNOWER	Feige						F		[15]	Died
DACHNER	Yochewed						F		[15]	Died
DAGAN	Yehezkel	KORNREICH					M		[11]	Survived
DAGAN	Joel	KORNREICH					M			
DAGAN	Berish						M		[11]	Survived
DAMASK	Shlomo						M		[12]	Survived
DAMASK	Eva						F		[11]	Survived
DAN	Wilhelm	.	1910				M		[7]	
DANENBERG	Leizer						M		[12]	Survived
DATNER	Roman						M		[12]	
DAWID	Yulek						M		[12]	
DAWID	Karl						M		[12]	
DAWID	Sara						F		[15]	Died
DAWID	Sara						F		[15]	Died
DEITELBAUM	Shmuel						M		[10]	Survived
DENNER	Hendel						F		[15]	Died
DENNER	Dwora						F		[15]	Died
DENNER	Mordechai						M		[15]	Died
DENNER	Zelig						M		[15]	Died
DENNER	Chana						F		[15]	Died
DENNER	Dwora						F		[15]	Died

List of Jews in Sandz   APP-21

Surname	First Name	Maiden Name	Birth Date	Residence	Father	Mother	Gender	Spouse	*Source	Remarks
DERSHOWICZ	Naphtali						M		[10]	Survived
DERSHOWICZ	Moshe-Max						M		[10]	Survived
DERSHOWICZ	Hena						F		[15]	Died
DERSHOWICZ	Meilech						M		[11]	Died
DERSHOWICZ	Roza						F		[11]	Died
DERSHOWICZ	Mela						F		[11]	Died
DERSHOWICZ	Bianka						F		[11]	Died
DESBERGER							M		[12]	
DEUTCH	Orna						F		[15]	Died
DIAMANT	Baruch						M		[15]	Died
DIAMANT	Rose						F		[11]	USA
DIRENFELD	Shlomo						M		[15]	Died
DOBRUSZ	Fela						F		[15]	Died
DOITELBAUM	Sala				Lwowska		F		[10]	Died
DOITELBAUM	Idek				Lwowska		F		[10]	Died
DOITELBAUM	Ahron				Lwowska		F		[10]	Died
DOLINSKI	Marcin		1925				M		[7]	
DOMINTZ	Haim						M		[12]	
DOMINTZ							M		[10]	Died
DORLICH	Hena						F		[15]	Died
DORMAN	Pinie						M		[12]	brother
DORMAN	Israel						M		[12]	brother
DORMAN	Naphtali						M		[4]	
DORTNER	Shlomo						M		[15]	Died
DORTNER	Pessah						M		[15]	Died
DORTNER	Gusta				Pijarska 34		F		[10]	Died
DORTNER	and wife				Kazimierz St				[10]	Died
DORTNER	Itzhak						M		[10]	Survived
DRANGER	Szimon						M		[15]	Died
DREIBAND	M						M		[12]	
DREILICH	Zipora	ZEIFERT					F		[11]	Died
DREILICH	Benyamin						M		[11]	Died
DREILICH	Ezriel						M		[15]	Died

List of Jews in Sandz   APP-22

Surname	First Name	Maiden Name	Birth Date	Residence	Father	Mother	Gender	Spouse	*Source	Remarks
DRENGER	Hersz		1915				M		[7]	
DREISSIGER	Lea						F		[15]	Died
DREKSLER	Leon						M		[11]	Died
DREKSLER	wife						F	Leon	[11]	Died
DREKSLER	Theodor						M		[11]	Survived
DREKSLER	Natan						M		[11]	Died
DREKSLER	Erna						F		[11]	Died
DREKSLER	Berta	FINK					F		[11]	Died
DREKSLER	Rosalia						F		[11]	Died
DREKSLER							M		[10]	Survived
DREKSLER	Dawid						M		[11]	Survived
DRENGER	Lezer						M		[15]	Died
DRENGER	Bat Shewa						F		[15]	Died
DRILICH	Golda		1901				F		[3]	Died
DRILICH							M		[12]	
DROBNY	Seller		1870				M		[2]	Died
DYM	Sara		1894				F		[3]	Died
DYM	Dow						M		[12]	
DYM	Beris						M		[15]	Died
DYM	Fela						F		[15]	Died
EBER	Awraham Sh.						M		[14]	Died
EBNER	Khana						F		[15]	Died
EBNER	Zygmunt		1909				M		[7]	
EHRLICH	Dow						M		[15]	Died
EHRLICH	Yaakow Sh.						M		[14]	
EHRLICH	Mendel						M		[4]	
EICHENSTEIN							M		[11]	Died
EICHENSTEIN	wife						F		[11]	Died
EICHENSTEIN	Moshe						M		[11]	Died
EICHENSTEIN	Eibisz						M		[11]	Died
EICHENSTEIN	Sheindel						F		[11]	Died
EICHENSTEIN	Hindel						F		[11]	Died
EICHENSTEIN	Moshe						M		[12]	

List of Jews in Sandz   APP-23

Surname	First Name	Maiden Name	Birth Date	Residence	Father	Mother	Gender	Spouse	*Source	Remarks
EICHENSTEIN	Hinde						F		[15]	Died
EICHHORN	Olek						M		[11]	Died
EICHHORN	Zinka						F		[11]	Died
EICHHORN	Sala						F		[11]	Died
EICHHORN	Zyga						M		[11]	Died
EICHHORN	Rachel						F		[11]	Died
EICHHORN	Sala					Rachel	F		[11]	Died
EICHHORN	Pinhas						M		[11]	Died
EICHHORN			1907				M		[2]	Died
EICHHORN							F		[2]	Died
EICHHORN			1907				M		[2]	Died
EICHHORN							F		[2]	Died
EICHHORN	Leopold						M		[12]	
EICHHORN	Frida						M		[12]	WIZO
EICHHORN	Pessah						F		[12]	
EICHHORN		LIPINSKI					M		[12]	
EICHHORN	Poldek						F		[12]	sport
EICHHORN	Dawid						M		[12]	Survived
EICHHORN	Eisik						M		[10]	Survived
EICHHORN	Moniek						M		[12]	
EICHHORN	Genia						M		[12]	Died
EICHHORN	Henick						F		[15]	Died
EICHHORN	Sala						F		[15]	Died
EICHHORN	Aharon						F		[15]	Died
EICHHORN	Eliahu						M		[15]	Died
EICHHORN	Zelig						M		[15]	Died
EICHHORN	Eliezer						M		[15]	Died
EICHHORN	Esther						M		[15]	Died
EICHHORN	Bluma						F		[15]	Died
EICHHORN	Hirsh						F		[15]	Died
EICHHORN	Hilel						M		[15]	Died
EICHHORN	Henoch						M		[15]	Died

Surname	First Name	Maiden Name	Birth Date	Residence	Father	Mother	Gender	Spouse	*Source	Remarks
EICHHORN	Chaja						F		[15]	Died
EICHHORN	Jehezkel						M		[15]	Died
EICHHORN	Minka						F		[15]	Died
EICHHORN	Nate						M		[15]	Died
EICHHORN	Sali						F		[15]	Died
EICHHORN	Akiva						M		[15]	Died
EICHHORN	Pesakh						M		[15]	Died
EICHHORN	Rakhel						F		[15]	Died
EICHHORN	Sheindel						F		[15]	Died
EICHHORN	Shmuel						M		[15]	Died
EICHHORN	Shymon						M		[15]	Died
EICHHORN	Aron						M		[15]	Died
EICHHORN	Moshe						M		[15]	Died
EICHHORN	Elimelech						M		[15]	Died
EICHHORN	Sala						F		[15]	Died
EICHHORN	Eisig						M		[15]	Died
EICHHORN	Hirsz						M		[15]	Died
EICHHORN	Blima						F		[15]	Died
EICHHORN	Pesha						F		[15]	Died
EICHHORN	Neche						F		[15]	Died
EICHHORN	Sara						F		[15]	Died
EICHHORN	Benjamin						M		[15]	Died
EICHHORN	Dawid						M		[10]	Survived
EICHHORN	Gitel						F		[15]	Died
EICHHORN	Yehosua						M		[15]	Died
EICHHORN	Neni						F		[15]	Died
EICHHORN	Araham		1887				M		[7]	Survived
EICHHORN	Jakob						M		[9]	Died 01/10/1942
EIGERMAN	Ruchele						F		[15]	Died
EIGERMAN	Bernard						M		[15]	Died
EILFERTIG	Rywka						F		[15]	Died
EILFERTIG	Shaul						M		[15]	Died

List of Jews in Sandz   APP-25

Surname	First Name	Maiden Name	Birth Date	Residence	Father	Mother	Gender	Spouse	*Source	Remarks
EINFELD	Mina						F		[11]	Died
EINFELD	Awraham						M		[11]	Died
EINFELD	Mina			Piotr-Skargi			F		[11]	Died
EINFELD	Dawid Menachem						M		[11]	Died
EINFELD	Rachel						F		[12]	
EINFELD	Awraham						M		[12]	
EINFELD	Leiser						M		[12]	Survived
EINFELD	Eliezer						M		[12]	
EINFELD	Eliezer						M		[12]	Survived
EINFELD	Manashik						M		[12]	Died
EINFELD	Henek						M		[12]	
EINICHT	Yochewed						F		[11]	Died
EINTZIGER	Natan						M		[11]	Died
EINZIGER	Dawid						M		[15]	Died
EINZIGER	Rena						F		[15]	Died
EINZIGER	Samuel						M		[15]	Died
EISEN	Feige	HADAR					F		[12]	Survived
EISEN	Mendel						M		[12]	
EISEN	Hanka						F		[12]	
EISEN	Hela						F		[15]	Died
EISEN	Frina						F		[11]	Survived
EISEN	N						F		[11]	Survived
EISENBACH	Sala						F		[6]	Survived
EISENBACH	Aaron						M		[12]	
EISENBACH	Emil						M		[12]	
EISENBACH	Mali						F		[12]	
EISENBACH	Moshe Meir						M		[15]	Died
EISENBACH	Anna						F		[15]	Died
EISENBACH	Sara						F		[15]	Died
EISENBACH	Jakob						M		[15]	Died
EISENBACH	Yekutiel						M		[10]	Survived
EISENBERG	Batsheva		1921				F		[7]	

List of Jews in Sandz APP-26

Surname	First Name	Maiden Name	Birth Date	Residence	Father	Mother	Gender	Spouse	*Source	Remarks
EISENHORN	Abraham						M		[15]	Died
EISENSHTEIN	Moshe						M		[12]	Died
EISENSHTEIN	Livia						F		[15]	Died
EISLAND	Liba						F		[15]	Died
EISLAND	Perla						F		[15]	Died
EIZEN	Mendel						M		[11]	Died
EIZEN	Gusta						F		[11]	Died
EIZEN	Rachel						F		[11]	Died
EIZEN	Chana						F		[11]	Died
ELLOWICZ	Sonia						F		[15]	Died
ELLOWICZ	Riwka						F		[15]	Died
ELOWICZ	Shalom						M		[15]	Died
ELSNER	Adolf						M		[15]	Died
ELSNER	Berta						F		[15]	Died
ENDE	Benek						M		[12]	Died
ENDE	Maks						M		[12]	
ENDE	Aaron						M		[12]	
ENGELBART	Zishe						M		[12]	
ENGELBERG	Shimon M.						M		[12]	
ENGELBERG	Mendel						M		[15]	Died
ENGELBERG	Mendel						M		[15]	Died
ENGELHARDT	Asher Leib		1904				M		[2]	Died
ENGELHARDT	Leon I.		1925				M		[3]	Died
ENGELHARDT	Samek		1921				M		[3]	Died
ENGELHARDT	Moshe						M		[12]	Died
ENGELHARDT	Yehiel						M		[12]	Died
ENGELHARDT	Leibek						M		[12]	Died
ENGELHARDT	Philip						M		[11]	Survived
ENGELHARDT	Isaac						M		[11]	Survived
ENGLANDER	Chaya Bracha	WOLF			Nissan Leib	Ella	F		[2]	Died
ENGLANDER	Moshe						M		[11]	Survived
ENGLANDER	Eber						M		[11]	Died
ENGLANDER	Rika						F		[11]	Died

Surname	First Name	Maiden Name	Birth Date	Residence	Father	Mother	Gender	Spouse	*Source	Remarks
ENGLANDER	Yossef						M		[11]	Died
ENGLANDER	Tzila						F		[11]	Died
ENGLANDER	Tziwi						F		[11]	Died
ENGLANDER	Jakob I		1921				M		[3]	Died
ENGLANDER	Eber						M		[6]	
ENGLANDER	Sarah						F		[12]	
ENGLANDER	Itzhak						M		[12]	
ENGLANDER	Sender						M		[12]	
ENGLANDER	Alexander						M		[12]	
ENGLANDER	Haya						F		[12]	
ENGLANDER	Yaakow						M		[14]	
ENGLANDER	Moshe						M		[14]	
ENGLANDER	Janek						M		[15]	Died
ENGLANDER	Itka						F		[15]	Died
ENGLANDER	Naftali						M		[15]	Died
ENGLANDER	Pinhas						M		[15]	Died
ENGLANDER	Israel						M		[15]	Died
ENGLANDER	Menachem						M		[15]	Died
ENGLANDER	Rosia						F		[15]	Died
ENGLANDER	Rachel						F		[15]	Died
ENGLANDER	Tzwi						M		[10]	Survived
ENGLANDER	Haya						F		[15]	Died
ENGLANDER	Hanina						M		[4]	
EPSTEIN	Hugo		1897				M		[7]	
ERRENREICH	Aaron						M		[11]	Died
ERRENREIICH	Leibish						M		[15]	Died
ERRENREIICH	Rachel						F		[15]	Died
ERRENREIICH	Chaskel						M		[11]	Survived
ERRENREIICH	Marcus						M		[11]	Survived
ETTINGER	Wolf						M		[11]	Died
ETTINGER	Rachel	BERGER					F		[11]	Died
ETTINGER	Arie						M		[11]	Died
ETTINGER	Israel						M		[11]	Died

List of Jews in Sandz   APP-28

Surname	First Name	Maiden Name	Birth Date	Residence	Father	Mother	Gender	Spouse	*Source	Remarks
ETTINGER	Moshe Abba						M		[11]	Died
ETTINGER	Shoshana						F		[11]	Died
ETTINGER	Wolf						M		[12]	
ETTINGER	Ponie	FEIGE					F		[12]	
ETTINGER	Ita						F		[15]	Died
FABER	Bernard						M		[11]	Died
FABER	Lisa						F		[11]	Died
FABER	Rachel						F		[15]	Died
FABER	Alter						M		[15]	Died
FABER	Itzhak						M		[15]	Died
FABER	Baruch						M		[15]	Died
FABER	Tauba						F		[15]	Died
FABER	Mojszez						M		[15]	Died
FABER	Reisla						F		[15]	Died
FABER	Salomon						M		[15]	Died
FABER	Keila						F		[15]	Died
FABER	Alter						M		[15]	Died
FABER	Reisel						F		[15]	Died
FABER	Itzhak						M		[15]	Died
FARBER	Bernard						M		[15]	Died
FARBER	Baruch						M		[15]	Died
FARBER	Fela						F		[15]	Died
FARBER	Rachel						F		[15]	Died
FARBER	Rebecca						F		[15]	Died
FARBER	Samuel						M		[15]	Died
FARBER	Aba						M		[15]	Died
FARBER	Leopold		1917				M		[7]	
FARBER	Yossef						M		[15]	Died
FARBER	Baruch						M		[15]	Died
FARBER	S						M		[11]	Survived
FAHRMAN	Abraham		1888				M		[7]	
FAHRMAN	Nina		1894				F		[7]	
FASS	Erna		1918				F		[7]	Survived

List of Jews in Sandz   APP-29

Surname	First Name	Maiden Name	Birth Date	Residence	Father	Mother	Gender	Spouse	*Source	Remarks
FASS	Regina		1921				F		[7]	Survived
FATEL	Low						M		[15]	Died
FEDERBUSH	Golda	BIRNBAUM	1904		Itzhak	Liba Ahuva	F		[2]	Survived
FEDERGRIN	Pessah						M		[11]	Died
FEDERGRIN	Itzhak						M		[11]	Died
FEDERGRIN	Israel						M		[11]	Died
FEDERGRIN	Riwka						F		[11]	Died
FEDERGRIN	Rachel						F		[11]	Died
FEDERGRIN	Israel						M		[11]	Died
FEDERGRIN	Shlomo						M		[11]	Died
FEDERGRIN	Shmuel						M		[11]	Died
FEDERGRUN	Israel						M		[15]	Died
FEDERGRUN	Izak						M		[15]	Died
FEDERGRUN	Chaim						M		[15]	Died
FEDERGRUN	Samuel						M		[15]	Died
FEIER	Yetta						F		[15]	Died
FEIER	Hersz						M		[15]	Died
FEIER	Taube						F		[15]	Died
FEIGENBAUM	Chaim		1894				M		[7]	
FEIGENBAUM	Chaia		1900				F	Chaim	[7]	
FEIGENBAUM	Markus		1926		Chaim	Chaia	M		[7]	
FEIGENBAUM	Pinkas		1917		Chaim	Chaia	M		[7]	
FEIGENBAUM	Regina		1934		Chaim	Chaia	F		[7]	
FEIGENBAUM	Naftali		1936		Chaim	Chaia	M		[7]	
FEIGENBAUM	Idek		1938		Chaim	Chaia	M		[7]	
FELBER	Markus						M		[7]	Died
FELBER	Chana						F		[15]	Died
FELBER	Leo						M		[11]	Survived
FELD	Hershel M						M		[12]	
FELD	Aaron						M		[12]	
FELDENGRUEN	Naftali						M		[15]	Died
FELDGRIN	Harry						M		[12]	Survived

Surname	First Name	Maiden Name	Birth Date	Residence	Father	Mother	Gender	Spouse	*Source	Remarks
FELDSCHREIBER	Erna						F		[11]	Died
FELKMAN	Fryda						F		[15]	Died
FELMAN	Moses		1905				M		[7]	
FELMAN	Lola		1905				F	Moses	[7]	
FELMAN	Regina		1936		Moses	Lola	F		[7]	
FELMAN	Brucha		1937		Moses	Lola	F		[7]	
FELSHEN	Chawa						F		[15]	Died
FENDLER	Baruch						M		[14]	
FENICHE	Freidel						F		[15]	Died
FENIGER							M		[12]	
FENSTERBLAU	Moshe						M		[11]	Died
FENSTERBLAU	Chana						F		[11]	Died
FENSTERBLAU	Yehoshua						M		[11]	Died
FENSTERBLAU	Israel						M		[11]	Died
FERBER	Yossef						M		[14]	
FERBER	Motel						M		[12]	
FERBER	Monie						M		[12]	
FERBER	Yeshayahu						M		[12]	
FERBER	Moshe						M		[12]	Died
FERBER	Rebeca						F		[15]	Died
FERBER	Ester						F		[15]	Died
FERBER	Riwka						F		[15]	Died
FERBER	Jakob						M		[15]	Died
FERDMAN	Tzwi						M		[10]	Survived
FERSHREIBER							M		[12]	
FERSTER	Rechel						F		[15]	Died
FERTIG							M		[12]	
FERTIG							M		[12]	
FERTIG	Wilek						M		[12]	
FERTIG	Malka						F		[12]	
FERTIG	Hela						F		[12]	
FERTIG	Nadzia						F		[12]	
FEUER	Yehuda						M		[15]	Died

List of Jews in Sandz   APP-31

Surname	First Name	Maiden Name	Birth Date	Residence	Father	Mother	Gender	Spouse	*Source	Remarks
FEUERLICHT	Leja						F		[15]	Died
FEUERZEIG	Leib		1908				M		[3]	Died
FIAKER	Shabtai						M		[14]	
FIBELS	Ela						F		[15]	Died
FINDER	Michael						M		[12]	
FINDER	Henrik						M		[12]	
FINDER	Ernest						M		[12]	
FINDER	Bronislaw						M		[12]	
FINDER		MISS					M		[12]	
FINDER	Henryk						M		[15]	Died
FINDER	Adolf Awraham						M		[9]	Died 03/9/1930
FINDER	GIZE						F		[15]	Died
FINK	Shimon						M		[12]	shot
FINK	Akiwa						M		[15]	Died
FINK	Gitel						F		[15]	Died
FINK	Dow						M		[15]	Died
FINK	Yaakow						M		[10]	Survived
FINKELSTEIN	Malka						F		[15]	Died
FINTZLER	Awraham						M		[12]	
FINTZLER	Haya						F		[12]	
FIRER	Dolek						M		[15]	Died
FIRER	Natan						M		[15]	Died
FISCH	Mechel		1917				M		[7]	
FISCH	Salomon		1910				M		[7]	
FISCH	Moshe						M		[11]	Died
FISCH	wife						F	Moshe	[11]	Died
FISCH	Leo						M		[11]	Survived
FISCH	Ester						F		[15]	Died
FISCH	Leon						M		[12]	
FISCH	Moshe						M		[14]	Poalei Zion
FISCH	Dawid						M		[4]	
FISCHER	Rosa						F		[15]	Died
FISHBEIN	Rachel						F		[15]	Died

List of Jews in Sandz   APP-32

Surname	First Name	Maiden Name	Birth Date	Residence	Father	Mother	Gender	Spouse	*Source	Remarks
FISHLER	Noah						M		[12]	
FISHLER	Blima						F		[12]	
FISKUS	Taube	ANISFELD					F		[11]	Died
FISZLER	Noah						M		[11]	Died
FLAKS	Sheindel						F		[15]	Died
FLASTER	Menashe						M		[14]	
FLASHEN	Blima						F		[15]	Died
FLASZEN	fam			Romanowskiego 4					[10]	Died
FLECHER	Dwora						F		[15]	Died
FLECK	S.						M		[12]	USA
FLINK	Naftali						M		[12]	
FLINK	Hanka						F		[12]	
FLOSHEN	Baruch						M		[12]	
FLOSTER	Mendel						M		[12]	
FOGEL	Itzhak						M		[11]	Died
FOGLER	Hershke						M		[12]	
FOLK	Feibish						M		[15]	Died
FOLKMAN	Berisz						M		[11]	Survived
FOLKMAN	Naphtali						M		[11]	Survived
FOLKMAN	Mordechai						M		[11]	Died
FOLKMAN	Rosa						F		[11]	Died
FOLKMAN	Chana						F		[11]	Died
FOLKMAN	Lonek						M		[11]	Died
FOLKMAN	Zigmunt						M		[11]	Died
FOLKMAN	Regina						F		[11]	Died
FOLKMAN	Ziska						F		[11]	Died
FOLKMAN	Itka						F		[11]	Died
FOLKMAN	Janek						M		[11]	Died
FOLKMAN	Frida						F		[11]	Died
FOLKMAN	Turka						F		[10]	Survived
FOLLMAN	Fruma						F		[15]	Died
FRANK	Moshe						M		[12]	shot
FRANK	Abraham						M		[15]	Died

List of Jews in Sandz   APP-33

Surname	First Name	Maiden Name	Birth Date	Residence	Father	Mother	Gender	Spouse	*Source	Remarks
FRANK	Rachel						F		[15]	Died
FRANK	Sheindel						F		[15]	Died
FRANK	Yankel						M		[15]	Died
FRANK	Abraham						M		[15]	Died
FRANK	Szeindel						F		[15]	Died
FRANK	Baruch		1907				M		[7]	Survived
FRANK	Mordechai						M		[15]	Died
FRANKEL	Hermann						M		[7]	Died
FRANKEL	Adolph						M		[11]	Died
FRANKEL	wife						F	Adolph	[11]	Died
FRANKEL	Stella						F		[11]	Died
FRANKEL	Yehudit						F		[11]	Died
FRANKEL	Chana						F		[11]	Died
FRANKEL	Sara						F		[11]	Died
FRANKEL	Awraham Mor						M		[11]	Died
FRANKEL	Mordechai						M		[11]	Died
FRANKEL	Yermiyahu		1880				M		[11]	Survived
FRANKEL	Itzhak						M		[12]	
FRANKEL	Yirmiyahu						M		[12]	active Zionist. Survived
FRANKEL	wife	FRIEDMAN					F	Yirmiyahu	[12]	
FRANKEL	Adolph						M		[12]	
FRANKEL	Yossef						M		[12]	
FRANKEL	Gita						F		[15]	Died
FRANKEL	Feige						F		[15]	Died
FRANTZBLAU	Hershel						M		[14]	
FRANTZBLAU	Yossef						M		[14]	
FREI	Markus		1918				M		[3]	Died
FREI	Neche						F		[15]	Died
FREI	Sara						F		[10]	Survived
FREILICH	Awraham						M		[11]	Died
FREILICH	Feige						F		[11]	Died
FREILICH	Rachel	SCHWIED					F		[11]	Died

List of Jews in Sandz   APP-34

Surname	First Name	Maiden Name	Birth Date	Residence	Father	Mother	Gender	Spouse	*Source	Remarks
FREILICH	Haim	LIMANOW					M		[12]	shot
FREILICH	Yaakow						M		[12]	died
FREILICH	Hersh						M		[15]	Died
FREIMAN	S.						M		[12]	sport. Survived
FRENKEL	Yehezkel						M		[14]	
FRENKEL									[1]	
FRIEDENBACH							M		[12]	
FRIEDENBACH	Markus						M		[10]	Survived
FRIEDENBACH	Winek				Wictor		M		[12]	Died
FRIEDENBACH	Moniek				Wictor		M		[12]	Died
FRIEDENBACH	Wictor						M		[12]	
FRIEDENBACH	Philip						M		[12]	
FRIEDHABER	Itzhak						M		[12]	
FRIEDHABER	Roza						F		[15]	Died
FRIEDLANDER	Yehudit						F		[15]	Died
FRIEDMAN	Ella						F		[11]	Died
FRIEDMAN	Itzhak						M		[11]	Died
FRIEDMAN	Shamai						M		[12]	
FRIEDMAN	Ela						F		[12]	
FRIEDMAN	Awraham						M		[12]	
FRIEDMAN	Shmuel						M		[12]	
FRIEDMAN	Moshe Wolf						M		[12]	
FRIEDMAN	Israel						M		[12]	
FRIEDMAN	Itzhak				Avraham		M		[12]	
FRIEDMAN	Awraham						M		[14]	
FRIEDMAN	Naftali						M		[15]	Died
FRIEDMAN	Aliza						F		[15]	Died
FRIEDMAN	Naphtali						M		[15]	Died
FRIEDMAN	Schragai						M		[15]	Died
FRIEDMAN	Taube						F		[15]	Died
FRIEDMAN	Naftali						M		[15]	Died
FRIEDMANN	Hirsch Wolf						M	Zeine	[5]	
FRIEDMANN	Zeine	BUKSBAUM					F		[5]	

Surname	First Name	Maiden Name	Birth Date	Residence	Father	Mother	Gender	Spouse	*Source	Remarks
FRIESEL	Matityahu-Mates		1920				M	Dawid	[14]	Survived
FRISCH	Esther						F		[11]	Died
FRISCH	Rachel						F		[11]	Died
FRISCH	Riwka						F		[11]	Died
FRISCH	Liba						F		[11]	Died
FRISCH	Berisz						M		[11]	Died
FRISCH	Moshe Dow						M		[11]	Died
FRISCH	Ekiasz						M		[11]	Died
FRISCH	Rachel	BLAUGRUND					F		[11]	Died
FRISCH	Moshe Daw						M		[11]	Died
FRISCH	Berisz						M		[11]	Died
FRISCH	Riwka						F		[11]	Died
FRIZEL	Dawid			Kazimeirz			M		[10]	Died
FROHLICH	Henry						M		[11]	USA
FUHRER	Ita						M		[12]	
FUHRER	Ita						F		[12]	
FUHRER	Ephraim						M		[12]	
FUHRER	Zalke						M		[12]	
FUHRER	Herman						M		[12]	
FUHRER	Shmuel						M		[15]	Died
FUHRER	Sara						F		[15]	Died
FUHRER	Ariel						M		[15]	Died
FUHRER	Nehemia						M		[15]	Died
FUHRER	Ida						F		[15]	Died
FUHRER	Mania						F		[15]	Died
FUHRER	Saul						M		[15]	Died
FUHRER	Harry						M		[11]	USA
FUHRER	Kuba						M		[10]	Survived
FUHRER	Zelda						F		[10]	Survived
FURMAN	Abraham		1915				M		[7]	
FURST	Pasah						M		[15]	Died
GANCWEICH	Wolf						M		[15]	Died

List of Jews in Sandz   APP-36

Surname	First Name	Maiden Name	Birth Date	Residence	Father	Mother	Gender	Spouse	*Source	Remarks
GANZWEICH	fam			Romanowskiego 4					[10]	Died
GARTNER	Wolf						M		[15]	Died
GASSNER	Hershel						M		[15]	Died
GEB	Leon						M		[15]	Died
GEBEL	fam			Romanowskiego 4					[10]	Died
GEHLER	Stefania						M		[2]	Died
GEHLER	Zygmunt						F		[2]	Died
GETZEHLIG	Eisik						M		[15]	Died
GELANDER	Moszko						M		[15]	Died
GELASSEN	Motel						M		[11]	Died
GELB	Zeev Wolf						M		[12]	
GELB	Adolf						F		[15]	Died
GELB	Regina						F		[15]	Died
GELB	Roman						M		[15]	Died
GELBAUM	Riwka						F		[11]	Survived
GELER	Rachel						F		[15]	Died
GELER	Josef						M		[15]	Died
GELERNTER							M		[12]	
GELERNTER		BILDER					M		[12]	
GELLER	Salomon		1905				M		[7]	
GELLER	Karpial		1918				F		[7]	
GELLER	Moshe						M		[12]	
GELLER	Moli						F		[12]	
GELLER	Shmuel						M		[12]	
GELLER	Blima						F		[15]	Died
GELLER	Abraham						M		[15]	Died
GELLER	Mosze						M		[15]	Died
GELLER	Pawel						M		[10]	Survived
GELLER	Yaakow						M		[10]	Survived
GELNER	Helena						F		[15]	Died
GENGER	Bronka						F		[12]	
GERSHON	Mordechai						M		[12]	died
GERSTEIN	Jczek		1933				M		[7]	

List of Jews in Sandz   APP-37

Surname	First Name	Maiden Name	Birth Date	Residence	Father	Mother	Gender	Spouse	*Source	Remarks
GERSTNER	Yossef						M		[11]	Died
GERSTNER	Rachel						F		[11]	Died
GERSTNER	Sala						F		[15]	Died
GERTNER	Elisza			Piotra			M		[10]	Died
GERTNER	Yehuda						M		[10]	Survived
GETS	Feige						F		[15]	Died
GETZ	Itsche						M		[12]	
GETZLER	Yuda						M		[15]	Died
GETZLER	Janina						F		[15]	Died
GEWIRTH	Jakub		1904				M		[7]	
GEWIRTH	Naftali		1908				M		[7]	
GEWIRTH	Bluma		1915				F		[7]	
GEWIRTZ	Sara						F		[15]	Died
GEWIRTZ	Rywka						F		[15]	Died
GEWIRTZ	Chaja						F		[15]	Died
GEWIRTZ	cHAJA						F		[15]	Died
GIB	Moshe						M		[11]	Survived
GINTER	Izak		1924				M		[7]	
GINTER	Mordechai						M		[11]	Died
GINTER	Melech		1911				M		[3]	Died
GINTER	Yehezkel						M		[12]	
GINTER	Hendel	WALDMAN					F		[12]	
GINTER	Sarah						F		[12]	Died
GINTER	Mordche						M		[15]	Died
GINTER	Meilech						M		[15]	Died
GINTER	Boris						M		[10]	Survived
GINTER	Moshe						M		[10]	Survived
GINZIG	Chaim		1910		Yechiel	Rachel	M		[2]	Died
GINZIG	Miriam	BUKSBAUM	1912				F		[2]	Died
GITTEL	Chawa						F		[11]	Died
GITTEL	Yehezkel						M		[11]	Died
GITTEL	Riwka						F		[11]	Died
GITTEL	Hinde						F		[11]	Died

Surname	First Name	Maiden Name	Birth Date	Residence	Father	Mother	Gender	Spouse	*Source	Remarks
GLASBERG	Hela						F		[15]	Died
GLASNER	Meir						M		[11]	Died
GLASNER	Rachel						F	Meir	[11]	Died
GLASNER	Shmuel				Meir	Rachel	M		[11]	Died
GLASNER	Feiga Gitel				Meir	Rachel	F		[11]	Died
GLASNER	Bernard						M		[11]	Died
GLASNER	Dwora						F		[11]	Died
GLASNER	Chana						F		[11]	Died
GLASNER	Moshe						M		[12]	
GLASS	Leib						M		[4]	
GLASSBERG	Peshe						F		[15]	Died
GLAUBIGER	Hena						F		[15]	Died
GLAZER	Sheindel						F		[15]	Died
GLAZER	Jurek						M		[15]	Died
GLAZER	Berl						M		[15]	Died
GLAZER	Sheindel						F		[15]	Died
GLICK	Sima			Kazimierz St			F		[10]	Died
GLINK	Cwi						M		[15]	Died
GLUCK	Adela						F		[15]	Died
GLUECK	Israel						M		[15]	Died
GLUECK	Israel						M		[15]	Died
GNIWILT	Shabtai						M		[14]	
GNIWILT	Itzhak						M		[14]	
GNIWILT	Meilech						M		[15]	Died
GOLD	Berl						M		[11]	Died
GOLD	Sara						F		[11]	Died
GOLDBERG	Leon						M		[11]	Died
GOLDBERG	wife						F	Leon	[11]	Died
GOLDBERG	Avraham						M		[11]	Died
GOLDBERG	Tautche						F	Avraham	[11]	Died
GOLDBERG	Retzka						F		[11]	Died
GOLDBERG	Henia						F		[11]	Died
GOLDBERG	husband						M		[11]	Died

Surname	First Name	Maiden Name	Birth Date	Residence	Father	Mother	Gender	Spouse	*Source	Remarks
GOLDBERG	Chaim						M		[11]	Died
GOLDBERG	wife						F	Chaim	[11]	Died
GOLDBERG	Adolph						M		[12]	
GOLDBERG	Hene						F		[12]	
GOLDBERG	Nachum						M		[12]	
GOLDBERG	Nachum						M	Nachum	[12]	
GOLDBERG	Wolf				Nachum		M		[12]	
GOLDBERG	Salek				Nachum		M		[12]	
GOLDBERG	Hershel						M		[12]	
GOLDBERG	Meir						M		[12]	
GOLDBERG	Solek						M		[12]	
GOLDBERG	Zigmunt						M		[12]	Died
GOLDBERG	Artek						M		[12]	brother
GOLDBERG	Izak						M		[12]	brother
GOLDBERG	Awraham						M		[12]	Died
GOLDBERG	Moshe						M		[12]	Died
GOLDBERG	wife						F		[12]	Died
GOLDBERG	Racke						F		[12]	Died
GOLDBERG	Sara						F		[15]	Died
GOLDBERG	Taube						F		[15]	Died
GOLDBERG	Jechiel						M		[15]	Died
GOLDBERG	Sara						F		[15]	Died
GOLDBERG	Samuel						M		[15]	Died
GOLDBERG	Shmuel								[15]	Died
GOLDBERG	Chana						F		[15]	Died
GOLDBERG	Helena						F		[15]	Died
GOLDBERG	Samuel						M		[15]	Died
GOLDBERG	Yehiel						M		[15]	Died
GOLDBERG	Salomon		1907				M		[7]	Survived
GOLDBERG	Yehiel						M		[15]	Died
GOLDBERG	Zelig						M		[15]	Died
GOLDBERG	Chaja						F		[15]	Died

List of Jews in Sandz   APP-40

Surname	First Name	Maiden Name	Birth Date	Residence	Father	Mother	Gender	Spouse	*Source	Remarks
GOLDBERG	Murray						M		[11]	USA
GOLDBERG	Itzhak						M		[10]	Survived
GOLDBERG	Shlomo						M		[10]	Survived
GOLDBERG	Tzila						F		[10]	Survived
GOLDBERGER	Leon						M		[11]	Died
GOLDBERGER	wife						F	Leon	[11]	Died
GOLDBERGER	Ratzel						F		[12]	
GOLDBERGER	Leon						M		[12]	
GOLDBERGER	Hene						F		[12]	
GOLDBERGER	Wolf						M		[15]	Died
GOLDBERGER	Shlomo						M		[15]	Died
GOLDBERGER	Mindel						F		[15]	Died
GOLDBERGER	Pepi						F		[15]	Died
GOLDBERGER	Leijbusz						M		[15]	Died
GOLDBERGER	Blime						F		[15]	Died
GOLDBERGER	Chaja						F		[15]	Died
GOLDBERGER	Khana						F		[15]	Died
GOLDBERGER	Feige						F		[15]	Died
GOLDBERGER	Yossef						M		[15]	Died
GOLDBERGER	Chana						F		[15]	Died
GOLDBERGER	Eliyahu						M		[15]	Died
GOLDBERGER	Mindel						F		[15]	Died
GOLDBERGER	Israel						M		[15]	Died
GOLDBERGER	pEPI						F		[15]	Died
GOLDBERGER	Leibusz						M		[15]	Died
GOLDBERGER	Bluma						F		[15]	Died
GOLDBERGER	Adolph						M		[11]	USA
GOLDBERGER	Irene						F	Adolph	[11]	USA
GOLDERN	Pessah						M		[12]	shot
GOLDFARB	Abraham						M		[15]	Died
GOLDFINGER	Welvel-Zew						M		[11]	Died
GOLDFINGER	Yaakow=Janek						M		[11]	Died
GOLDFINGER	Tzwi-Heshek						M		[11]	Died

List of Jews in Sandz   APP-41

Surname	First Name	Maiden Name	Birth Date	Residence	Father	Mother	Gender	Spouse	*Source	Remarks
GOLDFINGER	Chaya-Hela						F		[11]	Died
GOLDFINGER	Meriam-Man						F		[11]	Died
GOLDFINGER	Esther				Mordechai		F		[11]	Survived
GOLDFINGER	Shlomo						M		[11]	Died
GOLDFINGER			1865				M		[2]	Died
GOLDFINGER	Hindla						F		[2]	Died
GOLDFINGER	Mathilde		1903				F		[2]	Died
GOLDFINGER							M		[12]	
GOLDFINGER	Adela						F		[12]	
GOLDFINGER	Helena		1913				F		[7]	Survived
GOLDFINGER	Dwora						F		[15]	Died
GOLDFINGER	Emilia						F		[15]	Died
GOLDFINGER	Chaja						F		[15]	Died
GOLDFINGER	Drezdel						F		[15]	Died
GOLDFINGER	Lea						F		[15]	Died
GOLDFINGER	Moszek		1928				M		[7]	Survived
GOLDFINGER	Nachman						M		[15]	Died
GOLDFINGER	Drezdel						F		[15]	Died
GOLDFINGER	Itzhak						M		[10]	Survived
GOLDFINGER	Shmuel						M		[10]	Survived
GOLDFINGER	Mordechai						M		[10]	Survived
GOLDKLANG	Shimshon						M		[15]	Died
GOLDKLANG	Ester						F		[15]	Died
GOLDKLANG	Markus						M		[4], [12]	Noar Zion
GOLDMAN	Leon						M		[12]	Died
GOLDMAN	Abraham						M		[15]	Died
GOLDMAN	Gitel						F		[15]	Died
GOLDMAN	Joseph						M		[15]	Died
GOLDMAN	Samuel						M		[15]	Died
GOLDMAN	Yossef						M		[15]	Died
GOLDMAN	Bernard						M		[7]	Died
GOLDMAN	Reize						F		[15]	Died
GOLDMAN	Awraham						M		[15]	Died

List of Jews in Sandz APP-42

Surname	First Name	Maiden Name	Birth Date	Residence	Father	Mother	Gender	Spouse	*Source	Remarks
GOLDMAN	Elka						F		[15]	Died
GOLDSCHMIDT	Adela						F		[15]	Died
GOLDSTEIN	Yossef		.				M		[12]	
GOLDSTEIN	Yosef Shmu.						M		[12]	Died
GOLDSTEIN	Minka						F		[15]	Died
GOLDSTEIN	Jozef						M		[15]	Died
GOLDSTEIN	Bela						F		[15]	Died
GOLDSTEIN	Uri						M		[10]	Survived
GOLDSTEIN	Mordechai						M		[10]	Survived
GOLDSTEIN	Moshe Simshon						M		[10]	Survived
GOLDSTEIN	Shlomo Zalman						M		[10]	Survived
GOLDSTEIN	Markus		1926				M		[7]	
GOLFINGER	Awigdor						M		[12]	Died
GOLUCHOWSKI	Chana						F		[15]	Died
GOODMAN	Jack						M		[11]	Survived
GOREN	Avraham						M		[11]	Survived
GOTTCHRER	Abraham						M		[15]	Died
GOTTEHRER	Leopold						M		[15]	Died
GOTTHERER	Rywka						F		[15]	Died
GOTTHERER	Awraham						M		[11]	Died
GOTTLIEB	Yaakow						M		[15]	Died
GOTTLIEB	Moshe Eph.			Piotra			M		[10]	Died
GOTTLIEB	Mordechai						M		[15]	Died
GOTTLIEB	Shalom						M		[15]	Died
GOTTLIEB	Tzwi						M		[15]	Died
GOTTLIEB	Chana						F		[15]	Died
GOTTLIEB	Blima						F		[15]	Died
GOTTLIEB	Mordechai						M		[15]	Died
GOTTLIEB	Hersz						M		[15]	Died
GOTTLIEB	Jakob						M		[15]	Died
GOTTLIEB	Gittel						F		[15]	Died
GOTTLIEB	Chaim						M		[10]	Survived

List of Jews in Sandz   APP-43

Surname	First Name	Maiden Name	Birth Date	Residence	Father	Mother	Gender	Spouse	*Source	Remarks
GRAJMAN	Cyla						F		[15]	Died
GRANBART	Baruch		1899				M		[7]	
GRANBART	Anna		1899				F	Baruch	[7]	
GRANBART	Hedida		1929		Baruch	Anna	F		[7]	
GRANBART	Lida		1933		Baruch	Anna	F		[7]	
GRANCWEICH	Wolf						M		[15]	Died
GRASGRIN	Mendel						M		[11]	Died
GRASGRIN	Gita						F		[11]	Died
GRASGRIN	Sarah						F		[11]	Died
GRASGRIN	Chaim						M		[11]	Died
GRASGRIN	Yossi						M		[11]	Died
GRASGRIN	Tzwi						M		[11]	Died
GRASSGRIN	Chaim						M		[15]	Died
GREEN	Aharon						M		[15]	Died
GREEN	Wolf						M		[15]	Died
GREEN	David						M		[11]	USA
GREEN							F	David	[11]	USA
GREEN	Sam						M		[11]	USA
GREEN							F	Sam	[11]	USA
GREENBERG	Elias						M		[15]	Died
GREY	Hinde						F		[15]	Died
GRIBEL	Koiftche						M		[11]	Died
GRIBEL	wife						F	Koiftche	[11]	Died
GRIBEL	Yossef						M		[9]	
GRIBEL	Reuven		1907				M		[9]	Died 11/2/1968
GRIBEL	Feiga						F		[11]	Died
GRIBEL	Tania						F		[11]	Died
GRIBEL							M		[12]	
GRIBEL	Henek						M		[12]	
GRIEBEL							M		[12]	
GRIEBEL	Helena		1913				F			Survived
GRIEBEL	Wilhelm		1910				M		[7]	Survived
GRIN	Michael						M		[11]	Died

List of Jews in Sandz   APP-44

Surname	First Name	Maiden Name	Birth Date	Residence	Father	Mother	Gender	Spouse	*Source	Remarks
GRIN	Dawid						M		[11]	Died
GRIN	wife						F	Dawid	[11]	Died
GRIN	Fela						M			
GRIN	Fela						F			
GRIN	Moshe						M		[11]	Died
GRIN	Helena						F		[11]	Died
GRIN	Shlomo	RUBIN					M		[11]	Died
GRIN	Itzhak						M		[11]	Died
GRIN	Miriam						F		[11]	Died
GRIN	Ande						F		[11]	Died
GRIN	Frenia						F		[11]	Died
GRIN	Tzwi						M		[11]	Died
GRIN	Fanny						F		[11]	Died
GRIN	Sala						F		[11]	Died
GRIN	Simha						M		[12]	
GRIN	Dolek						M		[12]	
GRIN	Shmuel						M		[12]	
GRIN	Fela						M		[15]	Died
GRIN	Fela						F		[15]	Died
GRIN	Yossef						M		[15]	Died
GRIN	Mari						F		[15]	Died
GRIN	Symcha						M		[15]	Died
GRIN	Zalman						M		[10]	Survived
GRIN	Moshe						M		[10]	Survived
GRINBAL	Bluma						F		[15]	Died
GRINBAL	Symcha						M		[15]	Died
GRINBAL	Bluma						F		[15]	Died
GRINBERG	Abba						M		[11]	Died
GRINBERG	Blima						F		[11]	Died
GRINBERG	Moshe						M		[11]	Died
GRINBERG	Heike						F		[11]	Died
GRINBERG	Wilusz						M		[11]	Died
GRINBERG	Hersz						M		[11]	Died

List of Jews in Sandz   APP-45

Surname	First Name	Maiden Name	Birth Date	Residence	Father	Mother	Gender	Spouse	*Source	Remarks
GRINBERG	Frenia						F		[11]	Died
GRINBERG	Lolusz						M		[11]	Died
GRINBERG	Yaakow						M		[11]	Died
GRINBERG	Pola						F		[11]	Died
GRINBERG	Gerszon						M		[11]	Died
GRINBERG	Necha						F		[11]	Died
GRINBERG	Zindel						M		[11]	Died
GRINBERG	Malka						F		[11]	Died
GRINBERG	Heshek						M		[12]	Died
GRINBERG	Moshe						M		[12]	Died
GRINBERG	Sara						F		[15]	Died
GRINBERG	Pini						M		[10]	Survived
GRINBERG	Chune						M		[10]	Survived
GRINER	Moses						M		[15]	Died
GRINFELD	Chaim						M		[11]	Survived
GRINHUT							M		[12]	
GRINSHPAN	Alter						M		[15]	Died
GRINSHPAN	Chaja						F		[15]	Died
GRINSHPAN	Moshe						M		[15]	Died
GRINSHPAN	Itazhak						M		[15]	Died
GRINSPAN							M		[12]	
GRINSPAN	Rywka						F		[15]	Died
GRINSPAN	Helena						F		[15]	Died
GRINSTEIN	Ignac						M		[15]	Died
GROSS	Yossef						M		[15]	Died
GROSS	Lejbush						M		[15]	Died
GROSS	Nehema						F		[15]	Died
GROSS	Sara						F		[15]	Died
GROSS	Dwora						F		[15]	Died
GROSS	Rachel						F		[11]	Survived
GROSS	Simcha						M		[12]	
GROSS	Simcha						M		[15]	Died
GROSS	Menachem						M		[15]	Died

List of Jews in Sandz   APP-46

Surname	First Name	Maiden Name	Birth Date	Residence	Father	Mother	Gender	Spouse	*Source	Remarks
GROSS	Ester						F		[15]	Died
GROSS	Dawid						M		[15]	Died
GROSS	Gitel						F		[15]	Died
GROSS	Chaim						M		[15]	Died
GROSS	Nehema						F		[15]	Died
GROSS	Mosze						M		[15]	Died
GROSS	Abraham						M		[15]	Died
GROSS	Gitel						F		[15]	Died
GROSS	Yossef						M		[15]	Died
GROSS	Menachem						M		[15]	Died
GROSS	Sara						F		[15]	Died
GROSS	Dwora						F		[15]	Died
GROSS	Berny						M		[11]	Survived
GROSSBARD	Jakub				Chaim		M		[9]	Died 1932
GROSSBARD	Bertek						M		[12]	
GROSSBARD	Rachel L				Shmuel		F		[9]	Died 1935
GROSSBART	Zusanna		1930				F		[7]	
GROSSBART	Mendel						M		[15]	Died
GROSSBART	Rachel						F		[15]	Died
GROSSBART	Mendel						M		[15]	Died
GROSSMAN	Simha						M		[12]	
GROSSMAN	Aaron						M		[12]	
GROSSMAN	Max						M		[12]	USA
GROSSMAN	Moshe						M		[15]	Died
GROSSMAN	Riwka						F		[15]	Died
GROSSMAN	Yossef						M		[15]	Died
GROSSMAN	Hershel						M		[15]	Died
GROSSMAN	Aaron						M		[11]	Survived
GROSSMAN	Shirley						F	Aaron	[11]	Survived
GROSSMAN	Max						M		[11]	Survived
GROSSMAN							F	Max	[11]	Survived
GROSSMAN	Yehuda						M		[10]	Survived
GROSSWINTER							M		[12]	

List of Jews in Sandz   APP-47

Surname	First Name	Maiden Name	Birth Date	Residence	Father	Mother	Gender	Spouse	*Source	Remarks
GROSSWIRTH	Buna						F		[15]	Died
GRUBEL	Adolf		1910				M		[7]	
GRUBEL	Izaak		1887				M		[2]	Died
GRUBEL	Julia		1940				F		[2]	Died
GRUBEL	Rozalia		1882				F		[2]	Died
GRUBEL	Zygmunt I		1892				M		[3]	Died
GRUBEL	Klara		1914				F		[7]	Survived
GRUBEL	Henryk						M		[2]	Died
GRUNKART	Szmuel		1900				M		[7]	
GRUENSPAN	Miryam						F		[15]	Died
GRUN	Estera						F		[15]	Died
GRUN	Ester						F		[15]	Died
GRUN							M		[2]	Died
GRUNBERG	Nahum						M		[15]	Died
GRUNES	Fela						F		[15]	Died
GRUNGRASS	Pearl						F		[15]	Died
GUNSBERG	Ephraim						M		[7]	Died
GURFIN	Chana						F		[15]	Died
GUT	Yeshayahu			Piotra			M		[10]	Died
GUTFIRTD	Bara						F		[15]	Died
GUTFIRTD	Haim						M		[15]	Died
GUTFIRTD	Estera						F		[15]	Died
GUTFIRTD	Gitel						F		[15]	Died
GUTFIRTD	Rata						F		[15]	Died
GUTFIRTD	Naftali						M		[15]	Died
GUTFIRTD	Hersz						M		[15]	Died
GUTFIRTD	Gitel						F		[15]	Died
GUTFIRTD	Chaim						M		[15]	Died
GUTFREUND	Simcha						M		[12]	
GUTFREUND	Eva						F	Simcha	[12]	
GUTFREUND	Chune	NEHEMA			Simcha	Eva	M		[12]	
GUTFREUND	Ruza				Simcha	Eva	F		[12]	Died
GUTFREUND	Sala				Simcha	Eva	F		[12]	

Surname	First Name	Maiden Name	Birth Date	Residence	Father	Mother	Gender	Spouse	*Source	Remarks
GUTFREUND	Golda				Simcha	Eva	F		[12]	USA
GUTFREUND	Sabka				Simcha	Eva	F		[12]	
GUTFREUND	Yanek				Simcha	Eva	M		[12]	
GUTFREUND	Shmuel						M		[12]	
GUTH	Lieba						F		[15]	Died
GUTH	Chaja						F		[15]	Died
GUTH	AWRAHAM						M		[10]	Survived
GUTKIND	Henni						M		[7]	Died
GUTMAN	Chaim						M		[15]	Died
GUTMAN	Aron						M		[15]	Died
GUTMAN	Dawid		1928				M		[7]	Survived
GUTMAN	Chaim						M		[15]	Died
GUTMAN	Adela						F		[10]	Survived
GUTREICH	Moshe						M		[11]	Died
GUTREICH	Miriam Lea						F		[11]	Died
GUTREICH	Arie						M		[11]	Died
GUTREICH	Bela						F		[11]	Died
GUTREICH	Yehoshua						M		[11]	Died
GUTREICH	Hanina						M		[11]	Died
GUTREICH	Wolf						M		[11]	Died
GUTREICH	Bronka						F		[11]	Died
GUTREICH	Yoel						M		[11]	Died
GUTREICH	Mina						F		[11]	Died
GUTREICH	Mela						F		[11]	Died
GUTREICH	Idit						F		[11]	Died
GUTREICH	Hersz						M		[11]	Died
GUTREICH	Yehezkel						M		[11]	Died
GUTREICH	Itzhak						M		[11]	Died
GUTREICH	Chaim				Moshe		M		[9]	Died 19/4/1942
GUTREICH	Yehezkel				Simcha	Eva	M		[12]	
GUTREICH	Abraham						M		[10]	
GUTREICH	Lea	EDIGRIN					F	Abraham	[10]	
GUTREICH	Renee	ANISFELD			Avraham	Lea	F		[12]	

List of Jews in Sandz   APP-49

Surname	First Name	Maiden Name	Birth Date	Residence	Father	Mother	Gender	Spouse	*Source	Remarks
GUTREICH	Joel				Avraham	Lea	M		[12]	
GUTREICH	Chanina				Avraham	Lea	M		[12]	
GUTREICH	Jehezkel				Avraham	Lea	M		[12]	
GUTREICH	Aaron				Avraham	Lea	M		[12]	
GUTREICH	Itzhak				Avraham	Lea	M		[12]	
GUTREICH	Chaim				Avraham	Lea	M		[12]	
GUTREICH	Bronca	SHMUELI			Avraham	Lea	F		[12]	Survived
GUTREICH	Sala	TRAU			Avraham	Lea	F		[12]	Survived
GUTREICH	Chaja	SHLITTEN			Avraham	Lea	F		[12]	Survived
GUTREICH	Miriam Lea						F		[15]	Died
GUTREICH	Izaac						M		[15]	Died
GUTREICH	Mozes						M		[15]	Died
GUTREICH	Riwka						F		[10]	Survived
GUTTMAN	Chaskel		1914				M		[3]	Died
GUTWEIN	Shmuel	BELGIUM					M		[12]	
GUTWEIN	Yossef						M		[12]	
GUTWEIN	Michael						M		[15]	Died
GUTWIRTH	Awraham		1912		Tzvi Hersh		M		[9]	Died 1942
GUTWIRTH	Jozef		1935				M		[7]	
HAAS	Jakob I		1927				M		[3]	Died
HABER	Lila						F		[11]	Died
HADAR	Tzipora						F		[11]	Survived
HALBERSHTAM	Arieh Leibish	HALBERSHTADT					M		[2]	
HALBERSHTAM	Mrs						F		[2]	
HALBERSHTAM	Awigdor				Arieh Leib		M		[12]	
HALBERSHTAM	Chaim		1792		Arieh Leib		M		[10]	Died
HALBERSHTAM	Ruchel Feige	FRENKEL					F	Chaim	[10]	Died
HALBERSHTAM	Reitzel				Chaim	Ruchel Feige	F		[1]	married 1855
HALBERSHTAM	Miriam				Chaim	Ruchel Feige	F	Moshe	[10]	
HALBERSHTAM	Yetta				Chaim	Ruchel Feige	F	Eliezer Jeruchim	[1]	

Surname	First Name	Maiden Name	Birth Date	Residence	Father	Mother	Gender	Spouse	*Source	Remarks
HALBERSHTAM	Yehezkel Shra		1813		Chaim	Ruchel Feige	M		[10]	Died
HALBERSHTAM	Moshe				Yehezkel Shragai		M		[1]	
HALBERSHTAM	Simcha Yissachar				Yehezkel Shragai		M		[2]	
HALBERSHTAM	Shlomo				Yehezkel Shragai		M		[2]	
HALBERSHTAM	Naphtali				Shlomo				[10]	
HALBERSHTAM	Ben Zion				Shlomo				[10]	
HALBERSHTAM	Dawid		1821		Chaim	Ruchel Feige	M		[12]	Died
HALBERSHTAM	Naftali				Dawid		M		[2]	
HALBERSHTAM	Mendel				Naftali		M		[7]	
HALBERSHTAM	Meir Nussen				Chaim	Ruchel Feige	M		[12]	Died
HALBERSHTAM	Shloime		1847		Meir Nussen	Beila	M		[7]	
HALBERSHTAM	Chaya				Shloime	Rebecca Hen	F		[7]	
HALBERSHTAM	Ben Zion		1874		Shloime	Rebecca Hen	M		[7]	
HALBERSHTAM	Aaron		1826		Chaim	Ruchel Feige	M		[10]	Died
HALBERSHTAM	Shalom				Aaron	Chana Elke	M		[1]	Died
HALBERSHTAM	Moshe				Aaron	Chana Elke	M		[1]	Died
HALBERSHTAM	Ariel Leib				Aaron	Chana Elke	M		[1]	Died
HALBERSHTAM	Ephraim			Lwowska	Ariel Leibish		M		[10]	Died
HALBERSHTAM	Mordechai				Aaron	Chana Elke	M		[1]	
HALBERSHTAM	Moishele				Aaron	Chana Elke	M		[1]	

List of Jews in Sandz   APP-51

Surname	First Name	Maiden Name	Birth Date	Residence	Father	Mother	Gender	Spouse	*Source	Remarks
HALBERSHTAM	Shmelke				Aaron	Chana Elke	M		[1]	
HALBERSHTAM	Hersh				Aaron	Chana Elke	M		[1]	
HALBERSHTAM	Baruch		1826		Chaim	Ruchel Feige	M		[1]	Died
HALBERSHTAM	Elisha				Baruch	Pessel	M		[7]	
HALBERSHTAM	Shulem				Baruch	Pessel	M		[7]	
HALBERSHTAM	Yochewed				Baruch	Pessel	F		[7]	
HALBERSHTAM	Reisel				Baruch	Pessel	F		[7]	
HALBERSHTAM	Moshe		1850		Baruch	Pessel	M		[7]	
HALBERSHTAM	Chana		1853		Baruch	Pessel	F		[7]	
HALBERSHTAM	Zwi Hirsh		1858		Baruch	Pessel	M		[7]	
HALBERSHTAM	Yekutiel Y				Zwi Hirsh		M		[7]	Died
HALBERSHTAM	Tzwi Elimelech				Yekutiel Yehu		M		[1]	
HALBERSHTAM	Sinai		1869		Baruch	Pessel	M		[2]	Survived
HALBERSHTAM	Ruchama						F	Sinai	[2]	Survived
HALBERSHTAM	Aaron				Sinai	Ruchama	M		[2]	Died
HALBERSHTAM	Yaakow				Sinai	Ruchama	M		[2]	
HALBERSHTAM	Dawid				Sinai	Ruchama	M		[2]	
HALBERSHTAM	Baruch				Sinai	Ruchama	M		[2]	
HALBERSHTAM	Chaim Jud				Sinai	Ruchama	M		[2]	
HALBERSHTAM	Abraham Ab				Sinai	Ruchama	M		[2]	
HALBERSHTAM	Yehezkel				Sinai	Ruchama	M		[2]	
HALBERSHTAM	Pessel				Sinai	Ruchama	F		[2]	
HALBERSHTAM	Israel				Sinai	Ruchama	M		[2]	
HALBERSHTAM	Arieh				Sinai	Ruchama	M		[2]	
HALBERSHTAM	Chaim		1792		Arieh Leib		M		[2]	
HALBERSHTAM	Chaim		1792		Arieh Leib		M		[2]	
HALBERSHTAM	Fradel				Chaim	Rachel	F	Eliezer	[2]	
HALBERSHTAM	Nehema				Chaim	Rachel	F		[1]	Died
HALBERSHTAM	Gitel				Chaim	Rachel	F	Betzalel	[2]	Died
HALBERSHTAM	Tzila				Chaim	Rachel	F		[2]	

List of Jews in Sandz   APP-52

Surname	First Name	Maiden Name	Birth Date	Residence	Father	Mother	Gender	Spouse	*Source	Remarks
HALBERSHTAM	Shulem Eliezer		1862		Chaim	Rachel	M		[12]	Died
HALBERSHTAM	Bracha Sima				Shulem Eliezer	Sarah Miriam	F		[12]	
HALBERSHTAM	Chaim				Shulem Eliezer	Sarah Miriam	M		[2]	
HALBERSHTAM	Chaya Fr				Shulem Eliezer	Sarah Miriam	F		[2]	
HALBERSHTAM	Meshulem Zis				Shulem Eliezer	Sarah Miriam	M		[2]	
HALBERSHTAM	Adel				Shulem Eliezer	Sarah Miriam	F		[2]	
HALBERSHTAM	Isaac Yehosh		1864		Chaim	Rachel	M		[1]	
HALBERSHTAM	Hena				Isaac Yehosh		F	Menachem M	[7]	
HALBERSHTAM	Menachem M				Arie Leibush		M		[7]	
HALBERSHTAM	Haim		1793		Arie Leibush		M		[9]	Died 04/4/1876
HALBERSHTAM	Mordechai				Haim		M		[12]	
HALBERSHTAM	Aaron		1851		Aaron		M	Mordechai	[12]	
HALBERSHTAM	Ariel Leibish				Aaron		M		[9]	
HALBERSHTAM	Shalom				Aaron		M		[9]	
HALBERSHTAM	Ephraim			Lwowska	Arie Leib		M		[10]	Died
HALBERSHTAM	Hersh				Arie Leib		M		[12]	
HALBERSHTAM	Moshe				Aaron		M		[14]	
HALBERSHTAM	Arie Leibush				Moshe		M		[9]	
HALBERSHTAM	Mordechai Z.				Leibush		M		[9]	Died 25/4/1905
HALBERSHTAM	Baruch				Mordechai Z.		M		[9]	Died 25/4/1905
HALBERSHTAM	Hana Hersh						M		[14]	
HALBERSHTAM	Helen						F		[15]	Died
HALBERSHTAM	Beila						F		[15]	Died
HALBERSHTAM	Mordechai						M		[15]	Died
HALBERSHTAM	Hershel						M		[15]	Died
HALBERSHTAM	Sh. Rubin						M		[11]	USA
HALBERSHTAM	Szmaja			Kazimeirz			M		[10]	Died

Surname	First Name	Maiden Name	Birth Date	Residence	Father	Mother	Gender	Spouse	*Source	Remarks
HALBERSHTAM	Nafthali			Kazimeirz			M		[10]	Died
HALBERSTEIN	Hersh						M		[15]	Died
HALBERSTEIN	Ela						F		[15]	Died
HALBERSTEIN	Golda						F		[15]	Died
HALBERTAL	Lea						F		[11]	Died
HALBERTAL	Berisz						M		[11]	Died
HALBERTAL	Gitel						F		[11]	Died
HALBERTAL	Mendel						M		[11]	Died
HALBERTAL	Moshe						M		[11]	Died
HALBERTHAL	Emanuel						M		[12]	
HALBERTHAL	Lea					Emanuel	F		[12]	
HALBERTHAL	Haim						M		[12]	
HALBERTHAL	Haim						M		[12]	Survived
HALBERTHAL	Bernard						F		[15]	Died
HALTER	Feige						F		[15]	Died
HAMERSHLAG							M		[12]	
HAMMER							M		[12]	
HAMMER	Awraham						M		[15]	Died
HAMMER	Ida						F		[15]	Died
HAMMER	Yuda						M		[15]	Died
HAMMER	Blima						F		[15]	Died
HANDEL	Alfred						M		[11]	Survived
HANDEL	Erica						F	Alfred	[11]	Survived
HANNENBERG	Abraham						M		[15]	Died
HARBETHAL	Menahem						M		[3]	Died
HARTMAN	Menashe						M		[11]	Died
HARTMAN	Riwka Lea						F		[11]	Died
HARTMAN	Nahum						M		[11]	Died
HARTMAN	Chana						F		[11]	Died
HASENLAUF	Karol		1918				F		[7]	Survived
HAUPTSCHEIN	Israel						M		[15]	Died
HAUPTSTEIN	Shlomo						M		[15]	Died
HAUSENSHTOCK	Benyamin						M		[10]	Survived

List of Jews in Sandz   APP-54

Surname	First Name	Maiden Name	Birth Date	Residence	Father	Mother	Gender	Spouse	*Source	Remarks
HAUSNER	Shmuel						M		[12]	Survived
HAUSNER	Beile						F		[15]	Died
HAUSNER	Rachel						F		[15]	Died
HAUSNER	Sam						M		[11]	Survived
HAUSNER	Emma						F	Sam	[11]	Survived
HAUSNER	Helena		1905				F		[7]	
HAUSNER	Ignacy		1937				M		[7]	
HAUSSTOK	Izak						M		[15]	Died
HAUSSZTOCK	Gitel						F		[15]	Died
HAUSSZTOCK	Feige						F		[15]	Died
HAUSSZTOCK	Chaim						M		[15]	Died
HAYOS	Moshe						M		[10]	Survived
HECHMAN	Ch.						M		[12]	
HECHT	Mendel						M		[11]	Died
HECHT							M		[12]	
HECHT	Yaakow						M		[12]	
HECHT	Dora						F		[9]	
HECHT	Mindza			Romanowskiego 4			F		[10]	Died in Belzec 1942
HEFTEL	Israel						M		[10]	Survived
HEILMAN	Shlomom						M		[15]	Died
HEINIG	Yossef						M		[10]	Survived
HEIT	Hersh						M		[14]	
HEIZIGER	Melech						M		[10]	Survived
HEIZIGER	Dina						F		[10]	Survived
HEIZIGER	Hannah-Dwora						F		[10]	Survived
HEIZIGER	Taube						F		[10]	Survived
HEIZIGER	Rosalia						F		[10]	Survived
HELLER	Awraham						M		[12]	
HELMAN	Usher						M		[15]	Died
HELTZEL	Cila						F		[15]	Died
HENIG	Itzhak						M		[11]	Died
HENIG							M		[12]	

Surname	First Name	Maiden Name	Birth Date	Residence	Father	Mother	Gender	Spouse	*Source	Remarks
HENIG	Nathan						M		[12]	
HENNBERGER	Awraham						M		[15]	Died
HENNBERGER	Salomon						M		[11]	Survived
HENNBERGER							F	Salomon	[11]	Survived
HENOCH	fam			Romanowskiego 4					[10]	Died
HENOCH	Taube						F		[15]	Died
HENOCH	Nathan						M		[11]	USA
HERB	Leibish						M		[14]	
HERBACH	Hersz Tzwi						M		[15]	Died
HERBACH	Yehudit						F		[15]	Died
HERBACH	Ita						F		[15]	Died
HERBACH	Szlomo						M		[15]	Died
HERBACH	Yehudit						F		[15]	Died
HERBACH	Chaskel						M		[15]	Died
HERBACH	Ita						F		[15]	Died
HERBSMAN	Abraham						M		[15]	Died
HERBSMAN	Bluma						F		[15]	Died
HERBST							M		[11]	Died
HERBST	Leon		1909				M		[7]	
HERBST	Shmuel				Haim		M		[12]	died in Russia
HERBST	Shlomo				Haim		M		[12]	
HERBST	Moshe		1897				M		[2]	died in Russia
HERBST	Henrik						M		[12]	sport
HERBST	Harmiel						M		[12]	brother
HERBST	Hanoch						M		[12]	brother
HERBST	Abramtche						M		[12]	
HERBST	Henek				Abramtche		M		[12]	Died
HERBST	Masza				Abramtche		M		[12]	Survived
HERBST	Ignac				Abramtche		M		[12]	Died
HERBST	Henech						M		[12]	
HERBST	Yossef						M		[14]	
HERBST	Haim						M		[14]	
HERBST	Shlomo						M		[14]	

List of Jews in Sandz   APP-56

Surname	First Name	Maiden Name	Birth Date	Residence	Father	Mother	Gender	Spouse	*Source	Remarks
HERBST	Malka						F		[15]	Died
HERBST	Ruzia						F		[15]	Died
HERBST	Riza						F		[15]	Died
HERBST	Maksimilian						M		[7]	Died
HERBSTMAN	Naphtali						M		[11]	Died
HERBSTMAN	Tzwia						F		[11]	Died
HERBSTMAN	Sala						F		[11]	Died
HERBSTMAN	Naphtali						M		[15]	Died
HERBSTMAN	Zwi						M		[15]	Died
HERSHBERG	Hersz		1909				M		[7]	
HERSHEL	Leizer						M		[11]	Survived
HERSHKOWICZ	Eliyahu						M		[11]	Died
HERSHKOWICZ	Hadassa						F		[11]	Died
HERSHKOWICZ	Chaim						M		[11]	Died
HERSHKOWICZ	Naftali						M		[12]	Survived
HERSHKOWITZ	Chaim		1909				M		[3]	Died
HERSHSTAHL	Dow						M		[12]	Survived
HERSHSTAHL	Barak						M		[12]	
HERSHSTAHL	Heshek						M		[12]	Died
HERSHTAL	Yossef						M		[11]	Died
HERSHTAL	Liba						F		[11]	Died
HERSHTAL	Eliezar						M		[11]	Died
HERSHTAL	Tzwi						M		[11]	Died
HERSHTAL	Moshe						M		[11]	Died
HERSHTAL	Regina						F		[11]	Died
HERSHTEL	Cesia						F		[15]	Died
HERTZBERG	Hersz						M		[11]	Survived
HERTZBERG	Rywka						F		[15]	Died
HERTZBERG	H						M		[11]	Survived
HERTZBERG	Tzwi						M		[10]	Survived
HERTZBERGER	Gershon						M		[14]	
HERTZBERGER	Moshe						M		[10]	Died
HERTZBERGER	Mrs+child						F	Moshe	[10]	Died

List of Jews in Sandz   APP-57

Surname	First Name	Maiden Name	Birth Date	Residence	Father	Mother	Gender	Spouse	*Source	Remarks
HERZIG	Aaron						M		[15]	Died
HERZIG	Jakub		1896				M		[7]	
HERZIG	Zofia		1901				F		[7]	
HIESIGER-TEITELBAUM MEILECH			1893				M		[9]	Died
HILFSTEIN	Haim						M		[12]	
HILLEL	Naphtali	ABEK					M		[11]	Died
HILLEL	Czessia				Naphtali		F		[11]	Died
HILLEL	Abba						M		[12]	
HILLEL	Adolf		1915				M		[7]	
HILOWICZ	Towa						F		[11]	Died
HILOWICZ	Yossef						M		[11]	Died
HILOWICZ	Freidil						F		[11]	Died
HILOWICZ	Aaron Dow						M		[11]	Died
HILTZER	Yossef						M		[12]	
HINDBERG	Tunka						F		[12]	
HIRSCH	Abraham		1908				M		[2]	Died
HIRSCHEL	Aron						M		[15]	Died
HIRSCHEL	Mendel						M		[15]	Died
HIRSCHFELD	Sara						F		[15]	Died
HIRSH	Baruch						M		[11]	Died
HIRSH	Paula						F		[11]	Died
HIRSHFELD	Abraham						M		[15]	Died
HOBLENSTEIN	Aron Meir						M		[14]	
HOCHAJZER	Yehudit						F		[15]	Died
HOCHBERGER	Awraham						M		[11]	Died
HOCHBERGER	Lea	KEITELMAN					F		[11]	Died
HOCHBERGER	Gershon						M		[15]	Died
HOCHBERGER	Sara						F		[15]	Died
HOCHBERGER	Riwka						F		[15]	Died
HOCHBERGER	Ena						F		[15]	Died
HOCHENHAUSER	Dawid						M		[12]	Died

List of Jews in Sandz   APP-58

Surname	First Name	Maiden Name	Birth Date	Residence	Father	Mother	Gender	Spouse	*Source	Remarks
HOCHENHAUSER	Benjamin						M		[15]	Died
HOCHENHAUSER	Abraham						M		[15]	Died
HOCHENHAUSER	Moshe						M		[15]	Died
HOCHENHAUSER	Dawid		1893				M		[7]	Died
HOCHENHAUSER	Pinkas						M		[15]	Died
HOCHENHAUSER	Rysick		1934				M		[7]	
HOCHMAN	H.						M		[12]	
HOLCER	Rywka						F		[15]	Died
HOLCER	Ester						F		[15]	Died
HOLCER	Abraham						M		[15]	Died
HOLCER	Szmuel						M		[15]	Died
HOLCER	Szymon						M		[15]	Died
HOLCER	Shlomo						M		[15]	Died
HOLCER	Natan						M		[15]	Died
HOLDER	Leib						M		[15]	Died
HOLLANDER	Zigmunt						M		[11]	Died
HOLLANDER	Natan Dow						M		[11]	Died
HOLLANDER	Dawid						M		[12]	
HOLLANDER	Betta						F		[12]	
HOLLANDER	Minke						F		[12]	
HOLLANDER	Ruchtche						F		[12]	
HOLLANDER	Frania						F		[12]	shot
HOLLANDER	Jeruchim						M		[9]	Died
HOLLANDER	Amalia						F		[9]	Died
HOLLANDER	Awraham						M		[14]	
HOLLANDER	Josef						M		[15]	Died
HOLLANDER	Emilia						F		[15]	Died
HOLLANDER	Fania						F		[9]	Died
HOLLANDER	Aron						M		[15]	Died
HOLLANDER	Fela						F		[15]	Died
HOLLANDER	Feige						F		[15]	Died
HOLLANDER	H						M		[11]	Survived
HOLLANDER	Abraham						M		[11]	Survived

List of Jews in Sandz   APP-59

Surname	First Name	Maiden Name	Birth Date	Residence	Father	Mother	Gender	Spouse	*Source	Remarks
HOLLANDER	Abraham						M		[11]	Survived
HOLTZER	Zew						M		[11]	Survived
HOLTZER	Riwka						F		[11]	Survived
HOLTZER	Abba						M		[11]	Survived
HOLTZER	Gusta						F		[11]	Died
HOLTZER	Yehudit						F		[11]	Died
HOLTZER	Yehezkel						M		[11]	Died
HOLTZER	Menahem Me						M		[11]	Died
HOLTZER	Yohanan Wo						M		[11]	Died
HOLTZER	Chaim						M		[11]	Died
HOLTZER	Tzirel						F		[11]	Died
HOLTZER	Wolf						M		[11]	Died
HOLTZER	Esther Riwk						F		[11]	Died
HOLTZER	Gitel	KUS					F		[11]	Died
HOLTZER	Idit						F		[11]	Died
HOLTZER	Mendel						M		[11]	Died
HOLTZER	Esther						F		[11]	Died
HOLTZER	Schakne						M		[12]	Poalei Zion
HOLTZER	Riwkah						F		[12]	
HOLTZER							M		[12]	
HOLTZER	Reuven						M		[12]	Survived
HOLTZER	Male						M		[12]	
HOLTZER	Wilek						M		[12]	Survived
HOLTZER	Shachne						M		[12]	Died
HOLTZER	Haim						M		[12]	Died
HOLTZER	Shmuel						M		[14]	
HOLTZER	Natan						M		[15]	Died
HOLTZER	Reisla						F		[15]	Died
HOLTZER	Menashe						M		[15]	Died
HOLTZER	Bluma						F		[15]	Died
HOLTZER	Abba		1916				M		[10]	Survived
HOLTZER	Leib		1904				M		[10]	Survived
HOLTZER	Shimon						M		[10]	Survived

List of Jews in Sandz   APP-60

Surname	First Name	Maiden Name	Birth Date	Residence	Father	Mother	Gender	Spouse	*Source	Remarks
HOLTZER	Kalman		12/5/1905		Shimon		M		[9]	
HOLTZER	Yossef		1909				M		[10]	Survived
HOLTZER	Natan						M		[10]	Survived
HOLTZER	Fruma						F		[10]	Survived
HOLTZER	Lea						F		[10]	Survived
HOLTZER	Chaskel		1905				M		[7]	
HOLTZER-RIGGER	Malka						F		[12]	
HOLTZHEISER	Dawid						M		[12]	
HOLZER	Herman						M		[11]	Survived
HOMET	Awraham						M		[12]	
HONIG	Moses						M		[4]	
HORN	Abraham						M		[15]	Died
HORN	Rachel						F		[15]	Died
HORN	Samuel						M		[15]	Died
HORNER	Lea						F		[15]	Died
HORNSTEIN	Awraham	KORN					M		[11]	Died
HORNSTEIN	Yehudit						M		[11]	Died
HORNSTEIN	Tzwi Itz						M		[11]	Died
HORNSTEIN	Yossef						M		[11]	Died
HORNSTEIN	Chaya Ita						F		[11]	Died
HORNSTEIN	Feige						F		[11]	Died
HORNSTEIN	Esther						F		[11]	Died
HORNSTEIN	Rachel						F		[11]	Died
HORNSTEIN	Miriam						F		[11]	Died
HORNSTEIN	Sara						F		[11]	Died
HORNUNG	Yaakow						M		[11]	Died
HORNUNG	Berta						F		[11]	Died
HORNUNG	leopold		1919				M		[7]	
HOROWITZ	Beila						F	Meir Nussen	[2]	
HOROWITZ	ReiselSar				Sinai	Ruchama	F		[2]	
HOROWITZ	Aaron Dow						M		[11]	Died

List of Jews in Sandz   APP-61

Surname	First Name	Maiden Name	Birth Date	Residence	Father	Mother	Gender	Spouse	*Source	Remarks
HOROWITZ	Reisel						F		[11]	Died
HOROWITZ	Tzwi						M		[11]	Died
HOROWITZ	Chaim						M		[11]	Died
HOROWITZ	Awraham						M		[11]	Died
HOROWITZ	Chaim						M		[11]	Died
HOROWITZ	Zew						M		[11]	Died
HOROWITZ	Rachel						F		[11]	Died
HOROWITZ	Feige						F		[11]	Died
HOROWITZ	Itzhak						M		[11]	Died
HOROWITZ	Mchael						M		[11]	Died
HOROWITZ	Moshe Mend						M		[11]	Died
HOROWITZ	Sara						F		[11]	Died
HOROWITZ	Awraham	ABUSH					M		[11]	Died
HOROWITZ	Hena						F		[15]	Died
HOROWITZ	Toibe						F		[15]	Died
HOROWITZ	Meilech						M		[15]	Died
HOROWITZ	Sara						F		[15]	Died
HOROWITZ	Feige						F		[15]	Died
HOROWITZ	Samuel						M		[15]	Died
HOROWITZ	Reisel						F		[15]	Died
HOROWITZ	Dawid						M		[11]	Died
HOROWITZ	Abraham		1906				M		[3]	Died
HOROWITZ	Shmelke		1907				M		[3]	Died
HOROWITZ	Alish						M		[12]	
HOROWITZ	Dudel	HERTZOG					M		[12]	
HOROWITZ	Shmelke						M		[12]	
HOROWITZ	Max						M		[12]	
HOROWITZ	Luis						M		[12]	
HOROWITZ	Leon						M		[12]	
HOROWITZ	Edek						M		[12]	
HOROWITZ	Jakub	LEMBERG					M		[12]	
HOROWITZ		MOHRER					M		[12]	
HOROWITZ	Chaim						M		[15]	Died

Surname	First Name	Maiden Name	Birth Date	Residence	Father	Mother	Gender	Spouse	*Source	Remarks
HOROWITZ	Mindel						F		[15]	Died
HOROWITZ	Sara						F		[15]	Died
HOROWITZ	Berl						M		[15]	Died
HOROWITZ	Abraham						M		[15]	Died
HOROWITZ	Sara						F		[15]	Died
HOROWITZ	M						M		[11]	Survived
HOROWITZ	Sidney						M		[11]	Survived
HOROWITZ							F	Sidney	[11]	Survived
HOROWITZ	Aron Reuven				Asher Natan		F		[9]	
HOROWITZ	Regina		1873				F		[9]	Died 1937
HOTCHKE	Awraham						M		[12]	
HOWERS	Leib						M		[15]	Died
HUSCH	Henry						M		[11]	Survived
HUTA	Sara						F		[15]	Died
HUTA	Dawid						M		[15]	Died
IBEREICH	Frida						F		[11]	Died
IBEREICH	Malka						F		[11]	Died
IBEREICH	Sara						F		[11]	Died
IBEREICH	Freidil						F		[11]	Died
IBEREICH	Feivel						M		[11]	Died
IBEREICH	Yehezkel						M		[15]	Died
IBEREICH	Eliyahu						M		[15]	Died
IBEREICH	Shragai						M		[15]	Died
IBEREICH	Sara						F		[15]	Died
IBEREICH	Lea						F		[15]	Died
IBEREICH	Nataniel						M		[15]	Died
IBEREICH	Gitel						F		[15]	Died
IBEREICH	Melech						M		[12]	
IBEREICH	Neche						F		[15]	Died
IBEREICH	Samuel						M		[15]	Died
IBERRAICH	Abraham						M		[15]	Died
IBERRAICH	Herzel						M		[15]	Died

List of Jews in Sandz   APP-63

Surname	First Name	Maiden Name	Birth Date	Residence	Father	Mother	Gender	Spouse	*Source	Remarks
IBERRAICH	Hershel						M		[15]	Died
IBERRAICH	Karola						F		[15]	Died
IBERRAICH	Shaul						M		[15]	Died
INDIGO	Feiga		1887				F		[2]	Died
INDIGO	Samuel		1884				M		[2]	Died
IZKOWICZ	Shimon						M		[10]	Russia
ISAKOWICZ	Wolf						M		[15]	Died
ISAKOWICZ	Minka						F		[15]	Died
ISAKOWICZ	Rosa						F		[15]	Died
ISAKOWICZ	Hela						F		[15]	Died
IZAKOWICZ	Wof Dawid						M		[11]	Died
IZAKOWICZ	Mina						F		[11]	Died
IZAKOWICZ	Hela						F		[11]	Died
IZAKOWICZ	Roza			Lwowska 56			F		[11]	Died
IZAKOWICZ							M		[11]	Died
IZAKOWICZ							M		[12]	died
IZAKOWICZ	Hershel						M		[11]	Survived
IZAKOWICZ	Regine						F	Hersh	[11]	Survived
IZAKOWICZ	Shimon						M		[10]	Survived
JACHTZEL	Shimon						M		[14]	
JAKUBOWICZ	Aron						M		[15]	Died
JAKUBOWICZ	Mathilda						F		[15]	Died
JAKUBOWICZ	Mina						F		[15]	Died
JAKUBOWICZ	Matil						F		[15]	Died
JAKUBOWICZ	Rosalia						F		[15]	Died
JAKUBOWICZ	Matil						F		[15]	Died
JAKUBOWICZ	bARUCH		1916				M		[7]	
JARMIN	Melech						M		[15]	Died
JEDWAB	Breindl						F		[15]	Died
JEDWAB	Breindl						F		[15]	Died
JOSEFSTAL	Mendel						M		[15]	Died
JOSEFSTHAL							M		[2]	Died
JUNGMAN	Yehoshua						M		[15]	Died

List of Jews in Sandz APP-64

Surname	First Name	Maiden Name	Birth Date	Residence	Father	Mother	Gender	Spouse	*Source	Remarks
KAHANE				Kazimeirz			M		[10]	Died
KALB	Usher		1908				M		[3]	Died
KALBER	Moses						M		[11]	USA
KALECHSTEIN	Deborah						F		[15]	Died
KALECHSTEIN	Zwi						M		[15]	Died
KALFUSS	Ester						F		[15]	Died
KALTER	Zisel						F		[15]	Died
KALTER	Matateusz						M		[15]	Died
KALTER	Susla						F		[15]	Died
KAMHOLZ	Abraham						M		[4]	
KAMPF	Frania						F		[12]	
KAMPLBEAR	E.						M		[12]	USA
KAMPLER	Fanie						F		[15]	Died
KANENGEISSER	Awraham						M		[11]	Died
KANENGEISSER	Tzwi						M		[11]	Died
KANENGEISSER	Bluma						F		[11]	Died
KANENGEISSER	Moshe Jos.						M		[12]	Died
KANENGEISSER	Lewi			Romanowskiego 4			M		[11]	Died
KANENGEISSER	Mordechai				Yaakow	Ita	M		[2]	Survived
KANENGISSER	Dawid		1910				M		[3]	Died
KANNENGISSER	Abraham						M		[15]	Died
KANNENGISSER	Moshe						M		[15]	Died
KANNENGISSER	Josz			Kazimeirz			M		[10]	Died
KANNENGISSER	Yaakow				Lewi		M		[2]	Died
KANNENGISSER	Ita						F	Yaakow	[2]	Died
KANNENGISSER	Rachel				Yaakow	Ita	F		[2]	Died
KANNENGISSER	Moshe				Yaakow	Ita	M		[2]	Died
KANNER	Baruch						M		[6]	Died
KANNER	Yaakow						M		[12]	
KANNER	Raphael						M		[12]	
KANNER	Moshe					Raphael	M		[12]	
KANNER	Maria		1913				F		[7]	Survived
KANT	Fryda		1894				F		[2]	Died

List of Jews in Sandz   APP-65

Surname	First Name	Maiden Name	Birth Date	Residence	Father	Mother	Gender	Spouse	*Source	Remarks
KANT	Henryk		1872				M		[2]	Died
KANT	Yaakow						M		[15]	Died
KANTOR	Ester						F		[15]	Died
KAPLIANSKI							M		[12]	
KARKOWSKY	Lea	KORAL	1912		Dow Ber	Breine	F		[2]	Survived
KARMIN	Elka						F		[15]	Died
KATZ	Frida	BRADER					F	Itzhak	[11]	Died
KATZ	Itzhak						M		[11]	Died
KATZ	Awraham						M		[11]	Survived
KATZ	Moses						M		[2]	Died
KATZ	Shlomo						M		[6]	Israel
KATZ	Yankel						M		[12]	
KATZ	Aaron						M		[12]	
KATZ	Hertz						M		[12]	
KATZ	Zimel						M		[12]	Died
KATZ	Tovia						M		[14]	
KATZ	Yosef						M		[15]	Died
KATZ	Freide						F		[15]	Died
KATZ	Abraham						M		[15]	Died
KATZ	Freide						F		[15]	Died
KATZ	Moses						M		[11]	Survived
KATZ	Moshe						M		[10]	Survived
KATZ	Alwin						M		[10]	Survived
KATZ	Regina						F		[10]	Survived
KAUFER	Simcha						M		[11]	Died
KAUFER	Malka						F		[11]	Died
KAUFER	Yaakow						M		[11]	Died
KAUFER	Chana						F		[11]	Died
KAUFER	Mendel						M		[11]	Died
KAUFER	Riwka						F		[11]	Died
KAUFER	Herman		1898				M		[2]	Died
KAUFER	Markus		1871				M		[2]	Died
KAUFER	Mendel		1896				M		[2]	Died

Surname	First Name	Maiden Name	Birth Date	Residence	Father	Mother	Gender	Spouse	*Source	Remarks
KAUFER	Hirsh		1920				M		[3]	Died
KAUFER	Sala						F		[12]	
KAUFER	Yoel						M		[15]	Died
KAUFER	Rachel						F		[15]	Died
KAUFER	Moniek						M		[15]	Died
KAUFER	Rachel						F		[15]	Died
KAUFER	Stela						F		[15]	Died
KAUFER	Emil						F		[15]	Died
KAUFER	Stela						F		[15]	Died
KAUFER	Gershon						M		[15]	Died
KAUFER	Stella						F		[15]	Died
KAUFER	Zofia						F		[15]	Died
KAUFER	Mozes				Elias		M		[9]	Died
KAUFER	Shlomo						M		[15]	Died
KAUFER	Reuben						M		[10]	Survived
KAUFMAN	Gerszon						M		[15]	Died
KAUFTEIL	Yaakow L.						M		[12]	
KAUFTEIL	Kuba						M		[12]	Survived
KAUFTEIL	Doba						F		[15]	Died
KAUFTEL	Chaja						F		[15]	Died
KAUFTEL							M		[6]	
KAUL	Neche						F		[15]	Died
KAUL	Motel						M		[15]	Died
KAULBER							M		[12]	
KAULBER	Lewy						M		[12]	Died
KAULBER							M		[12]	
KAULBER	Moshe						M		[12]	Died
KEIL	Lea						F		[12]	
KEIL	Leibush						M		[12]	
KEIL	Yidel						M		[12]	Survived
KEIL	Salomea						F		[15]	Died
KEIL	Yeshayahu						M		[15]	Died
KEIL	Joseph						M		[11]	USA

List of Jews in Sandz   APP-67

Surname	First Name	Maiden Name	Birth Date	Residence	Father	Mother	Gender	Spouse	*Source	Remarks
KEIL							F	Joseph	[11]	USA
KETELMAN	Gerszon						M		[11]	Died
KETELMAN	Fela						F		[11]	Died
KELER	Israel Chaim						M		[11]	Died
KELER	Moshe		1914				M		[7]	Survived
KELER	Bracha						F		[15]	Died
KELER	Yaakov						M		[15]	Died
KELER	Abraham						M		[15]	Died
KELER	Emalia						F		[15]	Died
KELER	Sima						F		[15]	Died
KELER	Amalia						F		[15]	Died
KEMPINSKA	Regina		6/6/1913		Moshe		F		[9]	
KEMPLER	Tzwi						M		[11]	Survived
KEMPLER	Bluma						F		[11]	Survived
KEMPLER	Yohanan						M		[11]	Died
KEMPLER	Ryfka		1880				F		[2]	Died
KEMPLER	Miriam						F		[12]	
KEMPLER							M		[12]	
KEMPLER	Bluma						F		[12]	
KEMPLER	Herman						M		[12]	Survived
KEMPLER	Yossef						M		[15]	Died
KEMPLER	Fanie						F		[15]	Died
KEMPLER	Emil						M		[11]	USA
KEMPLER							F		[11]	USA
KEMPLER	Zeew						M		[10]	Survived
KEMPNER	Kalman						M		[15]	Died
KEONIG	Michael						M		[15]	Died
KERBEL							M		[12]	kehilla
KERBEL	Mauricy						M		[12]	
KESSAR	Moshe						M		[10]	Survived
KETTLER	Yaakow						M		[12]	
KETZEL	Itche						M		[12]	Died
KEZCAL	Israel						M		[12]	

List of Jews in Sandz   APP-68

Surname	First Name	Maiden Name	Birth Date	Residence	Father	Mother	Gender	Spouse	*Source	Remarks
KICHELMACHER	Ziga						F		[15]	Died
KICHELMACHER	Taube						F		[15]	Died
KINDERMAN	Peshke						M		[11]	Died
KINDERMAN	Peshke						F		[12]	
KINDERMAN	Yankel						M		[12]	
KINDERMAN	Cirl						F		[15]	Died
KINDERMAN	Anze						F		[15]	Died
KINDERMAN	Dov						M		[15]	Died
KINDERMAN	Yecheskel						M		[15]	Died
KINDERMAN	Menachem						M		[15]	Died
KINDERMANN							M		[2]	Died
KINDERMANN	Chaim Hersh		1910				M		[3]	Died
KINREICH	Dawid						M		[11]	Died
KINSTLER	Iza						M		[12]	sport
KIPPEL							M		[12]	Survived
KIPPEL							M		[12]	Survived
KIRSCHENBAUM	Hela						F		[11]	Died
KIRSCHENBAUM	Chaim						M		[15]	Died
KIRSCHENBAUM	Moshe						M		[10]	Survived
KIRSCHENBAUM	Livia						F		[10]	Survived
KIRSCHENBAUM	Chaim Yossef						M		[10]	Survived
KLAFTER	Markus I.		1905				M		[3]	Died
KLAFTER	Shlomo						M		[12]	
KLAFTER	Mina						F		[15]	Died
KLAFTER	Bronislawa						F		[15]	Died
KLAFTER	Yossef						M		[15]	Died
KLAFTER	Mindzia						F		[15]	Died
KLAFTER	Ester						F		[15]	Died
KLAGSBALD	Raja						F		[12]	
KLAGSBALD	Blima						F		[15]	Died
KLAGSBALD	Eisig						M		[15]	Died
KLAGSBALD	Baruch						M		[15]	Died
KLAGSBALD	Eber						M		[15]	Died

Surname	First Name	Maiden Name	Birth Date	Residence	Father	Mother	Gender	Spouse	*Source	Remarks
KLAGSBALD	Akiwa						M		[14]	
KLAGSBALD	Moshe				Akiva		M		[14]	
KLAGSBALD	Serenke						F		[15]	Died
KLAHR	Reisel						F		[11]	Died
KLAHR	Riwka						F		[11]	Died
KLAHR	Mela						F		[11]	Died
KLAHR	Abraham Ya						M		[15]	Died
KLAJERMAN	Gerszon		1922				M		[7]	Survived
KLAPHOLTZ	Frimet						F		[11]	Died
KLAPHOLTZ	Awraham						M		[11]	Died
KLAPHOLTZ	Elsa						F		[11]	Died
KLAPHOLTZ	Wolf						M		[11]	Died
KLAPHOLTZ	Rachel						F		[12]	
KLAPHOLTZ	Liba						F		[12]	
KLAPHOLTZ	Mendel						M		[12]	
KLAPHOLTZ	Mindel						F		[12]	
KLAPHOLTZ	Dawid						M		[12]	
KLAPHOLTZ	Leibish						M		[12]	
KLAPHOLTZ	Elisha						M		[12]	
KLAPHOLTZ	Moshe M.						M		[12]	
KLAPHOLTZ	Abish						M		[14]	
KLAPHOLTZ	Abraham						M		[15]	Died
KLAPHOLTZ	Aron						M		[15]	Died
KLAPHOLTZ	Dwora						F		[15]	Died
KLAPHOLTZ	Hershel						M		[15]	Died
KLAPHOLTZ	Yaakow						M		[15]	Died
KLAPHOLTZ	Mosze						M		[15]	Died
KLAPHOLTZ	Elias						M		[15]	Died
KLAPHOLTZ	Helena						F		[15]	Died
KLAPHOLTZ	Libi						F		[15]	Died
KLAPHOLTZ	Wolf						M		[15]	Died
KLAPTER							M		[12]	
KLASZ	Ester						F		[15]	Died

Surname	First Name	Maiden Name	Birth Date	Residence	Father	Mother	Gender	Spouse	*Source	Remarks
KLAUSNER	Moshe						M		[11]	Died
KLAUSNER	Malka						F		[11]	Died
KLAUSNER	Shlomo						M		[11]	Died
KLAUSNER	Sheindel						F		[11]	Died
KLAUSNER	Sara						F		[11]	Died
KLAUSNER	Itzhak						M		[11]	Died
KLAUSNER	Mania						F		[11]	Died
KLAUSNER	Zissel						F		[11]	Died
KLAUSNER	Awraham						M		[11]	Died
KLAUSNER	Rachel						F		[11]	Died
KLAUSNER	Yoel						M		[11]	Died
KLAUSNER	Hiel						M		[11]	Died
KLAUSNER	Chaim						M		[11]	Died
KLAUSNER	Rachel						F		[11]	Died
KLAUSNER	Ruzke						F		[12]	
KLAUSNER	Yochewed						F		[12]	
KLAUSNER							M		[12]	
KLAUSNER	Dawid						M		[14]	
KLAUSNER	Liba						F		[15]	Died
KLAUSNER	Shlomo						M		[15]	Died
KLAUSNER	Rosa						F		[15]	Died
KLAUSNER	Moshe						M		[15]	Died
KLAUSNER	Emalia						F		[15]	Died
KLAUSNER	Feivel						M		[15]	Died
KLAUSNER	Abraham						M		[15]	Died
KLAUSNER	Shlomo						M		[15]	Died
KLAUSNER	Etka						F		[10]	Survived
KLEIN	Benzion		1888				M		[2]	Died
KLEIN	Mirla		1898				F		[2]	Died
KLEIN	Polke						M		[12]	
KLEIN	Rafael						M		[12]	
KLEIN	Armin						M		[15]	Died
KLEIN	Henryka		1911				F		[7]	Survived

List of Jews in Sandz   APP-71

Surname	First Name	Maiden Name	Birth Date	Residence	Father	Mother	Gender	Spouse	*Source	Remarks
KLEIN	Tadek						M		[10]	Survived
KLEIN	Jozef		1912				M		[7]	
KLEINBERGER	Aron		1906				M		[3]	Died
KLEINBERGER	Awichail						M		[12]	Survived
KLEINBERGER	Awichail	.					M		[14]	
KLEINER	Szimon						M		[15]	Died
KLEINMAN	Edmund		1899				M		[7]	
KLEINMAN	Lidja		1930				F		[7]	
KLEINMAN	Mina						F		[12]	
KLEINMAN	Yankele						M		[12]	
KLEINMAN	Libi						F		[15]	Died
KLEINMAN	Abraham						M		[15]	Died
KLEINMAN	Regina						F		[15]	Died
KLEINMAN	Heleba						F		[15]	Died
KLEINZAHLER	Riwka						F		[11]	Died
KLEINZAHLER	Ydel						M		[11]	Died
KLEINZAHLER	Tania						F		[11]	Died
KLEINZAHLER	Pessia						F		[11]	Died
KLEINZAHLER	Mendel						M		[11]	Died
KLEINZAHLER	Salomon						M		[12]	
KLEINZAHLER	Abraham						M		[15]	Died
KLEINZAHLER	Esther						F		[15]	Died
KLEINZAHLER	Khaya						F		[15]	Died
KLEINZAHLER	Fajwel		1926				M		[7]	Survived
KLEINZAHLER	Fajwel		1923				M		[7]	Survived
KLEINZELLER	Yuda						M		[15]	Died
KLER	Rywka						F		[15]	Died
KLER	Gitel						F		[15]	Died
KLER	Reisel						F		[15]	Died
KLER	Rachel						F		[15]	Died
KLEZMER	Hershel						M		[14]	
KLIGER	Tovia						M		[14]	

List of Jews in Sandz   APP-72

Surname	First Name	Maiden Name	Birth Date	Residence	Father	Mother	Gender	Spouse	*Source	Remarks
KLIGER	Ita						F		[15]	Died
KLIMONT	Berisz						M		[15]	Died
KLIMONT	Jakob						M		[4]	
KLINGER	Sarah						F		[12]	
KLINGER	Zishe						M		[12]	Died
KLINGER	Yehoshua						M		[12]	Died
KLOTZ	Chiel						M		[11]	Died
KLOTZ	Nancy						F		[11]	Survived
KLUGER	Max						M		[12]	
KLUGER	Melech						M		[12]	
KLUGER	Yossef						M		[15]	Died
KNEBEL	Zahava-Lut	BUCHBAND					F	Yehuda	[11]	Survived
KNEBEL	Yehuda						M		[12]	Nowy Sacz Society. Survived
KNEBEL	Neche						F		[12]	
KNEBEL	Zahava	ZLATE					F	Yehuda		died
KNEBEL	Moshe						M		[10]	Survived
KNEBEL	Oscar						M		[10]	Survived
KNOBEL	Berish						M		[12]	
KNOBEL	Lea						F		[15]	Died
KNOBEL	Leja						F		[15]	Died
KNOBEL	Henia						F		[10]	Survived
KNOBEL	Zeew						M		[10]	Survived
KNOBLECH	Baruch						M		[11]	Died
KNOBLECH	Menahem						M		[11]	Died
KNOBLECH	Esther						F		[11]	Died
KOENIGSBERG	Szmuel						M		[15]	Died
KOENIGSBERG	Barbara		1916				F		[7]	Survived
KOFFER	Herman						M		[15]	Died
KOIFCZYIK	Rachela						F		[15]	Died
KOIFER	Itzhak						M		[12]	
KOLBER	Dawid						M		[11]	Died

List of Jews in Sandz APP-73

Surname	First Name	Maiden Name	Birth Date	Residence	Father	Mother	Gender	Spouse	*Source	Remarks
KOLBER	Baruch						M		[11]	Died
KOLBER	Awraham						M		[11]	Died
KOLBER	Pessel						F		[11]	Died
KOLBER	Arie-Leibisz						M		[11]	Died
KOLBER	Itzhak						M		[11]	Died
KOLBER	Chawa Sara						F		[11]	Died
KOLBER	Tzwi						M		[11]	Died
KOLBER	Mordechai						M		[11]	Died
KOLBER	Mindel						F	Mordechai	[11]	Died
KOLBER	Malcha						F		[15]	Died
KOLBER	Yaakov						M		[15]	Died
KOLBER	Markus						M		[15]	Died
KOLBER	Itzik						M		[15]	Died
KOLBER	Abraham						M		[15]	Died
KOLBER	Sheindel						F		[15]	Died
KOLBER	Zacharia						M		[15]	Died
KOLBER	Pesl						F		[15]	Died
KOLBER	Benjamin						M		[15]	Died
KOLBER	Aron						M		[15]	Died
KOLBER	Frida						F		[15]	Died
KOLBER	Max						M		[11]	USA
KOLBER	Regine						F		[11]	USA
KOLBER	Anna						F		[10]	Survived
KOLBER	Zissel						M		[10]	Survived
KOLBER	Dawid						M		[10]	Survived
KOLBER	Bluma						F		[10]	Survived
KOLBER	Mina						F		[10]	Survived
KOLBER	Yanka						F		[10]	Survived
KOLBER	Sima						F		[10]	Survived
KOLENDER	Jente						F		[15]	Died
KOLUSHNER	Moshe						M		[12]	
KONIGSBUCH	Mayer						M		[15]	Died
KONIGSBUCH	Dawid						M		[15]	Died

Surname	First Name	Maiden Name	Birth Date	Residence	Father	Mother	Gender	Spouse	*Source	Remarks
KONIGSBUCH	Miriam						F		[15]	Died
KONIGSBUCH	Shmuel						M		[15]	Died
KORAL	Yehuda Tzwi						M		[2]	Survived
KORAL	Chaya Riwka	BUKSBAUM	1880				F	Yehuda Tzwi	[2]	Died
KORAL	Chawa		1906		Dow Ber	Breine	F		[2]	Died
KORAL	Yehudit		1915		Dow Ber	Breine	F		[2]	Died
KORN	Shoshana						F		[11]	Survived
KORN	Natan						M		[11]	Died
KORN	Taama						F		[11]	Died
KORN	Leibel						M		[12]	Survived
KORN	Zigmund	ZIGA					M		[12]	died
KORN	Miriam						F		[12]	
KORN	Fela						F		[15]	Died
KORN	Ita						F		[15]	Died
KORN	Bela						F		[15]	Died
KORN	Ita						F		[15]	Died
KORN	Lucia						F		[15]	Died
KOREN	Asher						M		[11]	Died
KOREN	Bila						F	Asher	[2]	Died
KOREN	Lea				Asher	Bila	F		[2]	Died
KOREN	Hela				Asher	Bila	F		[2]	Died
KOREN	Sara				Asher	Bila	F		[2]	Died
KOREN	Srulik				Asher	Bila	M		[2]	Died
KOREN	Zaman				Asher	Bila	M		[2]	Died
KOREN	Awraham				Asher	Bila	M		[2]	Died
KOREN	Ysrael						M		[15]	Died
KOREN	Lutka				Ysrael	Lutka	F	Ysrael	[2]	Died
KOREN	Nusia				Ysrael	Lutka	F		[2]	Died
KOREN	Helenka				Ysrael	Lutka	F		[2]	Died
KOREN	Berta						F		[2]	Died
KOREN	Mida					Berta	F		[2]	
KOREN	Shlomo					Berta	F		[2]	

List of Jews in Sandz   APP-75

Surname	First Name	Maiden Name	Birth Date	Residence	Father	Mother	Gender	Spouse	*Source	Remarks
KOREN	Awraham						M		[2]	Survived
KOREN	Naphtali						M			
KOREN	Rachel						F	Naphtali		
KOREN	Polke				Naphtali	Rachel	M		[2]	Survived
KOREN	Shmulik				Naphtali	Rachel	M		[2]	Survived
KOREN	Sara				Naphtali	Rachel	F		[2]	Survived
KOREN	Yossef						M			
KOREN	Hela				Yossef		F		[2]	Survived
KOREN	Shlomo				Yossef		M		[2]	Survived
KOREN	Nissan						M		[12]	
KORNBROIT	Ithazk						M		[12]	
KORNBROIT	Sachne						M		[12]	
KORNBROIT	Fania						F		[15]	Died
KORNFEL	Itzhak						M		[12]	Survived
KORNFELD	A.						M		[12]	
KORNFELD							M		[12]	
KORNFELD	David						M		[11]	Survived
KORNFELD	Shmuel						M		[14]	
KORNGUT	Bracha						F		[15]	Died
KORNHAUSER	Etel						F		[11]	Died
KORNHAUSER	Pinkus						M		[12]	
KORNHAUSER	Zigmunt						M		[12]	
KORNHAUSER	Szimon						M		[15]	Died
KORNHAUSER	Sara						F		[15]	Died
KORNHAUSER	Gitla						F		[15]	Died
KORNHAUSER	Bracha						F		[15]	Died
KORNHAUSER					Shmaja		M		[9]	
KORNHAUSER	Felix						M		[14]	
KORNKROUT	Berta						F		[10]	Survived
KORNMAN	Elisha						M		[12]	
KORNMEHL	Chaim	DAGAN					M		[11]	Survived
KORNREICH	Yehezkel	DAGAN					M		[11]	Survived
KORNREICH	Yaakow		1907				M		[11]	Died

List of Jews in Sandz   APP-76

Surname	First Name	Maiden Name	Birth Date	Residence	Father	Mother	Gender	Spouse	*Source	Remarks
KORNREICH	Aaron						M		[11]	Died
KORNREICH	Chawa						F		[11]	Died
KORNREICH	Yoel						M		[11]	Died
KORNREICH	Bronia	STEINRICH					F		[11]	Died
KORNREICH	Awraham						M		[11]	Died
KORNREICH	Sara						F		[12]	
KORNREICH	Itzhak						M		[12]	Survived
KORNREICH	Salomon						M		[15]	Died
KORNREICH	Arthur		1909				M		[7]	Died
KORNREICH	M						M		[11]	Survived
KORNREICH	Nahum						M		[14]	
KORNWASSER	Jakob						M		[4]	
KOWALSKI	Malka						F		[15]	Died
KOZLOWSKA	Tzivia						F		[15]	Died
KRANC	Itzhak						M		[15]	Died
KRANTZBERG	Hanina						M		[12]	
KRAUSS	Stazek						M		[12]	
KRAUSS	Lea						F		[11]	Survived
KRAUT	Zew					Lea	M		[11]	Died
KRAUT	Adela					Lea	F		[11]	Survived
KRAUT	Yehuda						M		[11]	Died
KRAUT	Ada						F		[15]	Died
KRAUT	Chaja						F		[15]	Died
KRAUT	Yehuda						F		[15]	Died
KRAUT	Lucy						F		[15]	Died
KRAUT	Juda						M		[15]	Died
KRAUT	Hanina						M		[12]	
KRAUT	Alexander						M		[9]	Died 02/11/1935
KRAUTWIRTH	Abraham		1917				M		[7]	
KRAUTWIRTH	Pesia		1921				F		[7]	
KRAUTWIRTH	N\orbert		1902				M		[7]	
KREIS	Filip		1929				M		[7]	

List of Jews in Sandz   APP-77

Surname	First Name	Maiden Name	Birth Date	Residence	Father	Mother	Gender	Spouse	*Source	Remarks
KREIS	Estera		1905				F		[7]	
KREIS	Riwka						F		[15]	Died
KREISEL	Jacob						M		[15]	Died
KRESCH	Riesel						F		[15]	Died
KRESCH	Golda						F		[15]	Died
KRESCH	Jakob						M		[15]	Died
KRESCH	Rachelle						F	Jakob	[15]	Died
KRESCH	Bluma						F		[11]	Survived
KRESH	Gold						M		[15]	Died
KRIESER	Roza						F		[11]	Died
KRIESER	Gitel						F		[11]	Died
KRIESER	Akiwa						M		[11]	Died
KRIESER	Peschie						M		[15]	Died
KRIESER	Moses		1901				M		[7]	Survived
KRIESER	Mali						F		[15]	Died
KRISCHER	Efroim						M		[15]	Died
KRISCHER	Yossef						M		[15]	Died
KRISCHER	Haja						F		[15]	Died
KRISCHER	Paissah						M		[15]	Died
KRISCHER	Gitel						F		[15]	Died
KRISCHER	Moses		1908				M		[7]	Survived
KRISEL	Esther						F		[12]	
KRISHER	Rachel						F		[12]	
KRISHER	Sarah						F		[12]	sisters
KRISHER	Rurzke						F		[12]	sisters. Survived
KRISHER	Hanoch						M		[12]	
KRISHER	Ben Zion						M		[12]	
KRISHNER	Benjamin						M		[4]	
KRISSER	Golda						F		[15]	Died
KRITZMAN	Moshe						M		[10]	Survived
KRIZER	Feivel						M		[11]	Died
KRUMHOLTZ	Chana						F		[11]	Died

List of Jews in Sandz   APP-78

Surname	First Name	Maiden Name	Birth Date	Residence	Father	Mother	Gender	Spouse	*Source	Remarks
KRUMHOLTZ	Eber						M		[15]	Died
KUMER	Sidney						M		[11]	USA
KUNTZ	Ray	LONDONER					F		[11]	USA
KUNTZ	Moshe						M		[12]	Israel
KURTZ							M		[11]	Died
KURTZMAN	Frydek						M		[15]	Died
KURZER	Wilek						M		[12]	grandfather. Survived
LAKS	Maks						M		[12]	grandfather. Survived
LAKS	Kuba						M		[11]	Died
LAMPEL	Halinka						F		[11]	Survived
LAMPEL	Leibel						M		[12]	
LAMPEL	Leiba						M		[12]	
LAMPEL	Chanek						M		[12]	
LAMPEL	Kuba						M		[12]	
LAMPEL	Hersh Zwi						M		[15]	Died
LAMPEL	Szyja						M		[15]	Died
LAMPEL	Numa						F		[12]	
LANADAU	Hilary						F		[11]	Survived
LANCER	Berish						M		[11]	Died
LANDAU	Benjamin						M		[11]	Survived
LANDAU	Yehiel						M		[11]	Survived
LANDAU	Benyamin						M		[11]	Survived
LANDAU	Ella	FRIEDMAN					F		[11]	Died
LANDAU	Ruth Chaya						F		[11]	Died
LANDAU	Shmerl						M		[11]	Died
LANDAU	Chaya						F		[11]	Died
LANDAU	Sara						F		[11]	Died
LANDAU	Israel						M		[11]	Died
LANDAU	Itzhak						M		[11]	Died
LANDAU	Sheindel						F		[11]	Died

List of Jews in Sandz   APP-79

Surname	First Name	Maiden Name	Birth Date	Residence	Father	Mother	Gender	Spouse	*Source	Remarks
LANDAU	Yehoshua						M		[11]	Died
LANDAU	Benek						M		[12]	
LANDAU	Itzhak						M		[12]	Died
LANDAU	Benjamin						M		[12]	Survived
LANDAU	Hinde						F		[12]	sister
LANDAU	Sender						M		[12]	brother
LANDAU	Ruzke	SHIPPER					F		[12]	Died
LANDAU	Yehoshua						M		[12]	
LANDAU	Sima						F		[12]	
LANDAU	Dawid						M		[12]	
LANDAU	Esther						F		[12]	
LANDAU	M.D.						M		[12]	
LANDAU	Benyamin						M		[12]	
LANDAU	Haskel						M		[12]	
LANDAU	Isaak						M		[12]	
LANDAU	Malka						F		[15]	Died
LANDAU	Dawid						M		[15]	Died
LANDAU	Tova						F		[15]	Died
LANDAU	Dawid Berish						M			
LANDAU	Moshe Da						M		[15]	Died
LANDAU	Sara						F		[15]	Died
LANDAU	Chaim						M		[15]	Died
LANDAU	Hendel						F		[15]	Died
LANDAU	Ester						F		[15]	Died
LANDAU	Yehezkel						M		[15]	Died
LANDAU	Israel						M		[15]	Died
LANDAU	Dora						F		[15]	Died
LANDAU	Dawid						M		[15]	Died
LANDAU	Towa						F		[15]	Died
LANDAU	Israel						M		[12]	
LANDAU	Hersh				Israel		M		[12]	
LANDAU	Eisik						M		[12]	
LANDAU	Yehezkel						M		[12]	

Surname	First Name	Maiden Name	Birth Date	Residence	Father	Mother	Gender	Spouse	*Source	Remarks
LANDAU	Erna						F		[12]	Survived
LANDAU	Shlomo						M		[12]	
LANDAU	Meir						M		[12]	Survived
LANDERER	Aaron						M		[12]	
LANDERER	Zaharia						M		[12]	
LANDHER	Hela						F		[15]	Died
LANDRER	Henry						M		[11]	Survived
LANG	Chaya Sara						F		[11]	Died
LANG	Chaim Lew						M		[11]	Died
LANGER	Riwka						F		[11]	Died
LANGER	Frimet						F		[11]	Died
LANGER	Rachel						F		[11]	Died
LANGER	husband						M		[11]	Died
LANGER	Sara						F		[15]	Died
LANGER	Frimet						F		[15]	Died
LANGER	Alexander		1919				M		[7]	
LANGER	Wolf						M		[12]	Died
LANGFUSS	Wolf						M		[10]	Died
LANGSAM	Scheindel						F		[15]	Survived
LAUB	Moshe						M		[11]	Survived
LAUER	Nataniel			Romanowskiego 4			M		[10]	With family. Died
LAUER	Bluma						F		[11]	Died
LAUER	Aaron						M		[11]	Died
LAUER	Hinde						F		[11]	Died
LAUER	Riwka						F		[11]	Died
LAUER	Chaya						F		[11]	Died
LAUER	Towa						F		[11]	Died
LAUER	Rechel						F		[11]	Died
LAUER	Sara						F		[11]	Died
LAUER	Moshe						M		[11]	Survived
LAUER	Aron		1907				M		[3]	Died

List of Jews in Sandz   APP-81

Surname	First Name	Maiden Name	Birth Date	Residence	Father	Mother	Gender	Spouse	*Source	Remarks
LAUER	Shmuel						M		[12]	Survived
LAUER	Lewy						M		[12]	shot
LAUER	Rifka						F		[15]	Died
LAUER	Blima						F		[15]	Died
LAUER	Chaja						F		[15]	Died
LAUFER	Shmuel						M		[10]	Survived
LAUFER	Chana						F		[15]	Died
LEBOWITZ	fida						F		[15]	Died
LEDER	Hirsz		1923				M		[7]	
LEDERBERGER	Meir						M		[2]	Died
LEHRER	Frida	BUKSBAUM	1889		Avraham	Pearl	F	Meir	[2]	Died 1917
LEHRER	Meir						M		[12]	
LEHRER	Hershel						M		[14]	
LEHRER	Moshe						M		[14]	
LEHRER	Hersh						M		[14]	
LEHRER	Meir						M		[15]	Died
LEHRER	Awraham						M		[15]	Died
LEHRER	Ella						F		[15]	Died
LEHRER	Riwka						F		[15]	Died
LEHRER	Moshe						M		[10]	Survived
LEHRER	Bashe						F		[10]	Survived
LEHRER	Mordechai						M		[10]	Survived
LEHRER	Reuwen			Lacko			M		[15]	Died
LEIBEL	Reuben						M		[15]	Died
LEIBEL	Dwora		1887				M		[2]	Died
LEIBNER	Joseph Simche		1918				M	Israel	[2]	Died
LEIBNER	Izrael		1922				M	Israel	[2]	Died
LEIBNER	Ester		1926				F	Israel	[2]	Died
LEIBNER	Simche						F		[2]	Died
LEIBNER	Hudes						M		[2]	Died
LEIBNER	Izrael		1922				M		[2]	Died
LEIBNER	Chaja Malka		1924				F		[2]	Died
LEIBNER	Chaskel		1899				M		[2]	Died

Surname	First Name	Maiden Name	Birth Date	Residence	Father	Mother	Gender	Spouse	*Source	Remarks
LEIBNER	Nochem						M		[12]	
LEIBOWICZ	Yossef						M		[14]	
LEIZER	Moshe						M		[10]	Survived
LEOR	Sara						F		[10]	Survived
LEOR	Azias						M		[12]	Survived
LERNER	Yochewed						F		[15]	Died
LESER	Serl						F		[9]	
LESZKOWITZ	Eliakum						M		[15]	Died
LETZKI	Mordechai			Kazimierz St			M		[10]	Died
LEW	Dawid						M		[15]	Died
LEWANIOWSKI	Frida						F		[15]	Died
LEWANIOWSKI	Sheindel						F		[15]	Died
LEWANIOWSKI	Yehezkel						M		[15]	Died
LEWANIOWSKI	Chana						F		[15]	Died
LEWANIOWSKI	Shulem						M		[15]	Died
LEWANIOWSKI	Taube						F		[15]	Died
LEWANIOWSKI	Abraham						M		[11]	Survived
LEWENBER	Widow						F		[12]	
LEWIN	Ignac						M		[12]	Widower. Survived
LEWIN	Matchek						M		[12]	Widower. Survived
LEWIN	Raphel						M		[12]	
LEWINIANSKI	Chaskel		1905				M		[7]	
LEWKOWICZ	Deworah						M		[12]	shot
LEWNIAWSKI	Sheindel						F		[15]	Died
LEWNIOWSKI	Him						M		[12]	
LEWY	Markus		1904				M		[7]	
LIEZER	Naftali						M		[12]	Survived
LIBER	Awraham						M		[12]	shot
LIBERMAN	Beile						F		[15]	Died
LICHTENSTEIN	Miriam Lea						F		[15]	Died
LICHTMAN	Mordechai	LIMANOW					M		[12]	shot

List of Jews in Sandz   APP-83

Surname	First Name	Maiden Name	Birth Date	Residence	Father	Mother	Gender	Spouse	*Source	Remarks
LICHTREGER	Mania						F		[15]	Died
LIEBENHEIMER	Zosia						F		[15]	Died
LIEBENHEIMER	Salamon						M		[15]	Died
LIEBENHEIMER	Jozef		1905				M		[3]	Died
LIEBERMAN	Moshe						M		[12]	
LIMBER	Jozef		1908				M		[7]	Survived
LINDERBERGER	Chana						F		[11]	Died
LINKER	Itzhak						M		[11]	Died
LINKER	Yehudit						F		[11]	Died
LINKER	Gitel						F		[11]	Died
LINKER	Luba						F		[15]	Died
LINKER	Pepi						F		[15]	Died
LINKER	Mendel		1894				M		[7]	Survived
LINKER	Pepi						F		[15]	Died
LINKER	Gershon						M		[10]	Survived
LIPCZER	Beile						F		[15]	Died
LIPMAN	Shifra						F		[15]	Died
LIPSKEER	Aron						M		[15]	Died
LIPSKEER	Hershel						M		[15]	Died
LIPSKEER	Chyfra						F		[15]	Died
LIPSKEER	Mendel						M		[15]	Died
LIPSKEER	Lisa						F		[15]	Died
LIPSKEER	Hershel						M		[15]	Died
LIPSKER	Gersaon		1911				M		[7]	
LIPTACHER	Hinda		1916				F		[7]	
LIPTACHER	Paul						M		[11]	Survived
LIPTSCHER	Max						M		[11]	Survived
LIPTSCHER	Baruch						M		[12]	
LIPTZER	Necha						F		[15]	Died
LIST	Judith						F		[11]	USA
LITON	Yakow						M		[15]	Died
LOEW	Rachel						F		[15]	Died
LOEW	Lewy						M		[9]	Died

List of Jews in Sandz   APP-84

Surname	First Name	Maiden Name	Birth Date	Residence	Father	Mother	Gender	Spouse	*Source	Remarks
LOEW							M		[11]	Survived
LONDON	Ines						F		[11]	Survived
LUCKS	Ignacy		1915				M		[7]	
LUDNWER	Shoshana						F		[11]	Died
LUKS	Reisel						F		[11]	Died
LUKS	Rachel						F		[11]	Died
LUKS	Shmuel						M		[11]	Died
LUKS	Pinhas						M		[12]	
LUKS	Beni						M		[12]	Survived
LUKS	Aba						M		[15]	Died
LUKS	Shimon						M		[10]	Survived
LUKS	Jakub		1914				M		[7]	
LUSTBADER	Mala		1917				F		[7]	
LUSTBADER	Shlomo						M		[11]	Died
LUSTBADER	Zelig						M		[11]	Died
LUSTBADER	Chana						F		[11]	Died
LUSTBADER	Riwka						F		[11]	Died
LUSTBADER	Feige						F		[11]	Died
LUSTBADER	Itel						F		[11]	Died
LUSTBADER	Eidel						F		[11]	Died
LUSTBADER	Simon						M		[12]	
LUSTBADER	Awraham						M		[12]	
LUSTBADER	Ite						F		[12]	
LUSTBADER	Hershel						M		[14]	
LUSTBADER	Asher						M		[15]	Died
LUSTBADER	Abraam						M		[15]	Died
LUSTBADER	Regina						F		[15]	Died
LUSTBADER	Roman						M		[11]	USA
LUSTBADER	Zimel			Kazimeirz			M		[10]	Died
LUSTBADER	Kalman						M		[10]	Survived
LUSTBADER	Berl						M		[11]	Survived
LUSTGARTEN	Sara						F		[11]	Died
LUSTGARTEN	Moshe						M		[11]	Died

List of Jews in Sandz   APP-85

Surname	First Name	Maiden Name	Birth Date	Residence	Father	Mother	Gender	Spouse	*Source	Remarks
LUSTGARTEN	Shmuel						M		[12]	Survived
LUSTGARTEN	Benjamin						M		[12]	Survived
LUSTGARTEN	Reizi						F		[15]	Died
LUSTGARTEN	Taibe						F		[15]	Died
LUSTGARTEN	Brandel						F		[15]	Died
LUSTGARTEN	Moshe						M		[15]	Died
LUSTGARTEN	Itzhak						M		[15]	Died
LUSTGARTEN	Yossef						M		[15]	Died
LUSTGARTEN	Sam						M		[11]	Survived
LUSTGARTEN	Elsie						F	Sam	[11]	Survived
LUSTGARTEN	Chaim						M		[11]	Survived
LUSTIG	Zew						M		[11]	Survived
LUSTIG	Leon						M		[11]	Survived
LUSTIG	Salomon						M		[11]	Died
LUSTIG	Benyamin						M		[11]	Died
LUSTIG	Awraham						M		[11]	Died
LUSTIG	Shlomo Zal						M		[11]	Died
LUSTIG	Tzwi						M		[11]	Died
LUSTIG	Henia						F		[11]	Died
LUSTIG	Pepi						F		[11]	Died
LUSTIG	I.L.						M		[12]	
LUSTIG	Mendel						M		[12]	
LUSTIG	Moniek						M		[12]	Survived
LUSTIG	Baruch						M		[12]	Survived
LUSTIG	Leon						M		[12]	Survived
LUSTIG	Blima	MAHLER					F		[12]	
LUSTIG	Bolek						M		[12]	
LUSTIG	Simha						M		[12]	
LUSTIG	Malka	GELB					F	Simha	[12]	
LUSTIG	Wilek				Simha	Malka	M		[12]	Survived
LUSTIG	Minek				Simha	Malka	M		[12]	
LUSTIG	Azela				Simha	Malka	M		[12]	
LUSTIG	Zishek				Simha	Malka	M		[12]	

Surname	First Name	Maiden Name	Birth Date	Residence	Father	Mother	Gender	Spouse	*Source	Remarks
LUSTIG	Ruzka				Simha	Malka	F		[12]	
LUSTIG	Mila				Simha	Malka	M		[12]	
LUSTIG	Regina				Simha	Malka	F		[12]	
LUSTIG	Emanuel				Simha	Malka	M		[12]	Survived
LUSTIG	Dawid						M		[12]	
LUSTIG	Michael						M		[15]	Died
LUSTIG	Hinda						F	Michael	[15]	Died
LUSTIG	Moshe						M		[2]	Died
LUSTIG	Renata						F		[2]	Died
LUSTIG	Natan			Pioterskargi place			M		[10]	With family. Died
LUSTIG	Shyja			Romanowskiego 4			M		[10]	With family. Died
LUSTIG	Aron			Watowa St			M		[10]	With family. Died
LUSTIG	Shulem						M			
LUSTIG	Miriam	BRANDSTEIN		Romanowskiego 4			F		[10]	Died
LUSTIG	Riwka				Shulem	Miriam	F	Shulem	[2]	Died
LUSTIG	Yehezkel				Shulem	Miriam	M		[2]	Died
LUSTIG	Ita				Shulem	Miriam	F		[2]	Died
LUSTIG	Yehoshua				Shulem	Miriam	M		[2]	Died
LUSTIG	Aaron				Shulem	Miriam	M		[2]	Died
LUSTIG	Tzvi				Shulem	Miriam	M		[2]	Died
LUSTIG	Mordechai				Shulem	Miriam				
LUSTIG	Nathan				Shulem	Miriam				
LUSTIG	Anna						F		[15]	Died
LUSTIG	Leon						M		[10]	Survived
LUSTIG	Shimon						M		[10]	Survived
LUSTIG	Moniek						M		[10]	Survived
LUSTIG	Natan				Michael		M		[10]	Survived
LUSTIG	Leib Yehuda						M		[11]	Died
LUSTIGER	Miriam						F		[11]	Died
LUSTIGER	Yehoshua						M		[11]	Died
LUSTIGER	Aaron						M		[11]	Died

Surname	First Name	Maiden Name	Birth Date	Residence	Father	Mother	Gender	Spouse	*Source	Remarks
LUSTIGER	Yehezkel						M		[11]	Died
LUSTIGER	Riwka						F		[11]	Died
LUSTIGER	Nathan						M		[11]	Died
LUSTIGER	Itzhak						M		[11]	Died
LUSTIGER	Gusta						F		[11]	Died
LUSTIGER	Seymur						M		[11]	USA
LUX	Esther						F	Seymur	[11]	USA
LUX	Jakub						M		[2]	Died
MARIN				Kazimeirz			M		[10]	Died
MADER							M		[11]	
MAHER	Rafael						M		[11]	Survived
MAHLER	Suskind		1903				M		[3]	Died
MAHLER	Mina						F		[12]	
MAHLER	Gustave						M		[12]	
MAHLER	Yossi						M		[12]	
MAHLER	Sarah						F		[2]	Survived
MAHLER	Awrum						M		[2]	
MAHLER	Moshe Kalman	KARL			Awrum		M		[2]	
MAHLER	Eliezer						M		[12]	
MAHLER	Mordechai						M		[12]	
MAHLER	Michael				Mordechai	Sarah	M		[12]	
MAHLER	Riwka				Mordechai	Sarah	F		[12]	
MAHLER	Raphel						M		[12]	Poalei Zion
MAHLER	Sh						M		[12]	Poalei Zion
MAHLER	Sarah	LIBERMAN					M	Michael	[12]	
MAHLER	Heike				Itzhak Asher	Rachel	F		[12]	
MAHLER	Blime				Itzhak Asher	Rachel	F		[12]	
MAHLER	Petichya				Itzhak Asher	Rachel	F		[12]	Bialystok head
MAHLER	Anda	GRIN					F	Petichya	[12]	
MAHLER	Feige						F		[12]	
MAHLER	Itzhak Asher						M		[12]	

List of Jews in Sandz APP-88

Surname	First Name	Maiden Name	Birth Date	Residence	Father	Mother	Gender	Spouse	*Source	Remarks
MAHLER	Rachel						F	Itzhak Asher	[12]	
MAHLER	Haim						M		[12]	
MAHLER	Haya	SHPITMAN					F	Haim	[12]	Survived
MAHLER	Rafael						M		[12]	Survived
MAHLER	Kalman						M		[12]	
MAHLER	Sarah	RAPPORT			Moshe		F			
MAHLER	Jakub						M		[15]	Died
MAHLER	Klaman						M		[10]	Survived
MAHLER	Riwka				Itzhak Asher	Rachel	F		[12]	
MAHLER							M		[2]	Died
MAIBRUCH	Wolf						M		[15]	Died
MAIBRUCH	Malka						F		[15]	Died
MAIBRUCH	Bronka						F		[15]	Died
MAIBRUCH	Miriam						F		[15]	Died
MAIBRUCH	Chaija						M		[15]	Died
MAIBRUCH	Yossef						M		[15]	Died
MAIBRUCH	Itzhak						M		[15]	Died
MAIBRUCH	Wolf						M		[15]	Died
MAIBRUCH	Malka						F		[15]	Died
MAIBRUCH	Yakir						M		[15]	Died
MAIZELS							M		[11]	Died
MALEWITZ	Ruzka						F		[11]	Survived
MALEWITZ							M		[12]	
MALOZ	Yaakow						M		[11]	Died
MALTZ	Luba						F		[11]	Died
MALTZ	Keila						F		[11]	Died
MALTZ	Malka Reisel						F		[11]	Died
MALTZ	Deborah						F		[15]	Died
MALTZ	Sara	BEER					F		[2]	
MALTZ	Bronia						F		[15]	Died
MALTZ	Yehezkel						M		[15]	Died

List of Jews in Sandz   APP-89

Surname	First Name	Maiden Name	Birth Date	Residence	Father	Mother	Gender	Spouse	*Source	Remarks
MALTZ	Ben Tzion						M		[12]	Survived
MALTZ	Ernest						M		[15]	Died
MAN	Wolf						M		[15]	Died
MANDEL	Yossef						M		[11]	Died
MANDEL	Yaakow						M		[11]	Died
MANDEL	Feige						F		[11]	Died
MANDEL	Ruzke						F		[11]	Died
MANDEL	Yehuda						M		[11]	Died
MANDEL	Esther						F		[11]	Died
MANDEL	Wolf I.		1922				M		[3]	Died
MANDEL	Sheindel						F		[12]	
MANDEL	Moshe	SHAKED					M		[12]	Survived
MANDEL	Wolf						M		[12]	
MANDEL	Awraham						M		[12]	
MANDEL	Tzalke						M		[12]	Died
MANDEL	Riwkah						M		[12]	Died
MANDEL	Shlomo						M		[14]	
MANDEL	Yeshayahu						M		[14]	
MANDEL	Elimelech						M		[15]	Died
MANDEL	Ruzia						F		[15]	Died
MANDEL	Jakob						M		[15]	Died
MANDEL	Fela						F		[15]	Died
MANDEL	Yehuda						M		[15]	Died
MANDEL	Gitel						F		[15]	Died
MANDEL	Awraham						M		[10]	Survived
MANDEL	Sara						F		[10]	Survived
MANDEL	Itzhak						M		[15]	Died
MANDEL	Esther						F		[15]	Died
MANDEL	Sara						F		[15]	Died
MANDEL	Jacob						M		[11]	USA
MANDEL	Motke						M		[12]	Died
MANDELBAUM	Wolf						M		[12]	
MANDELBAUM	Meir						M		[14]	

List of Jews in Sandz   APP-90

Surname	First Name	Maiden Name	Birth Date	Residence	Father	Mother	Gender	Spouse	*Source	Remarks
MANDELBAUM	Lea						F		[15]	Died
MANDELBAUM	Moses		1923				M		[7]	
MANGEL	Anna						F		[12]	
MANHEIMER	Leon					Anna	M		[12]	
MANHEIMER	Yehoshua						M		[12]	
MANN	Frederyka						F		[15]	Died
MANNES	Yossef						M		[11]	Survived
MANSBACH	Yudel						M		[11]	Died
MAREK	Moshe				Israel		M		[11]	Died
MAREK	Chaim Itz				Israel		M		[11]	Died
MAREK	Tzwi				Israel		M		[11]	Died
MAREK	Yohanan Zew				Israel		M		[11]	Died
MAREK	Michal				Israel		F		[11]	Died
MAREK	Eda						F	Samuel	[2]	Died
MAREK	Samuel						M	Eda	[2]	Died
MAREK	Yankel						M		[12]	
MAREK	Pearl						F		[15]	Died
MAREK	Wolf						M		[15]	Died
MAREK	Chaim						M		[15]	Died
MAREK	Gitel						F		[15]	Died
MAREK	Joseph						M		[11]	USA
MAREK	Lisa						F	Joseph	[11]	USA
MAREK	Pol						M		[10]	Survived
MAREK	Joel						M		[12]	
MARGOLIES	Henrik						M		[12]	
MARGOLIES	Motel						M		[12]	
MARGOLIES	Joel						M		[12]	
MARGOLIES	L.						M		[12]	
MARGOLIES	Baruch						M		[12]	
MARGOLIES	Chaim Mordechai				Eliakim		M		[9]	
MARGOLIES	Lea				Israel Aron		F		[9]	Died 18/2/1917
MARGOLIES	Solomon						M		[11]	Survived

List of Jews in Sandz   APP-91

Surname	First Name	Maiden Name	Birth Date	Residence	Father	Mother	Gender	Spouse	*Source	Remarks
MARHOOR							F	Solomon	[11]	Survived
MARHOOR	Yankel				Mordechai N.		M		[12]	
MARIN	Nathan						M		[14]	
MARIN	Mordechai N.						M			
MARIN	Jetta						F		[15]	Died
MARIN	Israel						M		[12]	
MARK	Adolf						M		[15]	Died
MARKIEWICZ	Dawid						M		[10]	Survived
MARKUS	Mordechai				Shmuel		M		[12]	
MASHLER	Alexandrowicz				Shmuel		M		[12]	
MASHLER	Shmuel						M		[12]	died
MASHLER	Mina						F		[12]	died
MASHLER	Esther						F		[12]	died
MASHLER	Henrik		1908				M		[7]	Survived
MASHLER	Tinka						M	Shmuel	[12]	
MASHLER	Tinka				Shmuel		F		[12]	
MASHLER	Henryk						M	Shmuel	[10]	Survived
MASHLER	Michael						M		[11]	Survived
MASK	Zissel						F		[11]	Died
MASTBAUM	Eidel						F		[11]	Died
MASTBAUM	Chana						F		[11]	Died
MASTBAUM	Aaron						M		[11]	Died
MASTBAUM	Yehuda						M		[11]	Died
MASTBAUM	Yaakow	KATZ					M		[11]	Died
MASTBAUM	Malka						M		[11]	Died
MASTBAUM	Chana Sima						F		[11]	Died
MASTBAUM	Yehuda	KATZ					F		[11]	Died
MASTBAUM	Awraham						M		[11]	Died
MASTBAUM	Shlomo						M		[11]	Died
MASTBAUM	Shlomo Zalman						M		[11]	Died
MASTBAUM	Jakob						M		[15]	Died
MASTBAUM	Yossef						M		[10]	Survived

Surname	First Name	Maiden Name	Birth Date	Residence	Father	Mother	Gender	Spouse	*Source	Remarks
MASTBAUM	Hershel						M		[15]	Died
MAUER	Hershel M						M		[12]	
MAYERFELD							M		[12]	
MAYERFELD	Hershel						M		[12]	
MAYERFELD	I.						M		[12]	
MAYERFELD	Nathan						M		[12]	
MECHEL	Yehuda						M		[12]	
MEIR	Abush						M		[12]	
MEIR	Mania						F		[15]	Died
MEIR	Wolf Eliyahu						M		[15]	Died
MEIR	Ephraim						M		[11]	Died
METT	Motel						M		[11]	Died
METT	Bluma						F		[11]	Died
METT	Zew						M		[11]	Died
METT	Gitel						F		[11]	Died
METT	Wolf						M		[12]	
MELAWSKI	Sabina						F		[15]	Died
MELECH	Lubina						F		[15]	Died
MELETZ	Awichail						M		[14]	Died
MELITZER	Eliezer						M		[11]	Survived
MELTZER	Ben Tzion		1914		Eliezer		M		[11]	Survived
MELTZER	Moshe		1905		Eliezer		M		[11]	Survived
MELTZER	Yehuda		1908		Eliezer		M		[11]	Survived
MELTZER	Mozes						M		[15]	Died
MEMBER	Jakub		1895				M		[2]	Died
MENDLER	Tzwi						M			
MENDLER	Rachel				Nachum		F	Tzwi	[9]	Died 1937
MENDLER	Hersh						M		[12]	
MENKELE	Israel						M		[15]	Died
MESSENBERG	Moses						M		[11]	USA
METZLER	Itzhak				Avraham	Ita	M		[2]	Survived
MILLER	Sara Lea						F		[12]	
MILLER							M		[12]	

List of Jews in Sandz   APP-93

Surname	First Name	Maiden Name	Birth Date	Residence	Father	Mother	Gender	Spouse	*Source	Remarks
MILLER	Yaakow						M		[10]	Survived
MILLER	Sabina				Eliasz		F		[9]	Died 13/4/1961
MINC	Leibele						M		[14]	
MINTZBERG	Sara						F		[15]	Died
MINTZER	Broniek						M		[12]	
MOHR	Moniek						M		[12]	
MOHR		LEMBERG					F		[12]	
MOHR	Zigmunt						M		[12]	
MOHR	Marian						M		[12]	Survived
MOHR	Bronislaw						M		[12]	Died
MOHR	Antonia						F		[15]	Died
MOHR	Richard						M		[15]	Died
MOHR				Legionow St			M		[10]	
MONDERER	Berl						M		[11]	Survived
MORDECHAI	Nathan						M		[11]	Survived
MORGAN	Yetta						F		[11]	Survived
MORGAN	Rudek						M		[12]	
MORGENBESSER	Wolf						M		[11]	Died
MORGENSTERN	Rozalia						M		[12]	
MORGENSTERN	Regina						F		[15]	Died
MORGENSTERN	Janchale						F		[15]	Died
MORGENSTERN	Salome						F		[15]	Died
MORGENSTERN	Gizela						F		[15]	Died
MORGENSTERN	Yehuda						F		[15]	Died
MORGENSTERN	Mordechai						M		[15]	Died
MORGENSTERN	Rachel						M		[15]	Died
MORGENSTERN	Jakob						F		[15]	Died
MORGENSTERN	Josef						M		[15]	Died
MORGENSTERN	Mendel						M		[11]	Survived
MORGENSTERN	Caleb		1910				M		[7]	Survived
MORTENBAUM	Betzalel						M		[7]	
MOSKOWITZ	Aron		1840				M		[2]	

List of Jews in Sandz   APP-94

Surname	First Name	Maiden Name	Birth Date	Residence	Father	Mother	Gender	Spouse	*Source	Remarks
MOSKOWITZ	Dworah				Aron	Tzila	F		[2]	
MOSKOWITZ	Frimet						F		[15]	Died
MUELLER	Izrael		1921				M		[7]	
MUELLER	Ewa		1876				F		[2]	Died
MUHLBRUN	Kuba						M		[12]	
MUHLBRUN	Menahem M						M		[11]	Died
MUHLSTEIN	Fanny						F		[11]	Died
MUNDER	Emil						M		[12]	Died
NAGEL	Zelig						M		[15]	Died
NAJBUCH	Edward						M		[11]	Survived
NAMMY	Aleksander						M		[10]	Survived
NATEL	Wera						F		[10]	Survived
NATEL	Lea						F		[10]	Survived
NATEL	Hanna						F		[10]	Survived
NATEL	Israel		1885				M		[2]	Died
NATTEL	Naftali		1880				M		[2]	Died
NATTEL	Sabine						F		[12]	Israel
NATTEL	Miriam						F		[11]	Died
NEBEL	Zacharia						M		[11]	Died
NEBEL	Aron						M		[4], [12]	
NEBENZAHL	Romek						M		[15]	Died
NEBENZAHL	Eliahu						M		[15]	Died
NEBENZAHL	Henryk						M		[10]	Survived
NEIHEIT	Meir						M		[10]	Survived
NEIHEIT	mAYER						M		[15]	Died
NEIMAN	Maks						M		[10]	Survived
NEIMAN	Alter						M		[12]	
NETZMAN	Perla						F		[15]	Died
NEUGROSHEL	Moshe						M	Moshe	[12]	
NEUGROSHEL	Israel				Israel		M		[12]	
NEUGROSHEL					Israel		F		[12]	
NEUGROSHEL	Berek						M		[12]	
NEUGROSHEL	Nutek						M		[12]	

List of Jews in Sandz   APP-95

Surname	First Name	Maiden Name	Birth Date	Residence	Father	Mother	Gender	Spouse	*Source	Remarks
NEUGROSHEL	Haim Lei						M		[12]	Survived
NEUGROSHEL	Berish						M		[12]	
NEUGROSHEL	Israel				Berish		M		[12]	
NEUGROSHEL	Nunek	NATHAN			Berish		M		[12]	Survived
NEUGROSHEL	Mendel						M		[12]	Survived
NEUGROSHEL	Regine						F		[12]	
NEUGROSHEL	Israel						M		[11]	Died
NEUGROSHEL	Gitla				Israel		F		[9]	Died
NEUGROSHEL	Shmuel						M		[15]	Died
NEUGROSHEL	Haim						M		[15]	Died
NEUGROSHEL	Perla			Grybow			F		[15]	Died
NEUGROSHEL	Rosalia				Avraham		F		[9]	Died
NEUGROSHEL	Chaim				Avraham		M		[9]	Died
NEUGROSHEL	Ruchel				Avraham		F		[9]	Died
NEUGROSHEL	Bronia						F		[15]	Died
NEUGROSHEL	Herman						M		[15]	Died
NEUGROSHEL	Samuel						M		[15]	Died
NEUGROSHEL	Israel						M		[10]	Survived
NEUGROSHEL	Yaakow						M		[10]	Survived
NEUGROSHEL	Dawid						M		[10]	Survived
NEUGROSHEL	Samuel						M		[15]	Died
NEUGROSHEL	Eanuel						M		[11]	USA
NEUGROSHEL	Regine						F		[11]	USA
NEUGROSHEL	Alter						M		[11]	Survived
NEUMAN	Sara						F		[15]	Died
NEUSHTETEL	Aaron Tzwi						M		[11]	Died
NEUSTADT	Chana Rach						F		[11]	Died
NEUSTADT	Emannuel						M		[11]	Died
NEUSTADT	Faya						F		[11]	Died
NEUSTADT	Nina						F		[12]	sport
NEUSTADT	Awraham						M		[10]	Died
NEUSTADT	Mrs						F	Awraham	[10]	Died
NEUSTADT	Berta						F		[15]	Died

List of Jews in Sandz   APP-96

Surname	First Name	Maiden Name	Birth Date	Residence	Father	Mother	Gender	Spouse	*Source	Remarks
NEUSTETL							M		[12]	drowned
NEWHEIM	Sara						F		[15]	Died
NIDERMAN	Oskar		1916				M		[7]	
NICK	jozef		1914				M		[7]	
NICK	Rachel						F		[11]	Died
NISSENBAUM	Lea						F		[11]	Died
NISSENBAUM	Moshe						M		[11]	Died
NISSENBAUM	Tania						F		[15]	Died
NISSENBAUM	Dawid						M		[15]	Died
NORD	Pinhas						M		[15]	Died
NORD	Morris						M		[11]	Survived
NUDEL							F	Morris	[11]	Survived
NUDEL	Joseph						M		[11]	Survived
NUDEL	Margaret						F	Joseph	[11]	Survived
NUDEL	David						M		[11]	Survived
NUDEL							F	David	[11]	Survived
NUDEL	Shimon						M		[11]	Died
NUSSBAUM	Riwka						F		[11]	Died
NUSSBAUM	Awraham						M		[11]	Died
NUSSBAUM					Ariel		M		[2]	Died
NUSSBAUM	Rurzka						F		[12]	
NUSSBAUM	Sala						F		[12]	
NUSSBAUM	Jankel						M		[12]	
NUSSBAUM	Zishe						M		[12]	died
NUSSBAUM	Ariel						M		[12]	
NUSSBAUM	Moshe						M		[12]	died
NUSSBAUM							M		[12]	
NUSSBAUM	Awraham						M		[12]	
NUSSBAUM	Yossef						M		[12]	
NUSSBAUM	Shiek						M		[12]	
NUSSBAUM	Dvora						F		[15]	Died
ODERBERG	Abram						M		[15]	Died
ODERBERG	Jakob						M		[15]	Died

List of Jews in Sandz   APP-97

Surname	First Name	Maiden Name	Birth Date	Residence	Father	Mother	Gender	Spouse	*Source	Remarks
ODERBERG	Rozia						F		[15]	Died
ODERBERG	Sara						F		[15]	Died
ODERBERG	Mirel						F		[15]	Died
OHRSZTEIN	Chaim						M		[15]	Died
OHRSZTEIN	Szajndla		1905				M		[7]	
OLSZAWSKA	Heda						F		[15]	Died
OLSZWANGER	Abraham						M		[15]	Died
ORCHAN	Dawid						M		[15]	Died
ORCHAN	Abraham						M		[15]	Died
ORCHAN	Matel						F		[15]	Died
ORENSTEIN	Gitel						F		[15]	Died
ORENSTEIN	Sara Riwka	WAGSCHAL	17/6/1896		Aron	Rachel	F	Karl	[5]	
ORENSTEIN	Eva						F		[11]	Survived
ORNIANER	Josef I.		1916				M		[3]	Died
OSTERWEIL	Mosze						M		[15]	Died
OZER	Bluma						F		[15]	Died
OZER	Slenger			Zywiecka 20			M		[10]	Died
PALISNIOK	Yaakow						M		[12]	
PANTZER	Taibel						F		[15]	Died
PANZER							M		[12]	
PARDES							M		[12]	
PARNESS	Awraham						M		[12]	died
PARNESS	Shaul						M		[12]	Died
PARNESS	Natan						M		[12]	Died
PARNESS							M		[12]	
PATZANOWER	Eva	GUTERFREUND					F		[12]	
PATZNOWER	Haim						M		[15]	Died
PEARL	Hinda						F		[15]	Died
PEARL	Samuel						M		[15]	Died
PEARL	Riwka						F		[15]	Died
PEARL	Sara						F		[15]	Died
PEARL	Jacob						M		[15]	Died
PEARL	Lole						F		[11]	Survived

Surname	First Name	Maiden Name	Birth Date	Residence	Father	Mother	Gender	Spouse	*Source	Remarks
PEARL	Lea						F		[15]	Died
PEARLBERGER	Herz						M		[15]	Died
PEARLBERGER	Ita						F		[15]	Died
PEARLBERGER	Iziek						M		[15]	Died
PEARLBERGER	Riwka						F		[15]	Died
PENCAK							M		[12]	
PENDLER	Anita		1934				F		[7]	
PENNER	Lea						F		[12]	
PENTZAK							M		[12]	
PENTZAK	Frania	ABRAHAMOWICZ					M		[12]	
PENTZAK	Mala					Frania	M		[12]	
PENTZAK	Motek					Frania	M		[12]	Survived
PENTZAK	Zalman						M		[10]	Survived
PEPPER	Libe						F		[15]	Died
PERLSHTEIN	Chaim						M		[12]	
PETERFREUND	Braindl						M		[15]	Died
PETERFREUND	Beile						F		[15]	Died
PETERFREUND	Itzhak						M		[15]	Died
PETERFREUND	Gitel						F		[15]	Died
PETERFREUND	Zalkin						M		[15]	Died
PETERFREUND	Shalom						M		[15]	Died
PETERFREUND	Berta						F		[15]	Died
PETERFREUND	Szymon						M		[15]	Died
PETERFREUND	Chaja						F		[15]	Died
PETERFREUND	Sala						F		[15]	Died
PETERFREUND	Chaim Itzhak						M		[10]	Survived
PETERFREUND	Anton						M		[12]	Died
PETERFRIEND				Kolo Dunajewskiego			M		[10]	Died
PETERZAL	Peretz						M		[10]	Survived
PETERZAL	Mendel						M		[4]	Survived
PFEFFER	Berta						F		[11]	Survived
PFLASTER	Szimon						M		[11]	Died
PFLASTER	Hanke						F		[11]	Died

List of Jews in Sandz   APP-99

Surname	First Name	Maiden Name	Birth Date	Residence	Father	Mother	Gender	Spouse	*Source	Remarks
PFLASTER							M		[12]	
PFLASTER	Moshe						M		[9]	
PFLASTER	Nute						M		[12]	
PFLASTER	Menashe						M		[12]	
PFLASTER	Shimon						M		[12]	
PFLASTER	Regine						F		[15]	Died
PFLASTER	Shimon						M		[15]	Died
PFLASTER	Malka						F		[15]	Died
PFLASTER	Mendel						M		[4]	
PFLASTER							M		[13]	
PIDOWSKI	Hershel M						M		[12]	
PIEKIELENI	Gilda						F		[15]	Died
PILNIK	Khaim						M		[15]	Died
PINSEL	Miriam						F		[15]	Died
PINSEL	Mechele						M		[14]	
PIOK	Idel Nissel				Majer		M		[9]	
PIPERSBERG	Mosze						M		[15]	Died
POLAK	Lusia						F		[15]	Died
POLIWODA	Taube						F		[15]	Died
POLK	Morris						M		[11]	Survived
POLL	Feige						F		[15]	Died
POPIEL				Pijarski St			M		[10]	Died
PRAWER	Yzaydor		1907				M		[7]	
PRETSCHMAIER	Rachel						F		[11]	Died
PREMINGER	Tziwia Riwka	BIRNBAUM	1907		Itzhak	Liba Ahuva	F		[2]	Survived
PRIEL				Kazimeirz			M		[10]	Died
PROKSZO	Shoszana						F		[15]	Died
PTASZNIK	Dodo						M		[15]	Died
PTASZNIK	Shmuel						M		[15]	Died
PTASZNIK	Menahem						M		[11]	Died
PULMAN	Ruchcia						F		[15]	Died
PUTERMAN	Elieze						M		[10]	Survived

List of Jews in Sandz   APP-100

Surname	First Name	Maiden Name	Birth Date	Residence	Father	Mother	Gender	Spouse	*Source	Remarks
RABI	Ewa						F		[10]	Survived
RABI	Menachem						M		[15]	Died
RABINOVITS	Yehezkel						M		[12]	
RABINOWITZ	Malka						F		[15]	Died
RABINOWITZ	Menachem						M		[15]	Died
RABINOWITZ	Zion						M		[15]	Died
RAJBEN	Naftali Meir						M		[12]	
RAKAR	Helena		1918				M		[7]	
RAAP	Gita	ANISFELD					F		[11]	Died
RAPPAPORT	Shalom						M		[15]	Died
RAPPAPORT	Awraham						M		[15]	Died
RAPPAPORT	Szolom						M		[15]	Died
RAPPAPORT	Ben Zion	TARNOW			Moshe		M		[12]	Died
RAPPAPORT	Moshe				Ben Zion		M		[12]	Survived
RAPPAPORT	Dawid						M		[12]	
RAPPAPORT	Baruch		1906				M		[3]	Died
RAPPAPORT	Chune Henry		8/11/1883		Chune	Serli	M		[5]	Died
REBHUN	Beila Dwojre	WAGSCHAL	31/8/1876		Meir Izak	Chaje	F	Chune Henry	[2]	
REBHUN	Moshe (Mojzesz) Aron		1905		Chune	Beila Dwojre	M		[5]	
REBHUN	Stella	STOCK	1904			Beila Dwojre	F	Moshe Aron	[2]	
REBHUN	Israel (Sruleck)		Jan. 1907		Chune	Beila Dwojre	M		[5]	
REBHUN	Lishka Shulamit SHTILMAN	SHTILMAN					F	Israel (Sruleck)	[2]	
REBHUN	Naftali (Nacek)		1905		Chune	Beila Dwojre	M		[5]	Survived
REBHUN	Gizela	ENEHALT					F	Naftali (Nacek)	[2]	
REBHUN	Shlomo (Salomon)		1905		Chune	Beila Dwojre	M		[5]	Survived

Surname	First Name	Maiden Name	Birth Date	Residence	Father	Mother	Gender	Spouse	*Source	Remarks
REBHUN	Sofia Zochiya	GREENBERG					F	Shlomo (Salomon)	[2]	
REBHUN	Abraham		1913		Chune	Beila Dwojre	M		[5]	Died
REBHUN	Judith	VOGEL					F	Abraham	[2]	Died
REBHUN	Taube Jona		1905		Chune	Beila Dwojre	F		[5]	Died
REBHUN	Izak (Iczek)		1917		Chune	Beila Dwojre	M		[5]	
REBHUN	Clara	BRANDSTEIN							[2]	Survived
REBHUN			bef. 1906		Chune	Beila Dwojre	F		[5]	
REBHUN	Sol						M		[11]	Survived
REEFMAN	Benyamin						M		[12]	
REI	Leona		1899				F		[2]	Died
REIBSCHEID	Lieba		1913				F		[2]	Died
REIBSCHEID	Menke		1905				M		[2]	Died
REIBSCHEID	Sala		1890				F		[2]	Died
REIBSCHEID	Chana						F		[11]	Died
REIBSHEID	Herman						M		[11]	Died
REIBSHEID	Henryk						M		[11]	Died
REIBSHEID	Sarah						F		[11]	Died
REIBSHEID	Moshe						M		[11]	Died
REIBSHEID	Shamai						M		[11]	Died
REIBSHEID	Hela						F		[11]	Died
REIBSHEID	Chaim						M		[11]	Died
REIBSHEID	Yaakow						M		[11]	Died
REIBSHEID							M		[11]	Died
REIBSHEID							M		[12]	Died
REIBSHEID	Sara						F		[15]	Died
REIBSHEID	Roza						F		[15]	Died
REIBSHEID	Sara						F		[15]	Died
REIBSHEID	Aaron						M		[11]	Died
REICH	Ita						F		[11]	Died

Surname	First Name	Maiden Name	Birth Date	Residence	Father	Mother	Gender	Spouse	*Source	Remarks
REICH	Yaakow Wol						M		[11]	Died
REICH	Nechame						F		[11]	Died
REICH	Israel						M		[11]	Died
REICH	Naftali Hirsh		1911				M		[3]	Died
REICH	Regina		1908				F		[3]	Died
REICH	Itchele						M		[12]	
REICH	Yanek					Itchele	M		[12]	
REICH	Moniek					Itchele	M		[12]	
REICH	Nunik					Itchele	M		[12]	
REICH	Mania					Itchele	F		[12]	
REICH	Ruze					Itchele	F		[12]	
REICH	Fajge						F		[15]	Died
REICH	Haim						M		[15]	Died
REICH	Leib						M		[15]	Died
REICH	Riwka	INLANDER					F		[15]	Died
REICH	Feige						F		[15]	Died
REICH	Chaim						M		[15]	Died
REICH	Eliyahu						M		[15]	Died
REICH	Dawid			Joselowicz			M		[10]	Died
REICH	Arie						M		[10]	Died
REICH	Itzhak						M		[11]	Died
REICHER							M		[11]	Died
REICHER	Zigmunt						M		[14]	
REICHER	Sara						F		[15]	Died
REICHER	Julia						F		[15]	Died
REICHFELD	Gitel						F		[11]	Died
REICHMAN	Yossef				Chaim		M		[11]	Died
REICHMAN	Chaim						M		[11]	Died
REICHMAN	Gitel						F		[11]	Died
REICHMAN	Yossef						M		[11]	Died
REICHMAN	Czarna						F		[15]	Died
REID	Rachela						F		[15]	Died
REIHOLD	Julius		1926				M		[7]	

Surname	First Name	Maiden Name	Birth Date	Residence	Father	Mother	Gender	Spouse	*Source	Remarks
REIMER	Samuel						M		[11]	Survived
REISIG	Antonia						F	Samuel	[11]	Survived
REISIG							M		[12]	
REISS	Dawid						M		[15]	Died
REISS	Yehuda						M		[10]	Survived
REISS	Esther Erna	WAGSCHAL	20/101897		Aron	Rachel	F	Zvi	[5]	
REISS	Rachel						F		[15]	Died
RESLER	Sara						F		[15]	Died
RESLER	Hinda						F		[15]	Died
RHEINHOLD	Raizel						F		[15]	Died
RHEINHOLD	Sara						F		[15]	Died
RHEINHOLD	Shlomo						M		[15]	Died
RHEINHOLD	Boruch						M		[15]	Died
RHEINHOLD	Symche						M		[15]	Died
RHEINHOLD	Hilda						F		[15]	Died
RHEINHOLD	Isaac						M		[15]	Died
RHEINHOLD	Yidel						M		[15]	Died
RHEINHOLD	Moshe						M		[14]	
RHEINHOLD	Moshe Mendel						M		[10]	Died
RHEINHOLD	Mrs +child						F	Moshe Mendel	[10]	Died
RHEINHOLD	Lea						F		[15]	Died
RIBNER	Itzhak						M		[12]	
RICHTER	Rywka						F		[15]	Died
RIEGELBAUM	Mayer						M		[15]	Died
RIEGELHAUPT	Gitel						F		[15]	Died
RIEGELHAUPT				Kazimierz St			M		[1]	Died
RIF	Menahem						M		[11]	Survived
RIGELHAUPT	Ester						F		[15]	Died
RIGELHAUPT	Mojzes		1904				M		[7]	
RIGELHAUPT	Regina		1904				F		[7]	
RIGELHAUPT	Irena		1941				F		[7]	
RIGELHAUPT	Pesla		1932				F		[7]	

Surname	First Name	Maiden Name	Birth Date	Residence	Father	Mother	Gender	Spouse	*Source	Remarks
RIGELHAUPT	Romek		1945				M		[7]	
RIGELHAUPT	Malka-Emal						F		[11]	Died
RIGER	Esther-Stell						F		[11]	Died
RIGER	Yossef Yulik						M		[11]	Died
RIGER	Leon						M		[11]	Died
RIGER	Malka						F		[11]	Died
RIGER	Stella						F		[11]	Died
RIGER	Yulek						M		[11]	Died
RIGER	Ahuva						F		[11]	Died
RIGER	Nechame						F		[11]	Died
RIGER	Ludwik		1923				M		[3]	Died
RINDLER	Moshe						M		[12]	
RINDLER	Aaron						M		[12]	
RINDLER	Rachel						F		[15]	Died
RING	Chaim		25/5/1887						[9]	Died 10/8/1967
RING	Markus		1914				M		[7]	
RING	Emma						F		[12]	sister
RINGEL	Jehudit						F		[12]	sister
RINGEL	Aaron						M		[12]	brother
RINGEL	Emil						M		[11]	Survived
RINGEL	Emanuel						M		[12]	Poalei Zion
RINGELBAUM	Lushek						M		[12]	Died
RINGELBAUM	Sala	SHIPPER					F		[12]	Died
RINGELBAUM	Regina						F		[2]	Survived
RINGELHAFT	Baruch		1901							
RITTER	Shaye		1911							
RITTER	Abe						M		[11]	Survived
RITTERSTEIN	Israel						M		[12]	
ROB	Yosef						M		[12]	Died
ROGEL	Feige						F		[15]	Died
ROGEL	Yehuda						M		[10]	Survived
ROGEL	Henrietta						F		[15]	Died
ROMER							M		[2]	Died

List of Jews in Sandz   APP-105

Surname	First Name	Maiden Name	Birth Date	Residence	Father	Mother	Gender	Spouse	*Source	Remarks
ROPPER	Pinhas						M		[12]	Israel
ROSEGARTEN							M		[12]	
ROSEN	Asher						M		[15]	Died
ROSEN	Bronia						F		[15]	Died
ROSEN	Adolph						M		[15]	Died
ROSEN	Yossef						M		[10]	Survived
ROSENBACH	Yona						M		[10]	Survived
ROSENBACH	Moshe						M		[10]	Survived
ROSENBACH	Chaim						M		[10]	Survived
ROSENBACH	Yaakow						M		[10]	Survived
ROSENBACH	Abraham						M		[15]	Died
ROSENBAUM	Abraham						M		[15]	Died
ROSENBAUM	SABINA	POLL					F		[11]	Died
ROSENBAUM	Yochewed						F		[11]	Died
ROSENBERG	Shmuel						M		[11]	Died
ROSENBERG	Chaim						M		[11]	Died
ROSENBERG	Sima						F		[11]	Died
ROSENBERG	Riwka						F		[11]	Died
ROSENBERG	Shimon						M		[11]	Died
ROSENBERG	Dawid						M		[11]	Died
ROSENBERG	Sheindel						F		[11]	Died
ROSENBERG	Shmuel						M		[12]	
ROSENBERG	Awraham						M		[12]	
ROSENBERG	Shia						M		[12]	
ROSENBERG	Simon						M		[15]	Died
ROSENBERG	Jochewet						F		[15]	Died
ROSENBERG	Yochewet						F		[15]	Died
ROSENBERG	Feige						F		[15]	Died
ROSENBERG	Leib						M		[15]	Died
ROSENBLAT	Rachela						F		[15]	Died
ROSENBLAT	Itel						F		[15]	Died
ROSENBLAT	Lea						F		[15]	Died
ROSENBLUM	Margit						F		[15]	Died

List of Jews in Sandz   APP-106

Surname	First Name	Maiden Name	Birth Date	Residence	Father	Mother	Gender	Spouse	*Source	Remarks
ROSENBLUM	Moriz						M		[4]	
ROSENBLUT	Sera	KORAL	1908		Dow Ber	Breine	F		[2]	Survived
ROSENFELD	Rebecca Hen						F	Shloime	[7]	
ROSENFELD	Eliezer						M		[7]	
ROSENFELD	Chaim Ale.				Eliezer	Fradel	M		[7]	
ROSENFELD	Shlomo Re.				Eliezer	Fradel	M		[7]	
ROSENFELD	Naftali Tz				Eliezer	Fradel	M		[7]	
ROSENFELD	Sheindel				Eliezer	Fradel	F		[7]	
ROSENFELD	Rachel Dw.				Eliezer	Fradel	F		[7]	
ROSENFELD	Chaya				Eliezer	Fradel	F		[7]	
ROSENFELD	Malka				Eliezer	Fradel	F		[7]	
ROSENFELD	Baruch						M		[11]	Died
ROSENFELD	Bernard						M		[12]	Died
ROSENFELD	Heike						F		[12]	
ROSENFELD	Awraham						M		[12]	
ROSENFELD	Rena						F		[12]	Survived
ROSENFELD	Binem						M		[15]	Died
ROSENFELD	Bracha						F		[15]	Died
ROSENFELD	Rosa						F		[15]	Died
ROSENFELD	Sheindel						F		[10]	Survived
ROSENFELD	Beni						M		[10]	Survived
ROSENFELD	Yossef						M		[10]	Survived
ROSENFELD	Chaim Itz						M		[11]	Died
ROSENGARTEN	Esther Riwk						F		[11]	Died
ROSENGARTEN	Hula						F		[11]	Died
ROSENGARTEN	Pinhas					Hula	M		[11]	Died
ROSENGARTEN							F	Pinhas	[11]	Died
ROSENGARTEN	Pinhas						M			
ROSENGARTEN	Chaim						M			
ROSENGARTEN	Edek						M		[12]	Survived
ROSENTHAL	Rudek						M		[12]	Died
ROSENTHAL	Heshel						M		[12]	
ROSENTZWEIG	Yakow						M		[15]	Died

List of Jews in Sandz   APP-107

Surname	First Name	Maiden Name	Birth Date	Residence	Father	Mother	Gender	Spouse	*Source	Remarks
ROSENTZWEIG	Tzilish						M		[15]	Died
ROSENWASSER							M		[11]	Died
ROTH	Itzhak						M		[14]	
ROTH	Yossef						M		[14]	
ROTH	Josef						M		[15]	Died
ROTH	Fraidel						F		[15]	Died
ROTH	Abraham						M		[15]	Died
ROTH	Yossef						M		[15]	Died
ROTH	Dina						F		[15]	Died
ROTH	Hinda						F		[15]	Died
ROTH	Sara						F		[15]	Died
ROTH	Chaskel						M		[15]	Died
ROTH	Ester						F		[15]	Died
ROTH	Leib						M		[15]	Died
ROTHENBERG	Hershel M						M		[12]	
ROTHENBERG	Heshel						M		[12]	
ROTHENBERG	Moshe						M		[12]	
ROTHENBERG	Mania						F		[12]	shot
ROTHENBERG	Moses						M		[4]	
ROTHIRSZ	Zacharia						M		[11]	Died
ROTKOPF	Simon						M		[11]	Survived
ROTTER	Bertha						F		[11]	Survived
ROTTER	Adolph						M		[11]	Died
ROZEN	Mela Chaya						F		[11]	Died
ROZEN	Yaakow						M		[11]	Died
ROZEN	Feige						F		[11]	Died
ROZEN	Abraham						M		[15]	Died
ROZEN	Dawid						M		[15]	Died
ROZEN	Chaja						F		[15]	Died
ROZEN	Eliyahu			Piotr-Skargi			M		[10]	
ROZENBACH	Agusta						F		[9]	
ROZENWASSER	Lea	PRESSER					F		[11]	Died
ROZENZWEIG	Rafael	PRESSER					M		[11]	Died

List of Jews in Sandz   APP-108

Surname	First Name	Maiden Name	Birth Date	Residence	Father	Mother	Gender	Spouse	*Source	Remarks
ROZENZWEIG	Frida	PRESSER					F		[11]	Died
ROZENZWEIG	husband	PRESSER					M		[11]	Died
ROZENZWEIG	Mauric	PRESSER					M		[11]	Died
ROZENZWEIG		PRESSER					F	Mauric	[11]	Died
ROZENZWEIG	Chaim						M		[11]	Died
ROZENZWEIG	wife						F	Chaim	[11]	Died
ROZENZWEIG	Israel						M		[11]	Survived
ROZNER	Sima						F		[11]	Died
ROZNER	Sara Riw						F		[11]	Died
ROZNER	Shlomo Aar						M		[11]	Died
ROZNER	Itzhak Tuvia						M		[1]	
RUBIN	Moshe				Itzhak Tuvia	Nehema	M		[2]	Survived
RUBIN	Zwi Hersh				Itzhak Tuvia	Nehema	M		[2]	
RUBIN	Moshe						M		[12]	
RUBIN	A						M		[12]	Survived
RUBIN	Moshe						M		[14]	
RUBIN	Leibel						M		[15]	Died
RUBIN	Idek	MELTZER					M		[12]	
RUBINFELD	Haim						M		[15]	Died
RUBINSTEIN	Hinda						F		[15]	Died
RUBINSTEIN	Szyja						F		[15]	Died
RUBINSTEIN	Jekel						M		[15]	Died
RUBINSTEIN	Rifka						F		[15]	Died
RUBINSTEIN	Chaim						M		[15]	Died
RUBINSTEIN	Szyja						M		[15]	Died
RUBINSTEJN	William						M		[11]	Survived
RUCKEL	Anna						F	William	[11]	Survived
RUCKEL	Shewa	WOLF			Shaul	Shifra	F		[2]	Died
RUDKOWSKY	Zalman						M		[12]	
RUSLER	Abraham			Grybow			M		[15]	Died
RUTKOWSKI	Neche						F		[15]	Died

List of Jews in Sandz APP-109

Surname	First Name	Maiden Name	Birth Date	Residence	Father	Mother	Gender	Spouse	*Source	Remarks
SAFIR	Szymon						M		[15]	Died
SAFIR	Feige						F		[15]	Died
SAFIR	Yossef						M			
SAFIR	Yentel				Moshe		F	Yossef	[9]	Died 1930
SAFIR	Shmuel						M		[10]	Survived
SAKSZYIBEK	Salek						M		[15]	Died
SALAMON	Ruzia	ANISFELD					F	Awraham	[11]	Died
SALOMON	Awraham						M		[11]	Died
SALOMON	Moshe				Avraham	Ruzia	M		[11]	Died
SALOMON	Sara						F		[11]	Died
SALOMON	Chana						F		[11]	Died
SALOMON	Mania						F		[11]	Died
SALOMON	Mira						F		[11]	Died
SALOMON	Dawid						M		[11]	Died
SALOMON	Dawid						M		[12]	
SALOMON	Arie						M		[15]	Died
SALOMON							M		[12]	
SALPETER	Naphtali						M		[15]	Died
SALPETER	Ita						F		[15]	Died
SAMET	Betzalel						M		[15]	Died
SAMET	Bracha						F		[15]	Died
SAMUEL	Lea						F			
SAMUELI	Szymon		1916				M		[7]	Survived
SAMUELI	Ester						F		[15]	Died
SANDEL							M		[2]	Died
SANDER	Rachel						F		[11]	Died
SANDETZER	Meir						M		[11]	Died
SANDETZER	Dawid						M		[11]	Died
SANDETZER	Chaya Rac						F		[11]	Died
SANDETZER	Simon						M		[12]	
SAPHIR	Idel						M		[12]	
SAPHIR	Oscar						M		[12]	
SAPHIR	Mendel						M		[14]	

Surname	First Name	Maiden Name	Birth Date	Residence	Father	Mother	Gender	Spouse	*Source	Remarks
SAPHIR	Chawa						F		[15]	Died
SAUER	Abraham		1875				M		[2]	Died
SCHACHNER	Reizil						F		[15]	Died
SCHACHNER	Yaakow						M		[15]	Died
SCHACHNER	Isachar						M		[15]	Died
SCHACHTER	Neche						F		[15]	Died
SCHACHTER	Naftali						M		[15]	Died
SCHAGRIN	Taubi						F		[15]	Died
SCHAGRIN	Leon						M		[10]	Died
SCHAGRIN	Ryfka						F		[15]	Died
SCHANKER	Salomon						M		[15]	Died
SCHANKER	Nathan						M		[14]	
SCHANTZER	Haim						M		[15]	
SCHANTZER	Riwka						F		[10]	Survived
SCHANTZER	Meir						M		[11]	Survived
SCHAPIRA	Zipora						F		[11]	Died
SCHAPIRA	Leib						M		[11]	Died
SCHAPIRA	Moshe Men						M		[11]	Died
SCHAPIRA	Mendel						M		[11]	Died
SCHAPIRA	Frenia						F		[11]	Died
SCHAPIRA	Bluma						F		[11]	Died
SCHAPIRA	Shmuel						M		[11]	Died
SCHAPIRA	Yeshayahu N						M		[11]	Died
SCHAPIRA	Moshe Daw						M		[11]	Died
SCHAPIRA	Eisik						M		[11]	Died
SCHAPIRA	Esther						F		[11]	Died
SCHAPIRA	Tema						F		[11]	Died
SCHAPIRA	Meir						M		[10]	Survived
SCHAPIRO	Baruch						M		[10]	Survived
SCHAPIRO	Sarah						F		[11]	Survived
SCHARF	Shmuel						M		[15]	Died
SCHARF	Emil						M		[11]	Survived
SCHATTNER	Nissan						M		[11]	Died

List of Jews in Sandz   APP-111

Surname	First Name	Maiden Name	Birth Date	Residence	Father	Mother	Gender	Spouse	*Source	Remarks
SCHECHTER	Chana	.					F		[15]	Died
SCHECHTER	Rafael						M		[15]	Died
SCHECHTER	Chana						F		[15]	Died
SCHECHTER	Rafael						M		[15]	Died
SCHECHTER	Ethel						F		[11]	Survived
SCHEER	Lea						F		[11]	Died
SCHEER	ICCHAK						M		[9]	
SCHEER	Mendel						M		[15]	Died
SCHEIER	Zalman						M		[10]	Survived
SCHEIN	Mendel						M		[10]	Survived
SCHEIN	Isser						M		[10]	Died
SCHEIN	Abraham						M		[15]	Died
SCHEIN	Sima						F		[15]	Died
SCHEIN	Malka						F		[15]	Died
SCHEIN	Malka						F		[15]	Died
SCHEIN	Malka						F		[15]	Died
SCHEIN	Zalman						M		[10]	Survived
SCHEIN	Mendel						M		[10]	Survived
SCHEIN	Ysser						M		[10]	Survived
SCHEIN	Salamon						M		[15]	Died
SCHEINBERG	Menachem						M		[15]	Died
SCHEINBERG	Sheine						F		[11]	Died
SCHEINGUT	Taube						F		[11]	Died
SCHEINGUT	Yossel						M		[11]	Died
SCHEINGUT	Chaim						M		[11]	Died
SCHEINGUT	Feige						F		[15]	Died
SCHERMAN	Bernard						M		[15]	Died
SCHERMER	Mirla						F		[15]	Died
SCHERMER	Markus						M		[15]	Died
SCHERMER	Samuel		1907				M		[3]	Died
SCHIFF	Awraham						M		[14]	
SCHIFF	Abish						M		[14]	
SCHIFF	Shmelke				Abish		M		[14]	

Surname	First Name	Maiden Name	Birth Date	Residence	Father	Mother	Gender	Spouse	*Source	Remarks
SCHIFF	Paltiel						M		[14]	
SCHIFF	Shmelke						M		[15]	Died
SCHIFF	Sheindel						F		[15]	Died
SCHIFF	Paltiel						M		[15]	Died
SCHIFF	Abraham						M		[15]	Died
SCHIFFER	Lea						F		[15]	Died
SCHIFMAN	Moshe						M		[15]	Died
SCHIFMAN	Mordechai						M		[2]	Died
SCHIMEL	Chana	AMSTER					F	Mordechai	[2]	Died
SCHIMEL	Chune				Mordechai	Chana	M		[2]	Survived
SCHIMEL	Moshe				Mordechai	Chana	M		[2]	Survived
SCHIMEL	Sara				Mordechai	Chana	F		[2]	Died
SCHIMEL	Rachel				Mordechai	Chana	F		[2]	Died
SCHIMEL	Hadassah						F		[15]	Died
SCHIMEL	Meilech						M		[15]	Died
SCHIMEL	Bashe						F		[15]	Died
SCHIMEL	Yona						M		[15]	Died
SCHIMEL	Tzarne						F		[15]	Died
SCHIMEL	Minde						F		[15]	Died
SCHIMEL	Mendel						M		[15]	Died
SCHINDEL	Tzila						F		[15]	Died
SCHINDEL	Ephraim						M		[11]	Died
SCHIPER	Sara-Salom						F		[11]	Died
SCHIPER	Awraham						M		[11]	Died
SCHIPER	Sara						F		[11]	Died
SCHIPER	Shlomo						M		[11]	Died
SCHIPER	Riwka						F	Shlomo	[11]	Died
SCHIPER	Wolf						M		[11]	Died
SCHIPER	Chana						F		[11]	Died
SCHIPER	Liptche						F		[11]	Died
SCHIPER	Dawid						M		[15]	Died
SCHLACHET	Tunka						F		[11]	Survived
SCHLACHET	Pinhas						M		[15]	Died

List of Jews in Sandz   APP-113

Surname	First Name	Maiden Name	Birth Date	Residence	Father	Mother	Gender	Spouse	*Source	Remarks
SCHLACHET	Chaja						F		[15]	Died
SCHLACHET	Heshek						M		[11]	Died
SCHLACHET	Aaron						M		[11]	Died
SCHLACHET	Awraham						M		[10]	Survived
SCHLACHET	Leja						F		[15]	Died
SCHLANGER	Moshe						M		[10]	Survived
SCHLANGER	Shlomo						M		[10]	Died
SCHLANGER	Kiwa		1924				M		[3]	Died
SCHLEICHKORN	Joe						M		[11]	Survived
SCHLEIN	Kornelia		1851				F		[9]	Died 1932
SCHLEISSTEHER	Leibish						M		[15]	Died
SCHLENGER	Mina						F		[15]	Died
SCHLESINGER	Dora						F		[15]	Died
SCHLESINGER	Frania		1914				F		[7]	Survived
SCHLISEL	Dina						F		[11]	Died
SCHLISEL	Hinda						F		[11]	Died
SCHLISEL	Leon						M		[15]	Died
SCHLISEL	Riwka						F		[15]	Died
SCHLISEL	Arek						M		[15]	Died
SCHLISEL	Leon						M		[15]	Died
SCHLISEL	Heinrich		1901				M		[3]	Died
SCHLOSS	Herman						M		[15]	Died
SCHLUSSBERGER	Lea						F		[15]	Died
SCHMIDT	Ruchel						F		[10]	Died
SCHNITZER	Lea						F		[15]	Died
SCHOCHET	Josef						M		[15]	Died
SCHOENGUT	Nehema						F		[10]	Died
SCHOENGUT	Chaja		1918				F		[3]	Died
SCHON	Rachel						F		[15]	Died
SCHON	Baruch						M		[11]	Died
SCHONFELD	Herman						M		[15]	Died
SCHOSSBERGER	Awraham						M		[11]	Survived

List of Jews in Sandz   APP-114

Surname	First Name	Maiden Name	Birth Date	Residence	Father	Mother	Gender	Spouse	*Source	Remarks
SCHPILMAN	Chaim						M		[11]	Died
SCHPREI	Feige						F		[11]	Died
SCHPREI	Lola						F		[11]	Died
SCHPREI	Hersz						M		[11]	Died
SCHPRINGER	wife						F	Hersz	[11]	Died
SCHPRINGER	Mala						F		[15]	Died
SCHPRINGER	Regina						F		[15]	Died
SCHREIBER	Matel						F		[15]	Died
SCHREIBER	Eliyahu						M		[15]	Died
SCHREIBER	Aba						M		[9]	Died
SCHREIBER	Bumka				Itzhak		M		[9]	Died
SCHREIBER	Shlomo						M		[15]	Died
SCHREIBER	Josua						M		[15]	Died
SCHREIBER	Mojzesz		1909				M		[7]	
SCHREIER	Yossef						M		[11]	Died
SCHTEINER	wife						F	Yossef	[11]	Died
SCHTEINER	Moshe						M		[11]	Survived
SCHTEINER							M		[11]	Died
SCHTENGEL	Yehezkel						M		[11]	Died
SCHTURMAN	Mojsze						M		[15]	Died
SCHUSS	Roza		1924				F		[2]	Died
SCHUTZ	Shmuel						M		[12]	
SCHWARTS	Lucia						F		[11]	Survived
SCHWARTZ	Tzwi						M		[12]	
SCHWARTZ	Herman						M		[12]	
SCHWARTZ	Hershel						M		[12]	
SCHWARTZ	Rozia						F		[15]	Died
SCHWARTZKOPF	Sarah						F		[11]	Survived
SCHWEID	Menachem						M		[12]	
SCHWEID	Tzwi				Menachem		M		[12]	Survived
SCHWEID	Wolf				Menachem		M		[12]	
SCHWEID	Zalman				Menachem		M		[12]	Survived
SCHWEID							M		[11]	Died

List of Jews in Sandz   APP-115

Surname	First Name	Maiden Name	Birth Date	Residence	Father	Mother	Gender	Spouse	*Source	Remarks
SCHWIMMER	Isser						M		[15]	Died
SCHWINGER							M		[11]	Died
SEGAL							M		[12]	
SEGAL	Mordechai						M		[12]	
SEGULIS	Awraham						M		[12]	
SEGULIS	Debora						F		[15]	Died
SEIDEN	Dora						F		[15]	Died
SEIDEN	Zygmund						M		[15]	Died
SEIDENWORM	Zygmund						M		[15]	Died
SEIDENWURM	Smuel						M		[15]	Died
SEIFERT	Jadwiga						F		[2]	Died
SEIFERT	Miriam						F		[15]	Died
SEINFELD	Leon						M		[10]	Survived
SHAGRIN	Menashe						M		[11]	Survived
SHAKED	Samek						M		[6]	
SHAPIRO	Meir						M		[12]	Died
SHAPIRO	Racke	GOLDBERG					F		[12]	Died
SHAPIRO	Baruch						M		[12]	
SHAPIRO	Elimelech						M		[12]	
SHAPIRO							M		[12]	USA
SHAPIRO							M		[12]	drowned
SHECHTER	Isidor						M		[12]	shot
SHEIN	Lea						F		[15]	Died
SHEINBERG	Heshe						M		[12]	
SHEINFELD	Itzhak						M		[10]	Survived
SHEINFELD	Tzwi						M		[10]	Survived
SHEINFELD	Gusta						F		[10]	Survived
SHEINFELD	Tonka						F		[12]	
SHEINGUT	Nehemia						M		[10]	Survived
SHEINGUT	H.						M		[12]	
SHENFELD							M		[12]	
SHERADZIE	Jakub						M		[12]	
SHERMAN	Feige						F		[15]	Died

List of Jews in Sandz   APP-116

Surname	First Name	Maiden Name	Birth Date	Residence	Father	Mother	Gender	Spouse	*Source	Remarks
SHERMAN	Hene	.					F		[15]	Died
SHERMAN	Sara						F		[15]	Died
SHERMAN	Yudel						M		[12]	
SHIMEL	Haim L.						M		[12]	
SHINDEL	Meilech						M		[15]	Died
SHINDELHEIM	Ruzka						F		[12]	
SHIPER	Naftali						M		[12]	
SHIPPER	Moshe						M		[12]	
SHIPPER	Tulek				Moshe		M		[12]	died
SHIPPER	Ephraim						M		[12]	Survived
SHIPPER	Mathias						M		[12]	
SHLACHTER	Yudek						M		[12]	Survived
SHLACHTMAN	Awraham						M		[12]	
SHLAGER	Salomon		1926				M		[7]	
SHLANGER	Moshe						M		[12]	
SHLANGER	Roza						F		[15]	Died
SHLANGER	Dow						M		[15]	Died
SHLANGER	Sara						F		[15]	Died
SHLANGER	Esther						F		[15]	Died
SHLANGER	Shimon						M		[15]	Died
SHLANGER	Lea						F		[15]	Died
SHLENGER	Shlomo						M		[10]	Survived
SHLENGER	A.						M		[12]	
SHLISSEL	Nute						M		[12]	
SHLISSEL							M		[12]	
SHMALTZBACH							M		[12]	
SHMALTZBACH	Kuba						M		[12]	Died
SHMALTZBACH	Henek						M		[12]	Survived
SHMALTZBACH	Herman						M		[12]	
SHMALTZBACH	Moshe						M		[14]	
SHMAYAHU	Salo	LIMANOW					F		[12]	shot
SHNITZLER	Yidel	LIMANOW					M		[12]	shot
SHOCHAT	Aaron	LIMANOW					M		[12]	shot

List of Jews in Sandz   APP-117

Surname	First Name	Maiden Name	Birth Date	Residence	Father	Mother	Gender	Spouse	*Source	Remarks
SHOCHAT	Haim						M		[12]	
SHOR	Awraham						M		[12]	
SHOSS	Shmaya						M		[12]	
SHOSS	Moshe						M		[12]	shot
SHOSS	Rachel						F		[12]	shot
SHOSS							M		[12]	
SHOSSHEIM	Bela						F		[15]	Died
SHOUSTHEIM	Elchanan						M		[11]	Died
SHPILMAN	Lea						F		[15]	Died
SHPITZ	Gitel						F		[15]	Died
SHPITZ							M		[12]	
SHPRINGER	Mordechai						M		[10]	Survived
SHPRINGER	Asher						M		[10]	Survived
SHPRINGER	Eliyahu						M		[12]	
SHREIBER							M		[12]	
SHREIBER	Abba				Isak		M		[9]	Died
SHREIBER	Bumka				Isak		F		[9]	Died
SHREIBER	Shalom				Moshe		M		[9]	Died 03/7/1933
SHREIBER							M		[12]	
SHREIMER	Shalom						M		[12]	
SHTATER	Yudel						M		[12]	
SHTATER	Neche						F		[12]	
SHTATER	Bernard						M		[12]	
SHTATTER	Meshulem						M		[12]	
SHTATTER	fam								[2]	Survived
SHTEITELHAUF	Yankel				Yankel		M		[12]	
SHTEINABACH	Lola				Simha	Malka	F		[12]	Survived
SHTEINABACH	Eliezer				Eliezer		M		[12]	
SHTEINABACH	Feibish				Eliezer		M		[12]	
SHTEINABACH	Yehoshua				Eliezer		M		[12]	
SHTEINABACH	Yidel						M		[12]	
SHTEINABACH	Moniek						M		[10]	Survived
SHTEINBERG							M		[12]	kehilla head

Surname	First Name	Maiden Name	Birth Date	Residence	Father	Mother	Gender	Spouse	*Source	Remarks
SHTEINMETZ	Reuven						M		[12]	
SHTENER	Zeev						M		[12]	
SHTENGEL	Shanke						F		[12]	
SHTERLICHT	Hanine						M		[12]	
SHTERNLICHT	Yosef	LIMANOW					M		[12]	Died
SHTILL	Yaakow						M		[12]	brother
SHTILLER	Awraham						M		[12]	brother
SHTILLER	Dov						M		[12]	Survived
SHTOCK-SADAN	Beile						F		[15]	Died
SHTORK							M		[12]	
SHTRAUCHNER							M		[12]	
SHTRIK	Moshe Dawid						M		[14]	shot
SHTRUM	Sheindel		1915				F		[12]	
SHTUB	Majer						M		[3]	Died
SIERADSKI	Kalman						M		[11]	Died
SIERADZKI	Chana						F		[11]	Died
SIERADZKI	Eliyahu						M		[11]	Died
SIERADZKI	Sara						F		[11]	Died
SIERADZKI	Reisel						F		[11]	Died
SIERADZKI	Meir						M		[11]	Died
SIERADZKI	Paula						F		[11]	Died
SIERADZKI	Lea						F		[11]	Died
SIERADZKI	Lea	HOLLANDER					F		[11]	Died
SIERADZKI	Matilda						F		[11]	Died
SIERADZKI	Ernestina						F		[11]	Died
SIERADZKI	Hanna						F		[15]	Died
SIERADZKI	Lea						F		[15]	Died
SIERADZKI	Kalman						M		[15]	Died
SIERADZKI	Laike						F		[15]	Died
SIERADZKI	Chana						F		[15]	Died
SIERADZKI	Klaman						M		[15]	Died
SIERADZKI	Reisel						F		[15]	Died
SIERADZKI	Mayer						M		[15]	Died

List of Jews in Sandz APP-119

Surname	First Name	Maiden Name	Birth Date	Residence	Father	Mother	Gender	Spouse	*Source	Remarks
SIERADZKI	Awraham						M		[10]	Survived
SIGOLIM	Bronislawa						F		[15]	Died
SILBER	Adela		1881				F		[9]	Died 19/2/1935
SILBER	Rywka						F		[15]	Died
SILBERBERG	Shlomo						M		[15]	Died
SILBERBERG	Chaim						M		[4]	
SILBERMANN	Szymon						M		[15]	Died
SILBIGER	Eisik						M		[12]	Died
SIMANOWICZ	Mendel						M		[12]	Died
SIMANOWICZ	Itzhak						M		[13]	
SIMANOWICZ							M		[12]	
SIMANOWICZ	Adela						F		[9]	Died 1929
SIMANOWICZ	Zerah						M		[15]	Died
SIMCHOWICZ	Reisel						F		[15]	Died
SIMCHOWICZ	Bronia						F		[11]	Died
SINGER	Mela						F		[11]	Died
SINGER	Henrik						M		[11]	Died
SINGER	Aaron						M		[11]	Died
SINGER	SH.D.						M		[12]	Survived
SINGER	Syma						F		[9]	Died 29/10/1942
SINGER	Hersh						M		[12]	
SIROP	Sarah	ZOFIA					F	Hersh	[12]	
SIROP	Ruth				Moshe	Sarah	F		[12]	
SIROP	Rafael Eliezar				Moshe	Sarah	M		[12]	
SIROP	Huna						M		[15]	Died
SKLARZEWSKI	Elias I.		1917				M		[3]	Died
SKRZYPEK	widow						F		[12]	
SLEITERN	Bendek						M		[12]	
SLEITERN	Bronka	KERBEL					F		[12]	
SLEITERN	Samek						M		[12]	
SLEITERN	Max						M		[11]	Survived
SMALL	Symcha			Grybow			M		[15]	Died

List of Jews in Sandz   APP-120

Surname	First Name	Maiden Name	Birth Date	Residence	Father	Mother	Gender	Spouse	*Source	Remarks
SMUL	Menachem						M		[11]	Died
SOBEL	Matel						F		[11]	Died
SOBEL	Natan						M		[15]	Died
SOCHA	Mordechai			Kazimierz St			M		[10]	Died
SOFER	Dawid						M		[12]	
SOLOMON	Awraham				Dawid		M		[12]	
SOLOMON	Anna						F		[11]	Survived
SOLOMON	Taube						F		[11]	Survived
SOLOMON	Chawa						F		[15]	Died
SOMMER	Feige						F		[15]	Died
SOMMER	Mayer						M		[11]	Survived
SOMMER	Abraham						M		[11]	Survived
SOMMER	Dawid						M			
SONDERLING	Chawa	LEHRER			Meir	Frida	F	Dawid	[2]	Died
SONDERLING	Frida		1936		Dawid	Chawa	F		[2]	Died
SONDERLING	Reisel		1938		Dawid	Chawa	F		[2]	Died
SONDERLING	Isaak		1909				M		[3]	Died
SONDERLING	Reisel						F		[15]	Died
SONDERLING	Dawid						M		[15]	Died
SONDERLING	Dawid						M		[15]	Died
SONDERLING	Izaak						M		[15]	Died
SOROKIN	Lifka Elka		1923				F		[3]	Died
SPATZ	Rifka						F		[15]	Died
SPATZ	Matilda						F		[15]	Died
SPENDEL	Roza						F		[15]	Died
SPER	Taube						F		[15]	Died
SPERBER	Malia						F		[15]	Died
SPERBER	Hinda						F		[15]	Died
SPERBER	Miriam						F		[15]	Died
SPERBER	Henrik						M		[12]	Survived
SPERLING	Baruch						M		[11]	Survived
SPIRA	Heinrich						M		[15]	Died
SPREY							M		[11]	Died

List of Jews in Sandz   APP-121

Surname	First Name	Maiden Name	Birth Date	Residence	Father	Mother	Gender	Spouse	*Source	Remarks
SPRINGER	Berta						F		[15]	Died
SPRINGER	Mair						M		[15]	Died
SPRINGER	Natan						M		[15]	Died
SPRINGER	Chaskel						M		[15]	Died
SPRINGER	Fela						F		[15]	Died
SPRINGER	Hersh						M		[15]	Died
SPRINGER	Mala						F		[15]	Died
SPRINGER	Sarah Esther	BLEIWEISS					F	Chaim Yaak	[15]	Died
SPRINGER	Israel				Chaim Yaakow	Sarah Esther	M		[2]	
SPRINGER	Rosa	HERZ					F		[2]	
SPRINGER	Leon				Chaim Yaakow	Sarah Esther	M		[2]	
SPRINGER	Regina				Chaim Yaakow	Sarah Esther	F		[2]	
SPRINGER	Ester						F		[15]	Died
SRINGER	Asher						M		[11]	Survived
SRINGER	Sopia						F		[11]	Survived
SRINGER	Chaim Yaakow						M		[2]	Survived
SRINGER	Mordechai						M		[10]	Survived
SRINGER	Asher						M		[10]	Survived
SRINGER	Hersh						M		[12]	
STAHL	Mendel		1915				M		[7]	
STAMBERGER	Adolf		1906				M		[7]	
STAMBERGER	Lea						F		[15]	Died
STATER	Meshulem						M		[11]	Died
STATTER	Lea						F		[15]	Died
STATTER	Roza						F		[15]	Died
STATTER	Pessah						M		[11]	Died
STEIF	Yossef						M		[11]	Survived
STEIF	Hersz						M		[11]	Survived
STEIF	Arek						M		[11]	Survived
STEIF	Szimon						M		[11]	Died

Surname	First Name	Maiden Name	Birth Date	Residence	Father	Mother	Gender	Spouse	*Source	Remarks
STEIF	Bluma						M		[11]	Died
STEIF	Moshe Eliaz						M		[11]	Died
STEIF	Sara						F		[11]	Died
STEIF	Awraham						M		[11]	Died
STEIF	Yehezkel						M		[11]	Died
STEIF	Michael						M		[11]	Died
STEIF	Yaakow						M		[10]	Survived
STEIF	Sara						F		[15]	Died
STEIF	Golda	BLASENSTEIN			Benyamin	Shewa	F		[2]	Survived
STEIN	Itka						F		[15]	Died
STEIN	Moshe						M		[15]	Died
STEIN	Melech						M		[15]	Died
STEIN	Hanoch						M		[15]	Died
STEIN	Miriam						F		[11]	Died
STEINBACH	Yossef						M		[11]	Died
STEINBACH	Michael						M		[11]	Died
STEINBACH	Sara						F		[11]	Died
STEINBACH	Joel						M		[12]	
STEINBACH	Feibish						M		[12]	
STEINBACH	Mechel						M		[15]	Died
STEINBACH	Dawid						M		[12]	
STEINBERG	Aron						M		[15]	Died
STEINBERG	Shulem						M		[15]	Died
STEINBERGER	Yossef						M		[12]	
STEINER	Awraham						M		[12]	
STEINER	Noah						M		[12]	
STEINER	Ester						F		[15]	Died
STEINER	Joseph						M		[15]	Died
STEINER	Reuben Eli						M		[15]	Died
STEINER	Noah						M		[10]	Survived
STEINER	Shlomo						M		[10]	Survived
STEINER	Lea						F		[11]	Died
STEINFELD	Wolf						M		[15]	Died

List of Jews in Sandz APP-123

Surname	First Name	Maiden Name	Birth Date	Residence	Father	Mother	Gender	Spouse	*Source	Remarks
STEINFELD	Lea						F		[15]	Died
STEINFELD	Saul						M		[15]	Died
STEINFELD	Melech						M		[15]	Died
STEINFELD	Itzhak						M		[10]	Survived
STEINFELD	Tzwi						M		[10]	Survived
STEINFELD	Gusta						F		[10]	Survived
STEINFELD	Izaak						M		[15]	Died
STEINHOF							M		[2]	Died
STEINHOF	Alek						M		[15]	Died
STEINHOF	Sara						F		[15]	Died
STEINHOF	Chana						F		[15]	Died
STEINHOF	Lola						F		[10]	Survived
STEINHOF	Shoshana						F		[10]	Survived
STEINHOF	Yonina						F		[10]	Survived
STEINHOF	Yaakow						M		[10]	Survived
STEINHOF	Ester Rac.				Moshe		F		[9]	Died 1926
STEINHOF	Emil						M		[11]	Survived
STEINLAUF	Matia		1876				F		[9]	Died 08/8/1939
STEINLAUF	Lola						F		[10]	Survived
STEINLAUF	Shoshana						F		[10]	Survived
STEINLAUF	Yonina						F		[10]	Survived
STEINLAUF	Yaakow						M		[10]	Survived
STEINLAUF							M		[12]	
STEINMAN	Zofia						F		[15]	Died
STEINMETZ	Dawid						M		[15]	Died
STEINREICH	Feige						F		[15]	Died
STEINREICH	Szeindel						F		[15]	Died
STEINREICH	Roza						F		[15]	Died
STEINREICH	Yehuda Leib						M		[15]	Died
STEPEL	Baruch						M		[6]	Survived
STERN	Haya						F	Baruch	[6]	Survived
STERN	Shmuel						M		[9]	Died 17/9/1933
STERN	Berthold						M		[12]	

List of Jews in Sandz   APP-124

Surname	First Name	Maiden Name	Birth Date	Residence	Father	Mother	Gender	Spouse	*Source	Remarks
STERN	Aaron						M		[12]	shot
STERN	Moshe						M		[12]	shot
STERN	Hai Levy						M		[14]	
STERN	Josef						M		[15]	Died
STERN	Leon						M		[15]	Died
STERN	Yossef						M		[15]	Died
STERN	Yakow						M		[15]	Died
STERN	Shiya						M		[15]	Died
STERN	Leon						M		[15]	Died
STERN	Ester				Dow		F		[9]	Died 01/8/1932
STERN	Yaakov						M		[15]	Died
STERNHELL	Jacob						M		[11]	Survived
STERNLICHT	Moshe						M		[9]	
STERNLICHT	Ernestina	BRENDER					F	Herman	[11]	Died
STOF	Herman						M		[11]	Died
STOF	Ester						F		[9]	Died 15/5/1904
STOF	Leibele						M		[14]	
STRASSMAN	Yehoshua						M		[15]	Died
STRENGEC	Anita						F		[15]	Died
STTATER	Helena						F		[15]	Died
STTATER	Ludvik						M		[15]	Died
STTATER	Dawid						M		[15]	Died
STTATER	Yzak						M		[15]	Died
STUNHOF	Leib						M		[12]	
SUKMAN	Hersh		1920				M		[3]	Died
SUSSMAN	Hersz						M		[11]	Died
SYROP	Sofia						F		[11]	Died
SYROP	Ruth						F		[11]	Died
SYROP	Rafael Eliez						M		[11]	Died
SYROP	Pearl Gitel						F		[15]	Died
SZAGRIN	Israel						M		[15]	Died
SZAGRIN	Naftali						M		[15]	Died
SZAGRIN	Reisel						F		[15]	Died

List of Jews in Sandz   APP-125

Surname	First Name	Maiden Name	Birth Date	Residence	Father	Mother	Gender	Spouse	*Source	Remarks
SZAGRIN	Perl						F		[15]	Died
SZAGRIN	Moshe		1902		Elimelech		M		[9]	
SZAGRIN	Lazar		1906				M		[7]	
SZENIATYCKI	Mordko		1935	Pijarska 34			M		[7]	
SZENIATYCKI				Pijarska 34			M		[10]	Died
SZEINFELD	Wolf						M		[15]	Died
SZERMER	Dawid						M		[15]	Died
SZERMER	Awraham		1909				M		[7]	
SZERMER	Rachela		1916				F		[7]	
SZERMER				Kazimierz St			M		[10]	Died
SZIMEL	Chana F				Itzhac		F		[9]	Died 1903
SZITZER				Kazimierz St			M		[10]	Died
SZLANGER	Yaakow						M		[15]	Died
SZLAPOZNIK				Pijarska 34			M		[10]	Died
SZLEICHKORN	Hanoch						M		[12]	Died
SZPRAJ				Joselowicza			M		[10]	Died
SZTAIF	Perl						F		[15]	Died
SZTAIN	Cyla						F		[15]	Died
SZTAJN	Ignac						M		[15]	Died
SZTAJN	Henoch						M		[15]	Died
SZTAJN	Berl						M		[15]	Died
SZTAJN	Mosze			Kazimierz St			M		[10]	Died
SZTERN	Regina						F		[15]	Died
SZWEIT	Berl						M		[15]	Died
SZWEIT	Abraham		1904				M		[7]	
TANNENBAUM	Chaja						F		[15]	Died
TARLOWSKI	Szeindel						F		[15]	Died
TAUB							M		[12]	
TAUBES	Tobka						F		[12]	
TAUBES	Ida						F		[12]	
TAUBES	Tinka						F		[12]	
TAUBES	Witka						F		[12]	
TAUBES	Bernard		1901		Yossef Tzwi		M		[9]	

List of Jews in Sandz   APP-126

Surname	First Name	Maiden Name	Birth Date	Residence	Father	Mother	Gender	Spouse	*Source	Remarks
TEICHLER	Necha						F		[15]	Died
TEICHLER	Yuda						M		[15]	Died
TEICHTELL	Moses						M		[4]	
TEICHTELL	Sheindel						F		[2]	
TEICHNER	Berl		1907			Sheindel	M		[2]	Died
TEICHNER	Gita	FORSTENZER					F	Berl	[2]	Died
TEICHNER	Marcel/ Moshe						M		[2]	Died
TEICHNER	Sara Scheindel						F		[2]	Died
TEICHNER	Pessel						F	Baruch	[12]	Died
TEITELBAUM	Moshe						M		[11]	Died
TEITELBAUM	Bracha						F		[11]	Died
TEITELBAUM	yehezkel						M		[11]	Died
TEITELBAUM	Aaron						M		[11]	Died
TEITELBAUM	Yehezkel						M		[11]	Died
TEITELBAUM	Esther						F	Yehezkel	[11]	Died
TEITELBAUM	Israel Awra						M		[11]	Died
TEITELBAUM					Itzhak		M		[2]	Died
TEITELBAUM	Pessah						M		[12]	shot
TEITELBAUM	Shlomo						M		[12]	Died
TEITELBAUM	Yaakow						M		[12]	
TEITELBAUM	Issachar	TAMIR					M		[12]	Survived
TEITELBAUM	Leibek						M		[12]	Died
TEITELBAUM	Rachel						F		[15]	Died
TEITELBAUM	Aharon						M		[15]	
TEITELBAUM	Itzhak						M			
TEITELBAUM	Rachel						F		[15]	Died
TEITELBAUM	Simcha						M		[15]	Died
TEITELBAUM	Pesel						F		[15]	Died
TEITELBAUM	Wolf I.		1924				M		[3]	Died
TELLER	Tzwi						M		[12]	
TELLER	Szymon						M		[15]	Died
TELLER	Chaim						M		[15]	Died

List of Jews in Sandz   APP-127

Surname	First Name	Maiden Name	Birth Date	Residence	Father	Mother	Gender	Spouse	*Source	Remarks
TELLER	Tzwi						M		[10]	Survived
TELLER	Mrs						F	Tzwi	[10]	Survived
TELLER	Yaakow						M		[10]	Survived
TELLER	Lucia						F		[10]	Survived
TELLER	Shalom						M		[12]	died
TELLER-KARNIEL	Meir						M		[11]	Died
TELLERMAN	Riwka						F		[11]	Died
TELLERMAN	Frida						F		[11]	Died
TELLERMAN	Yehiel						M		[14]	
TEMPLER	Hermina						F		[15]	Died
TEMPLER	Yzydor		1892				M		[7]	
TEMPLER	Sholom						M		[15]	Died
TENCER	Shlomo						M		[11]	Survived
TENZER	Shulem						M		[11]	Died
TENZER	H.						M		[12]	
TENZER	Yona						M		[12]	
TENZER	Riwka						F		[15]	Died
TENZER	Szolom						M		[15]	Died
TENZER	Malka						F		[11]	Died
TEPFER	Zelig						M		[10]	Survived
TEPPER	Chaskel						M		[15]	Died
TESCHER	Chawa	BORENFREUND					F		[11]	Died
TESZLER	Mendel						M		[11]	Died
TESZLER	Gerszon						M		[11]	Died
TESZLER	Gershon						M		[14]	
TIEFENBRUNN	Yehuda Leib				Israel		M		[9]	
TIEFENBRUNN	Szimon						M		[15]	Died
TIMBERG	Lea						F		[15]	Died
TIMBERG	Eliyahu						M		[10]	Survived
TIMBERG	Eliyahu						M		[11]	Survived
TISH	A.						M		[12]	
TISH	Eliyahu						M		[12]	

Surname	First Name	Maiden Name	Birth Date	Residence	Father	Mother	Gender	Spouse	*Source	Remarks
TISH	Mechel		1920				M		[7]	
TOBIAS	Leibel						M		[12]	
TOBIAS	Yossef						M		[12]	Survived
TOBIAS							M		[10]	Survived
TOFFER	Mendel						M		[10]	Died
TOP	Rachel						F		[15]	Died
TOPFER	Malka						F		[15]	Died
TOPFER	Sara						F		[15]	Died
TOPFER	Zwi						M		[15]	Died
TOPFER	Janka						F		[15]	Died
TOPPER	Mordechai						M		[12]	
TOREM	Feigele	MAHLER					F	Mordechai	[12]	
TOREM	Yossik				Mordechai	Feigele	M		[12]	Died
TOREM	Sheindel	GOLDFINGER					F		[12]	
TOREM	Cila						F		[15]	Died
TRAIMAN	Hannah						F		[12]	
TRAUNFELTTER	Gittel						F		[12]	
TRAUNFETTER	H						M		[12]	Survived
TRAUNSTEIN	Esther						F		[11]	Died
TRAURIG	Tania						F		[11]	Died
TRAURIG	Emanuel						M		[15]	Died
TREBIC	Shlomo						M		[12]	
TREFER	Itche						M		[12]	
TREGER	Mark						M		[12]	Survived
TURER	Mendel						M		[11]	Died
TURM	Jakob		07/6/1889				M		[9]	Died 04/11/1918
TURYN	Mordechai Dov		1839				M	Mordechai Dov	[1]	
TWERSKI	Sarah Miriam		1861		Mordechai Dov	Reitzel	F		[7]	
TWERSKI	Aaron Elimelech		1864		Mordechai Dov	Reitzel	M		[7]	

List of Jews in Sandz   APP-129

Surname	First Name	Maiden Name	Birth Date	Residence	Father	Mother	Gender	Spouse	*Source	Remarks
TWERSKI	Miriam				Mordechai Dov	Reitzel	F		[7]	
TWERSKI	Esther		1865		Mordechai Dov	Reitzel	F		[7]	
TWERSKI	Chaim Moshe		1866		Mordechai Dov	Reitzel	M		[7]	
TWERSKI	Sarah Miriam						F	Shulem Eliezer	[12]	
TWERSKI	Leopold						M		[2]	Died
TYRKEL	Yaakow						M		[14]	
TZALMAN	YOssef						M		[14]	
TZANCER	Sheindel	SHANKE					F		[12]	
TZAPF	Jakob						M		[15]	Died
TZELNER	Mattityahu						M		[14]	
TZEMETBAUM							M		[12]	
TZERELE	Mina						F		[12]	
TZIGLER	Yaakow						M		[12]	Died
TZIGLER	Shimon						M		[12]	
TZIGLER							M		[12]	
TZIGLER	Kuba						M		[12]	Died
TZIGLER	Baruch						M		[11]	Survived
TZIMER	Mendel						M		[12]	
TZIMMBLER							M		[12]	
TZIMMBLER	Zinwil				Mendel		M	Mendel	[12]	
TZIMMBLER	Leibish				Mendel		M		[12]	
TZIMMBLER	Feige						F		[12]	
TZIMMER	Moshe						M		[14]	
TZIMMER	Mendel						M		[14]	
TZIMMER	Feige						F		[15]	Died
TZIMMER	Yossef						M		[15]	Died
TZIMMER	Frimet						F		[15]	Died
TZIMMER	Leizer						M		[12]	
TZIMMERMAN	Awraham						M		[12]	

Surname	First Name	Maiden Name	Birth Date	Residence	Father	Mother	Gender	Spouse	*Source	Remarks
TZIMMERSHPRITZ	Ruzka						F		[6]	
TZUKERMAN	Jakob						M		[15]	Died
TZUKERMAN	Malka						F		[15]	Died
TZUKERMAN	Meilech		1890				M		[7]	
UBERREICH	Mania						F		[11]	Died
ULLMAN	Dawid						M		[11]	Died
ULLMAN	Miriam						F		[11]	Died
ULLMAN	Leib						M		[11]	Died
ULLMAN	wife						F	Leib	[11]	Died
ULLMAN	Towa						F		[11]	Died
ULLMAN	Beila						F		[11]	Died
ULLMAN	Dwora						F		[11]	Died
ULLMAN	Yoel						M		[11]	Died
ULLMAN	Awraham						M		[12]	
ULLMAN	Sala						F		[12]	
ULLMAN	Wania						M		[12]	
ULLMAN	Taube						F		[15]	Died
ULLMAN	Leib						M		[15]	Died
ULLMAN	Josef		1910				M		[7]	Survived
UNGAR	Moshe						M		[12]	Died
UNGER	Rachel						F	Chaim	[2]	
UNGER	Rachel						M		[11]	Died
UNGER	Shlomo						F		[12]	Died
UNGER	Itzhak						M		[12]	
UNGER	Cyla						M		[15]	Died
UNGER	Roza						F		[15]	Died
UNGER	Dawid				Shlomo Tzwi		F		[15]	Died
UNGER	Achsah						M	Dawid	[9]	Died
UNGER	Gitel						F		[1]	1st wife
UNKNOWN	Helena						F		[15]	Died
							F		[15]	Died

List of Jews in Sandz   APP-131

Surname	First Name	Maiden Name	Birth Date	Residence	Father	Mother	Gender	Spouse	*Source	Remarks
UNKNOWN	Hana						F		[15]	Died
UNKNOWN	M.						M		[12]	
UNTERBERGER	Shlomo						M		[11]	Died
VOLKMAN	Ita Sara		1917				F		[3]	Died
VOLKMAN	Adlf						M		[7]	
VOLKMAN	Israel	KATOWICE					M		[12]	
VOLKMAN	Alek						M		[15]	Died
VOLKMAN	Hermina						F		[15]	Died
VOLKMAN	Rifka						F		[15]	Died
VOLKMAN	Yossef						M		[15]	Died
VOLKMAN	Leon						M		[15]	Died
VOLKMAN	Hela	LUSTGARTEN					F		[11]	Died
WACHTEL							M		[11]	Died
WACHTEL	Zeew						M		[15]	Died
WACHTEL	Helena						F		[15]	Died
WACHTEL	Ephraim						M		[12]	
WACHTER	Jachka						F		[15]	Died
WACHTER	Shimeck						M		[12]	
WADLER	Leon						M		[12]	
WADLER	Israel						M		[5]	
WAGSCHAL	Zerla						F		[5]	
WAGSCHAL	Meir Izak		1844		Israel	Zerla	M	Chaje	[5]	
WAGSCHAL	Chaje	FRIEDMAN	1845		Hirsch Wolf	Chaje	F	Meir Izak	[5]	
WAGSCHAL	Juda		1864		Meir Izak	Chaje	M		[5]	
WAGSCHAL	Cela Szena		1866		Meir Izak	Chaje	F		[5]	
WAGSCHAL	Aron		13/2/1868		Meir Izak	Chaje	M	Rachel	[5]	Survived
WAGSCHAL	Rachel	WAGSCHAL	21/11/1872		Aron Josef	Alte Broche	F	Aron	[5]	Survived
WAGSCHAL	Chaim Jecheskel		30/3/1899		Aron	Rachel	M		[5]	died aged 3
WAGSCHAL	Zerla Zella	WAGSCHAL			Aron	Rachel	F		[5]	died aged 19
WAGSCHAL	Roza		1870		Meir Izak	Chaje	F		[5]	
WAGSCHAL	Jzrael		1880		Meir Izak	Chaje	M		[5]	

List of Jews in Sandz   APP-132

Surname	First Name	Maiden Name	Birth Date	Residence	Father	Mother	Gender	Spouse	*Source	Remarks
WAGSCHAL	Frima						F		[12]	
WAGSHAL	Mendel						M		[14]	
WAGSHAL	Pearl						F		[15]	Died
WAGSHAL	Raizla						F		[15]	Died
WAJSBROT	Yaakow						M		[11]	Died
WAKS	Chawa	BLAUSENSTEIN					F		[11]	Died
WAKS	Sara	BROTMAN					F		[11]	Died
WAKS	Cima						M		[11]	Died
WAKS	Finkel						M		[11]	Died
WAKS	Shimon						M		[12]	
WAKS	Shimon						M		[12]	
WAKS	Nehema						F		[15]	Died
WAKS	Finkel						M		[15]	Died
WAKS	Shalom						M		[15]	Died
WAKS	Horsh						M		[15]	Died
WAKS	Naftali						M		[12]	
WAKSBERGER	Aaron						M		[12]	
WAKSLICHT	Haya						F		[9]	Died
WAKSLICHT	Golda						F		[15]	Died
WAKSLICHT	Chaja						F		[15]	Died
WAKSLLICHT	Shmuel						M		[15]	Died
WAKSMAN	Reisl						F		[15]	Died
WAKSMAN	Norton						M		[11]	
WAKSMAN	Leon						M		[12]	
WALDER	Shimek						M		[12]	
WALDER	Anda						F		[12]	
WALDER	Sala						F		[12]	
WALDER	Izaak		1900				M		[2]	Died
WALDMAN	Helena		1938				F		[2]	Died
WALDMAN	Mariem		1905				F		[2]	Died
WALDMAN							M		[12]	
WALTER	Herman						M		[12]	Survived
WALTER	daughter						F		[12]	

List of Jews in Sandz   APP-133

Surname	First Name	Maiden Name	Birth Date	Residence	Father	Mother	Gender	Spouse	*Source	Remarks
WALTER	Esther	LUSTGARTEN					F		[11]	Died
WAND	Yaakow						M		[12]	
WANDERER	Zisha						M		[15]	Died
WANDERER	Michael						M		[15]	Died
WANDERER	Hannah						F		[12]	Survived
WARMAN	Mendel						M		[10]	Died
WASNER	Szymon			Elowela			M		[10]	Died
WASNER	Sima						F		[15]	Died
WASSERLAUF	Naftali						M		[11]	Survived
WASSERLAUF	Shmuel						M		[11]	Died
WASSERLAUF	Michal						M		[11]	Died
WASSERLAUF	Riwka	GOLDFINGER					F		[11]	Died
WASSERLAUF	Chana						F		[11]	Died
WASSERLAUF	Aron		1919				M		[3]	Died
WASSERLAUF	Mechel						M		[12]	Died
WASSERLAUF	Syma						F		[15]	Died
WASSERLAUF	Chana						F		[15]	Died
WASSERLAUF	Michal						F		[15]	Died
WASSERLAUF	Riwka						F		[15]	Died
WASSERLAUF	Salomon						M		[15]	Died
WASSERLAUF	Anna						F		[15]	Died
WASSERLAUF	Izak						M		[15]	Died
WASSERLAUF	Lea						F		[15]	Died
WASSERLAUF	Sima						F		[15]	Died
WASSERLAUF	Benyamin						M		[15]	Died
WASSERLAUF	Nahum						M		[10]	Survived
WASSERLAUF		LIMANOW					M		[12]	shot
WASSERMAN	Mirel						F		[15]	Died
WASSERTEIL	Mendel						M		[11]	Died
WASSNER	Yonathan						M		[14]	
WEBER	Joachim						M		[2]	Died
WEBER	Yahad						M		[11]	Died
WECHTER	Reisel						F		[11]	Died

Surname	First Name	Maiden Name	Birth Date	Residence	Father	Mother	Gender	Spouse	*Source	Remarks
WECHTER	Shimon						M		[14]	
WECHTER	Shimon						M		[14]	
WEG	Aaron				Shimon		M		[14]	
WEG	Itzhak						M		[10]	Survived
WEIBERGER	Mechel						M		[12]	
WEICHERT	Hirshel						M		[15]	Died
WEICHMAN	Noach			Rynek			M		[10]	Died
WEICHMAN	Yaakow						M		[11]	Died
WEINBERG	Rachel						F		[11]	Died
WEINBERG	Ida						F		[11]	Died
WEINBERG	Ita						F		[11]	Died
WEINBERG	Yekel						M		[11]	Died
WEINBERG	Gershon						M		[12]	
WEINBERG	Ita						F		[15]	Died
WEINBERG	Itzhak						M		[10]	Survived
WEINBERG	Amalia						F		[15]	Died
WEINBERG	Ida						F		[12]	
WEINBERGER	Moshe						M		[12]	Survived
WEINBERGER	Ita						F		[12]	Survived
WEINBERGER	Ida						F		[12]	
WEINBERGER	Shmelke						M		[12]	
WEINBERGER	Gershon				Shmelke		M		[12]	
WEINBERGER	JAKOB						M		[15]	Died
WEINBERGER	Leon						M		[2]	Died
WEINBRENNER							M		[11]	Survived
WEINDLING	Nathan						M		[12]	Survived
WEINDLING	Isaak						M		[12]	Survived
WEINDLING	Hala						M		[12]	Survived
WEINDLING							M		[10]	Survived
WEINDLING	Abraham		1909				M		[3]	Died
WEINFELD	Majer I		1911				M		[3]	Died
WEINFELD	Mordechai						M		[10]	Survived
WEINFELD	Malka						F		[10]	Survived

List of Jews in Sandz APP-135

Surname	First Name	Maiden Name	Birth Date	Residence	Father	Mother	Gender	Spouse	*Source	Remarks
WEINFELD	Moshe						M		[10]	Survived
WEINFELD	Sara						F		[10]	Survived
WEINFELD	Dorka						F		[10]	Survived
WEINFELD	Hertzel						M		[10]	Survived
WEINFELD	Shimon						M		[10]	Survived
WEINFELD	Michael						M		[10]	Survived
WEINFELD	Mordechai						M		[10]	Survived
WEINGARTEN	Hersh						M		[15]	Died
WEINLISZ	Nathan						M		[6]	Died
WEINSHENKER	Herman		1924				M		[7]	Survived
WEINSTEIN	Henia						F		[15]	Died
WEINSTOCK							M		[12]	
WEINTRAUB	Shmuel						M		[12]	
WEINTRAUB	Kalman						M		[15]	Died
WEINTRAUB	Haja						F		[15]	Died
WEIS	Abraham						M		[15]	Died
WEISBARD	Eliezer						M		[15]	Died
WEISBARD	Chana Elke						F		[1]	Died
WEISBERGER	Itzhak						M		[11]	Survived
WEISS	Wolf		1904				M		[3]	Died
WEISS	Regina		1902				F		[7]	Survived
WEISS	Haim						M		[14]	
WEISS	Kraindel						F		[15]	Died
WEISS	Roza						F		[15]	Died
WEISS	Yehezkel						M		[15]	Died
WEISS	Rachela						F		[15]	Died
WEISS	Emalia						F		[15]	Died
WEISS	Luba						F		[15]	Died
WEISS	Ester						F		[15]	Died
WEISS	Chana						F		[15]	Died
WEISS	Reuwen						M		[15]	Died
WEISS	Zigusz						M		[15]	Died
WEISS	Wolf						M		[15]	Died

List of Jews in Sandz   APP-136

Surname	First Name	Maiden Name	Birth Date	Residence	Father	Mother	Gender	Spouse	*Source	Remarks
WEISS	Frenia						F		[15]	Died
WEISS	Itzhak						M		[11]	Survived
WEISS	Genia						F	Itzhak	[11]	Survived
WEISS	Itzhak						M		[10]	Survived
WEISS	Lea						M		[12]	
WEISSBROT	Rywka						F		[15]	Died
WEISSBROT	Meir						M		[6]	shot
WEITZMAN	Zaharia						M		[6]	
WEITZMAN	Sawa		1932				F		[2]	Died
WENCELBERG	Chaskiel						M		[15]	Died
WENGER	Szimon						M		[15]	Died
WENGER	Shmuel						M		[15]	Died
WENIGEREK	Riwka	BLASENSTEIN			Benyamin	Shewa	F		[2]	Survived
WENIR	Yossef						M		[11]	Died
WENTZELBERG	Israel						M		[11]	Died
WENTZELBERG	Moshe						M		[11]	Died
WENTZELBERG	Webel						M		[11]	Died
WENTZELBERG	Dora						F		[11]	Died
WENTZELBERG	Frida						F		[11]	Died
WENTZELBERG	Israel						M		[10]	Survived
WENTZELBERG	Israel		1892				M		[2]	Died
WENZELBERG	Awigdor						M		[12]	
WERNER	Hencia						F		[15]	Died
WERNER	Abraham						M		[15]	Died
WERNER	Yaakow						M		[15]	Died
WERNER	Jona						M		[15]	Died
WERNER	Szymon						M		[15]	Died
WESNER	Szymon						M		[15]	Died
WESSNER	Moshe						M		[12]	
WESTREICH	Izak		1923				M		[7]	
WESTREICH	Israel						M		[11]	Died
WICHNER	Rachel						F		[11]	Died
WICHNER	Hudes						F		[15]	Died

List of Jews in Sandz   APP-137

Surname	First Name	Maiden Name	Birth Date	Residence	Father	Mother	Gender	Spouse	*Source	Remarks
WIDAWSKI	Awraham						M		[10]	Survived
WIECZNER	Ital						F		[10]	Survived
WIECZNER	Itzhak						M		[12]	Survived
WIENDLING	Sol						M		[11]	Survived
WIENER	Riva						F	Sol	[11]	Survived
WIENER	Albert		1892				M		[7]	
WIESER	Gustaw		1894				M		[7]	
WIESER	Rosalia						F		[15]	Died
WIETCHNER	Dewora						F		[15]	Died
WIJNLIS	Majer		1919				M		[2]	Died
WILDFEUER	Sender						M		[2]	Died
WILDFEUER	Feige						F		[15]	Died
WILDFEUER	Rywka						F		[15]	Died
WILDFEUER	Frida						F		[15]	Died
WILDFEUER	Itzhak						M		[15]	Died
WILDFEUER	Ori						M		[15]	Died
WILDFIRE	Frida						F		[15]	Died
WILDFIRE	Genia						F		[15]	Died
WILDSTEIN	Itzhak						M		[10]	Survived
WILDSTEIN	Yossef						M		[15]	Died
WINCELBERGER	Naftali						M		[11]	USA
WIND	Israel						M		[11]	Died
WINIK	Hinda						F		[15]	Died
WINIK	Roman						M		[2]	Died
WINKLER	Moshe						M		[11]	Died
WINTER	Dora						F		[15]	Died
WIRZEBLOWSKI	Gitel						F		[11]	Died
WOHLMUT	Meir						M		[11]	Died
WOHLMUT	Sarah						F		[11]	Died
WOHLMUT	Moshe						M		[11]	Died
WOHLMUT	Chaim						M		[11]	Died
WOHLMUT	wife						F	Chaim	[11]	Died
WOHLMUT	Shaul						M		[2]	Died

Surname	First Name	Maiden Name	Birth Date	Residence	Father	Mother	Gender	Spouse	*Source	Remarks
WOLF	Shifra	BUKSBAUM			Moshe	Chawa	F	Shaul	[2]	Died
WOLF	Nissan Leib				Shaul	Shifra	M		[2]	Died
WOLF	Natan Mordechai				Shaul	Shifra	M		[2]	Died
WOLF	Moshe				Shaul	Shifra	M		[2]	Died
WOLF	Chaim Eliezer				Shaul	Shifra	M		[2]	Died
WOLF	Peshe	STEIN			Shaul	Shifra	F		[2]	Died
WOLF	Berish				Shaul	Shifra	M		[2]	Died
WOLF	Aron Itzhak				Shaul	Shifra	M		[2]	Died
WOLF	Malka	BARBER					F		[2]	Died
WOLF	Ella	WOLF			Moshe	Rachel	F	Nissan Leib	[2]	Died
WOLF	Pinchas				Nissan Leib	Ella	M		[2]	
WOLF	Menashe Is						M		[11]	Survived
WOLF	Moshe						M		[11]	Died
WOLF	Sara						F		[11]	Died
WOLF	Eliyahu						M		[11]	Died
WOLF	Tziporah						F		[11]	Died
WOLF	Moshe						M		[11]	Died
WOLF	Shlomo						M		[12]	
WOLF	Alek						M		[12]	
WOLF	Eliyahu						M		[12]	
WOLF	Itsche Meir						M		[14]	
WOLF	Cesia						F		[15]	Died
WOLF	Shaul						M		[15]	Died
WOLF	Shifra						F		[15]	Died
WOLF	Julia						F		[15]	Died
WOLF	Elimelech						M		[15]	Died
WOLF	Yossef						M		[15]	Died
WOLF	Hanoch						M		[15]	Died
WOLF	Sara						F		[15]	Died
WOLF	Moshe						M		[15]	Died
WOLF	Herman						M		[15]	Died

Surname	First Name	Maiden Name	Birth Date	Residence	Father	Mother	Gender	Spouse	*Source	Remarks
WOLF	Moshe						M		[10]	Survived
WOLF	Shlomo						M		[10]	Survived
WOLF	Ignacy						M		[2]	Died
WOLFSTAL	Jerzy						M		[2]	Died
WOLFSTAL	Wolf						M		[12]	shot
WOLOWSKI	Simek						M		[12]	shot
WOLOWSKI	Towa						F		[11]	Died
WORM	Chuma						M		[11]	Died
WORM	Roize						F		[11]	Died
WORM	Mendel						M		[14]	
WOSSNER	Shimon				Mendel		M		[14]	
WOSSNER	Nachman						M		[10]	Survived
WROBEL	Israel						M		[15]	Died
WULKAN	Karl						M		[11]	Survived
WUNDER	Ernestina						F	Karl	[11]	Survived
WUNDER	Abraham						F		[15]	Died
WURTZEL	Miriam						M		[11]	Survived
WURTZEL	Sigmunt						F	Abraham	[11]	Survived
WURTZEL	Henryk						M		[11]	Survived
WYGODA							M		[2]	Died
YALES	Moshe						M		[12]	
ZALTZMAN	Sara						M		[15]	Died
ZALTZMAN	Chana						F		[15]	Died
ZALTZMAN	Meir						F		[15]	Died
ZAMEND	Necha						M		[15]	Died
ZAMEND	Doctor						F		[15]	Died
ZANWELL							M		[12]	
ZAUER	Yehezkel						M		[12]	
ZAUER	Aaron						M		[12]	
ZAUER	Sara						F		[15]	Died
ZAUER	Rozalia		1924				F		[7]	Survived
ZAUKER	Chaim Itz						M		[11]	Died

List of Jews in Sandz   APP-140

Surname	First Name	Maiden Name	Birth Date	Residence	Father	Mother	Gender	Spouse	*Source	Remarks
ZBINCZIKI	Chana Tzerl						F		[11]	Died
ZBINCZIKI	Mechel Zeli						M		[11]	Died
ZBINCZIKI	Taube						F		[11]	Died
ZBINCZIKI	Sima						F		[11]	Died
ZBINCZIKI	Yossef						M		[11]	Died
ZBINCZIKI	Mordechai Da						M		[11]	Died
ZBINCZIKI	Breindl						F		[11]	Died
ZBINCZIKI	Aaron Meir						M		[11]	Died
ZBINCZIKI							M		[12]	
ZEEMAN	Eva						F		[15]	Died
ZEHNWIRTH	Miriam						F		[15]	Died
ZEHNWIRTH	Nina						F		[15]	Died
ZEIDENROSS	Nina						F		[15]	Died
ZEIDENROSS	Ydel Meir						M		[12]	
ZEIFERT	Benyamin						M		[11]	Died
ZEIFERT	Gitel						F*		[11]	Died
ZEIFERT	Hersz						M		[11]	Died
ZEIFERT	Yaakow						M		[11]	Died
ZEIFERT	Matilda						F		[11]	Died
ZEIFERT	Shmuel Daw						M		[11]	Died
ZEIFERT	Tziporah						F		[11]	Died
ZEIFERT	Sura						F		[11]	Died
ZEIFERT	Shmuel						M		[11]	Died
ZEIFERT	Pnina	REIZ					F		[11]	Died
ZEIFERT	Yaakow						M		[11]	Died
ZEIFERT	Matel						F		[11]	Died
ZEIFERT	Dow						M		[11]	Died
ZEIFERT	Naftali						M		[13]	Survived
ZEIFERT	Mania				Naftali		F		[13]	Survived
ZEIFERT	Gitel						F		[15]	Died
ZEIFERT	Pepka						F		[15]	Died
ZEIFERT	Benjamin						M		[15]	Died
ZEIFERT	Itzhak						M		[10]	Survived

List of Jews in Sandz   APP-141

Surname	First Name	Maiden Name	Birth Date	Residence	Father	Mother	Gender	Spouse	*Source	Remarks
ZEIFERT	Feiga						F		[15]	Died
ZEIMAN	Chaja						F		[15]	Died
ZELENFREUND	Chaim						M		[15]	Died
ZELLENFREUND	Neche						F		[15]	Died
ZELLENFREUND	Ffrieda						F		[15]	Died
ZELLENFREUND	David						M		[11]	Survived
ZELEERMAN	Chaja						F		[15]	Died
ZELLNER	Zalamon						M		[15]	Died
ZELLNER	Salomon						M		[15]	Died
ZELLNER	Mordechai						M		[15]	Died
ZELUCKIA	ROobert						M		[15]	Died
ZEMANEK	Yosef						M		[12]	shot
ZEMELMAN	Chaim		1887				M		[2]	Died
ZEUGER	Naftali						M		[12]	
ZIEGEL							M		[2]	Died
ZIEGLER	Estera		1909				F		[9]	Died 1938
ZIEGLER	Shimon						M		[11]	Died
ZIGLER	Bluma	FLASTER					F		[11]	Died
ZIGLER	Sabina	HESS					F		[11]	Died
ZIGLER	Mina	WESTREICH					F		[11]	Died
ZIGLER	Henrike						F		[11]	Died
ZIGLER	Henoch						M		[11]	Died
ZIGLER	Lonek						M		[11]	Died
ZIGLER	Golda						F		[15]	Died
ZIGLER	Menahem						M		[12]	died
ZILBER	Menahem						M		[12]	
ZILBER	Leibish						M		[12]	
ZILBER	Eliezar D.						M		[12]	
ZILBER	Dow						M		[12]	
ZILBER	Itsche						M		[12]	
ZILBERBACH	Yaakow						M		[12]	
ZILBERBACH	Hershel M						M		[12]	
ZILBERBACH	Lola						F		[11]	Died

Surname	First Name	Maiden Name	Birth Date	Residence	Father	Mother	Gender	Spouse	*Source	Remarks
ZILBERBUCH	Chana						F		[11]	Died
ZILBERBUCH	Yehuda						M		[11]	Died
ZILBERBUCH	Sara Riwka						F		[11]	Died
ZILBERBUCH	Dwora						F		[11]	Died
ZILBERBUCH	Peretz						M		[11]	Died
ZILBERBUCH	Naphtali						M		[11]	Died
ZILBERBUCH	Chaim						M		[11]	Died
ZILBERBUCH	Moshe						M		[11]	Died
ZILBERBUCH	Dow						M		[11]	Died
ZILBERBUCH	Regina						F		[15]	Died
ZILBERBUCH							M		[12]	
ZILBERMAN	Leon						M		[12]	
ZILBERMAN	Bernard						M		[12]	
ZILBERMAN	Haim						M		[12]	
ZILBERMAN	Ariel	LEON			Haim		M		[12]	
ZILBERMAN	Baruch	BERNARD			Haim		M		[12]	died
ZILBERMAN							M		[12]	
ZILBERMAN	Henek						M		[12]	
ZILBERMAN	Mendel						M		[11]	Survived
ZILBERSTEIN	Shimon						M		[11]	Died
ZILBIGER	Feige						F		[11]	Died
ZILBIGER	Chana						F		[11]	Died
ZILBIGER	Yakir						M		[12]	
ZILBIGER	Frimet						F	Yakir	[12]	
ZILBIGER	Wolf				Yakir	Frimet	M		[12]	
ZILBIGER	Dow				Yakir	Frimet	M		[12]	Survived
ZILBIGER	Awraham				Yakir	Frimet	M		[12]	Survived
ZILBIGER	Szhimon						M		[15]	Died
ZILBIGER	Henia						F		[15]	Died
ZILBIGER	Feige						F		[15]	Died
ZILBIGER	Rachel	KORAL	1910		Dow Ber	Breine	F		[2]	Survived
ZIMAN	Gitel						F		[15]	Died
ZIMAN	Sheindel						F		[15]	Died

List of Jews in Sandz APP-143

Surname	First Name	Maiden Name	Birth Date	Residence	Father	Mother	Gender	Spouse	*Source	Remarks
ZIMELS	Josef I.		1914				M		[3]	Died
ZIMERSPITZ	Eliyahu						M		[15]	Died
ZIMMER	Manle						F		[15]	Died
ZIMMER	Elke						F		[15]	Died
ZIMMERMAN	Israel						M		[11]	Died
ZINGER	Chaim						M		[15]	Died
ZINGER	Nissan						M		[10]	Survived
ZINGER	Yehoshua						M		[15]	Died
ZINS	Lea Zissa						F	Dawid	[7]	2nd wife
ZINZ							M		[4]	
ZOLLMAN				Kazimierz			M		[10]	Died
ZOMER	Ita						F		[10]	Survived
ZOMMER	Awraham			Pijarska			M		[10]	Survived
ZOMMER	Dow			Pijarska			M		[10]	Died
ZONDERLING							M		[11]	Died
ZONENBLICK	Pepi						F		[15]	Died
ZORN							M		[11]	Died
ZUPNIK	Aaron						M		[12]	
ZUPNIK	Ada						F		[12]	
ZUPNIK	Dow Ber						M		[12]	
ZUPNIK	Berl						M		[12]	
ZUPNIK	Usher						M		[15]	Died
ZWERLING	Awraham						M		[15]	Died
ZWETSHKENSTIEL	Regina		1880				F		[2]	Died
ZWIKLER	Rozalia		1900				F		[2]	Died
ZWIKLER	Zygmunt		1810				M		[2]	Died
ZWIKLER	Rachel						F		[15]	Died
ZWIKLER	Lea						F		[11]	Died
ZWINICKI	Eliezer						M		[15]	Died
ZWIRN	Chaje	JOSELOWICZA					F		[10]	Died

INDEX

A

B

I

J

K

M

N

Y

Z